¡Raza Sí! ¡Guerra No!

*Chicano Protest and Patriotism
during the Viet Nam War Era*

Lorena Oropeza

UNIVERSITY OF CALIFORNIA PRESS
Berkeley · Los Angeles · London

University of California Press
Berkeley and Los Angeles, California

University of California Press, Ltd.
London, England

© 2005 by The Regents of the University of California

Library of Congress Cataloging-in-Publication Data

Oropeza, Lorena, 1964–
    Raza sí!, guerra no! : Chicano protest and
    patriotism during the Viet Nam war era /
Lorena Oropeza.
        p. cm.
    Based on author's thesis (Ph. D.)—Cornell
    University.
    Includes bibliographical references and index.
    ISBN 0–520-22511-2 (cloth : alk. paper)—ISBN
    0–520-24195-9 (alk. paper)
        1. Mexican Americans—Civil rights—History—
    20th century. 2. Mexican Americans—Politics and
    government—20th century. 3. Patriotism—United
    States—History—20th century. 4. Vietnamese
    Conflict, 1961–1975—Protest movements. 5. Civil
    rights movements—United States—History—20th
    century. 6. Protest movements—United States—
    History—20th century. I. Title.

    E184.M5077 2005
    323.1168′72073′09046—dc22

                                    2004057996

Manufactured in the United States of America

14 13 12 11 10 09 08 07 06 05
10 9 8 7 6 5 4 3 2 1

This book is printed on New Leaf EcoBook 60,
containing 60% post-consumer waste, processed
chlorine free; 30% de-inked recycled fiber, elemental
chlorine free; and 10% FSC-certified virgin fiber, totally
chlorine free. EcoBook 60 is acid-free and meets the
minimum requirements of ANSI/ASTM D5634-01
(*Permanence of Paper*).

For my parents

Contents

Illustrations

Acknowledgments

In 2003, California's Lt. Governor, Cruz Bustamante, running as a Democratic candidate in a special election to recall Governor Gray Davis, confronted accusations from conservatives nationally that during the 1970s he was a member of a dangerous, extremist student organization called the Movimiento Chicano Estudiantil de Aztlán. Critics charged that MEChA was akin to the Ku Klux Klan or Nazi Party. Although Bustamante went down to defeat, the story continued in 2004, when Stanford students voted 1,357 to 1,329 to deny student funding for the same Chicano student group on the grounds that MEChA advocated racism.[1] Clearly, more than thirty years after the height of the Chicano movement, the history and legacy of Chicano activism remains controversial. My hope is that this book contributes toward a fairer and more balanced analysis of Chicano protest than that offered by some popular TV pundits and other media critics at the start of a new century. If it does, then certainly one reason is that so many people have nurtured me intellectually, financially, politically, and emotionally during its writing.

The book emerged from a dissertation written while I was a graduate student at Cornell University in the Department of History. I am deeply indebted to the three professors who chaired my dissertation committee and were my academic advisors throughout: Walt LaFeber, Tom Holloway, now my colleague at the University of California, Davis, and Debra Castillo, of Cornell's Department of Romance Studies. Each one demonstrated a great deal of patience as I made the transition from journalism to history. They opened a new world to me, and for that I remain extraordinarily grateful. Cornell also introduced me to a group of graduate students who became longtime friends. I especially want to thank Sayuri Shimizu, who encouraged me to write even when I would have preferred to do other things; Bob Bussell who planted in my brain the key words "legitimacy" and "military service"; and Shannon L. Smith, who, when I mentioned I was looking for some way to bring together Chicano history and the study of U.S. foreign policy, asked, "What about Viet Nam?"

Once at Davis, I likewise benefited from generous—and smart— colleagues within the history department and beyond. The *mujeres* associated with the Chicana/Latina Research Center provided a second home on campus. For that, I am grateful to Inés Hernández-Avila, Yvette Flores-Ortiz, Rafaela Castro, Raquel Scherr, Beatriz Pesquera, Adalijza Sosa-Riddell, and to Miroslava Chávez-García, my fellow Chicana historian and friend. Within the Davis history department, I wish to thank Beverly Bossler, Cynthia Brantley, Dan Brower, Joan Cadden, Susan Mann, Ted Margadant, Barbara Metcalf, and Ruth Rosen for their words of wisdom over the years on many matters. In addition, Alan Taylor and Joan Cadden helped me secure a year's worth of funding by reviewing what became a successful grant application; Karen Halttunen read the entire dissertation and provided excellent suggestions for each chapter; and Clarence Walker encouraged me to think more critically about race in many fruitful conversations that strengthened the manuscript throughout. I am also grateful to Cathy Kudlick whose company made long car trips shorter and to Krystyna von Henneberg for wonderful, wide-ranging conversations about history, husbands, and hats, among other things. In the special role of assistant professor compatriots were Steve Deyle and Kyu Hyun Kim. Special thanks to Andrés Reséndez, who also read the dissertation and every revised chapter afterward with great insight and care. I am grateful that he is my colleague and overjoyed that our families are friends. Finally, and most especially, I wish to thank Lucy G. Barber, who entered the history department with me, wrote her book, and then helped me write mine. That help ranged from handing out nearly daily doses of encouragement to suggesting an organizational strategy for Chapter 5. She is my Lucy Grace.

Many other scholars also offered me assistance and advice over the years. My thanks to Yolanda Broyles-Gonzales, Antonia Castañeda, Ed Escobar, Carlos Muñoz, Jr., Ramón A. Gutiérrez, Mario T. García, Vicki Ruiz, Ignacio M. García, Malaquiás Montoya, Rafael Pérez-Torres,

Brenda Gayle Plummer, Raul Ruiz, Chela Sandoval, Alex Saragoza, Devra Weber, and especially Laura Robinson, a friend from my hometown of Tucson, Arizona, who provided many helpful suggestions regarding revisions. In addition, readers for the University of California Press, David G. Gutiérrez and Matt Garcia, offered invaluable comments, especially regarding the Epilogue. The writings and wisdom of Jorge Mariscal, who also read the work in many incarnations, were foundational to the evolution of this project. My friend and academic collaborator, Dionne Espinoza, has been an intellectual and political mentor for nearly a decade.

I received institutional financial support from Cornell University in the form of fellowships and teaching assistantships; the University of California, Santa Barbara, where I spent a year as a Chicana Dissertation Fellow; and the Ford Foundation, which awarded me a postdoctoral fellowship. At the University of California, Davis, the Chicana/Latina Research Center, the Academic Senate, and the Dean's Office all provided research support. The Davis money funded research trips and, even more important, research assistance. I wish to thank the many graduate students who helped push this project toward completion, including David Barber, Chris Doyle, George Jarrett, Elena Gutiérrez, Jesus Francisco Malaret, Beth Slutsky, Lia Schraeder, and Teresa Sabol Spezio. I found star undergraduate assistants in José Escoto, Emily Erickson, Heather Heckler, and JoAnna Poblete.

Like so many historians, I depended upon the expert advice dispensed by librarians and archivists across the country. For their invaluable assistance, I wish to thank William M. Joyner at the National Archives; Beth Silbergleit at the Center for Southwest Research; Tom Kreneck of Special Collections at Texas A&M in Corpus Christi; Margo Gutiérrez of the Benson Collection at the University of Texas, Austin; Salvador Güereña of UC Santa Barbara's Davidson Library; Walter Brem at the Bancroft Library; and Lily Castillo-Speed, head of the Ethnic Studies Library at the University of California, Berkeley.

At UC Press, Monica McCormick and Randy Heyman have shepherded this project from the days when it was a dissertation to its final form. For that, I am grateful.

Without the generosity, patience, and courage of those people who allowed me to delve into their pasts, this book would never have been written. They opened their lives to me and trusted me to convey the spirit of their struggle. Among this inspirational group, I especially want to thank Betita Martínez, Enriqueta Vasquez, Rosalío Muñoz, and

Ernesto Vigil. Once the editor of one of the premier Chicano movement newspapers, *El Grito del Norte,* Betita helped me locate photographs for this work. Enriqueta's words not only enriched this project but also inspired another. Rosalío answered unending questions with infinite patience and, as an added bonus, introduced me to George Rodriguez, whose photographs grace this book. Ernesto was the first person I ever interviewed in relation to this research. I barely knew what I was doing, but he put up with me then and has been doing so pretty much non-stop since.

For the past ten years that Richmond, California, has been home, a tremendous circle of friends has contributed to this project by walking with me literally and metaphorically. The circle begins with Su Ping Huang and Marek Zelakiewicz, our first next-door neighbors, who offered words of encouragement and advice. I was fortunate to meet Valerie Mendoza and Lisa Chavez through a UC Berkeley campus group called Graduate Students por la Raza. They took me under their wings and became my dear friends. We have gone through graduations, weddings, motherhood, and the launching of new careers together. The same is true of Julia M. Aguirre. When she moved in next door, I gained a *comadre* who has sustained me intellectually, emotionally, and spiritually. I am so grateful that she, and now Jade, Alesandra, and Joaquín, are a part of my life. Finally, an unexpected benefit of raising children was meeting my sons' classmates and their really cool parents. I especially wish to thank Mogan Brown and Mitch Rudominer, the parents of Darius; Nicoletta Gherardi and Fernando Sannibale, the parents of Lorenzo and Flavia; and Sojeila Silva and Dan Ringer-Barwick, the parents of Tomás, for good food and good times. Dan also proved a terrific sounding board during the summer of 2003 as I made the final revisions. I cannot thank him enough, or Sojeila for volunteering his services!

Most important, I would like to thank my family. True to every stereotype, it is extended. So my thanks to my *tías,* my uncles, and my cousins, and to my brothers, Mark and Bob, and my sister-in-law, Marcie, for their love and support. I especially want to thank my brother Alex for being such a good friend for so long. Years ago, I won the in-law sweepstakes. For raising the man that I love and then deciding to love me too, I sincerely thank Catherine and James Byrd. The book is dedicated to my first teachers and friends, Celia S. and Armando C. Oropeza. They constantly went beyond the call of duty for my sake. Thus, my mother was a loyal research assistant in New Mexico one summer. My father built me a beautiful office *with* trapezoidal windows because I asked him to.

As parents and now grandparents, they have been an unending well of support, faith, and love. So has my husband, John M. Byrd, whose help in putting that office together is only one manifestation of the many ways he has taken care of me and our nest. My life has been immeasurably enriched by his strength, generosity, and good humor. Finally, I wish to thank my sons, Armando James and JuanMiguel Alejandro, for teaching this historian about the present. Although they did not hasten this book's publication in any way, they do fill me with the conviction that the messages it conveys are important.

Note on Terminology

This work employs many proper names and umbrella terms. To clarify, throughout the text I have used "Viet Nam," which is the preferred spelling of the Vietnamese, unless the word appeared as "Vietnam" in either a direct quotation or an organization's name. I have also used the terms "Anglos" and "Anglo American" more often than "white American." While I recognize the awkwardness of the terms, given that they include people who do not trace their ancestry from the British Isles, they nevertheless reflects the ethnic and racial categorizations of the U.S. Southwest. There, "Anglo" has long been a useful counterpoint to the term "Mexican American," especially because, for much of this history, many Mexican Americans have insisted that they were white. Within the book, I have used the term "Mexican American" as the most broad-based term to describe the U.S.-born population of Mexican origin. It is also the term I use to describe activists within this ethnic group who were not members of the Chicano movement. When describing a population that contained both persons of Mexican descent born in the United States and Mexican immigrants, I have tended to use the terms "ethnic Mexicans" and "people of Mexican descent." To distinguish participants in the Chicano movement from the broader Mexican American population, I have tried to restrict the terms "Chicanos" and "Chicanas" to them alone. Finally, the use of Spanish in the text also merits comment. While in the Spanish language the plural "Chicanos," refers to both a group of Chicano men and a mixed group of Chicanos and

Chicanas, I have sought to avoid any confusion in English by frequently employing instead such gender-neutral terms as "activists" and "movement participants." In addition, many Spanish words contain accents, and these appear in the text. However, in the case of people's first and last names, I have tried to follow the individual's or author's most frequent usage.

Introduction

When Delia Alvarez heard the news in August 1964 that her brother, Everett, a U.S. Navy pilot, had been captured by North Vietnamese forces, her first reaction was: "I wish I were a man." She wanted to enlist in the military, go to Vietnam, and rescue her brother.[1] Shot down in the Gulf of Tonkin, Everett Alvarez Jr. was to remain a prisoner of war for the next eight-and-a-half years. During his long captivity, he clung to a certain set of cherished values that he associated with being an American and a patriot: "duty, loyalty, unity, integrity, honor, allegiance, courage, and hope." As he wrote in his memoir, his sanity depended upon maintaining an "absolute belief" in these "core virtues."[2] In contrast, the longer her brother remained a captive, the more questions Delia Alvarez had about the war and her country. Initially uncritical about American involvement in Viet Nam, in 1970 she began to travel the country to speak out against U.S. military intervention. To a reporter, Delia Alvarez credited her shifting stance about the conflict as part of a larger political evolution. As she explained, "My involvement with the Chicano movement has done more than anything to open my eyes to things as they really are."[3]

Both Delia's anti-war activism and her politicization as a Chicana tested familial bonds between two siblings who had been exceptionally close as children. Growing up in the small town of Salinas, California, where she graduated from high school in 1959, Delia, the younger by three years, remembered being a tomboy so she could be like her brother. One of her earliest memories was of throwing a temper tantrum at the age of four because Everett was going to a basketball game without her. Family expectations united the pair even more. Repeatedly, their parents told them that family was important and that brother and sister should take care of each other. At the same time, the siblings shared their parents' expectations that they needed to succeed in the wider Anglo American world. As Delia remembered, the children were raised with "one foot in one culture and one foot in another." They were taught to be proud that they were "Mexicano," but also to realize that to get ahead they needed to be "white."[4]

The events of August 1964 placed the two on divergent paths. That night, sonar operators aboard the USS *Maddox* and USS *Turner Joy*, destroyers stationed in international waters off the coast of North Viet Nam, reported that the ships were under torpedo attack. North Vietnamese patrol boats had fired upon the *Maddox* two days before. After news of the second attack reached Washington, Congress passed the Gulf of Tonkin resolution endorsing President Lyndon B. Johnson's use of "all necessary measures to repel any armed attack against the forces of the United States." Serving aboard the USS *Constellation* in close proximity to the Gulf of Tonkin, Everett Alvarez was one of those first necessary measures. On August 5, he was among a group of U.S. Navy pilots ordered to bomb North Vietnamese targets in retaliation for the "deliberate and unprovoked" attacks. Information released later revealed a different story: before the first attack the *Maddox* had been conducting surveillance for the South Vietnamese; a second attack probably never occurred at all. This information came too late for Everett Alvarez. That night, his plane was shot down and he became a captive in North Viet Nam.[5]

At first, Delia Alvarez instinctively supported U.S. foreign policy toward Southeast Asia because she supported her brother. She had also grown up hearing about the domino theory, that communist aggression needed to be stopped or country after country would fall to communism like a row of dominoes. Vowing to avert that eventuality, President Johnson used the Gulf of Tonkin resolution to expand dramatically the American troop presence in Viet Nam beginning in 1965. For the Alvarez family, the widening war extinguished all hope for Everett's quick release. Every night, Delia recalled, the family gathered to watch television news reports about Viet Nam, and every night she felt "totally helpless" to aid her brother. Desperate to understand better his plight, Delia and her mother, Sally (short for Soledad), soon read everything they could about the history of Indochina and the conflict. Mother and daughter quickly concluded that the Americans were trying to repeat a failed French experiment, and worse, interfering in a civil war. They kept quiet. In the mid-1960s military families did not openly criticize the American government.[6]

Still, Delia Alvarez's doubts kept accumulating. Working as a social worker after college, Delia noticed that many of the impoverished Mexican American families she was helping had sons who were on their way to Viet Nam. While most of the young men had been drafted because they could not afford to go to college, and therefore did not qualify for student deferments, others had volunteered because they were unable to see any career options for themselves beyond serving in the military. Delia especially recalled one older teen who, not doing well in school, explained that he had decided to join the Army to fight for democracy and become a man. The combination of class vulnerability and naive patriotism among Mexican American youth ratified and strengthened Delia Alvarez's incipient opposition to the conflict. So did a long trip to Europe begun in mid-1967. Taken, in part, to escape the pressure that was building between her role as a public spokeswoman for a POW family, a role that mandated support for the war or silence, and her private qualms about American intervention, the trip revealed to Alvarez a continent awash in anti-American, anti-war demonstrations. Meeting a South Vietnamese man in a youth hostel in the south of France sealed her conviction that the conflict needed to be resolved by the Vietnamese themselves. From a wealthy family, the Vietnamese youth had avoided military service and was enjoying travel and study in Europe. Meanwhile, Delia's brother had been a prisoner of war for three years.[7]

Upon her return in early 1969 Delia Alvarez was determined to raise her voice in protest, despite the expectations placed on POW families. She soon found herself participating in not one but two social movements. At the same time that she joined the anti-war movement, she also joined other Mexican Americans in an unprecedented mass endeavor for equality that had erupted in her absence. Although members of the ethnic group had long sought equal treatment, the efforts by Cesar Chavez and Dolores Huerta to unionize California farmworkers marked the start of the most intense epoch of Mexican American political and cultural protest ever. Inspired by the farmworkers' struggle as well as a decade of social protest among African Americans, thousands of mostly young Mexican Americans began to organize on college campuses, in urban barrios, and in rural communities across the Southwest and beyond. They called themselves "Chicanos" and "Chicanas." Flourishing by 1969, the Chicano movement combined demonstrative politics and cultural affirmation in a dynamic endeavor to address such social injustices as poor educational equality, lack of political representation, poverty, and discrimination.

The movement also developed at the same time that U.S. military involvement in Southeast Asia was deepening and casualties were mounting. As a result, for many Chicano movement activists, domestic and international matters became inextricably linked. Delia Alvarez's political biography confirms the connection. Starting in 1969, she worked as coordinator and then interim director for a local program staffed by Chicano movement supporters that encouraged Mexican American college recruitment and retention. That same year, she was active in the founding of a Chicano organization in San Jose called La Confederación de la Raza Unida which pressed for better health care and improved housing for Mexican Americans. Soon afterward, Delia helped found an all-woman group called Chicanas de Aztlán, which sought an equal voice for Chicanas within the Chicano movement. In each case, her Chicano movement activism was inseparable from the wider context of the war. Unless more Mexican Americans entered the university, they would remain vulnerable to the draft. Like black activists, moreover, Chicano movement participants questioned the priorities of a society that spent so much on war when those funds could be put to use at home. Finally, Chicanas who questioned their subordinate role within the Chicano movement often looked to the prominent role that Vietnamese women played as National Liberation Front diplomats and soldiers. Delia Alvarez personally met with Indo-Chinese women twice, once at a women's conference in Vancouver in 1971 and the next year at a peace gathering in Paris.[8]

For many POW families, Delia Alvarez's anti-war activism was a betrayal. Committed to doing more to secure her brother's release, she sought at first to minimize controversy. In 1969 members of the extended family decided to start a petition respectfully asking President Richard M. Nixon to take "more positive forceful action" to speed Everett Alvarez's release. Generating a great deal of publicity, the petition collected more than seventy thousand signatures.[9] More provocative was Delia's decision to convert her status as a POW family member into an anti-war platform. Able to command media attention, she appeared on the Merv Griffin television talk show with Jane Fonda in 1971. That same year, she founded a group of anti-war POW families.[10]

While other families of POWs had started a campaign called "Have a Heart, Hanoi," which pleaded with the North Vietnamese government to improve the treatment of captives, Delia Alvarez's group traveled to Washington, D.C., to demand that the Nixon administration stop the war.[11] In 1972 she was a featured speaker at a West Coast anti-war demonstration in San Jose seeking an end to "war, racism, and repression." There, Delia condemned the war and, in particular, minority casualties.[12] Labeled a "communist" and worse, she persisted in her protest because she was certain that ending the war was the best way to secure her brother's release. She also knew that her mother, who had once told her that Vietnamese mothers cried for their sons the way that she was crying for her own, strongly supported her efforts.[13]

This book examines Chicano movement responses to the war in Viet Nam because these responses reveal the significance of the Chicano movement overall. The book argues that the war in Viet Nam fundamentally shaped the Chicano movement's challenge to long-held assumptions about the history of Mexican-origin people and their role within American society. Specifically, Chicano movement participants shared Delia Alvarez's willingness to dispute what Everett Alvarez proudly considered a "Hispanic tradition"—military service.[14] Eager to pursue an exciting career as a pilot, Everett Alvarez also admittedly joined the navy in the hope of smoothing out his "coarse country bumpkin" edges.[15] The military uniform provided a refuge for him from both an occasional sense of social awkwardness and from boyhood memories of anti-Mexican discrimination and rejection. In contrast, Chicano movement participants disputed the goal—and cost—of assimilation. By protesting the war, Chicano activists willingly forsook a venerable Mexican American civil rights tradition that had emphasized ethnic-group patriotism, especially as manifested through military service, in the hopes of obtaining first-class citizenship.

Instead, as they voiced their opposition to the conflict, the central refrain of anti-war Chicano activists was that Chicanos—and Chicanas—should struggle at home for their *raza*, their fellow Mexican Americans, not fight and die in a faraway land. Intensely critical of U.S. society and culture, they crafted a new understanding of themselves as a people of color, as a colonized people, and as women and men who had struggled against oppression for centuries. In the creation of each of these conceptions, moreover, movement activists gained critical inspiration and confirmation from examining the conflict in Viet Nam. As their opposition to the war grew, so too did their identification with a people that the American government insisted was the enemy. Thus, just as Delia Alvarez credited the Chicano movement with her politicization, with opening her eyes regarding the war, the Viet Nam conflict powerfully influenced the Chicano movement's forging of dramatic alternatives to prevailing notions about American citizenship and national belonging.

In sympathizing—and in many cases identifying—with the Vietnamese people, Delia Alvarez and her fellow Chicano activists were making the types of connections popular with other racial minorities in the country. The advent of black, red, yellow, and brown power not only paralleled the emergence of massive opposition to the war in Viet Nam, but different types of protests frequently overlapped.[16] Like Mexican Americans, African Americans and Asian Americans demonstrated against the war, and blacks, in particular, expressed concern about casualty rates.[17] As the title of the San Jose rally made clear, explicit linkages between racism at home and war abroad were also popular in the wider anti-war movement.[18] One of the goals of this book therefore is to examine the Chicano movement in relation to the era's other social protest movements.

Such an approach reveals the central role that opposition to the war played in the Chicano movement. To be certain, even as they championed their own history and culture, Chicano activists drew inspiration from African Americans and, in particular, from black power militants and their insistence upon race pride and political liberation.[19] Similarly, the leftist critiques popular within the national anti-war movement and elsewhere impressed many young Mexican Americans. Among the country's minority groups, however, only Mexican Americans active in the Chicano movement conducted a sustained campaign against U.S. policy in Southeast Asia through the founding of a minority-based anti-war organization, called the National Chicano Moratorium Committee. During 1970, more than a dozen Chicano Moratorium demonstrations were held across the country, culminating in a massive march in Los Angeles that August. Attracting between twenty thousand and thirty thousand people, the march was the largest anti-war march by any specific ethnic or racial group in U.S. history.[20]

These marches manifested a new and competing form of allegiance on the part of Mexican Americans. Instead of feeling patriotic toward the United States, Chicano movement participants directed their patriotic sentiments toward the Chicano struggle itself. This shift in loyalty, moreover, forced activists to reconsider their position vis-à-vis long-established hierarchies of race and gender, not only within U.S. society but also within their own Mexican American culture. First, the repeated identification with the Vietnamese contributed to the perception among those involved in the Chicano movement that people of Mexican descent constituted a race and not an ethnic group. They were brown, not white.[21] Second, the emergence of a Chicano anti-war movement prompted Chicanos and Chicanas to interrogate the meaning of masculinity for their struggle. Just as they no longer sought to be accepted as "white," no longer did their vision of equality rest upon demonstrated bravery in times of war.

This study, then, joins in a conversation with an extensive literature on American citizenship, race, and manhood.[22] Indeed, military service was a common denominator for these three concepts for most of the nation's history.[23] Serving in the U.S. military was traditionally not only an important marker of masculinity but also, throughout the long era of segregation, an important marker of whiteness. Despite the complications imposed by segregation, moreover, government leaders, military representatives, and social critics throughout the twentieth century proclaimed military service a powerful avenue toward furthering equality for ethnic and racial minorities alike.[24] The controversial war in Viet Nam presented Chicanos and Chicanas with the opportunity to reject this assumption and therefore to dispute the traditional parameters of citizenship. For these activists, Chicano cultural nationalism became a new form of patriotism that challenged the status quo. It even posited an alternative nation, Aztlán, to inspire a greater sense of belonging among members of a long-marginalized group. Ultimately, like the parallels that movement participants drew between themselves and combatants in a faraway war, cultural nationalism always functioned better as inspiration than as prescription. That fact, combined with massive institutional repression and sharp internal divisions, meant that the Chicano movement never accomplished all that the advocates of cultural nationalism hoped that it would. Nevertheless, Chicano movement participants did dramatically change the terms of their engagement with the majority society. Recognizing that movement participants operated in a local, national, and even international context, this study hopes to spur a greater appreciation of the movement's accomplishments in tandem with its limitations.

Toward that end, the book compares the Chicano movement with previous civil rights efforts among ethnic Mexicans. The first chapter examines the massive Americanization effort that accompanied the Second World War and its effect upon people of Mexican descent in the

United States. One major result was to inspire greater demands for equality. As one returning veteran put it, after "sweating it out" in "two major engagements in the Pacific," he was disappointed to find that "the racial war" still awaited him in Texas. "All we want is to be treated like American citizens and nothing less."[25] Like African Americans and other minorities and women of all racial backgrounds, Mexican Americans were less tolerant of second-class citizenship as a result of their war experience. Among people of Mexican descent, however, this renewed emphasis upon citizenship ran parallel with continuing immigration from Mexico, a phenomenon that inevitably complicated the ideal of Americanization.[26]

The second chapter then moves from the Second World War to the Viet Nam War era. It reveals not only the continuing relevance of the civil rights strategy that the WWII experience had cemented but also how tumultuous events domestically and abroad prompted the development of new strategies. Already divided over how best to benefit from reform programs pouring out of Washington during the 1960s, Mexican Americans were also of different opinions regarding the expanding war in Viet Nam. Indeed, given the centrality of military service to previous claims for equal treatment, the chapter argues that the war in Viet Nam accelerated a critical view of the nation and its foreign relations among members of the emerging Chicano movement and, consequently, magnified existing ethnic group divisions.

The third chapter traces the inspirational role the Vietnamese experience played within the Chicano movement. Having abandoned the political tactics of their Mexican American predecessors, Chicano activists also had grave reservations about the virtues of Americanization. Instead, they proclaimed their cultural inheritance a precious political resource—a means to build ethnic unity and, ultimately, power. With much enthusiasm, movement participants investigated and celebrated their indigenous heritage. Less well known is that many Chicano activists also drew historical parallels between themselves and the Vietnamese. From the perspective of some movement participants, not only was the United States guilty of allowing discrimination against minorities to flourish, it was also raining havoc upon a small, impoverished country filled with brown-skinned people like themselves.

The origins of the National Chicano Moratorium Committee in late 1969 in Los Angeles, detailed in Chapter 4, explains how and why antiwar protest moved to the Chicano movement's center stage. The chapter is also a study of the practical application of Chicano cultural nationalism. On the one hand, a nationalist appeal assumed a unanimity of interests that did not exist among Chicano movement participants opposed to the war, much less among Mexican Americans in general. On the other hand, anti-war Chicano activists brought a military conflict ten thousand miles away very close to home by emphasizing the war's deleterious effects upon ethnic Mexicans. In this way, moratorium organizers hoped to politicize an entire minority group not just against the war but also on behalf of the Chicano movement.

To their credit, organizers of the Chicano Moratorium launched the most massive demonstration in the history of the movement. The Chicano anti-war march that took place along East Los Angeles's Whittier Boulevard on August 29, 1970, was also one of the largest gatherings of Mexican Americans ever. A group that had once touted its patriotism now placed its protest on display. Yet an episode of police-instigated violence that day dashed the high hopes of moratorium organizers that the march would be only the beginning of a larger struggle. Chapter 5 examines the impressive coalition building that made the march possible and the tragic violence that day that cost three people their lives and ultimately destroyed the moratorium committee. Finally, against this painful denouement, the book's Epilogue evaluates the meaning of Chicano anti-war organizing for the nation's rapidly expanding Latino population at the start of a new century.

The legacy of this era of protest and patriotism certainly continued to affect the Alvarez family. Nearly thirty years after Everett Alvarez's release, brother and sister were personally close once again, although politically far apart. In 2000, at the Republican National Convention that nominated George W. Bush, Everett Alvarez led attendees in the Pledge of Allegiance. Meanwhile, Delia Alvarez, once a member of the Chicano political party La Raza Unida, was an independent who often voted Democratic. Looking ahead toward the 2004 presidential race, her favorite candidate was John Kerry, the Massachusetts Senator who had served as a Navy officer in Viet Nam and who had come back to oppose the war. As she looked back at her anti-war activism, Delia remained convinced that protesting the war was the right thing, the only thing, she could have done to help her brother. At the time, she had been prepared to accept his disapproval. Although Everett Alvarez did disapprove, deep bonds of affection and respect reconciled brother and sister. They agreed to disagree. Years later, Delia Alvarez also insisted that her protest was her patriotism. She had hated the war and loved her country.[27] Other Chicano movement participants were less willing to draw such distinctions. Regarding her opposition to the war in Viet Nam, another. Chicana commented, "We were proud to be traitors."[28] To understand better the complexities of Chicano and Chicana activism and, more broadly, the Mexican American experience since World War II, this book is a study of both protest and patriotism.

CHAPTER I

"To Be Better and More Loyal Citizens"

A Tradition of Mexican American Activism

In the opening scene of the 1945 film *A Medal for Benny,* Joe Morales, played by the Mexican-born actor Arturo de Córdova, is on his knees praying that his luck will change. Joe wants to marry the beautiful but distant Lolita Sierra (Dorothy Lamour), but like most Mexican Americans in the movie's fictional town of Pantera, Morales is poor. Worse, Lolita is already promised to Benny Martín, a young man renowned for his fat wallet and reckless charm, although he never appears on screen. Eventually, Morales's persistence wins Lolita's heart, yet before the couple can announce their engagement, word comes from overseas that Benny has been awarded the Congressional Medal of Honor for killing "nearly 100 Japs" in the Philippines. Proclaiming Pantera the birthplace of "America's number one hero," city boosters crank up a massive public relations campaign.

Here, the movie, based on a short story written by John Steinbeck, adopts a more serious tone. First, Charlie Martín, Benny's father, celebrates Benny's achievement for only a few moments before learning that his son was awarded the medal posthumously. Second, civic leaders are concerned that exposing Benny's impoverished origins on the Mexican side of town might undermine Pantera's image. They temporarily move Charlie to an elegant, Spanish-style villa and fill it with borrowed furniture in advance of a visit by the state governor and army brass. Convinced that his son's memory is being exploited more than honored, however, Charlie returns home. Finally, the media hoopla over Benny threatens the love affair between Lolita and Joe. The public relations campaign has nearly turned Lolita, although never a war bride, into a war widow.

Yet the movie ends on a patriotic note. When Charlie Martín ignores the invitation to appear at the official awards ceremony, the event travels to him. Although city officials protest, the visiting army general dismisses their concerns. "A lot of mighty fine Americans come out of shacks," he announces. Soon, a military parade is marching down the unpaved street in front of Charlie's home and saluting a teary-eyed Charlie. Meanwhile, Joe Morales discovers a solution to his own romantic dilemma: how to outdo Benny. He will join the army and obtain *two* Congressional Medals of Honor! Promising Lolita that he will return, Morales boards a train, as a crowd of well-wishers gathers. Although most wave small American flags at the soon-to-be-soldier, two hand-carried placards are also visible in the movie's final scene. One reads "Tokyo or Bust," the other, "Kick the Jap off the Map."[1]

One among hundreds of films that Hollywood produced between 1942 and 1945 in a determined effort to foster wartime unity, *A Medal for Benny* was nonetheless unique in featuring a story about Mexican Americans and in indicting the discrimination they faced.[2] At the same time, the movie presented a nation on the cusp of positive change regarding race relations between Anglos and this minority group. Initially assuming that the medal recipient was an Anglo—a MAR-tin versus a Mar-TEEN—by film's end Pantera's leading citizens have learned to acknowledge the presence and contributions of their Mexican-descent neighbors. Above all, the movie suggested, Mexican Americans like Benny and Joe made brave and loyal citizens despite the prejudices they confronted.

This central message of the movie was one that Mexican American civil rights activists had been articulating even before the advent of the Second World War. In the 1920s and 1930s ethnic leaders had insisted that Mexican Americans were loyal and exemplary citizens and, therefore, deserved to be treated as equals. As they made this argument, moreover, they were well aware of the racial hierarchy within the United States that privileged whiteness. *A Medal for Benny* captured that reality: Pantera's city leaders favored the descendants of "Spanish dons" over the offspring of Mexican immigrants. Nor was the use of the word "Japs" strictly a wartime phenomenon. In California and elsewhere, Asian immigrants had been systematically excluded from obtaining the rights and privileges of U.S. citizenship long before the war. In their quest for equal treatment before the Second World War, Mexican American civil rights activists tried to avoid racial discrimination by insisting that they were white.

Providing an unprecedented showcase for ethnic group patriotism and loyalty, the Second World War ushered in an era of significant civil rights progress. For members of a long disparaged and marginalized ethnic group, the war experience was also a tremendous source of ethnic pride. Between 250,000 and 500,000 Mexican Americans served in the military during the conflict.[3] Mexican American soldiers accrued a particularly commendable record, moreover, receiving eleven Congressional Medals of Honor for battlefield valor.[4] Although less celebrated, thousands of Mexican Americans also supported the war effort by working in defense industries. Aware of their contributions to the winning of the war abroad and at home, many people of Mexican descent gained a profound sense of themselves as legitimate and even important members of U.S. society. Consequently, in the postwar era, Mexican Americans launched an invigorated campaign to secure equal rights that included staging public protests, running for office, and suing for equal rights in court. In these endeavors, ethnic activists frequently mentioned the battlefield exploits of Mexican American soldiers as irrefutable proof that the ethnic group was deserving of first-class citizenship.

After 1945, therefore, many Mexican American activists continued to premise their struggle for equality upon the ethnic group's inherent worth. Before World War II, a primary goal of civil rights activists had been to make people of Mexican descent born north of the Rio Grande cognizant of their rights as Americans. The Second World War greatly accelerated the lesson. The result was increased political activism.[5] Wartime service now joined earlier claims of whiteness as evidence that Mexican Americans made first-rate citizens. Ignoring the complex racial inheritance of Mexican-origin people, such a strategy also inevitably focused attention on the Mexican-origin population itself rather than on the stubborn obstacles endemic within the United States, such as low wages and lingering prejudice. Thus, while World War II brought many positive changes to communities formed by people of Mexican descent, it also confirmed traditional patterns of supplication, embraced a narrow conception of citizenship, and mitigated criticism of U.S. institutions.

CLAIMING AMERICAN CITIZENSHIP

On the Fourth of July, 1941, the residents of Lockhart, Texas, were enjoying an outdoor celebration in honor of the nation's birthday. Several city blocks had been roped off to make way for a big band and dance along the town's main street. Late that evening, the bandleader came to the microphone. "I have been asked to make this announcement," he said. "All Spanish people gathered here must leave the block." The crowd's response was overwhelming approval. Listeners who were not "Spanish" applauded and cheered. "Since this is an American celebration, it is for white people only," the bandleader explained. The crowd again broke out in cheers.[6]

Just months before U.S. participation in World War II, the incident revealed that, in the minds of many Anglo Texans, people of Mexican descent were not Americans nor capable of becoming Americans. Whether born of immigrant parents or into families that had lived in the region for generations, they remained foreigners, in this case, "Spanish." Ironically, the bandleader had used an ethnic label that was frequently adopted by Anglo Americans, as well as some Mexican Americans, who wished to "lighten" people of Mexican descent by emphasizing Mexico's European cultural inheritance versus the indigenous ancestry of most ethnic Mexicans. But the announcement on the Fourth also underscored the limits of this social convention. Throughout the Southwest, Mexican Americans faced discrimination not just because they were culturally different but because they were racially mixed. In Lockhart, in 1941, not even "Spanish" people were white enough to be considered the social peers of Anglos. Instead, the prevailing Anglo-American sentiment refused to recognize Mexican Americans as equals, on the grounds that they were both excessively foreign and insufficiently Caucasian.

At the same time, Mexican Americans who chose to attend this Fourth of July dance apparently held a different opinion. By their very presence, Lockhart's Mexican Americans had laid claim to the heritage of the United States as their own. So, too, had Mexican Americans one hundred miles away in Poteet, who, in similar fashion, had attended an Armistice Day commemoration, although they too had been asked to leave.[7] Unfortunately, in neither case was the Mexican American reaction to their collective expulsion recorded. Nevertheless, the incidents in Lockhart and Poteet reveal that, despite Anglo-American prejudices, some Mexican Americans had begun to consider themselves integral members of U.S. society even before the Second World War. More often than not born in the United States, they increasingly saw their fortunes linked with the land of their birth rather than with the land that former generations had called home.[8]

Of course, those Mexicans who had first become Americans en masse as a result of the 1848 Treaty of Guadalupe-Hidalgo had never left their "home" country. But their numbers were quite limited, probably totaling no more than 100,000.[9] Constituting a despised and defeated enemy after the Mexican-American War, their incorporation into the United States was partial and conflict-ridden.[10] Despite some immigration during the late nineteenth century, the ethnic Mexican population within the United States remained relatively small until the 1910s and 1920s, when perhaps as many as one million Mexicans entered the country.[11] Fleeing the violence and poverty that accompanied the Mexican Revolution and drawn by the industrial jobs generated by the First World War, these immigrants found work in fields and factories from Los Angeles to Detroit. They also transformed the Mexican population north of the Rio Grande into a largely immigrant community for at least a generation.

The advent of the Great Depression, however, prompted the movement of people to reverse directions. According to one estimate, during the years of economic crisis between a quarter- and a half-million people of Mexican descent left the United States for Mexico.[12] Convinced that Mexicans were both a threat to labor and a social burden, local charity officials working with municipal authorities throughout the country encouraged the repatriation of legal aliens (and the expatriation of their American-born children) by paying bus and train fares to Mexico and threatening to cut off emergency cash and food supplies to impoverished families.[13] In addition, in Los Angeles in 1931, federal agents conducted several roundups of suspected aliens. Combined, these official efforts contributed to the mass return of Mexicans south across the border.[14] The emergence of a substantial native-born majority by 1940 was the result. While popular opinion continued to associate Mexican heritage with alien status, on the eve of World War II people of Mexican descent within the United States—perhaps as many as two-and-a-half million strong—were almost twice as likely to have been born north of the Rio Grande than south of it.[15]

Civil rights efforts among Mexican Americans began as early as the 1920s, largely among these U.S. citizens. Born, raised and, most importantly, intending to stay in the United States, ethnic activists argued that Mexican Americans were deserving of all the promises and privileges of their American birth. In the face of extensive Anglo-American prejudice, their primary strategy was to encourage Mexican Americans to assume the rights and responsibilities of American citizenship. Desiring to avoid the snare of segregation while maintaining a measure of pride in their ethnic background, Mexican American leaders sought acceptance of people of Mexican descent as equals.

The task before them was substantial. Repatriation efforts were the culmination of a severe anti-immigrant, anti-Mexican backlash that had swept the Southwest and the halls of Congress during the 1920s. Buttressing the backlash was eugenics theory, the latest attempt to place a scientific veneer on centuries-old notions of white supremacy. Eugenicists insisted that mixed races were both inherently degenerate and dangerously fertile, and they labeled Mexicans as a prime example of a dangerous "mongrelized" race. Immigration restrictionists lent a ready ear. Thus, in 1928, Congressman John Box of East Texas argued that the only way to protect "American racial stock" from Mexico's degrading "blend of low-grade Spanish, peonized Indian, and negro slave" was to bar all entries from the country.[16] Only intense lobbying from Western ranchers, farmers, and railroad men—all eager users of low-paid Mexican workers—successfully prevented the federal curtailment of immigration from Mexico.

In the decades before World War II, negative assumptions about people of Mexican descent were pervasive yet often contradictory. Despite the popularity of eugenics, racial prejudice against Mexicans also stemmed from the suspicion that the ethnic group was not mixed at all. Or, as one San Antonio constituent complained to Box, also in 1928, his way of life was under assault by a group he characterized as "worthless-despicable . . . impudent, sullen and obnoxious," namely, that "horde of Aztec Indians calling themselves Mexicans."[17] Employers were similarly at odds regarding Mexican labor. While some business interests regarded Mexicans as dangerously prone to labor agitation, others deemed the ethnic group remarkably submissive. In 1930 a list of California farm operators' objections to Mexican labor included that the population required "constant watching," was "untrustworthy and tricky" and tended to "strike readily." Yet, in the same report, at least one farm operator was certain that Mexican workers were "bovine and tractable individuals."[18] Meanwhile, popular stereotypes about Mexicans ranged from their being "dirty, shiftless and lazy," in the opinion of one urban reformer, to their being a cruel and hyperpassionate race that was prone to knifings and sex-crimes.[19]

Despite the clashing viewpoints, the result of such prejudices was consistent: before 1940 Anglo Americans seldom treated people of Mexican descent as equals before the law. Although, unlike African Americans, ethnic Mexicans did not encounter a system of segregation mandated by law, as the Lockhart Fourth of July dance revealed, the accumulation of local prejudices often resulted in similar practices. The situation was particularly oppressive in Texas, where many restaurants and barbershops routinely extended the state's southern heritage by refusing Mexican trade.[20] Across the Southwest, moreover, schoolchildren of Mexican descent, whether immigrant or native-born, English- or Spanish-speaking, usually attended segregated schools that were overcrowded and substandard. In addition, before World War II, labor unions, juries, and real estate covenants regularly excluded Mexican-origin people. Employers, meanwhile, not only routinely paid Mexican Americans and Mexican immigrants less than Anglo Americans for the same work, they also refused to hire people of Mexican descent for advanced positions, regardless of their nationality or on-the-job experience. Skilled work, most employers insisted, was a "a white man's job."[21]

Concentrated on the lowest rungs of the employment ladder, Mexicans in the United States—citizens as well as aliens—often endured economic hardship in the decades prior to World War II. Many lived in migrant agricultural camps and ethnic neighborhoods characterized by extreme poverty, lack of running water, overcrowded quarters, and, consequently, dirt and disease. Los Angeles and San Antonio, the two urban areas with the largest concentrations of people of Mexican descent, exhibited particularly appalling conditions.[22] In Los Angeles, during the 1910s and 1920s, the Mexican-origin population was congregated in a neighborhood called Sonoratown, which even Jacob Riis, the noted muckraker and photographer of urban ills, described as the "worse" slum he had ever seen.[23] Meanwhile, San Antonio in the 1930s had the nation's highest rates of tuberculosis infection and infant mortality, both of which took their heaviest toll among the city's ethnic Mexican population.[24] Already among the nation's poorest populations, people of Mexican descent fell into even more dire economic straits with the start of the Great Depression. One result was a decade of extraordinary strike activity among ethnic Mexican people in the United States, as pecan shellers in Texas, autoworkers in Michigan, coal miners in New Mexico, and thousands of farmworkers in California all went on strike and achieved some victories.[25]

Confronting poverty and prejudice both, most adults of Mexican descent during the 1930s concentrated on the more pressing issue, ensuring a livelihood for themselves and their children. Yet the 1930s also saw the rapid expansion of one of the earliest and most enduring Mexican American civil rights organizations, the League of United Latin American Citizens (LULAC), founded in Corpus Christi, Texas, in 1929.[26] From its origin the League promoted an understanding of Mexican Americans as American citizens foremost. The founders of the League encouraged Mexican Americans to present themselves as, in the words of the organization's founding document, "the best, purest, and more perfect type of true and loyal citizen of the United States of America."[27] The new emphasis on obtaining civil rights by practicing good citizenship proved popular: the league soon spread from its base in South Texas to form chapters throughout the state and, by 1940, throughout the Southwest.[28]

A first order of business was differentiating U.S. citizens of Mexican descent from more recent arrivals. League membership was restricted to American citizens. Although Mexicans and Mexican Americans shared a common culture, a common language, and, most fundamentally, a common experience of oppression, LULAC members, many of whom came from centuries-old Tejano families, quickly decided that the organization's detachment from immigrant concerns was a strategic necessity. The problem, they contended, was that not only did Anglo Americans generally consider all people of Mexican descent foreigners, many Mexican Americans also viewed themselves as a people apart from those they called *"los americanos."* The solution, according to the organization, was to encourage Mexican Americans to define and assert themselves as equals by claiming their full rights as citizens. League members also argued that once Mexican Americans did so they would be in a better position to help their immigrant cousins. Still, the decision to exclude non-citizens from membership illustrated how LULAC members negotiated the anti-immigrant backlash of the 1920s.

Determined to dispel the belief that all people of Mexican descent were foreigners, league members also hoped to counter a set of related assumptions that cast the ethnic group as a political "menace."[29] Acutely aware of South Texas's grand political tradition, whereby, according to one pithy phrase, "While blacks were not allowed to vote, Mexican Americans *were voted*," LULAC members vowed to pay their poll taxes and exercise the franchise responsibly.[30] The organization likewise sought to refute the notions—dating back centuries to the Black Legend but reinforced as a result of the violence and radicalism of the Mexican Revolution—that Latin Americans were both disloyal and subversive.[31] In particular, LULAC members vigorously shielded themselves from any hint of labor radicalism. During the pecan shellers' strike in San Antonio in 1938, for example, LULAC professed sympathy for the workers' desperate poverty but condemned the strike itself, citing the involvement of Communist Party members.[32]

Beyond endeavoring to refute the characterization of Mexican Americans as corrupt, disloyal, and radical, league members attempted to define what ethnic group members were. Most importantly, founding members of the league argued that Mexican Americans emulated the key standards of citizenship as confirmed by the nation's political, legal, and popular culture. Traditionally, the ideal citizen had been defined as white, male, and willing to serve his country in battle. Although only the first two attributes had been enshrined in the U.S. Constitution in 1789, all three had been self-reinforcing for much of U.S. history. Declaring in 1929 their "unquestionable loyalty to the ideals, principles, and citizenship of the United States of America," LULAC members systematically portrayed Mexican Americans as model citizen-patriots.[33]

At a time when "Mexican" and "American" referred as much to race as to nationality, LULAC members insisted that people of Mexican descent were white. Fully aware that first-class citizenship was reserved for white Americans, LULAC members maintained that Mexican Americans, despite their mixed indigenous and European heritage, properly fell within the favored category. Strengthening LULAC's case, the U.S. government, since the nineteenth century, had usually counted Mexican Americans as part of the country's "white population."[34] When the 1930 census placed people of Mexican descent into a racial category distinct from whites for the first (and only) time, which prompted local municipalities to follow suit, LULAC members strenuously—and successfully—objected.[35] In a 1930 court case in Del Rio, Texas, LULAC also protested the segregation of Mexican American children from "other white races."[36] In a similar vein, in 1939 a league member from New Mexico angrily condemned those academics who insisted that Mexicans were "non-white" or "colored." Outraged by the practice, he revealed the extent of his own racial prejudice: "Am I going to sit by and meekly allow this indignity, this insult to my blood, to my ancestors, to my very soul, go unchallenged?"[37] Not surprisingly, given such sentiments, LULAC members, before World War II, adamantly rejected any kind of political coalition with African American civil rights activists. Wishing to avoid the taint of foreign status as well as of radical politics, they also tried to avoid the taint of color.

Beyond whiteness, the league promoted a particularly masculinist and militaristic view of Mexican Americans. Notably, the league's original membership was entirely male. Women did not become voting members of LULAC until 1933. Even then, most LULAC women participated through ladies' auxiliaries that tended to undertake charitable and social work versus the political work of the male-dominated league councils.[38] Equally important, several founding members of the league were proud veterans of World War I, a status that both showcased their masculinity and cemented their citizenship claims.[39] Foreshadowing the effects of World War II, these members traced their interest in civil rights to their participation in the Great War. While, in 1917, the vast majority of people of Mexican descent in the United States were immigrants, and thus not required to serve, for the many Mexican Americans who did serve, military service set them apart as Americans.[40]

For LULAC members, moreover, military service became a way to exploit the gap between American creed and practice. In 1933, J. Luz Sáenz, a Texas educator and prominent LULAC member, published a volume entitled *Los méxico-americanos en la gran guerra y su contingente en pró de la democracia, la humanidad, y la justicia*.[41] Based on his personal diary, the book recounted the exploits of ethnic Mexican soldiers who had fought on behalf of "democracy, humanity and justice." The book also decried the absence of these same qualities at home. Indeed, shortly after the war's conclusion, the Anglo-American townspeople of Falfurrias, Texas, setting a precedent for the incidents at Lockhart and Poteet a generation later, had expelled Mexican American veterans from a Fourth of July dance.[42] In the face of such obstacles, the league continued to broadcast the essential credentials Mexican Americans brought to the task of being U.S. citizens, including their status as veterans.

Accepting the "male warrior as a central tenet of patriotic culture," league members attempted to emulate that central citizenship tripod of whiteness, masculinity, and military service.[43] The strategy, however, came at a substantial cost. LULAC members usually placed the onus for dismantling discrimination primarily upon Mexican-descent people. O. Douglas Weeks, a University of Texas political scientist, who wrote a scholarly article about the league's founding, certainly recognized the essence of LULAC's strategy. He concluded that "the greatest stumbling block" to equality was "the Mexican American himself who possesses no very clear conception of the significance of the privileges and duties of his American citizenship."[44] While harsh, Weeks's assessment mirrored LULAC's assumptions.

Inevitably, however, a strategy that targeted Mexican American "deficiencies," to borrow Weeks's term, minimized the role Anglo Americans played in maintaining the Southwest's system of political and social inequality. The strategy also ignored the fundamental problem of racial bias. After all, signs that read "No Mexicans" hardly meant that acculturated Mexican Americans were welcome. Although the organization sometimes pursued boycotts of local businesses, LULAC's primary hope was that, gradually, through ethnic uplift and assimilation, such signs might become less prevalent. Before World War II, the organization's philosophy was based on two interrelated assumptions—one, that if only Americans knew better, discrimination might disappear, and, two, that if only Mexicans knew better how to be Americans, then Americans might know better.

While circumscribed, LULAC's approach was not unique. To the contrary, in California, a student organization called the Mexican American Movement, founded in 1934, echoed many LULAC themes. Within a population that was making the transition from an immigrant majority to a native-born majority, both organizations struggled to define and defend the role of Mexican Americans as Americans first. Thus, in 1938 Felix Gutiérrez, the editor of MAM's newspaper, the *Mexican Voice*, expressed his sharp disagreement with the contention of the Mexican consul in Los Angeles that people of Mexican descent owed their first loyalty to Mexico. Acknowledging that Mexican immigrants had depended upon the consulate in times of trouble, Gutiérrez gave notice that times had changed. He invited the consul to witness how young people of Mexican descent "go around with American friends, taken for one, treated as one and feeling as one."[45]

Like LULAC, MAM also embraced an American identity and advocated ethnic self-improvement as the first step toward improved race relations. While both organizations emphasized citizenship, as a student group, MAM stressed scholastic achievement as well. Only through higher education, MAM members asserted, could Mexican Americans triumph against "prejudice, segregation, discrimination, social inequality," and, notably, what members labeled an ethnic-group "inferiority complex."[46] Although MAM members repeatedly professed faith in the ability of Mexican Americans to progress, their faith was matched by a concern about the ethnic group's "backward conditions."[47] As a result, MAM, again, like LULAC, placed the principal responsibility for dismantling race prejudice upon Mexican American shoulders. For both groups, the strategy reflected both the limited space in which these early organizations had to maneuver as well as a complicated mix of ethnic group pride and internalized racism among members.

An alternative vision of inclusion that neither made a distinction between immigrant and citizen nor placed the problem of discrimination wholly at the feet of the Mexican-origin population did emerge. Launched in 1939 in Los Angeles, El Congreso del Pueblo de Habla Española (the Congress of Spanish-Speaking People) was unique in stressing a pan-Latino unity rooted in the overwhelmingly working-class character of Spanish-speaking people in the United States. The organization also differed from LULAC and MAM because it officially endorsed women's equality and many of its key members were women.[48] Founded by labor activists with some support from the Communist Party, El Congreso thus sought equal rights for Mexicans from both sides of the border, men and women alike. According to congress members, Mexican-descent workers, whether native- or foreign-born, were vital contributors to the U.S. economy and society. Therefore, instead of asking ethnic Mexicans to showcase their loyalty and social value, the organization demanded that Anglo Americans prove they were good citizens by living up to the nation's democratic ideals. Standing somewhat apart from the Mexican American civil rights mainstream, El Congreso also favored direct action versus gradual acculturation. When the California assembly in 1939 threatened to exclude immigrants from relief rolls, for example, congress members engaged in protest tactics that foreshadowed the emergence of the Chicano movement a generation later: they participated in a hunger march, conducted a letter-writing campaign, and held a massive rally in Sacramento.[49] Although El Congreso did not survive the World War II era, its more aggressive attitude did, as the war spurred among Mexican-descent people within the United States not only an increased identification with the United States but also a growing impatience with the status quo.

A MINORITY AT WAR

In June 1942, one E. H. Johnson, an Albuquerque resident, dashed off a letter to U.S. Senator Dennis Chavez, accusing the New Deal Democrat of harping on "the non-existent subject of 'racial intolerance'" for political gain. In a characteristically direct response, Chavez affirmed his determination to see that President Roosevelt's Four Freedoms would "embrace everybody." He blasted the injustice of segregation by highlighting the sacrifices that had been made by men in battle, including, most recently, in the Philippines: "When New Mexico boys, relatives of those who died at Bataan, are denied the privilege of going into a

[Roswell, N.M.] swimming pool—a pool for which I tried to appropriate the money . . . because their names happened to be similar to mine, I am not going to stand by idly, regardless of what your opinion or anybody else's might be." No doubt counting the constituent's vote irretrievably lost, Chavez closed with this parting shot: "If you don't like the way I am doing things, well and good. As far as I am concerned, you can still have the privilege of burning another cross."[50]

Elected to the U.S. Senate in 1936 (and reelected every six years until his death in 1962), Chavez was the only Mexican American political actor on the national stage during the 1940s. His snappy response to Mr. Johnson reflected the impatience of a politician who, throughout his career, had encountered the insinuation, often intermixed with references to his ethnic background, that he was acting divisively if not disloyally by championing civil rights.[51] A descendant of a seventeenth-century New Mexican family, Chavez often countered such criticism by saying that he was "American before Plymouth Rock." More importantly, Chavez's reference to the Mexican American contribution to the war effort captured a major theme of the era. Repeatedly, Mexican American ethnic leaders argued that the fair reward for military service abroad was the dismantling of discriminatory practices at home. Like African Americans, they sought a "double victory."[52] During the war, masculinist and militaristic claims on citizenship proliferated, as Mexican American soldiers amply demonstrated the ultimate proof of patriotism: the willingness to give their lives for their country. Some ethnic activists, like Chavez, also drew explicit linkages between the domestic struggle for equality and U.S. wartime objectives. In both cases, Mexican American leaders challenged the United States to make real the ideals that the country proclaimed at home and abroad.

At the same time, federal and local governments, seeking to foster national unity during wartime, took unprecedented, if tentative, steps toward addressing minority concerns. Even before the fighting started, President Roosevelt, under considerable pressure from black civil rights leaders, ordered defense industry work open to racial and ethnic minorities and set up the Fair Employment Practices Committee to investigate workplace inequality. In addition, Mexican Americans were the unique beneficiaries of Washington's 1942 decision to establish a Spanish-speaking People's Division within the wartime Office of the Coordinator of Inter-American Affairs (CIAA). While the CIAA's prime responsibility was to maintain friendly relations within the hemisphere, the Spanish-speaking People's Division attempted to further that task by ameliorating tensions within the United States between ethnic Mexicans and Anglos.[53] Combined, these government programs aimed to promote the acceptance of Mexican Americans as integral and valuable members of U.S. society.

That message certainly got through to many Mexican Americans as a result of their wartime experience. Ethnic leaders rejoiced in what they saw as a central accomplishment of the war: a shift in self-perception among members of their ethnic group, from "Mexican" to "American." During the conflict, thousands of ordinary Mexican Americans—men and women alike—donned hard hats and trousers to work in critical defense industries centered out West. These workers expressed new confidence in their contribution to American society and their rightful place within it.[54] An even more important symbol of inclusion was the military uniform that was donned by nearly an entire generation of young Mexican American men. As one Mexican American Movement leader enthused, military service provided Mexican Americans with "a chance to fit into the scheme of things, a chance to belong."[55] Unlike African Americans, who were shunted into segregated, and usually service, units for most of the war, and who had to, in the words of one advocate, "fight for the right to fight for democracy," Mexican Americans participated in combat as equals.[56] In addition, a small number of Mexican American women enlisted without restriction as Army WACS, Navy WAVES, and members of the Marine Corps' Women Reserve.[57] The upshot, for many, was a burgeoning recognition of themselves as Americans.

Military life, in particular, often proved a personal revelation. The war took thousands of Mexican Americans away from the Southwest and its complicated pattern of social difference, and exposed them to the rough equality of the armed forces. While incidents of discrimination occurred, Mexican Americans also met people from different parts of the country who accepted them as just another group of ethnic Americans instead of the specific targets of segregation they had been at home.[58] "The rest of the world isn't like Descanso," noted one California-born soldier, who thought about moving back East, where his girlfriend's family lived.[59] Similarly, another young Californian declared that his military experience had renewed his faith in his country and himself. Angry about the racism that had blighted his life before the war, he had flirted with *sinarquismo*, the Mexican fascist movement (with a small American following) that anticipated the return of the American Southwest to Mexico once the Nazis triumphed. But his politics changed after he got drafted because "the Army has treated me swell. I feel like I amount to something now."[60]

Military service also offered more concrete benefits to a disadvantaged ethnic group. For the most impoverished and unschooled Mexican Americans, the armed services provided a measure of nutritional as well as educational luxury: three full meals a day plus on-the-job training. Moreover, many Mexican Americans hoped that the knowledge they gained in the fields of mechanics, electronics, and aeronautics might serve to jump-start their careers once they were back home.[61] According to the Office of Inter-American Affairs, in 1943 the U.S. Army also arranged bilingual basic training—that is, a chance to learn some English—for at least fifty-four U.S.-born, Spanish-speaking soldiers of Mexican descent. Representative of this group was one Ricardo Noyola, a Texas native who at the age of twenty-six had spent half his life harvesting wheat and cotton and had never attended school. In a revealing boast about the era's newfound impulse toward social reform and inclusion, a government publication noted, "It took war to bring about a change for Noyola and his people, to give him a chance."[62] Of course, the cost of belonging was high: soldiers risked death, the most equalizing experience of all.

Yet, in a strange way, combat was also an opportunity. In the words of one writer: "The war gave much to the Mexican American soldier. Here he was judged as a man and a fighter."[63] With good reason, Mexican American soldiers—indeed, the entire Mexican American population—took extraordinary pride in their wartime sacrifices and accomplishments. Early in the war, for example, Mexican Americans endured some of the most brutal fighting when artillerymen from two former National Guard units from New Mexico participated in the battles for Bataan and Corregidor. These units had been sent to the Pacific theater specifically because so many of their soldiers were Spanish-speakers who could communicate with their Filipino allies. During the fighting and the subsequent Bataan Death March, one official source noted, "New Mexico gave the fullest measure of devotion—one quarter of the 9,000 men from the mainland lost."[64] Also celebrated was the bravery of the men of Company E, another former National Guard unit comprised entirely of Mexican Americans from the same El Paso, Texas, neighborhood. They were the first U.S. troops to land on Italian soil. As one veteran recalled: "The Germans thought they had the Mexican Army fighting because we all spoke Spanish." Company E led the army's costly and ultimately futile attempt in January 1944 to reach Rome by crossing the swollen Rapido River despite heavy Nazi defenses.[65] The most impressive testament to Mexican American heroism and sacrifice was, of course, the bestowal of the Congressional Medal of Honor, the nation's highest military commendation. Of the eleven medals given to Mexican Americans for their World War II exploits, six were awarded posthumously.[66]

During World War II, the frequent appearance of Spanish-surnamed soldiers on casualty and awards lists soon attracted attention beyond the ethnic group. Beatrice Griffith, a sociologist who investigated Mexican American life in Los Angeles, concluded in her 1948 book *American Me* that this ethnic group had made a disproportionate sacrifice in the war effort. Knowing that Mexican Americans accounted for roughly 10 percent of the Los Angeles population, Griffith had looked randomly at ten casualty lists published in city newspapers. She discovered that about 20 percent of the casualties had Spanish surnames, as well as about 20 percent of those who were listed for awards.[67] Other writers noted that Mexican Americans were also probably disproportionately represented among the casualties in the Philippines, given the great number of New Mexicans involved in the fighting, and, within that group, the great number of Mexican Americans.[68] Nearly ten years after the war, an Anglo observer describing "Spanish American" life in New Mexico shared what had become the conventional wisdom concerning the patriotism of the state's Spanish-surnamed inhabitants during World War II: "In many villages," the draft board had nothing to do, because "each boy volunteered as soon as he was acceptable."[69] Unfortunately, given the lack of army documentation, obtaining precise information about Mexican Americans who served and died in World War II is difficult.[70] Such oft-repeated assertions that Mexican Americans served, died—and even received military commendations—in disproportionate numbers were more important for their implication of Mexican American valor than for their numerical specificity, however.

For many Mexican Americans, here was a story of the underdog coming out on top. One of the most compelling figures in Mexican popular culture is the underdog. Plays and stories about the altar boy who knows more than the priest, the Indian who outwits the Spaniard, the country yokel who proves to be more sophisticated than the urban dweller are profuse.[71] In the case of World War II, many Mexican American soldiers considered their modest backgrounds an advantage. As one Tejano veteran contended, years of hard labor at menial jobs had suddenly proved useful, once the shooting started: "When we were told to dig a trench or fox hole there was no question about who was superior behind the business end of the shovel."[72] More importantly, humble men often turned out to be dedicated warriors. For example, in 1943 a Colorado sugar-beet worker, a mere private, found himself on the snow-covered Aleutian island of Attu, leading the charge that would eventually capture an important mountain pass. For his bravery in the face of massive enemy fire, Joe P. Martinez—at the cost of his life—became the first draftee to be awarded the Congressional Medal of Honor.[73] In a similar topsy-turvy fashion, an unpresuming lane, unpaved and less than two blocks long, in the town of Silvis, Illinois, earned the sobriquet "Hero Street" during World War II because of the extraordinarily high participation rate of its residents in the armed forces. Settled during the 1930s by Mexican immigrant families who had migrated north to work on the railroad, the street's twenty-five houses sent an amazing forty-five young men off to the war, six of whom never returned. One family sent six sons, another seven, as younger siblings resolutely followed their older brothers to war.[74]

Yet another Mexican cultural tradition, in George Mariscal's phrase, "warrior patriotism," considers the willingness to risk one's life for one's country a commendable and even essential male attribute.[75] Certainly, many Mexican American veterans saw their service in that light. For example, Silvestre Herrera, a recipient of the Congressional Medal of Honor (see Fig, 1), justified his decision to enter a minefield and single-handedly attack an enemy stronghold in France as the product of his cultural upbringing. As he explained to a journalist fifty years after his feet were blown off, "I am a Mexican-American and we have a tradition. We're supposed to be men, not sissies."[76] Likewise, Mexican American paratroopers boasted that their ethnic group was especially well represented within that branch of the service because members were drawn to such hazardous missions as jumping out of airplanes. As one young enlistee explained, "When they told us at the induction centers that the Paratroopers was the toughest of all to get in and stay in— we decided that was for us."[77] Three decades after the war, a Mexican American who became a career army man remained convinced that Mexican American fighting men had demonstrated a unique talent in combat: "Every platoon, every rifle [squad] had a Rodriguez or Martinez [who] was an outstanding soldier. . . . There was something about this fighting business that we ate up! Perhaps we welcomed the chance to show this nation that we were loyal, faithful and could be depended

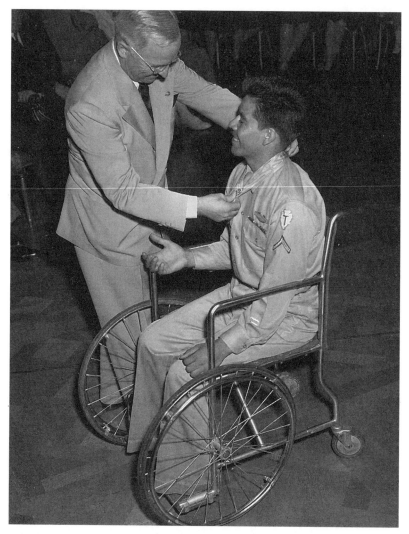

Figure 1. President Harry S. Truman awards the Congressional Medal of Honor to Silvestre Herrera. Herrera's valor on the battlefield during World War II, like the courage of the ten other Mexican American recipients of the award during that conflict, became both a source of ethnic pride and a way for such groups as LULAC and the American G.I. Forum to argue for equality for all Mexican Americans. Source: National Archives.

upon given the opportunity."[78] Invariably, such unmuffled expressions of ethnic pride carried a political charge: Mexican-flavored patriotism became all-American patriotism as ethnic group members rested their hopes of being recognized as equals upon their military contributions to the war.

After some struggle, supporting evidence could be found on the home front. When the war began, defense industry employers often flatly rejected Mexican Americans on the grounds that they were physically weaker, less intelligent, and less responsible than Anglo workers. Mexican and Mexican American alike were also dismissed as foreigners.[79] Nevertheless, wartime labor shortages not only spurred the importation of temporary contract workers from Mexico, under what popularly became known as the Bracero Program, but the labor crunch also opened new jobs for many groups that historically had faced workplace discrimination, including Mexican Americans. In 1943, Carlos Castañeda, a professor of history at the University of Texas at Austin and, during World War II, a regional director of the Fair Employment Practices Division, noted that Mexican Americans were finding work in "the shipyard, the airship factories, the oil industry, the mines, [and] the munitions factories." Still, he reported, most employers continued to relegate Mexican Americans to less skilled positions.[80] The limited effectiveness of the FEPC was not surprising: endowed with only investigative authority, it could expose discrimination but not punish it.[81]

Despite (or perhaps because of) persistent obstacles to full equality, many Mexican American workers valued their contribution to the war effort and were proud of their accomplishments. While still likely to hold unskilled positions, these workers nevertheless usually enjoyed better-paying jobs than they had held before the war. On the factory floor and in special training schools established during the conflict, they also gained specialized skills.[82] Certainly, complaints registered with the FEPC and the Spanish-speaking People's Division of the CIAA during the war revealed the deeply entrenched nature of discrimination against Mexican Americans. They also suggested, however, an increased expectation of fair treatment among some Mexican American workers. As one Mexican American woman later explained, four years of defense work had granted her and her colleagues "new job skills, self-confidence, and a sense of self-worth."[83] In the words of another worker, after having worked so hard to win the war, discrimination now struck her as "totally unfair."[84] Imbued with a new sense of belonging, these Mexican American workers demanded to be treated as equals.

Given a measure of progress on the employment front and notable achievements on the battlefield, many Mexican Americans were disappointed to see that it was the zoot-suiters, and not soldiers or workers, who were grabbing national headlines during the summer of 1943. The longish coat and pegged pants of the zoot suit had become a popular style among many young Mexican Americans, a minority of whom wore the outfit as a distinct symbol of rebellion and gang membership. Although not every zooter was criminally inclined, nor was every zoot-suiter a Mexican American, by the summer of 1943, thanks to critical press reports and mass arrests such as those that occurred in the infamous Sleepy Lagoon Case, an image of Mexican American youth as "forming roving gangs of blood-thirsty, marihuana-crazed young men [and] committing arson, rape and robbery" had been well set in the public's mind.[85] Long-simmering racial tensions erupted that June after newspapers reported that a gang of zoot-suiters had assaulted some Navy soldiers. For the next five days, sailors, joined by soldiers and marines, took the law into their own hands by conducting massive sweeps of Mexican neighborhoods and beating up Mexican-descent youths. The local police response was to arrest the instigators of the violence. Fortunately for the Mexican American community, the State Department, after receiving a request from the Mexican ambassador to investigate the riots, placed pressure upon the respective branches of the military to control their men. Military officials then forbade servicemen from entering what had become a virtual battleground in Los Angeles. The riots stopped.[86]

While the riots prompted the Los Angeles Mexican American community to organize defense committees, many individuals nonetheless expressed frustration at the young people involved. Dependent upon newspapers from the states, for example, Raul Morin, a World War II veteran, related how other Mexican American soldiers "felt uncomfortable" when they heard about the riots, especially when they were asked by Anglo servicemen, "What kind of citizens are those Mexican Zoot-Zooters that would beat up our own Navy Men?"[87] Closer to home, the Los Angeles Spanish-language newspaper *La Opinión* also pointed the finger of blame at Mexican American youth. Although some innocent youths had been beaten and therefore "the just [had] paid for the sinners" (*pagaron justos por pecadores*), one editorial stated, the zoot-suiters had invited the wrath of U.S. servicemen upon the entire Mexican American community.[88] Even a Mexican American who served on a youth advocacy board suggested that all juveniles "between sixteen and eighteen years of age should be summarily placed into military reserve organizations."[89] Presumably, he meant juveniles of Mexican descent. In the wake of the riots, the central concern of Los Angeles's Mexican Americans was rehabilitating the image of their youth. Significantly, as part of this endeavor and in an echo of a pre-war civil rights strategy, local activists spent much of their time insisting that Mexican Americans were white and therefore not the legitimate targets of discrimination.[90]

In the effort to convey that members of their ethnic group were excellent citizenship material, the Mexican American soldier was, of course, a more helpful image than that of the Mexican American zoot-suiter. Indeed, LULAC members strongly suggested that, by serving their country, Mexican Americans had proved themselves to be both real men and real Americans. Although the organization experienced declining membership during the war years, a core group of members in South Texas that monitored instances of discrimination embraced that argument. Reporting how a planned 1943 farewell celebration for departing soldiers had been thrown into disarray when they and their companions had been denied entrance to not one but two public swimming pools in Welasco, for example, one Hector Valdez praised Mexican Americans soldiers as "proud young fighters [on behalf] of Democracy and Liberty."[91] That same year, Leocardio Duran, of Fort Bend, appealed to the Texas governor for anti-discrimination legislation, "in the names of our sons, brothers, and other dear ones who are at present in the battle field (and from this County there are so many) so that Democracy . . . may exist."[92] For his part, John J. Herrera, an early leader of LULAC whose own patriotism prompted him to christen his son Douglas MacArthur, claimed an all-American identity for boys of Mexican descent that rested upon military service and sports.[93] In a letter lamenting widespread discrimination in the small towns of New Gulf and Boling, Herrera complained that Mexican Americans at the local high school were generally not allowed to play on the football team, even though football was "a game which I love and every American boy loves." For a while, he wrote, the rule apparently had been bent for a talented player named Albino Campos, a Mexican citizen, who had been Boling High's star football player until he had been kicked off the team for protesting the exclusion of other ethnic Mexicans. Herrera explained that he had advised Campos, who had decided to join the Marines, to focus on his military future, not the discriminatory past: "You are leaving next week to fight with the Marines, the proudest branch of our armed forces, but you will be fighting for the real Americans, not the people [who] call themselves Americans and live in this community; remember, Albino, you are fighting for the typical American which you don't find in New Gulf or Boling."[94] In Herrera's opinion, a Mexican boy who played the all-American game of football and opted to serve his adopted country made a better American than the U.S.-born purveyors of prejudice.

The circumstances of the war buttressed the argument. Whereas the United States at least had been founded upon the ideal that "all men were created equal," Nazi Germany promoted the concept of a master Aryan race. Like other minorities, Mexican Americans therefore contended that clinging to notions of racial superiority during the war was tantamount to siding with the enemy. According to LULAC members, for example, segregationists were "Anglo American saboteurs" and "bad citizens" who were "using the weapon of race prejudice to bring about disunity and dismay."[95] Still another LULAC member labeled discrimination "the underhand[ed] work of some persons, who are masquerating [*sic*] [as] loyal American citizens, but who, in fact are either spies or traitors to our Country."[96] Meanwhile, in Los Angeles, Manuel Ruiz Jr., an attorney who represented many young people during the riots, suggested that interethnic intolerance dangerously undermined the war effort by providing fodder for propaganda-makers in "Rome, Tokyo and Berlin."[97] Ruiz's comment made clear the enduring connections between the struggle for Mexican American civil rights at home and the goals and implications of American foreign policy.

So too did the Bracero Program. Even at a time of war-induced hyper-Americanization, Mexican Americans often found their plight indivisible from that of Mexican immigrants, especially in Texas. In June 1943, Mexico decided against sending contract workers to Texas, given the pervasiveness of anti-Mexican discrimination and segregation in the state. In an attempt to mollify the Mexican government, Governor Coke Stevenson set up a Good Neighbor Commission, a state agency that took its title directly from the Roosevelt administration's foreign policy goal of being a "good neighbor" to Latin America. Thus, the Good Neighbor Commission was dedicated both to promoting "friendship, understanding, and respect between Anglo American and Latin American citizens of the community" and to ensuring "cordial relations between Texas and Mexico." Immediately, Tejanos bombarded the commission with complaints of second-class treatment. Like their Fair Employment Practices Commission counterparts on the federal level, however, state commissioners lacked any authority beyond the power to investigate. And even in this task, they were hamstrung by a dearth of money and staff.[98] Not

surprisingly, the Mexican government remained unmoved. Again seeking to persuade Mexico to reverse its decision, the state legislature then
passed the Caucasian Race Resolution, which explicitly forbade the segregation of white people. The resolution's tacit inclusion of ethnic Mexicans within the privileged category was made clear by its stated intent
of fostering hemispheric cooperation during wartime. Thus, the resolution solemnly pronounced the segregation of Caucasians to be a violation of the Good Neighbor Policy, even as it implicitly endorsed the continued segregation of African Americans. Although the resolution
echoed the insistence of many Mexican Americans civil rights leaders
that their ethnic group was racially white, at a time when few Anglo Texans agreed, the resolution amounted to no more than a public relations
ploy, and an unsuccessful one at that.[99]

Nevertheless, the theme of hemispheric solidarity was one that Mexican Americans activists across the Southwest frequently adopted as they
diligently pursued equality during wartime. At the beginning of the war,
for example, Tucson activist Vicente Alfaro pleaded with the governor of
that state for integration of training schools, based upon the country's
promise to be a "good neighbor."[100] Similarly, in 1943 LULAC executive secretary Manuel C. Gonzales warned that incidents of discrimination against Mexican Americans "were surely perturbing the good relations between the residents of Mexico and the United States."[101] Yet,
even Mexican Americans also seemed to recognize that placing their
appeal within an international context had limits. Thus, another LULAC
member, outraged that he and his companions had been barred from a
public swimming pool in Fort Stockton, could only ask rhetorically,
"What of the Good Neighbor Policy then?" Notably, the barred man,
one M. R. González, recited a theme that Chicano movement participants were to adopt a generation later in regard to Viet Nam: "I told the
Sheriff that I would prefer to fight and die . . . here in my own hometown
than have to go and die in Guadalcanal or in North Africa, because here
was where we [Mexican Americans] had the worst enemies."[102]
González put an unusual twist on the standard formula by indicating that
both his patriotism and patience were finite. More commonly, during
World War II, Mexican Americans emphasized their unwavering adher-
ence to the American cause, in contrast to the racists who were undermining the twin goals of national unity and inter-American solidarity.

Among Mexican Americans, no one promoted these twin goals more,
or saw them as intertwined, as Senator Chavez of New Mexico. Yet the
proposition was always a tricky one. At the same time that Mexican

American activists insisted upon their status as American citizens, quite a few of them also claimed a role as informal representatives of Latin America within the United States. The second claim seemed to contradict the first, or at least contribute to the still lingering notion that all people of Mexican descent were foreigners. Yet Chavez powerfully reconciled the two positions by linking the domestic problem of discrimination to the integrity and credibility of U.S. leadership abroad. As the war drew to a close in 1945, Chavez warned that unless a remedy were found for the domestic problem of racial injustice, not only did "national disaster loom," but also, because racism undermined the U.S. reputation abroad, "world peace" was at stake. During the war, Chavez had held a series of Senate hearings to keep the spotlight focused on workplace discrimination. This alternative forum was necessary because administration officials often blocked regular meetings of the Fair Employment Practice Committee as detrimental to the war effort.[103] In contrast, Chavez upheld fair employment practice as "a cornerstone of foreign policy." In a 1945 speech with that title, he pressed for a permanent FEPC by reminding his Senate colleagues that among the flag-raisers at Iwo Jima there had been a soldier of "Latin ancestry" as well as a "full-blooded Pima Indian from Arizona."[104]

While the connection between battlefield sacrifice and home front equality was a common one, Chavez stood apart from many of his contemporaries by insisting that prejudice was not an aberrant phenomenon but one at the core of the American experience:

> I have heard it said a hundred times . . . that it is unfair, indecent, and un-American to deprive a man of his job because of his racial, religious, or political origins or persuasion. On the contrary, my fellow Americans, racial and ethnic prejudice are common among us, they are even characteristic of us. They most certainly are unfair and indecent, but they are not un-American . . . when examined in the light of everyday American practice. . . . Intolerance, prejudice, bigotry and discrimination are as American as a hot-dog.

Indicating the heightened sense of urgency felt by Mexican Americans, Chavez contended that condemning discrimination as "un-American" was no longer sufficient. Instead, federal legislation was necessary.[105]

THE FIGHT FOR CIVIL RIGHTS

Arturo Músquiz came home to West Texas adorned with five medals on his chest and scars above. In Germany, shrapnel had shattered part of his cheekbone and left him blind in one eye and deaf in one ear. To Pauline R. Kibbe, chair of the Texas Good Neighbor Commission, the soldier's multiple injuries "offered mute testimony" to his status as an "American hero." Many locals, however, disagreed. Restaurants and barbershops refused his business, and the only theater in town continued to seat "Mexicans" in the balcony. Although speech was still a struggle for him, Músquiz haltingly recalled for Kibbe that in the army a greater goal had prevailed: "All of us were against the Nazis, but good." So, he asked in a sudden burst of effort, "What's the matter with Texas?"[106]

Músquiz's evident battlefield service and his deep dismay regarding race prejudice at home illuminate the ways in which the Second World War energized the struggle for civil rights among people of Mexican descent. Cognizant of their contributions to the war effort, returning veterans and others reinvigorated and broadened the civil rights crusade. They demanded an end to discrimination, based upon the status of Mexican Americans as citizens who, moreover, had just served their country in war. As the LULAC *News* declared in 1946, World War II had achieved the "primary and general objective of the league, to teach Americans of Latin origin to be better and more loyal citizens. They have met the test with flying colors."[107] Through public protest and litigation, Mexican American activists in the decade after World War II successfully dismantled much of the segregation that the veteran Músquiz had encountered. Emphasizing Mexican American patriotism and military service, they achieved notable successes, despite the constraints imposed upon all activism by the domestic Red Scare. Indeed, ethnic leaders often presented Mexican Americans as committed Cold Warriors ready to serve their county again.

After the Second World War, Mexican American civil rights efforts more than ever hinged upon the demonstrated fealty of Mexican American soldiers. A prominent example was the 1948 book *Are We Good Neighbors?* Written by Alonso S. Perales, a founding member of LULAC, the book collected affidavits by Mexican Americans who had experienced discrimination in employment, housing, and at public establishments over the previous seven years. As Perales explained in the book's introduction, Mexican Americans had been "trying to make progress . . . ever since the end of the last World War [World War I] by means of cooperation and education," to no avail. Now they were insisting upon state and federal legislation to outlaw discrimination.[108] The affidavits demonstrated a clear pattern. If the person who had suffered discrimination was a soldier or a veteran, he invariably mentioned in which branch of the military he had served, the injuries he had received, and the medals he had been awarded. Those who were not soldiers offered similar information about their husbands, brothers, or sons who had gone to war. The message was clear: military service should merit peacetime equality.

As Perales knew, the irony of wartime heroes suffering second-class treatment was hard to ignore. That Governor Sidney Preston Osborne of Arizona should declare a Silvestre Herrera Day to honor the Congressional Medal Honoree was a point of pride. That the governor was forced to order Phoenix businesses to take down signs that read "No Mexican Trade Wanted" in advance of that day was a powerful commentary on the racism that remained embedded in American society.[109] Similarly, within a year after he returned home, Sgt. Marcario García, another Congressional Medal of Honor recipient, was refused service in the Oasis Cafe in Richmond, Texas. The fighting spirit of García, and, more broadly, the growing unwillingness of Mexican Americans to tolerate such abuse, was soon evident: García got into a scuffle with the cafe owner.[110] A national audience then heard about the injustice when Walter Winchell, the well-known radio personality, broadcast a story about it. Although peeved Richmond authorities later arrested the war hero on charges of "aggravated assault," Mexican Americans had won a public relations victory.[111]

After the war, Mexican American women also protested in the names of their loved ones who had gone off to war. In 1947, for instance, Mexican American men and women alike angrily responded to a Mrs. Charles Keller, the wife of an "American war veteran." Keller had written to her local newspaper in Edinburg, Texas, to complain that after a two-year absence during the war she had returned to find that the town had "become completely Mexican." Upset about a housing crunch, Keller suggested that the Mexicans should "go back over where they were before the war" in order to "give the American boys and their families a chance; [as] they gave their best to us." Of the dozen replies to Keller that appeared in the newspaper, Mexican American women wrote half. Mary L. Martínez, who had several relatives who were veterans, pointed out that "there were no restricted areas . . . in the battlefields. Everybody was the same, used the same weapons, and fought for the same cause." With more vehemence, Bertha Villareal, "a sister of a boy who lost his life fighting for this country," was glad to hear the Kellers were having difficulty finding a place to live. "It's a good thing," she wrote. "I am afraid there will never be a place in this part of the country for people like you, Mrs. Keller."[112]

No doubt the most well-publicized event that fused the battlefield sacrifices of Mexican American men with the protests of Mexican American women was the case of Pvt. Felix Longoria. Nearly four years after his combat death in 1945 in the Philippines, his remains were finally found. His body was shipped to Three Rivers, Texas, where the local funeral home denied his family the use of the funeral home's chapel and prepared to bury him in a segregated Mexican cemetery. The manager of the Rice Funeral Home explained to a curious news reporter that such segregation was no more than tradition: "We just never made it a practice to let them [Mexican Americans] use the chapel and we don't want to start now."[113]

Yet what had been common practice before the war was no longer acceptable to many Mexican Americans, including Longoria's widow, Beatrice. Upon her sister's suggestion, she contacted Dr. Hector P. Garcia, the founder of a veterans group called the American G.I. Forum, in nearby Corpus Christi. Within twenty-four hours, Garcia had arranged a protest meeting and alerted local newspapers of the incident. He had also telegraphed a complaint to Texas Senator Lyndon B. Johnson, pointing out that the funeral home's action was "a direct contradiction of those principles for which this American soldier made the supreme sacrifice."[114] For her part, Beatrice Longoria disregarded the funeral home's feeble and belated excuse that a simple misunderstanding had occurred. Instead, she accepted Johnson's prompt offer that her husband be buried at Arlington National Cemetery.[115] The Longoria case underscored the aversion of Mexican Americans to second-class treatment after the war, the group's greater willingness to resort to public protest, and the overall effectiveness of emphasizing the military contributions of Mexican Americans in order to obtain redress.

The incident also provided the American G.I. Forum with a mission. Founded as small veterans group in 1947 to secure benefits for its members, after the Longoria affair the organization emerged as one of the foremost Mexican American advocacy groups of the postwar era, with nearly twenty-five thousand members in thirteen states by the mid-1950s.[116] As they tackled the problem of discrimination, Forum members naturally referred to their status as former military men. A 1949 Forum report on school segregation in Texas, for instance, flatly pronounced that Mexican Americans "did not fight a system like the Nazi Socialist system in order to come back . . . and tolerate such humiliation and suffering of our own children."[117] The centrality of military service to the Forum's civil right strategy was apparent in Hector P. Garcia's prompt refutation of a draft board clerk's suggestion, shortly before the Korean War, that young men of Mexican descent were shirking their duty by pretending to be illiterate. Not only was the heroic record of Mexican Americans well known, Garcia said, but also the "vicious system of segregation" in Texas promoted illiteracy by offering Mexican-origin children an inferior education. If only state officials would end segregation, he maintained, "we would have more enlightened citizens ready and willing to serve and die for our Country—The United States of America."[118]

Like LULAC, therefore, the Forum advocated—both through its reform efforts and its organizational framework—a particularly male-dominated and militaristic form of American citizenship. As a veterans' organization, the Forum readily broadcast the patriotism of Mexican American men. Although individual Mexican American women sometimes linked their civil rights fortunes to Mexican American servicemen, within the organization, Forum women—like lady LULACers—mainly participated via ladies' auxiliaries. The auxiliaries concentrated on organizing social events, including picnics and bake sales, versus pursuing political work.[119] As evidenced in the organization's newsletters and other publications, another popular, but ancillary, role for many young women was to be crowned as festival queens.[120] What diminished slightly in the postwar era was an automatic emphasis on whiteness.

To be sure, some racial attitudes and strategies stayed the same. During the 1940s and 1950s, activists continued to protest whenever local police, health department officials, or prison administrators classified Mexican Americans as anything other than "white."[121] Moreover, individual Mexican Americans, like Pedro Ochoa of Dallas, might hold virulent anti-black attitudes. A publisher of a small weekly Spanish-language newspaper called the *Dallas Americano* during the 1950s, Ochoa advocated an American identity for all Mexican Americans that rested upon a powerful sense of white supremacy. Tellingly, however, Ochoa also condemned LULAC and the American G.I. Forum as "nigger groups" (*agrupaciones niggeranias*). Not only had leaders of both organizations repeatedly called for an end to segregation, including against black people, but, as Ochoa noted and criticized, Mexican American activists had allied themselves with the National Association for the Advancement of Colored People to seek redress in court.[122]

By doing so, Mexican Americans issued a sweeping and precedent-setting challenge to segregation. Civil rights activists before World

War II had contended—mostly in the court of public opinion—that Mexican Americans were racially white and therefore rightfully excluded from segregation's grasp. In the postwar era, however, Mexican American activists made the more fundamental legal case that segregation constituted a violation of the Constitution's equal protection clause. For example, in California's 1946 Mendez vs. Westminster, Orange County, School District Mexican American parents petitioned the court that the Fourteenth Amendment be applied to their children's education and received a landmark favorable ruling banning school segregation. A similar victory for Mexican Americans followed two years later in Texas. Although other hurdles remained, together these cases narrowed the pedagogical justifications that had been used by school systems to keep Mexican-descent children segregated.[123] Furthermore, in 1954 the same Mexican American lawyer who had sued the courts in Texas regarding school segregation argued before the U.S. Supreme Court that his client had not received a fair trial as provided by the equal protection clause of the U.S. Constitution. Attorney Gus García showed that, despite a large local Mexican American population, no Spanish-surnamed person had served on a jury in Jackson County, Texas, during the past 20 years. Pete Hernández, sentenced to life imprisonment on a murder conviction, therefore had been denied a trial by a jury of his peers, García argued. Texas officials countered that, as "whites," Mexican Americans had been fairly represented by Anglo American jurors. The Supreme Court, however, sided with García and ordered a new trial.[124]

Along with court victories, another visible achievement of the postwar era was the election of Mexican Americans to office. Gus García, for example, a member of both LULAC and the American G.I. Forum, won a seat on the San Antonio School Board in 1948. Some veterans were expressly moved by their wartime experience to seek elective office. As one California veteran explained: "I'm glad I'm going to have one of those little [service] buttons to wear in my coat. And a flock of foliage to put on my uniform for Armistice Day parades. I'm going into politics. There's seven or eight of us, all from Southern California, who've talked it over. Things are going to happen in these colonies [Mexican neighborhoods, *colonias*] and we're going to see that they do."[125] In the twenty years following the war, dozens of Mexican Americans won positions on local school boards and a few gained positions on city councils.[126] Successful candidates, moreover, were often backed by new organizations, including most notably the Community Service Organization, whose founding helped elect Edward Roybal, a liberal Democrat and another

World War II veteran, to the Los Angeles City Council in 1948.[127] In Texas, Henry B. Gonzalez, a member of the American G.I. Forum (although he had worked stateside during the war) and also a liberal Democrat, won election to the San Antonio city council in 1953, and the Texas senate in 1956, where he conducted a record-breaking twenty-two-hour filibuster against a school segregation bill. Both Royal and Gonzalez, moreover, won election to Congress in the early 1960s. These electoral victories, combined with litigation and public protest, as in the Longoria affair, were all part of a multifaceted campaign for equality that Mexican Americans waged in the postwar era.

Aiding that campaign was a more favorable racial climate within the United States. After the war, the horrors of Nazism combined with persistent demands for equality from their fellow citizens convinced more Americans than ever before to consider the harm done by race prejudice within their own country. The newfound willingness of Mexican American civil rights groups to cooperate with their African American counterparts no doubt reflected this shift. In Southern California, for example, the post–World War II period saw the emergence of Unity Leagues—interracial coalitions whose members worked together to fight segregation and increase minority political representation.[128] Change was also evident in the highest branches of government. In late 1946 President Harry S. Truman appointed a federal civil rights committee to investigate the problem of prejudice. Its report the following year, *To Secure These Rights*, outlined the need for civil rights legislation. In 1948 Truman ordered the gradual end to segregation in the armed services. Also in 1948 the Democratic Party platform included a strong plank in support of civil rights. Resistance, of course, remained. Southerners in Congress blocked the recommendations that had been made by the authors of *To Secure These Rights*, while delegates from Mississippi and Alabama bolted from the 1948 Democratic convention in protest. Still, candidate Truman continued to position himself as a liberal on civil rights. In the final week of the campaign, he declared his support for the "goal of equal rights and equal opportunities" for every American.[129] Truman was speaking to a Harlem audience, but the growing opposition to race prejudice benefited Mexican Americans, too. Indeed, in the Southwest, Mexican Americans generally made faster inroads than did African Americans.

Skin color helped account for the difference. As Governor Coke Stevenson commented in 1943 when he established the Good Neighbor Commission in Texas, "Meskins is pretty good folk. If it were niggers, it'd be different."[130] With more precision, in 1954, John H. Burma, a sociologist and the author of *Spanish-Speaking Groups in the United States*, argued that discrimination against people of Mexican descent was a function of "both color and acculturation." Whereas the lightest and most acculturated "are accepted almost without discrimination," he contended, "the darkest and least acculturated are treated but a little better than the Negro."[131] As Burma's schema indicated, prejudice against dark-skinned Spanish-speaking Mexicans was similar to that experienced by African Americans, yet overall, the group's experience was not as severe. Certainly, segregation aimed at Mexican Americans was dismantled sooner. A comparison illustrates the point. In 1954 in Winslow, Arizona, Mexican Americans were allowed to use the city swimming pool only one day of the week. That day was Wednesday, the day before the water was drained and the pool was refilled with fresh water. Still, when local activists filed suit, city officials quickly agreed to integrate the pool before the case went to court. The Winslow pool, moreover, was one of the last city facilities in the Southwest to maintain a segregationist policy against Mexican Americans.[132] In contrast, the bus boycott in Montgomery, Alabama, begun by African American activists in 1955, encountered intense resistance and reprisals from local segregationists lasting an entire year. The buses were integrated only after a U.S. Supreme Court ruling.[133]

Beyond a narrow form of skin privilege, Mexican Americans benefited, as did many Americans, from government programs aimed at veterans and from the affluence of the postwar era. The G.I. Bill, in the words of one veteran, "was the Emancipation Proclamation for Mexican Americans, thousands of whom used it to attend college for the first time."[134] Educational achievement, in turn, triggered economic mobility. Helpful, too, were Veterans Administration loans that made homeownership easier. In addition, Mexican Americans, concentrated mostly in Texas and California, the two states awarded the greatest number of defense industry contracts, were well positioned to find better-paying jobs within the military-industrial complex. These jobs continued to draw Mexican Americans from rural areas to cities, which offered comparatively more economic and educational opportunities. For all these reasons, Mexican Americans saw their incomes rise between 1945 and 1960, less dramatically than those of Anglo Americans, but faster than those of African Americans.[135] As one Texas official boasted in 1952, "The Mexican American is more prosperous than he has been ever before. Even the poorest elements have radios, automobiles, washing machines, refrigerators—and you guessed it, television." Yet even this state booster noted a singular exception: "Wetbacks live . . . without civil protection" and earn "a much lower wage than any United States citizen."[136]

The nation's unprecedented postwar prosperity acted as a magnet for a renewed burst of immigration from Mexico. Not only was the Bracero Program renewed after 1947, but illegal immigration also flourished. In 1946, for example, the Border Patrol had apprehended 91,000 Mexicans attempting to enter the country illegally. In 1953 the number was 865,000.[137] The inevitable backlash within the United States mixed old fears about Mexicanization of the country with Cold War concerns that the southern border was open to communists. Responding to a perceived communist threat, in 1952 Congress passed the McCarran-Walter Act, which greatly facilitated the deportation of aliens and made permissible the denaturalization of immigrants who had become Americans. In an attempt to curb illegal Mexican immigration specifically, the Immigration and Naturalization Service in 1954 launched Operation Wetback, a massive deportation campaign that included dragnet operations in factories, fields, and neighborhoods.[138]

In response, most Mexican American groups, committed to presenting Mexican Americans as idealized American citizens, tried to maintain their distance from immigrants. The division was sometimes artificial. Even as activists upheld Mexican American recipients of the Congressional Medal of Honor as the ultimate American patriots, for example, at least two, Marcario García and Silvestre Herrera, were proud Americans born in Mexico.[139] More important, Mexican Americans were often the children of Mexican immigrants. According to 1950 census data, the combined population of "resident Mexican aliens and Mexican Americans with at least one parent who had been born in Mexico" amounted to an estimated 55 percent of the total ethnic Mexican population in the United States.[140] Still, only the Community Service Organization championed naturalization. LULAC and the American G.I. Forum, in contrast, strongly endorsed Operation Wetback. Opposition to the Bracero Program after the war, moreover, was universal. Members of LULAC, the Forum, and the CSO, as well as most Mexican American unionists, opposed the program, on the grounds that braceros lowered wages and took jobs away from U.S. citizens. Nor did ethnic organizations immediately criticize the McCarran-Walter Act, although the legislation would soon create havoc for a mixed Mexican-origin population of citizens and immigrants. When LULAC finally did speak out, it was forced to acknowledge the situation's complexity. As league members noted in a 1953 resolution condemning the act, "There are thousands [of Mexican nationals] who have intermarried with Americans citizens [and] are now parents of members of the United States Armed forces." Significantly, the league chose to emphasize the outstanding citizenship qualities that, at the very least, the children of Mexican immigrants had demonstrated. By virtue of their children's military service, LULAC argued, many Mexican immigrants merited protection from summary deportation.[141]

Not surprisingly, a civil rights strategy that repeatedly touted military service also influenced how most Mexican American civil rights activists viewed the Korean War. The anticommunist stance of the American G.I. Forum was evident from its founding: it barred communists or members of any "conspiracy that advocates the overthrow of the United States" from joining.[142] While the organization therefore backed the conflict, it also demanded Mexican American representation on draft boards, contending that young men of Mexican descent were once again serving in disproportionate numbers.[143] Honoring those that served was also a priority for the organization. In October 1953, for example, the Forum joined the League of United Latin American Citizens to host a welcoming reception for Cpl. Abel Garcia, who had been held a prisoner of war by "North Korean and Chinese Communist forces." Several thousand people in Fort Stockton, Texas, attended the homecoming.[144] Mexican American women, meanwhile, saw the conflict as another opportunity to mark the sacrifices of their sons. In 1951, on May 10, the date Mother's Day is celebrated in Mexico, California's Society of Mexican Mothers erected a nearly life-sized statue of a Mexican American soldier in the state's Capitol. According to the dedication, the monument was meant to honor all the young men who had given their lives "on the altar of liberty."[145] Korea increased that tally. Mexican American leaders were proud that Mexican American soldiers once again served with valor. "Hero Street" in Silvis, Illinois, sent a dozen men to Korea, two of whom died, one of whom was a World War II veteran. Mexican American soldiers, furthermore, received six Congressional Medals of Honor in the conflict.[146]

Once again, a less celebratory perspective existed, but it was short-lived. The Asociación Nacional México-Americana, founded in 1949 to be the political arm of the International Union of Mine, Mill, and Smelter Workers, a largely Mexican American union, had been red-baited out of existence by 1954. Best understood as the ideological heir of El Congreso del Pueblo de Habla Española, ANMA at its height had attracted several thousand members. The organization presented an important counterpoint to LULAC and especially to the American G.I. Forum. First, ANMA refused to draw a sharp divide between immigrants and citizens. Second, women played essential leadership roles within the organization, which also formally endorsed equality for women. Finally, and perhaps most controversially, ANMA members dared to be critical of U.S. military intervention in Korea, labeling it "unjust and unnecessary." Like Chicano movement participants twenty years later protesting the Viet Nam War, ANMA members complained that Mexican Americans were being used as "cannon fodder." At a time when the Federal Bureau of Investigation was spying even on LULAC and the American G.I. Forum, ANMA's leftist politics made it an easy target.[147] In 1954 the U.S. Attorney General deemed ANMA a subversive organization. By then, the persistent harassment of members by the Immigration and Naturalization Service—including the deportation of some leaders—had already fatally weakened the organization.[148]

Both before and after World War II, most ethnic activists sought "the perfection of our American democracy," in the words of one American G.I. Forum member.[149] In essence, ethnic activists had to resolve the central contradiction between the ideals of American society and the abrogation of those ideals experienced by many people of Mexican descent. Beginning in the 1930s, a central ethnic response was the insistence that Mexican Americans were legitimate—and even ideal—U.S. citizens and thus deserving of equality, liberty, and freedom. World War II cemented that strategy. While the alienation and violence of the so-called zoot-suit riots, as well as workplace discrimination, pointed to deeper problems, this strategy did achieve some remarkable court victories in the two decades after the end of World War Two. Indeed, by 1960, some leaders of LULAC were prepared to disband the organization, convinced that the combination of court victories, the dismantling of formal segregation, and economic improvement meant their job was done.[150]

The award-winning film *Giant,* released in 1956, captured that confidence. The film is both a saga of a Texas family, headed by Jordan "Bick" Benedict (Rock Hudson), and a portrait of improving race relations between Anglos and Mexicans. Based on a novel by Edna Ferber, who had spent three weeks accompanied by Hector P. Garcia, the Forum's founder, as she traveled the state and learned about race relations in Texas, the film begins in the 1920s, when Mexicans on Benedict's ranch lived in desperate poverty and beneath the rancher's contempt. The longest scene that features Mexican Americans in the movie marks the beginning of a shift in Benedict's racist attitudes, when he attends the burial of young Angel Obregón, a ranch hand who had gone off to fight in World War II. Obregon's funeral is attended both by his family and by a number of Anglo servicemen: his death in combat thus serves as a powerful and familiar turning point of improved race relations. The movie closes with a scene of interethnic harmony. The aging Benedict and his wife look down upon their two grandchildren, who are sharing the same playpen. One is blond and blue-eyed, and the other resembles his mother, a dark-skinned Mexican American woman. Although "Bick" Benedict expresses his amazement that one of his grandchildren looks like a "wetback," he is willing to accept the situation.[151] While the movie sought a happy conclusion, as Carl Gutiérrez-Jones in his careful analysis observed, the use of the term "wetback" suggested that, in the movie, people of Mexican descent had obtained only a "conditional citizenship" at best.[152]

A minor incident in Golden, Colorado, a year after the movie's release underscored that exact point about the place of Mexican Americans during the 1950s. A local chapter of the Daughters of the American Revolution objected when a boy of Mexican descent was designated to carry the American flag in a local school's celebration of President Lincoln's Day. Although acknowledging that the student was probably American-born, the local DAR chair insisted that he was nevertheless "really a Mexican" because he was probably the child of Mexican immigrants. "I wouldn't want a Mexican to carry Old Glory," she stated. "Would you?" While her remarks proved to be an acute embarrassment to the DAR national office, they nonetheless made clear that, despite real progress on the civil rights front after World War II, the Mexican American claim to citizenship remained contested at mid-century.[153] Although generally optimistic about race relations, Mexican American activists stood primed to defend themselves against Anglo Americans who issued such discriminatory challenges.[154]

They were ill prepared, however, to contend with fellow ethnic group members who similarly doubted the legitimacy of Mexican-origin people asserting an American identity. Within a decade, and to the great surprise of an earlier generation of activists, many young Mexican Americans would offer a stiff challenge to a civil rights strategy that emphasized Americanization. Influenced by a different war, these young people began to abandon the political tactics that World War II had made popular, to object to the sense of victory that existed among older, more established ethnic group leaders, and even to dispute wartime sacrifice as a source of ethnic group pride. Calling themselves Chicanos and Chicanas, they were no longer convinced that the route to equality, liberty, and freedom in the United States should rest on military service, unquestioning patriotism, and devotion to the nation. Indeed, they began to argue the opposite.

CHAPTER 2

"New Wind from the Southwest"

Questioning a Political Tradition

In May 1966 the *Nation* ran an article on Mexican Americans entitled "New Wind from the Southwest." Written by Joan W. Moore and Ralph Guzman, academic collaborators on a massive study of Mexican Americans sponsored by the Ford Foundation, the article declared: "Today a new purposefulness is appearing in the forgotten ghettos of the Southwest. The new hope lies in a discovery by the Mexican of himself as a minority." Wrongly characterizing the Mexican American population as historically politically "passive," Moore, a sociologist, and Guzman, a political scientist, nonetheless noted several indications that a "new militancy" was afoot. Initially, the article noted, the spotlight had been on the small South Texas town of Crystal City, where in 1963 a slate of Mexican American candidates had won control of the city council, a phenomenon that had not been seen since the nineteenth century. More recently, during the 1966 Easter season, the article went on, a Lenten march through California's San Joaquin Valley by striking Mexican and Filipino farmworkers had made the front page of the *New York Times*. Under the leadership of Cesar Chavez, Dolores Huerta, and Larry Itliong, union members had been employing new tactics, such as marches and boycotts, to draw attention to their plight. Finally, Moore and Guzman noted, just eleven days after farmworkers started their march, some fifty leaders from established Mexican American organizations had staged a protest during a meeting in Albuquerque with federal representatives. Dismayed about what they considered only a token effort to address their concerns regarding job discrimination, the leaders walked out within an hour of convening the meeting.[1]

Colleagues on the "Mexican-American Study Project" at the University of California at Los Angeles, Guzman and Moore offered several reasons to explain the greater willingness of Mexican Americans to challenge the status quo. They noted the political experience that Mexican Americans had gained through appointments to War on Poverty programs; their continuing integration into the American mainstream since the end of World War II; and, finally, the reigning liberal climate in the United States, which had allowed minority protest to flourish. Moore and Guzman lamented, however, that, compared to African Americans, Mexican Americans in 1966 still lacked "a mass movement with mass organization." They predicted that such a movement, if it ever developed, "was far in the future."[2]

Their prediction proved to be inaccurate. The "new wind" was to blow a lot harder than they had expected. The erroneous prognostication was understandable, however: the Mexican American population during the mid-1960s was undergoing a major political transition. Impressed by the political victories of the African American freedom struggle, Mexican Americans leaders were eager to see federal attention directed toward their ethnic group, too. During the 1960s, Mexican American leaders sought to enjoy the bounty of the Great Society and to ensure that the civil rights legislation crafted in response to black Americans' demands also met the needs of Mexican Americans. Toward these ends, ethnic leaders from established organizations often reinvigorated familiar patterns of petition. Still framing their politics in terms of their World War II experience, they touted the deserving nature of the ethnic group, especially as evidenced by Mexican American military service. On rare occasions, they engaged in public protest. These tactics engendered a measure of success: at mid-decade, a few, select ethnic leaders were able to exert unprecedented influence on Lyndon B. Johnson's presidential administration.

Against the backdrop of a different and more unpopular war, however, participants in an emerging Chicano movement were issuing bold new demands. Inspired by Cesar Chavez and other Mexican American heroes, as well as the tactics and language of black power advocates, young Mexican Americans from urban and rural pockets across the Southwest were moved to protest. More so than any group of activists before them, they engaged in mass demonstrations, uncompromising speech, and an open celebration of their cultural inheritance to denounce inferior schools, paltry political representation, job discrimination, and abusive treatment by law enforcement. Both the size and the scope of their protest were unparalleled.[3]

Because Mexican American activists since before the Second World War had used their service in the U.S. military as a justification for their demands for equal treatment, the war in Viet Nam was a defining event for this switch in political tactics. For activists who continued to support the traditional basis for their political claims, the war in Viet Nam and other groups' opposition to it became another way to prove their loyalty. In contrast, for activists critical of this strategy, who questioned whether a Mexican American's willingness to die for his country was the only way to win equality, the war in Viet Nam helped inspire a rethinking of the position of Mexican Americans within society. Given the long duration of the earlier civil rights strategy, this break was neither immediate nor complete. Nevertheless, for many Chicano movement participants, opposition to the war accelerated the transition from the politics of supplication to the politics of confrontation. Although Guzman and Moore perceived a new wind as blowing from the American Southwest, also affecting Mexican Americans during the 1960s were the winds of war blowing from Southeast Asia.

VIVA LBJ

Students who sat in the combined fifth-, sixth-, and seventh-grade "Mexican" school classroom in 1928 remember a teacher who often extolled the brave defenders of Texas freedom against the bloodthirsty Santa Anna and who was wont to punish them if they spoke Spanish on the school grounds.[4] Yet their instructor, energetic and just twenty years old, also liked to proclaim that any one of them could grow up to be a lawyer some day or maybe even President of the United States. Although not particularly culturally sensitive, the young Lyndon Baines Johnson clearly favored incorporating Mexican Americans into the American— and Texas—mainstream. Forty years later, President Johnson often traced his desire to eradicate poverty and racism nationwide to the deprivation he had witnessed among the Mexican American children in the small South Texas town of Cotulla on the eve of the Depression.[5]

Not surprisingly, given Johnson's eventual rise to the nation's highest office, the relationship between Johnson and Mexican Americans during much of the 1960s reflected its original distribution of power, when Johnson had stood at the head of the class and Mexican Americans had vied for the teacher's attention. During the Johnson presidency, Mexican Americans lobbied hard for presidential recognition, political appointments, and Great Society program funding from Washington. Trying to curry presidential favor, some ethnic leaders offered new evidence of ethnic group good behavior: they pointed to the maintenance of calm in Mexican American barrios during the 1960s, especially when compared to the riot-torn African American ghettos. Above all, they emphasized Mexican American support for U.S. military intervention in Southeast Asia. In 1967 the politics of supplication achieved a singular victory when Johnson established a special cabinet-level agency to address the concerns of Mexican Americans.

When Johnson first entered the White House, some Mexican American activists worried about his Southern background, but others, familiar with Johnson's decades-long career, concluded that they had a friend in the Oval Office. A master politician, Johnson often had been quick to demonstrate that he considered Mexican Americans an "estimable class of Texas citizens."[6] In the 1930s and 1940s he had campaigned hard for Mexican American votes during runs for the U.S. House of Representative and, later, the U.S. Senate. The burial of Pvt. Felix Longoria in 1949 was also the start of a close and friendly working relationship between Johnson and Hector P. Garcia, the founder of the American G.I. Forum. Familiar with Mexican American military accomplishments, Vice President Johnson graciously agreed to write a brief introduction to *Among the Valiant,* a book written by Raul Morin, also an American G.I. Forum member, which chronicled Mexican American accomplishments during World War II and the Korean War. Although Johnson's own military career during the Second World War had been exceedingly and deliberately brief, he was effusive in his praise:

> As a Navy officer and as a member of Congress during World War Two, I had occasion to become familiar on numerous occasions with the contributions made during that conflict by American soldiers of Mexican origin. . . . The American soldiers of Mexican origin served with distinction. They fought courageously. They gave their lives, when need be, valiantly. . . . It is a privilege to pay tribute to these my fellow Americans. I salute them as brave men who did credit to the flag they followed into battle.[7]

The politically astute Johnson no doubt saw such favors as a good election time investment. Yet, once he became president, Johnson's personal commitment to equality reaped him wider Mexican American support. President Johnson moved quickly to sponsor and sign the Civil Rights

Act of 1964 and the Voting Rights Act of 1965. This landmark legislation, which put an end to segregation and other forms of legalized discrimination, applied to Mexican Americans as well as other racial and ethnic groups.

Intimately familiar with poverty as well as prejudice, Mexican Americans also benefited from Johnson's plans to help America's poor. The War on Poverty held an understandable appeal to an ethnic group that continued to lag far behind the general population according to most socioeconomic indicators. Despite considerable progress made during the 1940s and 1950s, the United States Census Bureau showed that "Spanish-surnamed" people in the Southwest began the 1960s poorer than the majority population and in some respects worse off than African Americans. Although likely to earn more money than African Americans, Mexican Americans were less educated on average and more likely to live in overcrowded, dilapidated housing.[8] Totaling billions of dollars in federal spending, the War on Poverty directly aided impoverished Mexican Americans through such programs as Head Start early education, health care coverage, legal aid, and food stamps.[9] Initially, therefore, many Mexican American political activists found much to admire in Johnson's domestic agenda.

Aware that the black experience lay at the heart of the American racial dilemma, many Mexican American leaders similarly admired the African American civil rights movement, even as they pondered, with a touch of envy, how to replicate its moral force and vigor among people of Mexican descent. As early as 1963, for example, a longtime California activist acknowledged that many Mexican Americans felt a combination of "fascination" and "resentment" at the "momentum" of the civil rights movement. Nevertheless, she declared, the problems that afflicted African Americans and Mexican Americans shared "one common source—race prejudice."[10] Two years later, moreover, after a pair of civil rights workers had been killed in Alabama, the Mexican American Political Association in California, an electoral advocacy group, extended its sincere condolences. Vowing that the victims' "blood has not been shed in vain," MAPA members pledged to support the civil rights movement's "unfinished work of democracy."[11]

While sympathetic to the black civil rights movement, by mid-decade some Mexican American leaders were beginning to express concern that Washington appeared oblivious to the plight of Mexican Americans. Especially in the wake of the Watts uprising in 1965, they wondered whether Johnson's War on Poverty programs targeted the problems of urban African Americans to the detriment of urban Mexican Americans. The six-day riot in South-Central Los Angeles wrecked nearly a thousand buildings, resulted in four thousand arrests and, ultimately, cost thirty-four people their lives.[12] As Mexican Americans noted, afterward, the Watts area experienced a massive infusion of federal funds, even though East Los Angeles, where the city's Mexican American population was concentrated, was a far poorer area.[13] Watts, moreover, was only the first of many urban revolts. Although smaller in scale, nearly two hundred similar uprisings occurred during the summers of 1966 and 1967, prompting the outlay of additional federal funds to help these largely African American communities. Adding to the dismay of many Mexican American leaders, these riots coincided with the rise of black power militants who championed the right to defend themselves against white oppression "by any means necessary."[14] Quite a few Mexican Americans concluded that the seeming reward for both the rhetoric of violence and the actual violence of urban riots was more federal and media attention directed toward African Americans.

In an era that paid new attention to the problem of racial discrimination, ethnic group leaders confronted the shortcomings of a strategy that insisted that Mexican Americans were white. Despite a sympathetic Texan in the White House, Mexican Americans discovered that they lacked recognition in Washington as a minority group that shared many of the same problems as African Americans.[15] The concentration of Mexican Americans in the Southwest, far from the centers of the national media and federal government, only compounded their seeming invisibility. The national president of LULAC expressed his doubts concerning the efficacy of the Mexican American political moderation and patience in 1965: "What does it take? What must we do? While I do not condone violence, it may be that we too should resort to marches, sit-ins, and demonstrations."[16]

Compounding the dilemma was the politically weak position of Mexican Americans throughout the decade, despite recent helpful legislation. In 1964 the Twenty-fourth Amendment had finally outlawed the poll tax. The next year, the Voting Rights Act, which ended literacy and other tests that had been used to bar people from voting, also included provisions to extend the franchise to non-English speakers. In both cases, Mexican Americans stood to gain. Yet other obstacles remained that dramatically undercut Mexican American political clout. The problems were most acute where the ethnic group posed the greatest threat—South Texas and Southern California, where roughly 80 percent of the

Mexican-origin population in the United States lived.[17] Thus, in South Texas, Mexican Americans who wished to vote confronted bossism, threats, job loss, and complicated residency requirements. In addition, in smaller communities elections were routinely scheduled during the harvest season, when resident farmworker families were out of town following the crop migrant trail.[18] Meanwhile, in Southern California, a central obstacle was gerrymandering. According to the 1960 census, an estimated six hundred thousand persons of Mexican descent called the greater Los Angeles area home, the largest concentration of them living in East Los Angeles.[19] Already straddling county and city jurisdictions, East Los Angeles was further fragmented, according to the state apportionment scheme for the 1960s, into nine state assembly districts, seven state senate districts, and six congressional districts.[20] As one male resident complained, "Even if all the women, children and dogs in East Los Angeles voted, we couldn't elect anybody."[21]

Consequently, despite a series of local electoral victories after World War II, rarely was Mexican American political representation close to proportional during the decade of the 1960s. In 1967, for example, just as the Chicano movement was gaining national attention, Texas had ten state legislators of Mexican descent, Arizona four, Colorado one, and California, despite the size of its Mexican American population, none. At the federal level, of the four states, Texas had just two Mexican American members of the U.S. House of Representatives, while California had one.[22] Meanwhile, Mexican Americans represented between 12 and 15 percent of the regions' populations.[23] Only in New Mexico, where Hispanos had constituted a significant voting bloc since territorial days, was state political representation close to proportional.[24] New Mexico was also the only state to send a Spanish-surnamed person to the U.S. Senate consistently.

Feeling ignored by Washington and largely thwarted in the electoral arena, some Mexican Americans leaders returned with a new intensity to pleading for equality while showcasing Mexican Americans as good and deserving citizens. A particularly revealing example was a resolution that MAPA members drafted in October 1965 in which they complained of the government's willingness to address the "economic plight of the Negro in urban areas," whereas the "economic problems" of Mexican Americans had "discreetly or inadvertently been swept under the carpet." Signed as well by California representatives from LULAC, the American G.I. Forum, and the Community Service Organization (CSO), the resolution emphasized that Mexican Americans deserved better because they were upstanding, law-abiding citizens. Implicitly condemning civil rights and black power protests, urban riots, and even demonstrations against the war in Viet Nam, a handful of which had occurred earlier that year, the resolution contended, "The Hispanic and Mexican-American citizen subscribes to the proposition that old wrongs and new fears cannot justify the breaking of the law." Therefore, the resolution noted, Mexican Americans shunned participation in "civil disobedience manifestations" and "picket lines [that risked] the safety of our country."[25]

Offering another example of good behavior, the resolution emphasized that Mexican Americans had been brave and loyal soldiers and, more ludicrously, staunch Cold War allies of the United States since the early 1800s. Boasting that Mexican Americans had "received more Congressional Medals of Honor than any other ethnic group during World War II and the Korean Conflict," the resolution noted for good measure that "not a single Spanish-surnamed person became a turncoat" during these conflicts. The resolution continued: "Over 150 years ago, Spanish-speaking Mexican Americans stopped the Russian colonial advance and conquest from Siberia and Alaska and preserved the Western portion of the United States for our country." Once again, ethnic leaders rested the reach for equality upon Mexican American military accomplishments. In this case, however, they presented a tortured reading of the past to portray the Spanish-speaking residents of California as the dedicated defenders of the United States, against Russian aggression no less, more than a century before the Cold War had begun. Not surprisingly, the resolution glossed over the American conquest of the northern third of Mexico by 1848. Instead of referring to war, the author of the resolution wrote more obliquely of the area's "incorporation" into the United States. Given the group's long desire for approval and recognition from Washington, historical accuracy was less important than enumerating the exploits that people of Mexican descent had performed on behalf of the United States. At least one MAPA member, however, begged to differ. Recognizing that the resolution's historical analysis was "weird to say the least," she suggested that sometimes "the squeaking wheel gets the grease."[26]

In fact, quick dabbles in protest politics proved effective. The Albuquerque walkout mentioned by Guzman and Moore occurred during a March 1966 meeting between Mexican Americans and representatives from the U.S. Equal Employment Opportunities Commission. The commission had been established under the 1964 Civil Rights Act specifically to investigate job discrimination. Already concerned that the EEOC was paying scant attention to Mexican American grievances, ethnic activists were dismayed to discover upon arriving at the meeting that only a single EEOC commissioner had bothered to attend. They left the gathering in disgust.[27] Shortly thereafter, Mexican American leaders filed a complaint with the U.S. Commission of Civil Rights that charged the Equal Employment Opportunity Commission with "insincerity" in addressing Mexican American civil rights problems. The very agency assigned to enforce equal employment opportunity lacked Mexican American staff, the complaint asserted, and therefore was focusing attention on "only one racial group," namely African Americans.[28] In another display of jealousy and frustration, staff from the Washington office of the American G.I. Forum picketed the White House Civil Rights Conference in June 1966 because the meeting was dedicated to addressing only African American concerns.[29] Taking a cue from the larger African American civil rights struggle, even as they felt overshadowed by it, some Mexican American members of established ethnic organizations were willing to confront Johnson directly.

These new methods captured Johnson's attention. He started a campaign to woo Mexican Americans back to him. Twice in 1966, the president met with ethnic representatives from established groups. To their great pleasure, Johnson promised to hold a special conference on the Mexican American.[30] Since 1965, ethnic group leaders had looked forward to such an event as the ultimate bestowal of legitimacy that would finally place the ethnic group on a par with African Americans in terms of federal recognition. Mexican Americans were likewise pleased, in April 1967, when Johnson elevated Vicente T. Ximenes, a World War II veteran and American G.I. Forum member, to a seat on the EEOC. Better yet, that June the president established the Inter-Agency Committee on Mexican American affairs and named Ximenes as its chair.[31] The committee was charged with coordinating the hiring of more Mexican Americans by the federal government and ensuring that more federal funds reached Mexican American organizations.[32] The main beneficiaries were LULAC and the American G.I. Forum, both mainstream organizations that White House policymakers favored for the duration of the administration.[33] To at least one observer in August 1967, Johnson's courting efforts appeared spectacularly successful. As a representative of the Democratic National Committee who attended the G.I. Forum's national convention gleefully reported, the "whole convention was 99.9 percent safely pro-Johnson."[34]

The White House conference, however, remained a sore spot. Despite earlier promises, at the end of 1966 Johnson decided that a White House conference represented too much of a potential political headache. He wrote to a staff member, "We better get away from this—I don't want any Mexican meetings at all," concluding, "The more you have, the more trouble you have."[35] The Secretary of Health, Education and Welfare, John W. Gardner, agreed. As he wrote Johnson, "White House conferences are inevitably risky with groups of this sort. The temptation is great to use the conference as a means of belaboring the Administration."[36] Other "groups" were African American and Puerto Rican civil rights organizations that were also pressing upon the Johnson White House with their own demands. Around the same time, two Mexican Americans irritated the president by insisting that members of the ethnic group should play a major role in the planning of any conference, lest it be unsatisfactorily "imposed from above."[37] The ultimatum left Johnson spluttering; he directed his staff to "keep this trash out of the White House."[38] The incident revealed that Johnson's tolerance for aggressive demands had limits.

Yet the limits of the politics of supplication were also apparent. One of Vicente Ximenes's first responsibilities as chair of the new Inter-Agency Committee on Mexican American Affairs was to plan an acceptable substitute for a White House conference in order to get the "administration off the hook" regarding its earlier promises.[39] Flattering members of established Mexican American organizations by working closely with them, Ximenes arranged for a series of hearings in El Paso instead that brought together more than one thousand ethnic representatives and dozens of federal officials. Representatives from LULAC and the American G.I. Forum each chaired conference sessions. So did the Political Association of Spanish-Speaking Organizations (PASSO), an electoral advocacy group based in Texas, as well as California's Community Service Organization. Although not the desired White House conference, the American G.I. Forum's newspaper still labeled the gathering "historic."[40]

For some grateful Mexican American leaders, the hearings in El Paso provided a forum to revive traditional forms of petition. Testifying about job discrimination, for example, Albert Armendariz, a former LULAC national president, emphasized that Mexican Americans were upstanding, loyal citizens. According to Armendariz, Mexicans Americans were reliant upon the kindness of Anglos, and, failing that, government help, because "we are not a militant group, because we are too proud, too shy or too scared to join many marches, [and] because we know that our advances in our society must be achieved in a dignified manner."[41] As it turned out, this statement was one of the last hurrahs for the politics of supplication. In the wake of the Chicano movement, even moderate Mexican American leaders developed a taste for more fiery language.[42] Armendariz's decision to add the qualifier "many" in front of "marches" suggested that he too realized that times were changing.

The evidence was hard to ignore. Across town, several hundred Mexican Americans, including members of MAPA and a few emerging Chicano movement groups, were attending a competing conference called La Raza Unida in protest of the official event. Participants disrupted the opening of the government hearings by marching with signs that read "Today we demonstrate, Tomorrow we revolt," "Don't ask rich Mexicans to talk for the poor," and *"Conferencia de titeres"* (Conference of puppets).[43] By accusing the government of sticking with "safe" ethnic leaders in planning the event in El Paso, the signs revealed an impatience with the Johnson administration's pace of reform. They also echoed the frustrations of black activists who were discovering that the legislative triumphs of the Civil Rights and Voting Rights Acts had done little to address the problem of widespread African American poverty. For the poor, African American and Mexican American alike, the War on Poverty had failed to deliver as much as it had promised.[44]

Indeed, impatience with the Johnson administration's stalled domestic agenda topped the list of grievances at the Raza Unida conference. Announced as a massive, long-term, multifaceted attack on the root causes of poverty in 1964, the War on Poverty had fallen under the budgetary ax a mere two years later. Funding for the Office of Economic Opportunity, which coordinated the entire effort, had been slashed by nearly 25 percent, while funding for community action programs, which had brought an infusion of federal funds directly into the barrios of the Southwest, had been cut by a third.[45] MAPA president Bert Corona later summarized his disappointment regarding the War on Poverty and his reason for walking out of the official conference: "We were expecting an elephant to be born, instead we got a flea."[46] Indeed, even within the halls of the government-sponsored conference, flashes of discontent were on display. According to the *El Paso Times*, "anti-LBJ pins were widely distributed that said, '*Primero la Raza, Después Viva LBJ*' (First La Raza, then Viva LBJ)."[47]

While impatience was widespread, the Viet Nam War played a far more prominent role at the Raza Unida conference. Like Martin Luther

King Jr. in his famous April 1967 speech against the war in Viet Nam, participants drew a direct link between domestic budget cuts that hurt impoverished minorities and the cost of the ongoing war in Viet Nam.[48] In El Paso at the time of the hearings, Corona complained to reporters, "They [government officials] should direct some of their funds from Viet Nam to aid poverty in the United States."[49] New Mexican land-grant activists participating in a Raza Unida march through the impoverished south side of El Paso made the same connection. "War in Vietnam does not help the Mexican American," one placard proclaimed, while another declared, "Justice—Not War." Still another sign denounced "Johnson's Unholy War."[50] With questions about tactics and styles already dividing Mexican Americans, these signs suggest how the war in Viet Nam operated as a wedge issue widening that split. Advocates of tactics that had been cemented during the World War II era could not oppose the conflict without disregarding their own logic that demonstrated patriotism, especially in time of war, was the best tactic for achieving ethnic group goals. In contrast, those who were ready to abandon the politics of supplication, with its emphasis upon respectful petition, in favor of direct confrontation found it difficult to ignore the American military commitment to defeat North Viet Nam and the protest against that commitment that was burgeoning across the country.

A GREAT DIVIDE

In early 1968 a Phoenix reporter asked Vicente Ximenes about anti-war protesters who burned their draft cards. He answered that as a Mexican American he did not have much to say: "We don't burn draft cards because we have none to burn—we volunteer." Although an exaggeration, Ximenes's quip received warm applause from the largely Mexican American audience. In a February note to the president, Ximenes passed along the anecdote and suggested that Johnson incorporate a similar nod to the ethnic group the next time the president was at the LBJ ranch or in San Antonio.[51]

Ximenes, however, was mistaken in his boast that all Mexican Americans backed the war. At the time Ximenes spoke, at least one Mexican American had already refused to serve in Viet Nam. Although he did not burn his draft card, Ernesto Vigil, a native of Denver, Colorado, did mail it back to the Selective Service, along with letter that explained his "dissatisfaction and disaffection" with the war. During his first semester at Vermont's liberal Goddard College in 1966, Vigil had grown to oppose the war. Shocked to learn in January 1968 that Dr. Benjamin Spock was facing prison time for advocating draft resistance, Vigil took more definitive action. He immediately wrote a letter to the Selective Service, in which he described the United States as "unjust, hypocritical, deceitful, inadequate, and detrimental to the happiness and best interests of its own people and the people of the other nations of the world." Returning to Denver, he joined a civil rights organization called the Crusade for Justice. In the pages of the organization's newspaper a few months later, Vigil explained that his refusal to serve was directly linked to his own ongoing political—and identity—transformation (see Fig. 2). "I did not do this for kicks," he wrote. "I oppose the war as a Mexican American, a Chicano."[52]

During the late 1960s, Ximenes and Vigil represented the spectrum of Mexican American opinion regarding U.S. military involvement in Southeast Asia. Just as the war was to spur bitter debate within the country as a whole, Mexican Americans likewise developed clashing opinions. On the one hand, many ethnic leaders familiar with the civil rights tradition emerging out of the Second World War strongly endorsed the U.S. support of South Viet Nam. Patriotism and anti-communism illustrated their devotion to the American cause. On the other hand, as the 1960s progressed, a growing number of Mexican Americans at home and abroad proved willing to break with tradition. A particular concern for many was the Selective Service System and the egregious class biases of the draft. As one early critic of U.S. intervention in Viet Nam later explained, his opposition to the war developed precisely because "our kids were getting killed out there."[53]

The transition from a cold war to hot one had been a long time coming in Southeast Asia. After the end of the Second World War, Harry S. Truman had refused to recognize an independent Viet Nam and instead acquiesced in the return of French troops to Indochina. These decisions effectively meant the rejection of Ho Chi Minh, the charismatic Vietnamese leader who had been struggling against French domination since 1912. Determined to secure French cooperation at the dawn of the Cold War, Truman favored the colonizer over the colonized because Ho was a communist and therefore, from an American point of view, potentially "Moscow-directed."[54]

By 1954, the central goal of U.S. policy in the region had become the continuance of an independent, non-communist government south of the 17th parallel. That year, the defeated French had withdrawn from Indochina under an agreement that temporarily divided Viet Nam in

Figure 2. Ernesto Vigil, May 1968. This picture appeared on the front page of *El Gallo*, the newspaper of Denver's Crusade for Justice. The newspaper had reprinted a letter that Vigil sent to the Selective Service to explain his reasons for refusing to be inducted into the Armed Forces. The article was one of the first public statements of organized resistance by a Mexican American to the Viet Nam War. Vigil's youth—he was twenty when he made his declaration—was typical of many Chicano movement participants. Source: Ernesto Vigil, "First Chicano in Southwest Refuses to Kill in Viet Nam," *El Gallo*, May 1968, 1.

two and ceded the northern portion to Ho's control. Determined to prevent another "domino" from "falling" to communism, the Eisenhower
administration offered enormous amounts of military and economic aid
to South Viet Nam.[55] Nevertheless, its military was soon under attack
by southern communist guerrillas aided by North Viet Nam. Confronted with a deteriorating situation, President John F. Kennedy eventually increased the number of U.S. military advisors in Viet Nam from
800 to 16,000.[56]

By the time Johnson occupied the White House, the long-term investment of American resources and prestige had become yet another reason for remaining involved. Just like "every American president" since
1954, Johnson explained, he would honor a "national pledge" to support South Viet Nam.[57] After doubling and then tripling the American
presence to no avail, Johnson announced in mid-1965 the commitment
of 125,000 additional American combat troops.[58] Despite grave private
doubts, Johnson insisted the expansion was prudent, necessary to fight
communism, and likely to beget success.[59] Three years later, the number
of American troops in Viet Nam topped half a million and victory
remained elusive.[60] At home, the anti-war movement staged massive
protests.[61]

Initially, however, Johnson enjoyed a great deal of support for his
Viet Nam policy from Americans, including a significant number of
Mexican Americans who shared the president's strong opposition to
communism. Strategically useful for most of the twentieth century,
when "to be a Mexican and a radical was to be doubly suspect," anti-
communism also genuinely represented the outlook of many Mexican
Americans who were influenced by national priorities and rhetoric during the Cold War.[62] The highest-ranking Mexican American elected official, for example, U.S. Senator Joseph M. Montoya, Democrat of New
Mexico, was an early supporter of U.S. intervention in Viet Nam. In
1965, he declared that, "no matter what the cost," the war was necessary "to halt the contamination of new areas of the world by communism." Two years later, Montoya blasted anti-war protest as bordering
on "the thin edge of treason."[63] Sharing Montoya's views was Ignacio
Lozano Jr., the publisher of Los Angeles's *La Opinión*, the nation's
largest Spanish-language daily since 1953. Founded by his father and
originally "a Mexican paper in the United States," the U.S.-born Lozano
explained that under his leadership *La Opinión* had become "an American paper in the Spanish language."[64] Vilifying Cuba as "that poison-
ous pustule of communism" in the Americas, throughout the 1960s *La*

Opinión strongly supported the U.S. military effort "to bring peace and prosperity" to Southeast Asia.[65] In Texas, another fervent backer of U.S. intervention was John J. Herrera, a World War II veteran and longtime LULAC activist. In 1966, Herrera noted with pride that "our [Mexican American] boys die every day in [the] jungles and rice paddies" of Viet Nam.[66] Such sentiments were apparently widespread in some Mexican American activist circles. As the founder of the American G.I. Forum, Hector P. Garcia, enthusiastically described the state of Mexican American opinion in an April 1967 letter to the President: "As far as I know the majority if not the total Mexican-American people approve of your present course of action in Vietnam."[67]

By far, Johnson's most organized and loyal base of support among Mexican Americans for the war effort was the American G.I. Forum. In fact, the first public demonstrations that Mexican Americans planned regarding the Viet Nam War were Forum-sponsored marches backing U.S. intervention. According to *Carta Editorial,* in 1965 a few members of the G.I. Forum, among others, planned a brief Thanksgiving Day march in Los Angeles "to support our servicemen in Vietnam."[68] The following year, a much larger Forum-sponsored event took place in Austin, Texas. In July 1966, more than two hundred Mexican Americans marched through downtown Austin carrying signs that read "Support LBJ all the Way," "Help the South Vietnamese Remain Free," and "We Resist Communism." Still other participants in the Forum march carried signs championing "La Huelga," a Rio Grande Valley strike by farmworkers who had been inspired by the unionizing efforts in California. This overlap illustrated that Forum members in 1966 drew clear distinctions between domestic and foreign policy. Challenged by a grand total of six, presumably Anglo, anti-war activists that afternoon, Forum members easily shouted the counter-demonstrators down. They accused them of being "pinkies" and "chicken" and asked, "Why don't you cowards join us?"[69] Such comments suggested how Forum members saw anti-war demonstrators as both un-American and unmanly.

In contrast, Forum members sought official recognition of the patriotic service of Mexican American soldiers in Viet Nam. Throughout the conflict, the organization maintained lists of Mexican American casualties as a means of tallying the ethnic group's sacrifices on behalf of the war effort.[70] Representatives of the Forum also joined bereaved families at the airport as they awaited the arrival of a loved one's coffin; and they regularly attended the funerals of Mexican American war dead. At graveside, officials from the Forum would typically salute the slain serviceman and present "a wreath to the mother and the [American] flag to the wife."[71] In a 1967 letter sent to Secretary of Defense Robert McNamara, Ximenes praised the American G.I. Forum's "tremendous service for our country" by noting how the organization had helped countless families "through the most difficult time of their [lives]—the burial of a son."[72] Prompting the letter was Hector P. Garcia's request that a Spanish-speaking troupe of musicians and singers be sent to Viet Nam for the benefit of Mexican American soldiers. Ximenes's letter secured the Secretary of Defense's approval for such a visit.

Taking place in January 1968, the tour became another means of confirming the Forum's analysis of the war. Upon returning to Corpus Christi, the excursion's leader, Domingo Peña, a local television and radio celebrity, assured residents that their "sons and husband and nephews are being taken care of. . . . You should see the morale. It is just tremendous. Our men are 100 percent with our government." Peña added, "They don't mind being there. Some are back for their second or third times. We even talked to wounded ones who would gladly do it again."[73]

Some letters that Garcia collected from soldiers in Viet Nam appeared to back Peña's interpretation. In particular, two letters written by Mexican Americans in 1967 reveal a strong commitment to the military's role in Southeast Asia and deep impatience with those who questioned it. Writing to his eleven-year-old son in December 1967, for example, S. B. Sanchez, a Texan stationed in Saigon, explained that he was overseas as part of his responsibility as a "good citizen," just as the war itself was part of America's responsibility as a "great country." American citizens enjoyed "great advantages and opportunities," Sanchez wrote to his son, but they also bore "great responsibilities," among these, sharing with "all the people of the world . . . our great advantages and opportunities." Championing a global mission for the country, Sanchez was nonetheless willing to concede that problems existed on the home front. "Sometimes in our communities the ugly head of racism and discrimination arises," he wrote, but he encouraged his son to allow nothing to deter him from "the path of being a good American." An advocate for traditional notions of belonging, Sanchez explained that practicing good citizenship meant treating everybody, no matter their status or skin color, with "respect and courtesy," and being willing, if necessary, to "bear arms . . . to defend our freedom and heritage." Not surprisingly, Sanchez had little patience for those who he believed strayed from the path he outlined. He encouraged his son to study hard "because this country needs . . . engineers, doctors, lawyers, accountants, chemist[s] [and] economist[s]. . . . [and] not any more thieves, murderers, dope addicts, beatniks, draft card burners and peace demonstrators."[74]

Similarly, Lance Cpl. Patrick Vasquez Jr., a Marine from San Jose, California, staunchly defended the role of the United States within Southeast Asia while objecting to anti-war critics. Answering a letter from his "Pop" in April 1967, Vasquez agreed with a point that his father had raised in a previous letter: many parents who had lost sons in Viet Nam had turned against the war. According to the younger Vasquez, however, anti-war demonstrators were to blame. By "carrying banners like they do at Berkeley College [the University of California at Berkeley] supporting the V.C. [Viet Cong], or carrying 'Ban the bombings' sign[s]," protestors convinced parents that "their sons had died for something worthless," Vasquez wrote, when, in reality, the fate of the "Free World" was at stake. Apparently, the older Vasquez needed convincing on that exact point, however: much of the soldier's letter emphasized the threat posed by communist expansion and the necessity of American military intervention. "I want peace probably more than you do," Vasquez wrote to his father, but "if we don't stop the Red Empire somewhere, it'll never end."

More poignantly, the letter also revealed the powerful commingling of national and personal pride that motivated many young Mexican Americans to join the military in the first place. "Maybe you might think I'm nuts or something, but in a way I'm glad I was sent over here," Vasquez wrote. A combat rotation, he told his father, "really gives me the chance to see what I can do for myself and what I can do for my country." At the same time, Vasquez, already twice-wounded, tried to allay his parents' concerns about his safety. He offered that, "God will lead me to my destiny . . . if I should die over here, I'll be proud [to] know that I died for my country and I hope that you'll be proud of me too, for I'm a <u>Marine</u>." Underlining the last word for emphasis, Vasquez met his destiny three months later: killed in action in Che Sanh.[75]

Moved by Patrick Vasquez's words, the state chairman of the California G.I. Forum praised him as an outstanding example of Mexican American patriotism and sacrifice. While making arrangements to establish a Forum presence at Patrick Vasquez's funeral, Mario R. Vasquez of San Jose (apparently no relation) decided to forward to President Johnson a copy of the slain Marine's missive. In his own explanatory cover letter to the president, Mario Vasquez contended that the dead soldier represented a broader tradition among Mexican Americans. "Mr. President," Mario Vasquez wrote, "Mexican-Americans have died in many wars in our fight to preserve freedom." Drawing the contrast with anti-war protesters, he emphasized, "I hope that you have taken notice, that to date, no Mexican American has refused service to his country." Although incapable of knowing the actions of every single young Mexican American male regarding conscription, the Forum leader was right that as of the summer of 1967 none had attracted notice for refusing the draft. Implicitly referring to urban uprisings as well as anti-war demonstrations, he concluded, "If the people who are now rioting in this country had the same thoughts as Patrick, I am sure we could go about making the United States the country that it should be."[76]

As the war grew increasingly unpopular, the temptation for ethnic activists familiar with the politics of supplication was to boast that members of their ethnic group remained loyal at home and abroad. That was the message behind Vicente Ximenes's encounter with the Phoenix reporter. That was the distinction that Mario Vasquez upheld in his letter to the president. Similarly, in April and November 1967, newspaperman Lozano published editorials that celebrated the "loyalty of Mexican American youth" as compared to the "excesses" of anti-war activists.[77] When in June of that year anti-war activists planned an unfriendly reception for the president, *La Opinión* boasted that no Mexican Americans would disrupt the Johnson visit to Los Angeles because of their sense of decorum and their sincere appreciation of Johnson's civil rights record. The prediction apparently proved to be correct. No one arrested during the anti-war gathering was Spanish-surnamed.[78]

Yet the senior Vasquez's perception also had been correct: as casualties mounted, Mexican American doubts about the conflict began to accumulate. One early critic of the "bloodshed in Vietnam" was Francisca Flores, editor of the newsletter *Carta Editorial* and a founding member of the Mexican American Political Association. Born of immigrant parents in 1913, her political leanings were far removed from the politics of supplication. One early influence was the Mexican Revolution. Suffering from tuberculosis, Flores had spent the decade between 1926 and 1936 in a sanatorium outside of San Diego, California, along with many veterans of that struggle. They inspired her with their stories: one of her first acts upon leaving was to organize a labor strike by the facilities' nurses. Always a strong supporter of labor, during the 1940s Flores had also been a member of the Sleepy Lagoon Defense Committee that successfully appealed the murder convictions of eight Mexican

American youths. During the 1950s, she had arranged underground screenings of the blacklisted film *Salt of the Earth,* which celebrated a lengthy strike by Mexican American members of the International Union of Mine, Mill and Smelter Workers. As part of MAPA, Flores had also played an important role in California Democrat Edward Roybal's winning 1962 bid for a seat in the U.S. Congress.[79]

Three years later, Flores made clear her opposition to the war in Viet Nam. In the pages of *Carta Editorial,* she found fault with the planned 1965 Thanksgiving Day march by Mexican Americans in Los Angeles to "support our servicemen." To Flores, such an event was tantamount to "cheering [Mexican American soldiers] on to bigger and better fighting, to bigger and better battles, and as a consequence, to more and more deaths." Troubled by reports from Viet Nam of the deaths of two Mexican American solders who were only eighteen and twenty-two years old and lamenting the "many more that will occur," she went on: "If the loss of these lives . . . were actually in the defense of democracy, one could almost justify them." But such was not the case, Flores maintained. The South Vietnamese government was "a series of dictatorships" held in place solely by "American guns and men." Her conclusion: "The real support our servicemen in Viet Nam need is pressure by us here at home on our government to pull them out of the morass to which they have been sent for no good reason."[80]

Within MAPA, however, members were split over the war. While Flores was an early opponent, in August 1965 San Jose *mapistas,* several of whom were also Forum members, introduced a resolution expressing "unconditional support for President Johnson's war in Vietnam." According to Flores, the organization tabled the resolution for fear that, "once the issue of foreign policy was opened up," the "unity" that members had achieved on "questions of special importance to Mexican Americans" would be imperiled.[81] In a seeming reversal, the following year MAPA's executive board introduced a resolution criticizing the war. But other MAPA members successfully urged the organization to remain "patriotic" and reject the resolution. The inability of members of the Mexican American Political Association to come to any agreement on the war was made even more apparent in 1967 when resolutions condemning and supporting the war both failed to muster majorities. Not until 1968 did MAPA agree on a resolution, one that condemned the war. According to Bert Corona, a long-time opponent of the war who was then the organization's president, the main reason the organization finally took a stand on the war was that "more and more

Chicanos were coming home in body bags."[82] Although for several years divided about the war, by 1968 most *mapistas* agreed that the toll the conflict was taking upon young lives made it a matter "of special importance" to the organization.

Increasingly, the war and its impact upon Mexican Americans as a group were also attracting the attention of the handful of Mexican American elected officials in Washington. Edward R. Roybal, the original chair of MAPA and the politician most closely associated with the organization, made his opposition to the war known by mid-1967. He, along with Representative Henry B. Gonzalez of Texas, were among sixty-seven House Democrats who wrote to Johnson asking the president to renew his efforts to seek peace through the United Nations.[83] In addition, both members of Congress had started to investigate the Mexican American casualty rate. Gonzales's office had collected some disturbing data: according to one source, in 1966, 62.5 percent of the Viet Nam casualties from San Antonio were Spanish-surnamed, whereas Mexican Americans made up only 41 percent of the city's population.[84]

A well-circulated report by Ralph Guzman confirmed that the war was taking a disproportionate toll upon Mexican Americans. As part of his ongoing work with the Ford Foundation's Mexican-American Study Project, Guzman had examined the names of Viet Nam war dead from January 1, 1961, to February 28, 1967, comparing the numbers to U.S. census data from 1960. Estimating that Spanish-surnamed "males of military age" made up 13.8 percent of the total population in the Southwestern states of Texas, New Mexico, Arizona, California, and Colorado in 1960, Guzman found that Spanish-surnamed individuals accounted for 19.4 percent of the war dead from these states during the period studied. Although later modified by other scholars, his conclusion at the time was stark: "American servicemen of Mexican descent have a higher death rate in Vietnam than all other G.I.s."[85] Furthermore, Guzman insisted that unjust social circumstances compelled many Mexican Americans to enlist. As a historically "suspect 'foreign' minority," they felt a need to prove their loyalty, he wrote, while as an impoverished and disregarded group, they sought the social status and economic benefits that a military career provided. Finally, Guzman pointed out, Mexican Americans also felt compelled to uphold a powerful tradition, one of "impressive records of heroism in times of war."[86]

Eventually, Chicano movement anti-war activists were to appropriate Guzman's data and analysis. Initially, however, Mexican Americans concerned about casualty rates blamed the lack of ethnic group representation on draft boards. Empowered to decide who stayed and who went to Viet Nam, local draft boards across the country were "overwhelmingly controlled by conservative, white [and] prosperous men."[87] Consequently, many Mexican Americans feared that draft boards were more apt to excuse middle-class Anglo Americans and draft the poor and minorities. This potential for injustice prompted concern once again among members of the American G.I. Forum. They demanded inclusion in the draft process while continuing to support U.S. intervention in Southeast Asia. As early as 1966 Forum founder Garcia wrote a letter in a "spirit of cooperation and understanding" to the Texas State Director of the Selective Service requesting a meeting to discuss a lack of Mexican American representation on draft boards. Garcia took pains to explain that the Forum's purpose was not "to cause any embarrassments" but "to get a solution to our problem."[88] Two years later, however, a solution still seemed far away. In a letter drafted directly to President Johnson, Garcia pointed out that in several Rio Grande Valley counties where Mexican Americans comprised more than 50 percent of the population, not one Mexican American sat on local draft boards.[89] The situation was not so different in California. According to one survey of the San Francisco Bay area in early 1968, of forty local draft board members only one was Spanish-surnamed.[90] Garcia's assessment of such figures was blunt; the matter was "serious, urgent and explosive . . . [and] must be remedied.[91] Fully aware of the charge that minorities were dying in disproportionate numbers in Viet Nam, by 1966 the White House had attempted to rectify the situation. The official emphasis, however, was on placing more African Americans on draft boards.[92]

The class—and racial—biases of the Selective Service System, however, extended far beyond the question of draft board representation. As Christian Appy argued, these biases guaranteed that the fighting in Viet Nam was done by a "working-class military," poorer, less educated, and, initially at least, less white than their counterparts who stayed out of the service.[93] Affecting poor people of all backgrounds, student deferment constituted the most extreme form of privilege. Until 1970, full-time college students automatically escaped the draft pool. Until 1967, moreover, those continuing their studies at the graduate level extended their immunity. Yet few Mexican Americans were eligible for student deferments because few were enrolled in college, much less graduate school. At a time when the Mexican-origin population of Los Angeles was the third largest in the hemisphere, after Mexico City and Guadalajara, the Mexican American student population at the University of California at Los Angeles, with a total enrollment of 26,000, was exactly 70 students.[94] The tragic flip side of student deferment, meanwhile, was a program called Project 100,000. In 1966, the military, ostensibly to provide Great Society "opportunity" to young men from families "caught up in the downward spiral of decay," decided to lower the standards on the Armed Forces Qualification Test. The project's goal was to draft into the services 100,000 young men each year who had previously been rejected as scoring too low on this basic entrance exam.[95] Such programs reinforced the opinion of Mexican Americans that because they were poorer and less educated than the general U.S. population they were more likely to be drafted.

If the G.I. Forum protested politely about draft boards and selective service policy, other Mexican Americans took a more confrontational tone. In 1966 *El Malcriado*, the newspaper of striking California farmworkers, visually portrayed Mexican American vulnerability to the draft. In June, the newspaper ran two drawings that compared the effects of the draft upon the son of a big grower versus a son of a poor laborer. In each panel, the father gives his child a farewell pat on the shoulder, but the grower's son holds a suitcase marked "Stanford U.," while the farmworker's son is carrying a suitcase marked "Army." A "labor of love" on the part of union leader Cesar Chavez, the paper's title alone was a challenge to the status quo: a *malcriado* is a poorly behaved child, especially a mouthy one. Reprinting statistics from an unnamed "government memorandum," an April 1967 article declared that, of the five states of the U.S. Southwest, all, except New Mexico, had "flunk[ed] miserably" the test of proportionate ethnic draft board representation." The headline blared: "If you are a chicano, the draft deck is stacked against you."[96]

THE POLITICS OF CONFRONTATION

On the morning of June 5, 1967, about twenty armed members of La Alianza Federal de Pueblos Libres (the Federal Alliance of Free Towns) entered a courthouse in the tiny New Mexico town of Tierra Amarilla, determined to make a citizen's arrest of District Attorney Alfonso Sanchez.[97] Frustrated that Sanchez was not in the building, Alianza members started shooting, firing upon a janitor and a deputy sheriff. The insurgents then pistol-whipped another deputy and took two hostages before fleeing the building. By the time the hostages were released a few hours later, the state of New Mexico had launched the

largest manhunt in its history. All told, at least 350 National Guardsmen, as well as scores of "heavily-armed" representatives from the New
Mexico State Police, the New Mexico Mounted Patrol, and the Apache
Tribal Police, joined the search for the participants in the courthouse
raid, particularly the Alianza's charismatic leader, Reies López Tijerina.
With helicopters flying overhead, state law officials brusquely rounding
up suspected Alianza members in rural areas, and jeeps and even two
tanks rolling across the northern hills of the state (see Fig. 3), "a large
part of New Mexico was treated as if it were an enemy country in the
process of occupation."[98] The eerie parallel to another conflict across
the globe was unmistakable, even to a small boy. "Hey, if you want to
fight," a young Alianza supporter shouted to a tank driver, "trade places
with my brother Mario in Vietnam."[99]

The young boy was not alone in making the comparison. A native of
Texas and a former traveling preacher, Tijerina had founded the Alianza
in 1963 to advance the interests of the descendants of Spanish and Mexican property-holders whose families had lost title after the American
conquest. Accusing the United States of stealing from a conquered people, Tijerina's demand for the return of ancestral holdings approached
advocacy of a separate homeland. That goal, in turn, shaped his attitude
about the war in Viet Nam. To Tijerina and many of his followers, the
Vietnamese were not the enemy because *aliancistas* were not necessarily
Americans. As Tijerina contended during a protest rally in Albuquerque, "Our sons are being sent to Vietnam illegally, because many of
these land grants are free city states and are independent."[100] He also
asserted that the conquered people of the Southwest and the embattled
people of Southeast Asia shared some common experiences. Responding to recent press reports that New Mexico Hispanos were disproportionately represented in Viet Nam, in combat and among the dead and
injured, Tijerina angrily concluded: "They are sending your children to
die in Vietnam and won't give you a decent living here. They have
attempted to destroy your culture, now they are sending your boys over
there to destroy another culture. They are not satisfied with having
stolen all the land from us here, they send our boys to bloody death so
that they can take more land away from the poor people over there."[101]
For Tijerina, opposition to the war in Viet Nam was an integral part of
his confrontational politics. Those confrontational politics, in turn,
were the hallmark of the emerging Chicano movement.

The most intensive and widespread effort by Mexican-origin people
to combat social injustices in the history of the United States, the Chi-

Figure 3. National Guard troops aboard tank confront Hispano farmer astride horse, New Mexico, June 1967. This incongruous meeting took place in the midst of the massive manhunt for Reies López Tijerina and his supporters after they had conducted a shootout and then fled the Tierra Amarilla courthouse. Photo courtesy *The Santa Fe New Mexican.*

cano movement provoked a new awareness of Mexican Americans across the country.[102] Even before Tijerina catapulted onto the nation's front pages in June 1967 with his courthouse raid, the strikes and protests of the United Farm Workers union in California, headed by Cesar Chavez, had attracted sustained national attention to the plight of farmworkers for the first time. Although the farmworkers' strike always remained Chavez's first priority, La Huelga, inspirational and well publicized, soon became impossible to separate from what people, within the movement and beyond it, were beginning to call La Causa, the wider aspirations of Mexican Americans for recognition, respect, and fair treatment.[103]

The Chicano movement represented a major shift in the style and substance of ethnic group activism. Most significantly, the Chicano movement looked upon the bonds of culture and history as a political resource. Unlike earlier Mexican American activists who had kept ethnic pride primarily a private affair, Chicano activists publicly linked their political crusade to their cultural inheritance. The farmworkers' union was a premier example. Whenever the striking farmworkers marched, they carried a banner of the Virgen de Guadalupe. This was the same image carried by the native followers of Father Miguel Hidalgo as he launched Mexico's quest for independence from Spain in 1810 and the same one held aloft by the troops of General Emiliano Zapata during the Mexican Revolution a century later. Historically, therefore, the Virgin was not just the patron saint of the Americas but, just as important, the defender of poor brown people struggling for social justice. The union president also highlighted the shared Catholic tradition when he broke his long fasts with the consumption of the communion host during the mass. Similarly, the union tapped into a venerable Mexican political practice when it issued *El Plan de Delano,* a ringing plea for dignity and equality for all farmworkers. Many figures of the Mexican Revolution had likewise issued "Plans," which typically melded political demands with a call for social justice. Given these repeated public references to the culture and history of Mexico, it is little wonder that the farmworkers' struggle became identified in the public mind with a broader impulse toward reform on the part of all Mexican Americans.

Beyond embracing their cultural heritage, Chicano movement participants also employed militant words and actions. Tijerina's courthouse raid was the most spectacular example, but the peaceful marches and boycotts of the United Farm Workers were likewise unprecedented in their sheer number of supporters and organizational reach. Indeed, many young Chicanas and Chicanos cut their political teeth participating in UFW-sponsored picket lines at local grocery stores. Although not all the student volunteers agreed with Chavez's pacifism, with the notable exception of the Tierra Amarilla incident, Chicano movement participants usually shunned the use, although not necessarily the threat, of violence. In Los Angeles, for example, the group of young people who formed the Brown Berets in late 1967 called themselves a "self-defense organization" and, borrowing a line from black power advocates, vowed to obtain justice for Mexican Americans "by all means necessary."[104] The organization's image as comprising the fearless shock troops of the movement inspired dozens of Beret chapters to open across the Southwest.

The predominance of youth within the Chicano movement marked another new development in ethnic group activism. Although the early heroes of the movement were middle-aged men, the bulk of movement participants were young men and women in their late teens and twenties. The age of participants was a reflection of the overall ethnic Mexican youth population; according to the U.S. Census, the median age of Mexican Americans at the start of the 1960s was twenty years.[105] Not surprisingly, much Chicano activism was centered on college and even high school campuses. In March 1968, more than one thousand Mexican American high school students walked out of Lincoln High School in East Los Angeles to register their dissatisfaction with what they considered a second-rate facility, insensitive and even racist faculty, and a curriculum that consistently overlooked their experiences as people of Mexican origin. "How can they expect to teach us if they do not know us?" they asked.[106] Planned with the help of sympathetic Chicano college students, such high school "blowouts" or "walkouts" soon spread to other schools in the Los Angeles area and beyond. In Texas, for example, the Mexican American Youth Organization (MAYO) launched an impressive total of thirty-nine high school boycotts between 1968 and 1970.[107] Critical of mainstream ethnic organizations, MAYO had been founded in the summer of 1967 by a handful of young men who, during informal get-togethers at a campus bar near St. Mary's University in San Antonio, had begun to envision a Chicano "revolution" in Texas.[108]

This combination of youth, militancy, and cultural pride resulted in an intensely nationalistic movement that in many respects paralleled the black power movement. The opportunities for influence were many. Chicano activists not only paid attention to news reports about black power and read books by black nationalists, but the two minority movements also intersected.[109] Members of the Berets and the Black Panthers, for example, came together to sign mutual non-aggression pacts.[110] As soon as the Brown Berets opened a coffeehouse in East Los Angeles in 1967, moreover, black power leaders began to drop by to meet with Chicano youth.[111] That same year (and just a week before the federal government's hearings on the Mexican American in El Paso), the Alianza in New Mexico invited Ralph Featherstone of the Student Non-Violent Coordinating Committee and Ron Karenga of the black nationalist group US (United Slaves) to a land-grant convention. Attendees alternated shouts of "¡Poder negro!" (Black power!) with "¡Viva Tijerina!"[112] Finally, the following summer, Reies López Tijerina led New Mexico's contingent to the Poor People's March on Washington. The event, sponsored by the Southern Christian Leadership Conference and headed by the Rev. Ralph Abernathy after the assassination of Martin Luther King Jr., also drew many top members of the Crusade for Justice in Colorado, as well as ethnic Mexican migrant farmworkers from Wisconsin.[113] To be sure, moments of collaboration between brown power and black power, two nationalist movements, also generated conflict: at the Poor People's Campaign, for example, Hosea Williams, an African American leader, complained that Chicanos were getting disproportionate media attention, to which Corky Gonzales instantly warned that Williams had better respect his "manhood."[114] Despite such tensions, brown power brought Mexican Americans into closer political alliance with African Americans than ever before.[115]

Also to a greater extent than ever before, Chicano movement activists took critical aim at the prejudices and endemic structural disparities confronting Mexican Americans. Whereas the main thrust of most previous civil rights efforts had been to stress the potential of Mexican Americans to be good citizens and assimilate into the American nation, the Chicano movement rejected joining the Anglo American mainstream as a laudable goal. They looked at American society with a critical eye. Inequalities in education, housing, and employment, Chicano movement participants argued, were the product of a flawed nation, not a flawed ethnic group. Likewise, neither the under-representation of Mexican Americans in higher education nor their over-representation in jail cells was the result of inherent ethnic group deficiencies. Instead, Chicano movement participants were certain that the root cause was a racist and economically exploitative American nation. This disapproving and unrelenting examination of American institutions, moreover, extended beyond the borders of the United States.

To many Chicano movement participants, opposition to the war in Viet Nam was an integral part of their political protest. Notably, by 1966, the early heroes of the movement—Tijerina, the pacifist Chavez, and Colorado's Rodolfo "Corky" Gonzales, founder of Denver's Crusade for Justice—had each voiced his opposition to the U.S. military intervention in Viet Nam.[116] As the decade progressed, moreover, young Mexican American men and women began to appear with greater frequency at anti-war rallies, especially in California and Colorado. College students also organized the first Mexican American-led march against the war, in San Francisco on Thanksgiving Day 1967.[117] At the same time, because anti-war sentiment not only challenged a proud ethnic group tradition of soldiering but also implicitly threatened a generation's worth of civil rights gains based on that tradition, the war remained a deeply divisive matter for the Mexican American population overall.

Such hesitancy was incomprehensible to Corky Gonzales, a former featherweight boxer of national caliber and a self-made businessman, a seller of bail bonds, who had long been a popular personality in the barrios of his hometown of Denver. Although not a veteran himself, he helped found the Colorado G.I. Forum, the state branch of the national group. Gonzales had run unsuccessfully for the Denver city council on the Democratic Party ticket in 1955. In 1960 he had rallied the city's Mexican American population by leading the local Viva Kennedy! campaign, the first massive get-out-the-vote effort among Mexican Americans.[118] Four years later, he made another unsuccessful bid, this time for a seat in the U.S. House of Representatives. During the Johnson administration, Denver Mayor Tom Corrigan appointed Gonzales to be director of an agency called the Neighborhood Youth Corps, as well as chair of the city's local War on Poverty board. A year later, the city's conservative paper, the *Rocky Mountain News,* accused Gonzales of favoring Mexican American groups in the dispersal of federal funds. Fired by the mayor after he organized a boycott of the newspaper in the city's Mexican American neighborhoods, Gonzales announced in disgust his complete rejection of traditional politics, existing political organizations, and the Great Society's promises. Instead, Gonzales launched an independent civil rights organization that was particularly concerned with the issues of educational opportunity and police brutality. Featuring a "Pig of the Month" award, the organization's newspaper, *El Gallo,* engaged in confrontational politics from the start.

From the start, the Crusade for Justice was also an anti-war organization.[119] Personally, Gonzales suspected that all wars were waged solely to benefit "people who are capitalistic."[120] Touching upon this theme, Gonzales contended as early as April 1966 at an anti-war rally that the "economic stabilization of our country" depended upon waging war.[121] Notably, when draft resister Ernesto Vigil decided to join the Crusade, Gonzales made certain that Vigil's story appeared on the front pages of *El Gallo.* The headline proudly announced, "First Chicano in Southwest refuses to kill in Vietnam."[122] Gonzales flatly rejected military service as a testing ground for Mexican American manhood. Asserting that young Mexican American men had been entering the services to prove their "machismo and courage," he asked them to apply these same attributes to the Chicano movement instead.[123]

Similarly, Ezequiel "Kelly" Lovato, a founding member of the Crusade and one of the lead writers for *El Gallo,* encouraged members to join anti-war rallies. Describing a recent confrontation between police and peace advocates in an *El Gallo* article during the summer of 1967, Lovato offered a new arena in which Mexican American men could express their manhood. The thrill of battle could be found in attending peace rallies, he suggested. "You Chicanos who might . . . have up to now thought that peace marchers are sissies and cowards," Lovato wrote, "come to the next rally and face 'the Man's' goons." Referring to the police, Lovato continued: "By not supporting a rally you show your support for 'the man,' the same guy who beats you, jails you and sends you up or shoots your brother in the back." In an almost offhand manner, Lovato also disputed traditional claims of whiteness on the part of many Mexican Americans. "All this is true of our black brothers, too," he wrote. "Wake up minorities, unite."[124] Lovato's article indicated the far-reaching implications of Chicano movement politics and anti-war protest combined. No longer willing to try to convince white Americans that Mexican Americans were loyal citizens, Lovato also suggested that the group's more natural allies were other people of color.

Of course, such a stance made some Mexican Americans outside the Chicano movement—and some within—uncomfortable. While Cesar Chavez was an early opponent of the war, other farmworkers had their reservations. In 1965 eager student volunteers from San Francisco Bay Area college campuses had been among the first volunteers to travel to Delano, the headquarters of the strike. There, they had been shocked to discover that many farmworkers believed that criticizing the war was "unpatriotic."[125] Moreover, as late as mid-1967, at least one Fresno farmworker who called himself a *chavista*, a follower of Cesar Chavez, complained in a letter to the editor of *El Malcriado,* "You are not always the 'Voice of the Farm Worker' that you pretend to be. Stories about Negroes in Atlanta and soldiers in Vietnam have nothing to do with Mexican and Filipino farmworkers here in California and down in Texas."[126]

A farmworker from Laredo, Texas, who had attended the Raza Unida conference in El Paso that October drew a similar distinction between domestic and foreign policy. Writing a letter to President Johnson, Jesus Hernandez explained that his decision to protest the official hearings and attend the alternative gathering had been strictly a result of his hope "to develop a program . . . to help my people come out of the poverty level and have [a] better education." He added, by way of an apology: "Probably you are disgusted with us because we demonstrated in El Paso, but I want you to know that I will never join a group that is against the draft, because I believe in democracy and that we should fight for our freedom. I assume you know that Mexican Americans are brave; just recently two Laredo Mexican-American soldiers were killed in Vietnam."[127] Though Hernandez was ready to take to the streets on domestic issues, he still emphasized that he was a loyal and patriotic citizen, as demonstrated by his support for the American war policy.

A reluctance to criticize the war in Viet Nam could also be found among Mexican Americans on college campuses. Draft resister Salomón Baldenegro found this out when members of the Mexican American Students Association at the University of Arizona in Tucson—a group he helped form—banned him from the group because he continued to speak out at campus anti-war rallies.[128] Similarly, according to Carlos Montes, one of the original members of the Brown Berets, in 1967 some Mexican American students at the University of California at Los Angeles refused to join an anti-war march organized by local peace activists. Undeterred, the Brown Berets not only attended, they picketed the Mexican American Political Association's convention that year because the organization had not yet denounced the war.[129] Meanwhile, in Texas, Homer Garcia, a native of San Antonio, a former member of that town's Mexican American Youth Organization (MAYO), and an opponent of the war, recalled having received special instructions from MAYO leaders after his arrival at the University of Texas in Austin. If he wished to attend anti-war rallies, he remembered, he was told to do so as an individual student and not as a representative of the group.[130]

Although MAYO was fast gaining a reputation for confrontational speech and radical politics, members refused to protest the war, in part because Anglo Americans dominated the anti-war movement. MAYO feared that engaging in any anti-war protest was likely to blur the line between "Mexican American" and "gringo" that the organization was working to establish.[131] Adopting a finger-pointing, take-on-the-gringo approach, MAYO members indulged in inflammatory nationalistic speech, most notably when José Angel Gutiérrez, one of the group's founders, advocated that "Mexicanos . . . come together, resist, and eliminate the gringo."[132] When accused of "reverse racism" by such established Mexican American political figures as Congressman Henry B. Gonzalez of San Antonio, the organization was unapologetic because, members maintained, the "gringo" was the enemy. Although members sometimes drew finer distinctions between sympathetic and racist Anglo Americans, the organization's aim was to present a clear choice to Mexican Americans in South Texas: Did they stand with

MAYO or with the enemy?[133] Given this strategy and the "enemy's" involvement in anti-war work, the organization insisted that the conflict in Viet Nam was not a Chicano movement concern but a "white issue."[134]

MAYO members also realized that protesting the war meant contesting the deeply held patriotism that Mexican Americans, and particularly Tejanos, felt for the nation overall. To many Mexican American men from impoverished South Texas, the military remained a recognized path of upward mobility. Years later, for example, one Korean War-era vet still recalled the thrill he had felt as a former migrant worker when he had traded in "my cotton-picking sack for a [U.S.] Navy blue suit."[135] Especially in the San Antonio area, patriotism among Mexican Americans was intensified by the frequent employment of ethnic group members at one of the four military bases that surrounded the city.[136] Ireneo Garcia, for example, Homer Garcia's father, worked as an upholsterer at Kelly Air Force Base, patching the airplane seats in B-52 bombers that flew over Viet Nam. While his doubts about the conflict grew, Homer recalled, his father cheered on Chicago Mayor Richard Daley for unleashing the Chicago police against anti-war demonstrators during the Democratic Convention in August 1968. To older Mexican Americans like Ireneo Garcia, student protesters were "spoiled rich kids" with "long hair who didn't bathe" and probably used drugs to boot.[137] As Mario Compean, another founding member, later summarized the situation: "If MAYO would have spoken out against the war in the barrios, it would have been run out immediately."[138]

Compean stressed another reason MAYO stayed away from anti-war protest: any alliance between the anti-war movement and the Chicano movement was bound to be a partnership between unequals. Compean, who had developed a personal distrust of Anglos based upon his experiences in San Antonio schools, likewise tended to distrust the anti-war movement.[139] Years later, he explained why. Anti-war protesters were always happy to accept Chicano help, but he believed they were unlikely to return the favor. Once the war ended, anti-war protesters would then be free to celebrate, whereas Mexican Americans would likely be stuck in the same miserable conditions as before.[140] Therefore, although many MAYO members personally were opposed to the war and quite a few sought to avoid the draft, they refrained from contesting the war in any organized fashion.[141]

The determination of MAYO activists to avoid the war debate was evident at the second Raza Unida conference in 1968, a follow-up to the original protest gathering in El Paso. The conference once again attracted hundreds of ethnic leaders from across the Southwest, but MAYO members made sure the conference participants did not stray from an agenda that was focused largely on domestic concerns. In attendance, however, were two members of a San Antonio-based group called the Federation for the Advancement of Mexican Americans that had worked closely with anti-war groups throughout the decade. Disturbed by the mounting war casualties, certain that the conflict had devolved into a bloody stalemate, and asked by Anglo-American anti-war friends to introduce a peace resolution at the conference, the two FAMA members complied.[142] The student caucus was their forum. According to one news reporter, the counter-response was swift: "MAYO jefes intervened by removing the two men from the room."[143] Indeed, the only mention of the Viet Nam War within the conference proceedings was when evidence of disproportionate casualty rates was offered as proof of ethnic group loyalty. The proceedings noted: "We still confront insensitive and stupid people who entertain doubts as to our loyalty to citizenship and to our country. Let us remember: the best answer that we can possibly give them is to point to the disproportional number of Mexican-American casualties in the war in Vietnam."[144]

In 1968 MAYO's influence at a national gathering of Mexican Americans helped assure that the ethnic group seemed to have even less to say about the war in Viet Nam than they had the year before. Nevertheless, Chicano anti-war activism continued and became increasingly important to most Chicano movement participants. The transition from a politics of supplication to a politics of confrontation could be seen in the way these activists reframed the meaning of the statistics indicating disproportionate casualty rates. Instead of using these numbers to prove Mexican American patriotism and loyalty, Chicano activists held up the same statistics as further evidence of the nation's relentless exploitation of Mexican Americans. Yet, opposition to the war in Viet Nam was so integral to the political outlook of so many Chicano movement participants that Chicano anti-war activism was always more than just a matter of how many Mexican Americans were dying. As more and more young Mexican Americans joined a movement whose first building block was ethnicity, they asked themselves again and again: "What is a Chicano?" Searching for an answer, they continued to look at events in Viet Nam.

CHAPTER 3

"Branches of the Same Tree"

Aztlán and Viet Nam

Salomón Baldenegro lived through a political and identity transformation shared by many young Mexican Americans in the late 1960s. As he put it, he and many others went from being "students who happened to be Mexican Americans" to "Chicanos who happened to be students."[1] Although the term "Chicano" had been used interchangeably with "Mexicano" by some Mexican Americans for most of the twentieth century, in the 1960s students and non-students embraced the label to indicate their own expanding social consciousness. Ethnicity not only moved to the foreground during the Chicano movement, it became highly politicized. Recognition and pride in one's ethnic and racial background formed the cornerstone of Chicano cultural nationalism, or *chicanismo*. To activists, this nationalism was essential if a united Mexican American population was to gain, in the words of one of the founding movement documents, "total liberation from oppression, exploitation, and racism."[2] Within their history and culture, movement participants believed, was the raw stuff of political and social transformation. A crucial first step was to understand the significance of proclaiming oneself a Chicano or a Chicana. As a writer for the Brown Beret paper *La Causa* later explained, "Before we could move on the system that oppressed us, we first had to realize our identity."[3]

The urgency that accompanied this search for identity indicated the sense of uncertainty that many Mexican Americans in their teens and twenties felt regarding their ethnic background. Overwhelmingly second- and third-generation Americans, many were less familiar with the traditions and even the language of Mexico than their parents and grandparents had been.[4] Even those who maintained a strong sense of their Mexican heritage experienced little appreciation for that culture or history outside their immediate circle of family and friends. In an Anglo-dominated world, moreover, Mexican Americans in college faced particular hurdles. On the one hand, they represented a small, privileged group compared to the rest of the Mexican American population. In 1960 Mexican Americans averaged a seventh-grade education across the Southwest.[5] On the other hand, while education aided economic progress, like military service, it was also traditionally a means of assimilation. Some young people feared that success in Anglo-America might mandate a further erasure of their ethnic identity. At best, one Chicano student leader recalled, student life for him meant a constant and exhausting "negotiation" between his "Mexican culture" and the university's "gringo culture."[6]

Unsure of their position within U.S. society and sometimes uncertain of their place even within their own ethnic group, youth in the movement responded powerfully to a poem, written in 1967 by Corky Gonzales, called *I Am Joaquin*. It began, "I am Joaquin / lost in a world of confusion / caught up in the whirl of gringo society." Yet the poem ultimately held out hope about the resilience of the Chicano community: "I refuse to be absorbed / The odds are great but my spirit is strong . . . I SHALL ENDURE! / I WILL ENDURE!" Mentioning episodes from Mexican and then Mexican American history, the poem reassured young people that they and their ancestors had already endured much: "the muck of exploitation / the fierce heat of racial hatred," lands lost, a culture raped, tyranny, and poverty. By implication, Chicanos were capable of continuing to win "the struggle for cultural survival."[7]

Still, the poem raised the question: What culture was surviving? Joaquin lamented that he lived in a country that had "wiped out all my history, / stifled my pride" and burdened him with a "new load" of "inferiority."[8] Activists who sought to reclaim their culture and history also, by necessity, engaged in a creative process. Rejecting pluralism for nationalism, they struggled to define a new position for themselves in relation to the majority society, within the sweep of American and Latin American history, and even as members of a global community.

The identity that Chicano movement activists chose was almost the obverse of that promoted by Mexican American activists in preceding years. They celebrated their mestizo heritage; their predecessors had downplayed it. Chicano youth emphasized that they were brown, not white. They were native to the continent, not immigrants. Their allegiance was to those who had suffered conquest, not to the conquerors, whether Spanish or Anglo. Even as they sought political recognition and social equality within the United States, Chicanos and Chicanas conceived of themselves as a people apart. Seeking a source of pride and inspiration, Chicano activists principally studied the Aztecs, who had resisted so ferociously the Spanish. They even adopted the ancient Aztec homeland, Aztlán, as their own imaginary national space.

As a war raged in Southeast Asia, movement participants also looked to the Vietnamese for inspiration. Chicanas and Chicanos repeatedly drew parallels—political, emotional, and cultural—between the inhabitants of Aztlán and the inhabitants of Viet Nam. Unconvinced by the stated aims of U.S. involvement, movement activists were more impressed by battlefield horrors than heroics. As a result, Chicano movement participants contested not only the value of military service but also traditional notions of manhood. Opposition to the war forced movement participants to break apart narrow conceptions of citizenship and national belonging that had privileged whiteness, masculinity, and military service. In their place, they struck entirely new claims for legitimacy and belonging for Chicanos and Chicanas alike, and for the movement they were spreading across the country. Ironically, as these activists tried to create a vision of a United States that would include them without destroying them, they looked abroad to a country under attack by the United States.

PRE-COLUMBIAN CHICANOS

For many movement participants, the sympathetic connection between Aztlán and Viet Nam began with the adoption of a new name. Throughout the twentieth century, Mexican-origin working-class people in the United States had called themselves "Chicanos." Yet some Mexican Americans had used the term pejoratively to refer to lower-class ethnic-group members as well as recent arrivals from Mexico. Other Spanish-speakers refused to use "Chicano" at all because it was not a "proper" word but a slang term that probably derived from the shortening of the word *mexicano*.[9] For Chicano movement participants, adopting the label was an act of identification and rebellion. In their minds, "Chicano" came to mean a proud and politically independent people descended from indigenous populations who had lived in the Americas long before any Europeans arrived. To Bob Morales, whose work appeared in Los Angeles's *La Raza*, the term was meaningful because young people had chosen it for themselves to denote a newfound political identity and, above all, commitment. "We plant the flag of self-description and allow it to fly defiantly in the winds of opposition," Morales wrote. To call oneself a "Chicano" or a "Chicana," he explained, was to support "your people's steady advance along the paths of positive and progressive change" and to "lend your total being to the family of La Raza Nueva."[10]

"La Raza Nueva," in turn, referred to a renewed, reinvigorated Mexican American population that Chicano activists saw resulting from a spreading sense of ethnic pride and unity. Eager to reinterpret their role in the United States, movement participants explored and celebrated their own history and culture. In doing so, they forcefully rejected the traditional standards of belonging that Anglo-American society had set forth and that many members of an earlier generation of Mexican American activists had attempted to emulate. Specifically, Chicanos abandoned the quest for whiteness in favor of a recognition of and even a celebration of their indigenous inheritance. Although José Vasconcelos, the Mexican philosopher and educator, had proposed as early as 1925 that the blend of European and Native American cultures in Mexico and throughout Latin America had resulted in a powerful and even superior *raza cósmica*, Chicano movement participants seeking a *raza unida* conceived of themselves first and foremost as indigenous to the Americas.[11] In doing so, they purposefully blurred the sharp divide that U.S. society had imposed, and that many ethnic activists readily had accepted, between Mexican immigrants and Mexican American citizens. As Ruben Salazar, a *Los Angeles Times* journalist who helped introduce and interpret the Chicano movement to a broader public, succinctly explained, "A Chicano is a Mexican American with a non-Anglo image of himself."[12]

This new vision depended on a revamped racial identity. Whereas an earlier generation of activists had emphasized their membership within the "white race," Chicanos took a cue from African Americans and the tumultuous politics of the 1960s. Instead of black power, Chicanos championed "brown power" and proudly declared themselves a "bronze people."[13] As the prime minister of the Los Angeles-based Brown Berets once explained, the color of their caps was deliberate: "Brown is the color of our skin and our pride."[14] During the movement, alternative newspapers with such titles as *Bronce* and *Raza de Bronce* flourished.[15]

And just as black power advocates announced that "black is beautiful," Chicano movement participants maintained that they, too, were physically attractive. Thus, Mexican American high school students in Crystal City, Texas, demanded equal access to the Anglo-American-dominated cheerleading squad in 1970 by carrying signs that read "Brown legs are beautiful too!"[16] While hardly a challenge to the objectification of women, such sentiments revealed the profound racial repositioning occurring among Chicano movement participants.

Through the color brown, moreover, activists literally asserted their presence against the majority. Again in Crystal City, movement participants angry with local officials decided to Chicano-ize the town's statue of the cartoon character Popeye using brown paint.[17] So altered, Popeye not only represented the town's boast that it was the Spinach Capital of the World but also acknowledged the labor of the Mexican-origin farmworkers whose work made the boast possible. Similarly, in Mission, Texas, Chicano activists spray-painted a life-size gray stone statue of the Virgin Mary bronze to protest Church neglect of Mexican American needs.[18] Moreover, this new racial affirmation quickly became an explicit part of Chicano opposition to the war in Viet Nam. In 1969, after anti-war protestors on the University of Arizona campus set up a series of white crosses on the main campus mall to signify the number of war dead, Salomón Baldenegro, in a midnight run, painted roughly 20 percent of the crosses brown to emphasize Chicano casualties.[19]

At the same time that Chicano movement participants upheld brown skin as a marker of race, they also tended to view race as an important marker of culture. Seeking a linkage to a pre-Columbian past beyond mere biology, many activists insisted that political legitimacy—and even psychic well-being—rested upon the reclamation of what they proposed was a still vibrant indigenous cultural inheritance. To Santiago, a Chicano writer who preferred to use only his first name, a prior reluctance to acknowledge their Indian ancestry had caused Mexican-origin people on both sides of the border to suffer "psychological agonies." Exhibiting a penchant for cruder language than earlier activists, Santiago allowed that in some cases, "the Indianism has [been] diluted with white crap," but he maintained that the physical and spiritual beauty of native people remained.[20] Luis Valdez, who founded the well-known Teatro Campesino in support of the United Farm Workers, agreed. Although Valdez lamented that the Spanish conquest "shattered our ancient Indian universe," he insisted that "more of it was left above ground than beans and tortillas."[21] In fact, according to Enriqueta Vasquez, a columnist for the

New Mexican newspaper *El Grito del Norte*, people of Mexican descent, by virtue of their "Indian family roots," formed part of a larger whole that extended past the borders of the United States. "We are so brainwashed, we keep thinking that we are a minority," Vasquez asserted, "and this is one thing we have to begin to tell our people, that we are not a minority! We are a majority in this hemisphere."[22]

In identifying with their native instead of their European heritage, Chicanos were balancing the scales. Traditionally, Mexican Americans had proclaimed themselves as the proud inheritors of two great civilizations: the Spanish and Aztec. A Mexican's "rich heritage of rich Aztec and Spanish blood has provided him with characteristics born of a high cultural civilization," a member of the student Mexican American Movement had written in 1938.[23] The tendency among most Mexican American activists both before and after World War II, however, had been to consider the European legacy the better of the two. For example, Andrés de Luna of the League of United Latin American Citizens, speaking before the Daughters of the American Revolution, had once paid tribute to "civilized Mexico." Yet what made the mestizo nation notable in de Luna's estimation was that the Spanish had introduced to Mexico, and thus to the Western Hemisphere, such European inventions as the printing press and the university.[24]

Dismissing the "superiority" of European civilization, Chicanos instead described a pre-Columbian past that contained nearly Edenic qualities. Indeed, an advantage to the term "Chicano," from the viewpoint of many movement participants, was that it avoided any reference to the American nation, as suggested by the term "Mexican American," as well as excising any reference to Europe, as in "Spanish-surnamed" or the doubly distasteful "Spanish American." Instead of looking to the United States or Spain, writers and poets celebrated Aztlán, the original homeland of the Aztecs before they had migrated southward to build their capital of Tenochtitlán (latter-day Mexico City). In what one scholar labeled *chicanismo*'s "most brilliant political maneuver," movement participants appropriated Aztlán as their origin myth to create a unique basis for ethnic identity and unity.[25] Although the exact location of Aztlán was uncertain even before the arrival of the Spanish, within the Chicano movement Aztlán became geographically synonymous with the U.S. Southwest.[26] As such, the term underscored the Chicano contention that the unwelcome conqueror was the Anglo American as much as the Spaniard. Equally significant, Aztlán referred to a people who had deep and—so they asserted—more legitimate ties to the region. The existence of Aztlán, after all, greatly antedated the border between Mexico and the United States. Tired of being perceived as foreigners and no longer willing to present themselves as model citizens, participants at a massive March 1969 gathering of Chicanos in Denver instead proudly announced, "We are Aztlán."[27]

The determination of movement participants to carve a new political and cultural space for themselves was readily apparent at that 1969 Denver gathering. Sponsored by the Crusade for Justice, the first Chicano Youth Liberation Conference drew an estimated 1,500 young people from across the country. Participating in various workshops and caucuses, the attendees made an initial effort to outline the goals of the movement. Their findings, in turn, were consolidated in a document entitled *El Plan Espiritual de Aztlán*. A foundational blueprint for the Chicano movement, the plan advocated "nationalism" as the means to secure complete Chicano "control of our barrios, campos, pueblos, lands, our economy, our culture, and our political life."[28] Just as important, the plan presented the Chicano quest for self-determination as a justifiable attempt by ethnic Mexicans in the United States to gain what had been stolen from them. As the opening words of the preamble announced, Chicanos comprised "a new people that is conscious not only of its proud historical heritage, but also of the brutal 'gringo' invasion of our territories." Asserting an ethnic-group claim to the American Southwest that predated 1848, the preamble also left no doubt that Chicano ownership of Aztlán extended into the present day. Offering a bow of recognition to the hard labor performed within the United States by Mexican-origin people from both sides of the border, the preamble continued: "Aztlán belongs to those who plant the seeds, water the fields, and gather the crops and not to the foreign Europeans."[29]

While a powerful statement of Chicano self-discovery and pride, the preamble, written by Alurista, a leading movement poet, also evinced poetic license. Despite its characterization of Mexican Americans as an agricultural people tied to the land, by 1960 nearly 80 percent of the Mexican American population was living in urban areas.[30] Just as the precise historical location of Aztlán was of secondary importance, so too was the actual urban-to-rural ratio of the Mexican-origin population. That most Mexican Americans dated their arrival in the United States to well after the 1846–48 war was also beside the point: the inhabitants of Aztlán did not recognize "capricious frontiers" on the "bronze continent."[31] As mestizos twice over, Spanish and Indian, Mexican and American, Chicano activists wanting to revitalize their culture

emphasized those aspects that they found most liberating. Most important for movement participants based upon the lives they knew, the history they were uncovering, and the myths they were appropriating was
that they were a pre-Columbian and agrarian people whose ancient and
deep connection to the land trumped any American claim to the same
territory.

Eager to make this alternative political vision a reality, Chicano movement participants upheld their culture as a force of liberation against
American domination, especially American "economic control." Although *El Plan Espiritual de Aztlán* emphasized ethnic unity instead of
class struggle as the primary means of achieving political power, Denver
conference participants nevertheless dedicated themselves to defeating
the "gringo dollar value system." Their weapons were such Chicano
"cultural values" as an appreciation of "life, family, and home" and an
embrace of "humanism" versus "materialism."[32] Ironically, even as
movement participants sought to distinguish themselves from Anglo-
American society, this collection of presumably unique cultural traits
made clear that, just as black power had influenced the Chicano movement, so too had the social protest of the white radical youth who dominated the New Left and the counterculture. Echoing the counterculture's
rejection of consumerism (and reaffirming the Chicano movement's contention that brown was beautiful), for example, Maria Varela, a veteran
of the Student Non-Violent Coordinating Committee struggle in
Alabama and Mississippi, described the Denver gathering this way:
"'Conference' is a poor word to describe those five days. . . . It was in
reality a fiesta: days of celebrating what sings in the blood of a people
who, taught to believe they are ugly, discover the true beauty in their
souls during the years of occupation and intimidation. . . . Coca Cola,
Doris Day, Breck Shampoo, the Playboy Bunny, the Arrow Shirt man, the
Marlboro heroes, are lies."[33] As Varela's comments suggested, Chicano
movement participants frequently professed their opposition to American consumer society—and, implicitly, to capitalism—as much as to
American racism. Although not mostly rural, the Mexican American
population was overwhelmingly working-class or poor. Among many
activists who knew poverty firsthand, pro-labor and anti-consumerist
sentiments flourished. For them, the promise of American assimilation
had been an economic failure as well as a cultural one.

At the most basic level, however, conference participants declared
themselves to be liberated from long-held feelings of inferiority. Consequently, unlike earlier activists who had kept ethnic pride primarily a pri-

vate affair, Chicano activists publicly and proudly linked their political crusade to their cultural inheritance. Indeed, as the cultural contrasts contained within *El Plan Espiritual de Aztlán* suggested, movement participants often favorably compared an idealized Chicano lifestyle to what they considered the worst aspects of a hostile Anglo-American society. Anglos were individualists and materialists, movement activists maintained, whereas Chicanos held a deep respect for the community and—as a native people—for the natural world. Thus, in *I Am Joaquin* the narrator had been "unwillingly dragged by that / monstrous, technical / industrial giant called Progress" and had consequently faced "the sterilization of the soul" demanded by Anglo success. But Joaquin had chosen a different path: "I withdraw to the safety within the / Circle of Life / MY OWN PEOPLE."[34] Against a fast-paced, urbanized, technocratic, and profit-driven Anglo-American world, movement activists asserted, Chicano culture offered sanctuary and protection.

Other Chicano writers broke down Chicano culture into what they saw as its most important constituent parts: an appreciation for family and, most of all, for the land. Writing in 1976, José Armas, editor of the journal *De Colores,* continued to celebrate these attributes as the basic building-blocks of a life-affirming Chicano culture. As opposed to the Anglo drive for "material things, money, [and] social status," Armas wrote, Chicanos recognized the worth of "*familia* values," which included "cooperation, unity, respect, dignity and honor [for] individuals." Anglos were atomized in their cities, Armas continued, but Chicanos, even barrio Chicanos, drew their "nourishment from the *tierra* [land] and the plant of life, the *Familia.*"[35] Enriqueta Vasquez, in a 1970 column that championed Chicano culture, also brought together the motifs of families and the land. Born in rural Colorado, she paid tribute to the "*viejitos,*" her elders, who had taught her an appreciation of "*la madre tierra; la santa tierra; la tierra sagrada*" (the mother earth, the holy earth, the sacred earth). In contrast to "Gringo society," which "does not make a place for HUMANS in relation to NATURE," Vasquez contended, people raised in a Chicano cultural world "learned that the earth gives life and feeds us. . . . We learned to respect the food on our table and we learned to respect and love the laborer and the campesino."[36] Apart from being the basis for fond recollections, however, culture within the movement was always politically charged. Just as ties to the land reinforced the Chicano claim to Aztlán, the image of a strong and cohesive Chicano family hinted at the potential for unity across the entire ethnic group.

This Chicano identity, indigenous and rooted in tradition and the land, had immediate implications for how movement participants viewed the war in Viet Nam. Already exposed to anti-war sentiment on campus and often genuinely horrified by the devastation produced by the bombing, some movement participants identified with the invaded rather than the invader, in Viet Nam as well as in Aztlán. Brown Beret founder David Sanchez was one. Talking about Viet Nam on a radio program in April 1968, Sanchez put a literal spin on the term "brother," based upon his understanding of the origins of the Chicano people. On the air, Sanchez complained that "the man" was exploiting the fighting capabilities of young Chicanos and young African Americans by sending them to fight against the Vietnamese. Sanchez made clear that not only did he favor a closer alliance between brown and black, but he also believed that Chicanos and the Vietnamese were biologically connected: "We figure that since Chicanos came down through the Bering Straits part Oriental, and that honkie, what's his name? Cortés, came across over and raped our women, so we're half mongoloid and half causcasoid, that makes the Viet Cong our brothers."[37] On a more allegorical level, in December 1967 the Crusade for Justice newspaper *El Gallo* wrote about the courage of Cuauhtemoc, Moctezuma's nephew, who had refused to submit to Spanish authority despite having had his feet roasted by Cortés. The moral of the story, the paper concluded, was that Chicanos should pattern their lives after the Aztec prince by fighting against the cruel "European foreigners" at home, and not on their behalf "in an unjust war like Viet Nam."[38]

In a similar fashion, Manuel Gómez declared in a letter to his draft board in December 1969, "My fight is here." That declaration was more than mere metaphor. A leader of the Chicano movement in the San Francisco Bay area, Gómez had undergone a personal and political metamorphosis from scholarship boy to committed revolutionary. Deeply affected by the social, political, and cultural ferment of the Bay area during the late 1960s, in his letter Gómez offered a radical Chicano's understanding of events in Viet Nam. Movement themes of condemnation of Anglo-America, a special connection to the land, and, most important, an identification with the Vietnamese found expression in the missive. The Vietnamese were not his foes, he argued. To the contrary, they were "brothers involved in the same struggle for justice against a common enemy," namely, the United States.[39]

In many ways, Gómez's opposition to the war in Viet Nam was the culmination of his radicalization. Born into a migrant family (four of eight siblings were born in California, the other four in Colorado), Gómez had been a straight "A" student and student body president while in high school. After arriving on the California State University at Hayward campus in 1965, he had helped found the Mexican American Student Confederation (MASC), which lobbied for more Mexican American faculty, staff, and students. He also picketed supermarkets in support of the United Farm Workers grape boycott. Later, after the unexplained—and uninvestigated—shooting death of a young Mexican American in Hayward by police officers, he took up the issue of police brutality. Eventually, he became a member of a Bay Area chapter of the Brown Berets. Yet his experience also revealed multiple points of overlap between the Chicano movement and the era's other social protest movements. As a student assistant to Theodore Roszak, author of the 1969 book *The Making of a Counter Culture,* for example, Gómez remembered conducting research as a participant as much as an observer. He came to admire the Oakland-based Black Panthers. He attended the founding convention of the Peace and Freedom Party in the East Bay town of Richmond in 1968. Soon Gómez was reading all the socialist literature he could find, although as he later recalled, "I was never really a dedicated Marxist, I was a dedicated Chicano."[40]

Years later, Gómez remained certain that the war in Viet Nam had been the "single most significant, overall event that radicalized my consciousness."[41] As a result of learning about the history of American involvement in Southeast Asia, Gómez became convinced that the Chicano plight was not unique but part of a bigger, systematic oppression by a brutal empire. The bombing of Viet Nam reminded him of the U.S. invasion of Mexico more than a century before. He came to view the mounting Chicano combat casualties as an eerie echo of the unexplained Chicano deaths at the hands of police at home. In his letter refusing induction, Gómez thus angrily contended that American society was characterized by violence and treachery that Chicanos, Native Americans, and the people of Viet Nam had experienced firsthand: "It is well known that Mexicans were among the first victims of your empire. . . . The Treaty of Guadalupe Hidalgo is a lie, similar to all the treaties signed with our Indian brothers." Linking that troubled history with events in Viet Nam, Gómez asserted that, in both cases, the Anglo-American penchant for bloodshed was the culprit. "This society with its Texas Rangers and Green Berets has never allowed our people to live in peace," he continued. Now the Vietnamese were bearing the brunt of American ruthlessness: "My ears hear the screams of the fatherless children, my head hurts with the tears of mothers moaning for their sons, my soul shrinks from the knowledge of the unspeakable horrors of Song My and the rest to come."[42]

Anglo Americans were guilty of destroying not just lives, but the environment, according to Gómez. Within his letter, the counterculture's emphasis on the environment intermingled with the Chicano movement's appreciation of the land. Although he might have mentioned herbicides raining down upon Southeast Asia, Gómez concentrated on the effects of urbanization on the U.S. Southwest. In particular, he lamented the introduction of the concept of "private property." Without specifically referring to the struggle in Viet Nam, he thus indirectly suggested that communism and the *ejido* concept of Mexico, in which grants of land were given in perpetuity to the inhabitants of a village and their descendants, were not far apart: "In the short time [that] you have held the land we have felt the pain of seeing beautiful lands turn into parking lots and freeways, of seeing the birds disappear, the fish die and the waters become undrinkable, seeing the sign 'Private Property' hung on a fence surrounding lands once held in common, and having our mountains become but vague shadows behind a veil of choking smog." The message was clear: before the Anglo-American occupation, Aztlán had been a paradise. And whereas the Anglo wreaked destruction upon the natural world, a bond rooted in nature united Chicanos and Vietnamese. "I cannot betray the blood of my brothers, Gómez explained. "We are all branches of the same tree, flowers of the same garden, waves of the same sea."[43]

Despite referring to the Vietnamese as "brothers," for Gómez, identification with the people of Southeast Asia was primarily the result of shared circumstances not shared biology. To be certain, Gómez greatly appreciated that some of his distant ancestors had originated in Asia. In the process of what he later described as "unwinding my own umbilical cord," Gómez had made pilgrimages during college summers to well-known indigenous ruins in Peru, Guatemala, and Mexico. A later trip to Spain, moreover, was taken with one goal in mind: "to piss on Cortez's grave." While proud of his mestizo heritage (Gómez did not urinate on that grave after all because he realized Spain's language and even its surnames were a part of him), Gómez also insisted that the Chicano movement's cultural celebration must look outward not inward.[44] For that reason, in his letter to the Selective Service Gómez offered a subtle reinterpretation of the meaning of *la raza*. Rather than refer to Mexican Americans alone, Gómez used the term to signify something closer to "the human race." "In my veins runs the blood of all the people in the World," he wrote. "I am a son of La Raza, the universal children, and cannot be trained and ordered to shoot my brother."[45] A few months before, while attending the 1969 Chicano Youth Liberation Conference as a member of the Northern California Caucus (soon reconstituted as the Revolutionary Caucus), Gómez had made a similar point. "Because we know who we are," he had written, "our nationalism becomes an internationalism."[46]

PEOPLE JUST LIKE US

With a dictionary at her side, twenty-year-old Valentina Valdez (later Valdez Martinez; see Fig. 4) was struggling through *Vietnam: The Inside Story of the Guerrilla War* by Wilfred Burchett, the Australian-born, left-wing journalist. It was mid-1969, and already several former classmates from the tiny community of San Luis, Colorado, had died in Viet Nam. Valdez was determined to learn about the origins of the fighting. A member of La Alianza Federal de Pueblos Libres, she had moved to northern New Mexico two years earlier to volunteer full-time for the land-grant group. Initially, she had modestly assumed that her talents might lie in cleaning the Alianza's main office in Española, but Valdez had instead become a regular contributor to *El Grito del Norte,* the newspaper conceived as the "Voice of the Alianza." Accustomed to providing personal reminiscences, folk tales, and recipes, nearly thirty years later she still vividly recalled the tremendous challenge that Burchett's 1965 account of Vietnamese resistance to French and later American military forces had posed for her. Stopping to look up the meaning of every fifth or sixth word meant that reading the book "took me forever the first time." Intrigued and outraged, however, Valdez immediately re-read Burchett's work, as well as Felix Greene's 1966 pictorial and explicitly anti-war history, *Vietnam! Vietnam!*[47] "Now when I hear that a boy of our Raza, a poor boy who doesn't know anything about the Vietnam War has been drafted or enlists, it burns me, I feel terrible," she confided to *El Grito del Norte* readers a few week later. "The people they are sent to fight are poor people, just like us."[48]

Sharing her newfound opposition to the war in a series of articles for the newspaper, Valdez succinctly captured three major and frequently overlapping strands of Chicano anti-war sentiment.[49] First, Valdez lamented the death and destruction rained down by U.S. bombs. Her articles included several graphic photographs that highlighted the dev-

Figure 4. Valentina Valdez Martinez, November 1968. Valdez's writings for *El Grito del Norte* provided an eloquent and celebratory voice on Chicano culture and movement activities from 1968 to 1972. Just eighteen when she became a full-time volunteer for the Alianza, New Mexico's land-grant organization, she shared on the pages of the paper her own political evolution, including her dismay at the war in Viet Nam, and her belief that at the root of both conflicts was a people's just desire for land. Source: *El Grito del Norte*, November 27, 1968. Photo by Jane Lougee.

astation. Horrified by the carnage inflicted by the American war machine, Chicano activists like Valdez demanded an immediate end to the war. Second, Valdez denounced U.S. foreign policy as imperialistic. "Imperialism," she told her readers, "is when a large country, like the United States, exploits the people and natural resources of a smaller country."[50] Many Chicano anti-war activists agreed with her point. Like Manual Gómez in his letter refusing the draft, they often directly linked U.S. territorial conquests of the 1840s and U.S. military interventions of the 1960s to insist that Chicanos and the Vietnamese were kindred spirits, both victims of U.S. domination. This identification with the Vietnamese was the third, and by far the most prominent, theme of Chicano anti-war writings.

Indeed, opposition to the war in Viet Nam often moved in tandem with the emergence of a Chicano and Chicana identity as anti-war activists like Valdez drew specific comparisons between events overseas and incidents in Mexican American history or contemporary Chicano life. Similar to the lot of Chicanos, Valdez wrote, Vietnamese peasants had suffered the loss of their lands at the hands of the government. Referring to a land-grab that had taken place during the Ngo Dinh Diem regime in the name of agrarian reform, Valdez related how greedy government officials, whom she called *"vendidos"* (sell-outs), had taken land away from the people through trickery and harassment. She then asked, "Don't all these tactics sound familiar to you? The way the U.S. Government robbed our ancestors of their land? The forests were ours once too."[51] Valdez likewise noted that "anyone who fights for his land and what belongs to him . . . is called a communist." Thus, the South Vietnamese government disparagingly labeled its opponents "Viet Cong," while in the United States, Reies López Tijerina, Cesar Chavez and, until his assassination, Martin Luther King Jr., had all been labeled communists, too.[52]

These feelings of closeness and historical connection added to the genuine sympathy that many Chicano movement participants expressed for the Vietnamese victims of war. Tanya Luna Mount, a high school student at Los Angeles's Roosevelt High School, for example, wrote an exposé for a Chicano movement publication in September 1968 in which she labeled napalm as "America's shame." Describing in horrific detail the damage inflicted upon combatants and non-combatants alike by napalm bombs, including "severe burns, loss of tissue, bone damage, and amputation of arms and legs," Luna Mount asked her fellow students, "Do we stand and watch this un-declared war bring down our pride in America[?]"[53] Although her patriotic overture was to become a rarity within the movement, a feeling of outrage at the devastation that had been unleashed by American bombs remained. News of American atrocities magnified that sentiment. As a Texas editor of an alternative movement publication noted, reading about the My Lai massacre had made him "sick to his stomach." Halfway through a *Harper's* magazine article reporting on the 1968 event, he had put down the magazine because "my eyes were so full of tears I had to go to wash my face."[54] For their part, Católicos por la Raza, a Los Angeles organization committed to making the Roman Catholic Church more responsive to the poor, included two points about Viet Nam in a list of demands the organization submitted in late 1969 to the Archdiocese of Los Angeles. The organization insisted that the Church should not only be concerned about the number of Chicano war dead, but also that clergy should work to end "the Viet Nam War in all its hideous aspects."[55]

While movement participants often liked to compare the Chicano experience to the situation in Southeast Asia, many also recognized that the Vietnamese alone suffered the horrors of modern warfare.[56] In a 1971 poem that employed both English and Spanish, for example, Luis Valdez commended the Vietnamese for having endured bombings, mines, and biological warfare without having been *"tragados por el ODIO"* (devoured by HATE). The lesson for Chicanos was to replicate this *"espíritu positivo"* (positive spirit) by not "let[ting] the enemy *robarnos* [rob us] of our humanity with a little racism and police brutality." After all, Valdez asserted, "Compared to the Vietnamese, our life in the hands of the gringo has been a *tardeada con pura música de acordeón*" (an afternoon stroll set to accordion music).[57] An account of one of the first Chicano anti-war protests, in December 1969, made a similar comparison by juxtaposing scenes of a clapping and chanting movement crowd in Los Angeles with scenes "from that other place," of "burning grass huts," "volleys of gunfire," and "a young girl [who] screamed" upon being orphaned. Offended by both sets of sufferings, the writer disputed any description of the war as "honorable." More important, the two-track vignette made clear that, even as Chicanos protested the number of minorities dying in Viet Nam, the Vietnamese were bearing a comparatively greater burden within their war-torn homeland.[58]

In addition to objecting to the war on humanitarian grounds, Chicano movement activists often shared a worldview that was both critical of U.S. foreign policy and sympathetic to "Third World" struggles for liberation across the globe. Although first used to refer to underdeveloped nations, the term "Third World" within the United States soon took on connotations of color. Thus, in the late 1960s Mexican Americans joined African Americans and others minorities in Third World Liberation Fronts on several California campuses to demand higher minority admissions and more classes pertinent to them.[59] With a war raging in Southeast Asia, moreover, such protest politics naturally affected how students of color perceived U.S. foreign policy as well as the university. From a radical perspective, Chicanos and the Vietnamese were both members of the Third World in that both were a non-white people suffering from the exploitative nature of U.S. imperialism and capitalism. From this perspective, moreover, the Chicano claim to the land was an anticolonial struggle similar to the one that the Vietnamese were waging.

Indeed, influenced by events in Viet Nam and elsewhere, beginning in the early 1970s movement scholars advanced a sociological and historical interpretation of Mexican Americans as constituting a colonized people. As a seminal article on the topic explained, the long-term subjugation of Mexican Americans stemmed from the American conquest of the northern portion of Mexico. Just as Indochina was once an external colony of France, Chicanos since 1848 had comprised an "internal colony" of the United States. Consequently, they had endured "a lack of control over those institutions which affect their lives" and "constant attack from a racist society."[60] In a similar manner, Juan Gómez-Quiñones, one of the first scholars to grapple with defining the field of Chicano history, maintained in a 1971 article that, as the result of conquest, Chicanos formed "a minority-territorial enclave . . . analogous to other colonial cases in different parts of the world."[61] Finally, according to Rodolfo Acuña, author of the founding textbook of Chicano history, *Occupied America,* published in 1972, the conquest had not only been the key turning point in Chicano history, it had been brutal. "The Anglo-America invasion of Mexico was as vicious as that of Hitler's invasion of Poland and other central European nations, or, for that matter, U.S. involvement in Vietnam," Acuña contended in the first edition of the book. Like other colonized people around the globe, he stated, Chicanos had survived conquest, invasion, repression, and subsequent political and economic powerlessness.[62]

The crystallization of an academic theory reflected the broader anti-imperialist ethos of the Chicano movement. Movement activists readily partook of the era's brew of anti-imperialist politics as represented by the New Left (and revived "Old Left"), the anti-war movement, and black power. In conjunction with studying their own history, many Chicano movement participants therefore became familiar with—and sympathetic to—the vocabulary and ideas of anti-imperialism. In December 1970, for example, an article appearing in the Brown Beret's newspaper, *La Causa,* lamented the fact that "millions of people around the world suffer the agonies of oppression by U.S. imperialism and its lackeys."[63] More concretely, because Cuba had escaped American domination and survived years of American opposition, many participants looked to the island nation as an inspirational model.[64] As early as 1964, Luis Valdez returned from a trip to Cuba convinced that he, as a Chicano, could not serve in Viet Nam. It was no coincidence that the Brown Berets, as well as a lesser-known Chicano group, the Black Berets, paid sartorial homage to Che Guevara. For her part, Enriqueta Vasquez, after visiting the island in early 1969, wrote a two-part series for *El Grito del Norte*, whose title announced her admiration for the ten-year-old revolution: *¡Qué Linda es Cuba!* (*How Beautiful Cuba Is!*).[65] Similarly, Gina Gonzales, the daughter of Corky Gonzales, explained in 1972 that her support for the Cuban revolution echoed her support of the Vietnamese revolution. In a concern voiced by other movement participants, she also raised the specter of future "Vietnams in Latin America against my brothers and sisters." Examining the country's foreign policy, Gonzales concluded that the United States was a "monster."[66]

Yet neither vigorous condemnation of U.S. foreign policy nor genuine enthusiasm for the Vietnamese and Cuban revolutions necessarily translated into immediate support for socialism or communism among most movement participants. Although by the early 1970s several Chicano Marxist groups had formed, the Chicano movement always remained predominantly a cultural-nationalist movement. Moreover, in an echo of sectarian debates that had arisen among different social movements across the country, tensions between cultural nationalists and Marxists often surfaced, both between Chicano organizations and other left-wing groups and within the Chicano movement itself.[67] Among cultural nationalists, a major concern was that while white-dominated radical left groups appeared eager to recruit Chicano activists as members, white radicals also seemed likely to subordinate the Chicano movement agenda to their own.[68] Mario Compean, of course, had expressed a similar wariness about Anglo-American anti-war activists in Texas. A second source of tension also displayed nationalistic roots. Some activists doubted whether political theories that originated in the United States or, worse, Europe, could speak to the Chicano experience. Complicating the debate was that even within a single Chicano organization, members did not always agree. In California, the frequently feuding Brown Berets were a prime example. On the one hand, the group's paper *La Causa* denounced imperialism and capitalism. On the other hand, as late as 1971, the paper took Los Angeles Police Chief Edward Davis to task for mislabeling the Berets "communists": "If Chief Davis calls us 'communists,' he too is subconsciously aligning himself with the White revolutionaries in misunderstanding the fact that the Nahuas, the Huicholes, [and] the Yaquis were all sharing the land when his people were 'witches' in Europe."[69] Not surprisingly, given such divisions, movement participants who wrote about the Viet Nam conflict in any detail tended to sidestep explicitly ideological debates.

In New Mexico, for example, *El Grito del Norte*'s coverage of the Viet Nam conflict employed familiar Chicano themes of land and brown skin, of conquest and struggle, and of pride and determination. Unique among movement publications for the amount of attention it paid to international issues, the tone of the paper was largely set by editor Elizabeth "Betita" Martínez, who had arrived in New Mexico from New York a committed critic of U.S. foreign policy. As she was well aware, however, she was also politically to the left of the majority of her readers. Indeed, she later recalled, the rural residents of northern New Mexico who comprised the Alianza membership often called repressive law enforcement agents "communists" because the word, loaded with negative connotations in their experience, was the worst insult they knew.[70] Martínez therefore preferred to explain her opposition to the war by drawing linkages between events in Southeast Asia and the land struggle in New Mexico. As she later explained, these linkages were important as a "teaching tool" and more effective than an assault of "isms" such as imperialism, capitalism, and socialism.[71] Writers like Martínez thus promoted a Chicano/Chicana identity at the same time that they disseminated their anti-imperialistic and pro-socialist ideals.

The politics of identity that infused much of *El Grito del Norte*'s international coverage accurately reflected Martínez's own political journey. Born in 1925 to a Mexican father who had worked for the Mexican embassy in Washington and an Anglo American mother who was a high school Spanish teacher, Martínez recalled that her interest in politics and the international arena was probably shaped by the close attention she paid, while still in her late teens, to the events of World War II. Her first job out of college also had an international angle: for several years she had worked for the United Nations as a researcher. During the mid-1960s, she became an editor with Simon and Schuster. She also became involved with the East Coast brand of protest politics. Martínez was a member of New York Radical Women, an early feminist group, as well as a member of a support committee called Friends of SNCC. In 1965 she edited a book on the Student Non-Violent Coordinating Committee called *Letters from Mississippi*.[72] In addition, in 1965 and 1966 Martínez participated in some of the earliest anti-war demonstrations held in the city. During this time, she was developing her interest in socialism. As an editor, Martínez made it a point to travel to socialist countries such as Hungary, Poland, and the Soviet Union to find authors. She traveled to Cuba for the first time just after the 1959 revolution and eventually made six more trips there. In 1969 Martínez wrote a sympathetic book about the "youngest revolution."[73]

Upon arriving in New Mexico to launch the Alianza's newspaper, Martínez soon underwent another political awakening closer to the heart of *chicanismo:* she began to recover her Mexican roots. After a brief meeting in 1968 with Tijerina in New York City, Martínez had agreed to come to New Mexico for a short visit to investigate the possibility of editing a newspaper for the Alianza. "I came for two weeks and stayed for eight years," she recalled. By changing her name, Martínez demonstrated her adaptation to the Chicano movement. She had started her career under the name "Sutherland," a family name on her mother's side, because it impressed her as sounding appropriately "literary." Later, Martínez acknowledged that she had probably taken the name because she suffered from some internalized racism.[74] The SNCC book had been published under the Elizabeth Sutherland name. The book on Cuba, however, and a later book Martínez co-authored on the Chicano movement had both appeared under the name Elizabeth Sutherland Martinez. Eventually, Martínez dropped the "Sutherland" entirely.

As she embraced her ethnic identity, she also came to see the history of "her people" being repeated in Viet Nam. During the spring of 1970, Martínez visited North Viet Nam as part of a small delegation that was performing a letter-exchange for prisoners of war and their families.[75] Describing the trip for *El Grito del Norte* readers a few months later, Martínez began with the scenery. "There are mountains and valleys and caves and big skies and glowing sunsets, as in New Mexico," she wrote. "There are also things we do not have here—palm trees, animals like the water buffalo, crops like rice." But Martínez was more taken by the similarities. The Vietnamese were *"campesinos"* (literally, people of the *campo*, or countryside) who loved their land. Eastern medicine was like "our *curanderismo"* (folk-healing). And, in some respects, the North Vietnamese enjoyed benefits not available to the people of New Mexico. "The Vietnamese have a real bi-lingual education program for the [country's] minorities," Martínez wrote. What most impressed Martínez, however, was the spirit of the Vietnamese despite the ravages of war. Surveying the ruined buildings and the craters formed by bombs, she wrote: "The spirit of the people was like a force of nature itself, creating life in the shadow of death. The white people of the West with their unnatural soul and their unnatural weapons are a death people. . . . The Vietnamese are a life people. And anybody who thinks that

a life people can really be conquered is a fool."[76] Leaving no doubt as
to the type of enemy Chicanos faced at home, Martínez offered the Vietnamese struggle as an inspiration to all Chicanos, who were also a "life
people."

Martínez appeared to be saying that, together, Chicanos and Vietnamese shared a simple, pristine, country-based existence that unnatu-
ral-death people were incapable of appreciating. The cover of the issue
of *El Grito del Norte* that contained this article conveyed the same message through pictures. A special issue printed to coincide with a massive
Chicano anti-war demonstration that took place in Los Angeles on
August 29, 1970, the cover showed three pairs of photographs. The
headline read: "Vietnam War—Why?" and then, "Their People" and
"Our People." The first pair of photos featured the smiling faces of children from North Viet Nam and New Mexico. The second pair of photos compared the "*campesinos* of North Vietnam," a group of Vietnamese walking alongside their water buffalo, with the "campesinos of
Northern New Mexico," a group of New Mexicans in a similar com-
position walking alongside their horses. The final photo pair showed
two domestic scenes, "A North Vietnamese Woman" and "La Chicana," each working in an outdoor, rudimentary kitchen, each with her
long dark hair tied back.[77] The likenesses were striking, deliberate, and
underscored Valdez's earlier statement about "people just like us."

In California, thanks to the policies of the Richard Nixon administration, the Teatro Campesino was able to make its own set of connections between the people of Viet Nam and the people of Aztlán. Its 1970
play *Vietnam Campesino* condemned the administration's policies at
home and in Viet Nam. Its strong anti-war message in part reflected the
established anti-imperialistic sentiments of Luis Valdez, the founder of
the theater group. As early as 1964, Valdez had held Fidel Castro up as
a leader for all Mexican Americans and had denounced the history of
the U.S. Southwest as "a brutal panorama of nascent imperialism."[78]
Yet the play also captured the general sense of outrage among farmworkers about Nixon's anti-union policies. Campaigning for president
as a law-and-order candidate, Nixon had labeled the UFW's boycott of
table grapes as "illegal." Once president, Nixon had ordered the
Department of Defense to increase dramatically its purchase of the boy-
cotted produce to send to the troops in Viet Nam. Between 1968 and
1969 the Department of Defense nearly quadrupled its purchases, from
555,000 to 2,167,000 pounds of table grapes.[79] Despite this obstacle,
the United Farm Workers brought the grape growers to the table in

1970, hammered out an agreement, and almost immediately launched a boycott of lettuce to force lettuce growers to the table. In an instant repeat, the Defense Department soon started buying large amounts of non-union lettuce.[80] As a result, the play's anti-war message was impossible to separate from its pro-union one. Instead, by showing how the Chicano struggle mirrored and intersected the struggle in Viet Nam, *Vietnam Campesino* drove home its central contention that the fight for Chicanos was not in Southeast Asia, populated as it was by farmworkers like themselves, but in the southwestern United States.

Suggesting that the people of Viet Nam and Chicanos were natural allies, *Vietnam Campesino* also effectively caricatured their respective enemies, "General Defense" and "Butt Anglo," the latter character's name a deliberate reference to the name of the lettuce supplier, Bud Antle, Inc. The overlapping nature of the farmworkers' struggle and the anti-war crusade was made clear in the play's first scene: peace marchers are picketing the grower and union members are picketing the general. "Why are you yelling at me about the war in Vietnam?" Anglo asks. "I'm just a poor grower." "Why are you yelling at me about that farm labor strike?" General asks. "I'm a general." The picketers respond with their own questions: "What are you doing about the control of pesticides?" "How many Chicanos are dying in Vietnam?" "How many scab grapes did the Pentagon buy from Delano?" Assaulted by picketers, the General and Anglo are delighted to find each other, and they hammer out an agreement on the purchase of lettuce.[81]

Events in Southeast Asia and in the San Joaquin Valley intertwine even more as the play continues. Little Butt, the son of the grower, is a crop duster at home and a pilot in Viet Nam. Don Coyote, the labor contractor who hires strikebreakers for Butt Anglo, later comes back on stage as, in quick succession, President Ding Dong Diem, President Hu Nos Hu, and President Dan Ky Ho Ti (Don Quijote) of the South Vietnamese government. Also on stage are two couples, one Mexican and the other Vietnamese. Ordered by the General to burn the house of some farmworkers, the son of the Mexican couple heads toward his parent's corner of the stage, until the General says, "Not those farmworkers, stupid," and, pointing to the Vietnamese, explains, "These farmworkers." The Chicano soldier follows orders and is killed by the Vietnamese man. Little Butt then kills both sets of farmworkers by dropping pesticide-laced lettuce bombs and returns home a hero. But the end of the play shows the dead coming back to life. The Chicano soldier appears once more on stage and tells the audience: "The war in Vietnam continues, *asesinando* [assassinating] families *inocentes de campesinos* [innocent and farm-working]. *Los Chicanos mueren en la guerra, y los rancheros se hacen ricos* [Chicanos die in the war, and the ranchers get rich] selling their scab products to the Pentagon. The fight is here, Raza! *En Aztlán.*" "*En Aztlán*" echo his parents and the couple from Viet Nam from opposite ends of the stage as they rise to their feet.[82]

THE BATTLE IS HERE

In another Teatro Campesino play, *Soldado Razo,* Johnny, a high school dropout heading for Viet Nam, enjoys the respect and affection he receives the night before he leaves. "My son is a man," his mother concludes upon seeing that Johnny has donned military dress for his last night at home. "He looks so nice in that uniform." Proud that his son is going off to war, his father also describes Johnny as "*bien macho el cabrón*" (a real man's man, the son of a gun). For her part, Johnny's fiancée, Cecilia, fantasizes about their wedding day, when she will wear a bridal gown and he his uniform. Even Cecilia's parents are impressed that their daughter's suitor, who seemed to be without prospects, is about to serve his country. But the happiest character by far is Muerte (Death) who throughout the play applies white powder to Johnny's face, slowly turning him into a ghost. Muerte gleefully assures the audience that the soldier did receive a "first-class" exit from Viet Nam: his funeral boasted a "military coffin, *muchas flores* [a lot of flowers], [an] American flag, *mujeres llorando* [women crying] and a trumpet playing taps with a rifle salute at the end."[83]

The play took its title from a popular World War II song that celebrated all those Mexican American soldiers who bravely went off to war, leaving their dear mothers and crying sweethearts behind. Yet the message of the play was entirely different. Johnny's death makes a mockery of the cast's enthusiasm for his going off to war. Despite their multiple pronouncements, this youth who spent his entire life in a small California town will never become a man. Rejecting a set of cultural values held by many Mexican Americans that equated military service with manhood, the play also implicitly critiqued what had been a prominent civil rights strategy for an earlier generation of activists.

As Chicano movement participants continued to identify with the Vietnamese and condemn U.S. military aims, they inevitably questioned this earlier civil rights strategy and source of ethnic pride. Just as movement activists no longer considered themselves "white," they likewise contested the other two traditional parameters of belonging, military service and manhood, which along with whiteness had composed the traditional tripod of American citizenship. In their place, Chicanos, and especially Chicanas, struggled to define a new role for men and women alike within the movement. They also strove to convince the broader Mexican American population that the battle was indeed at home and not in Viet Nam. As José Angel Gutiérrez, founder of the Mexican American Youth Organization, summarized his take on the war in Viet Nam in 1970: "Chicanos have to fight here, not over there."[84]

Gutiérrez's comment suggested that even MAYO activists in Texas were promoting a reconsideration of military service. Previously, most MAYO members had shunned anti-war dissent as counterproductive to their greater goal of ethnic empowerment. Wanting to protect their own agenda, they had also decided against cooperating with Anglo-American anti-war activists. Yet in October 1969 Mario Compean, then MAYO state chairman, was a featured speaker at a San Antonio anti-war rally, one of dozens coordinated across the country by the Vietnam Moratorium Committee. He forcefully stated that now was the time for "all Chicano brothers, to manifest themselves in opposition to the Vietnam War, and give up all this patriotic . . ." (the newspaper covering the event printed ellipses rather than print Compean's apparent obscenity). Compean's presence at the rally hinted at rising anti-war sentiment among Mexican Americans in Texas; certainly, MAYO members no longer feared alienating their base of support by speaking out against the war. To the contrary, Compean made clear that it was his concern for the welfare of the ethnic group that had prompted his anti-war stance. Showing his ultimate loyalty to *chicanismo* over Americanism, he added, "If it weren't for Chicanos dying, I wouldn't care if the war lasted another 10 years."[85]

Although Compean's statement was unusual within a movement that often expressed solidarity with the Vietnamese, his emphasis upon the toll the war was taking upon Mexican Americans proved popular in Texas. The following month, for example, about 150 MAYO members participated in an anti-war, anti-draft protest in the Rio Grande Valley town of McAllen. The protest once again stressed Mexican American casualties and also accused local draft boards of targeting Chicanos. Similarly, when MAYO's political offshoot, the Raza Unida Party, gained control of the school board in Crystal City, Texas, the school board passed a series of measures aimed at stemming the flow of young men from Crystal City, where high school dropout rates topped 70 percent, to South Viet Nam.[86] In 1970 school board members barred army recruiters from visiting the campus, prohibited district employees from serving as registrars for the Selective Service System, and hired a draft counselor. [87] The counselor discovered upon his arrival that the high school's English teachers had routinely assigned the U.S. Army admissions manual as a textbook.[88] While opposition to the war in any form called into question the value of military service, Raza Unida schoolboard members, accountable to their constituents, broached the topic with care by focusing exclusively—and least controversially—upon reducing Chicano casualties.

The experiences of the man hired as the Crystal City draft counselor appeared to confirm the wisdom of some circumspection. Despite growing anti-war sentiment, Erasmo Andrade discovered that the traditional equation between manhood and military service continued to carry weight in Texas. A Korean War-era veteran, Andrade himself had turned against the war by 1967, convinced that U.S. intervention in Viet Nam had devolved into a bloody stalemate. Upon his arrival in Crystal City, he found that many young men in the town also considered the conflict pointless; at least, they had no desire to go themselves. Tellingly, however, few potential draftees were interested in obtaining conscientious objector status. Instilled from a young age with the idea that Mexican Americans were patriotic and brave, Andrade recalled, most believed that C.O. status was a category for cowards. Instead, they sought and— by virtue of the precarious livelihood offered by the migrant trail—often received economic deferments.[89] Notably, this legal alternative to the draft cemented their status as family providers, an accepted and valued role for a man.

In Northern California, Lea Ybarra and Nina Genera also shared legal alternatives to the draft in their work as members of Chicano Draft Help, one of the movement's longest-running anti-draft efforts. Ybarra and Genera had founded the organization to channel their fierce opposition to the war. The pair had met at the University of California at Berkeley, where both had been sociology students with brothers serving in Viet Nam and, in Ybarra's case, more than a dozen first cousins serving there as well. A transfer student from California State University at Fresno, where she had volunteered on behalf of the United Farm Workers, Ybarra had arrived at Berkeley to find the campus shut down in response to the Tet offensive in January 1968. Just as the UFW had helped raise her consciousness about domestic injustice, Ybarra recalled that the Berkeley student scene raised her awareness about the war in Viet Nam.

A member of the Movimiento Estudiantil Chicano de Aztlán, Ybarra remembered Chicano and Chicana students engaging in long discussions about imperialism and the war and drawing "connections" between their own oppression and that borne by the Vietnamese.[90] For her part, Genera attributed her anti-war stance largely to the influence of her father, a veteran of Pancho Villa's revolutionary army and a consistent critic of American foreign policy. Opposition turned to activism, however, only after her younger brother had been shipped off to Viet Nam despite the family's best efforts to secure a hardship deferment for him. As Genera recollected, the local Selective Service board of Yolo County, dominated by conservative Anglo Americans, did not seem to care that their mother was terminally ill.[91] When in early 1970 Ybarra invited her fellow *mechistas* to join her in taking a training course for draft counselors offered by the American Friends Service Committee, Genera decided to do so.

Afterward, the two women literally began to run interference at the Oakland Army Induction Center. Stationed out front by 6 a.m., they would greet the buses arriving from such agricultural towns as Watsonville and Salinas that boasted large Mexican American populations. Faced with large numbers of draftees and little time, their aim was not to raise consciousness but to save lives. For that reason, they did not debate the war but concentrated instead on persuading the young men not to enter the building. Their main tactic was to "bombard" the men with visions of their own mortality in hopes that they would at least stop and examine their available options. "We would say, 'Do you want to die?'" Genera recalled, and mention evidence of disproportionate Chicano casualty rates.[92] Although the vast majority of men completed the short walk from the buses to the induction center, some turned around. The women provided these men with basic information about possible deferments. As Ybarra later explained, "We knew it takes a political consciousness to resist. But it doesn't take a political consciousness to take a legal deferment."[93]

At the Oakland Induction Center the women vividly saw how poverty and minimal education exacerbated ethnic-group vulnerability to the draft. Years later, Ybarra remembered how she was able to obtain conscientious objector status for one young man who, although philosophically a pacifist, had no idea what "conscientious objector" meant.[94] In a similar manner, Genera recalled pulling another soon-to-be draftee out of line who later discovered that he had spondylitis, a back ailment that disqualified him from military service. From a poor family, he had never

seen a doctor until after Genera convinced him to delay reporting for
duty. According to Genera, yet another potential inductee was married
with a pregnant wife. Not knowing what to do, he had appeared for his
induction when Genera persuaded him to step out of the line. That man
later received a deferment for fathers.[95]

Despite such individual triumphs, Genera and Ybarra soon grew
frustrated with the slow progress they were making. Instead of inter-
ceding at the last moment, they embarked on a more preventive
approach—taking their anti-war message directly to the Mexican American population. The method they chose was theater. Joined by María
Elena Ramirez, a dramatic arts major, Ybarra and Genera performed
anti-war *actos* at high schools, community centers, and even in people's
homes throughout the Bay area and beyond. One of their most successful skits was based upon "The Ballad of Richard Campos," by Daniel
Valdez, also of the Teatro Campesino.[96] The piece told the story of a
young man, killed in Viet Nam, whose body was kept at the Oakland
Air Terminal for two weeks because he had no family to claim him. The
climax of the ballad was: "Now should a man, should a man have to kill
in order to live like a human being in this country? You are dead,
Richard Campos, you are gone."[97] Concurrent with those three words,
"You are dead," each member of Chicano Draft Help would watch jaws
drop as they pointed directly to a young man in the audience who
looked to be of draft age.[98]

Together, Genera and Ybarra also co-authored a bilingual anti-draft
booklet entitled *La Batalla Está Aquí* (see Fig. 5). While outlining in
great detail the "Legal Ways to Stay Out of the Military," the booklet
also served as an unsurpassed Chicano movement anti-war manifesto.
It appealed to "the entire Mexican American community, both young
and old, male and female" to turn against what the authors considered
an immoral war. Touching upon many familiar themes, the text first
labeled the war as "a direct imperialist intervention by the United
States." The anti-draft booklet then directly linked the ongoing war to
the historical experience of Chicanos: "Just as the North Vietnamese are
accused of 'invading' a city in their own country, (which in reality the
American government has invaded) so are Chicanos considered foreigners in our own country—the land that originally belonged to our
own forefathers." Beyond encouraging Mexican Americans to identify
with the Vietnamese, the pair aimed to compel ethnic group members to
sympathize with them.[99] Ybarra later pinpointed another source of Chicano movement anti-war activism: "A lot of us were feeling badly about

Figure 5. Cover of *La Batalla Está Aquí: Chicanos and the War.* Originally published in 1970 by Lea Ybarra and Nina Genera and then reprinted in 1972, the pamphlet was an impassioned plea to Mexican American young men not to participate in what the authors called an "imperialistic intervention." It contained a brief history lesson on the Viet Nam War, a critique of Mexican American military service, and a primer on the legal alternatives to the draft. Malaquías Montoya, a Chicano artist and activist, was responsible for the pamphlet's dramatic cover image. Source: Lea Ybarra and Nina Genera, *La Batalla Está Aquí* (copy in author's possession).

the Vietnamese."[100] Asking Mexican Americans to consider the suffering of the Vietnamese as much as the dangers faced by their relatives in combat, *La Batalla Está Aquí* featured several horrific photographs of dead or wounded Vietnamese children, all victims of American bombing raids.[101]

Through such graphic images the authors also hoped to erode the automatic respect with which many Mexican Americans had long regarded military service. First, *La Batalla Está Aquí* acknowledged that Mexican Americans had played "major heroic roles" in earlier conflicts. In their anti-war work, moreover, the pair had encountered fathers who called their sons cowards for not wanting to go into the army, mothers who hoped that army discipline would straighten out their sons, and girlfriends who, as in *Soldado Razo*, admired their boyfriends in uniform.[102] Ybarra also never forgot a Mexican American army officer who, in a dispute over her presence at the Oakland Induction Center, had pointed to his uniform and stated with pride, "This makes me a man."[103] Yet by supporting the maiming and killing of countless Vietnamese men, women, and children, the authors contended, Mexican Americans "only lose—our men and our own honor and our pride." Representing a dramatic break with earlier attempts to claim citizenship based upon military service and wartime sacrifice, *La Batalla Está Aquí* forthrightly challenged Mexican Americans to rethink what truly made a man "courageous and honorable."[104]

In the place of military service, Ybarra and Genera offered an alternative vision of manhood, of "machismo," that was soon echoed by others. Instead of encouraging young Mexican American men "to prove their manhood ('machismo') by fighting and dying in a war we have no business in," they wrote, young Mexican American men needed to use their "potential here at home in constructive ways that will help our Raza."[105] Even more emphatically, a Chicana student in Southern California declared that "machismo" could not be proven by joining the armed forces. In the service, and especially in Viet Nam, Corinne Sanchez wrote in 1970, the presumed fearlessness of Mexican Americans only awaited exploitation. The solution was to redirect that male energy. According to Sanchez, "Manliness is a beautiful cultural concept that should be utilized for the betterment of our people and not for the destruction of another people." Chicanos and Chicanas needed to work together to change "those institutions in this country that have oppressed our people," she wrote.[106] Men in the movement made a similar argument. Thus, another writer, dismayed at the injustices he encountered every day in the barrio, also rejected the notion that Chicanos could prove themselves to be "real men" in the military. "You're not much of a man if you let your own people go hungry, live in poverty and get ripped off by this country. Our people need you to fight for our freedom right here," he asserted, adding, "Dig man, something's wrong when you live in a country that offers people a better life in the Army than at home."[107]

The writer's final comment contained a central irony to which activists repeatedly took exception: why was it, they asked, that Mexican American men rarely experienced equality or attracted federal attention they were needed as cannon fodder? A writer who crafted a short poem about receiving his draft notice emphasized the last point: " . . . yesterday my Uncle Sam wrote. / He says he wants me. / He didn't say much else. / He never does." Still another Chicano author noted the discrepancy between the racial prejudices that Mexican Americans confronted at home versus the official welcome they received on the war front. "History calls me a Mexican (an excuse for wetback)," he wrote. "The military calls me a Caucasian." As Chicano activists reclaimed their "brown" and mestizo identity, the racial transformation wrought by the military no longer had the appeal it once had. Whereas an earlier generation of Mexican Americans had latched on to military service as a vehicle of ethnic uplift, this Chicano generation swore to defend their people at home. At least one military man agreed with this shift in priorities and racial consciousness. In 1970, a Mexican American Marine stationed in Viet Nam wrote an anonymous letter to a Los Angeles Chicano movement publication. "I'm being treated like an animal over here," he complained. "I know this is not the Brown Man's war. If I had a second chance I wouldn't have come over."[108]

The determination to craft a new vision of manhood that would stand apart from military service, however, proved challenging for antiwar activists. From the start, the Chicano movement had embraced a celebration of masculinity and patriarchy. Many of the movement's earliest cultural productions had been uncritical presentations of male supremacy. Particularly recurrent in movement literature and art was the archetype of the male warrior, one that dated back to the glorious Aztecs and extended to modern-day Chicano G.I.s, with whom movement participants, even as they protested the war, still sympathized. Also abounding as image and metaphor was the concept of *la familia de la raza*. The concept not only maintained that all Chicanos were a family, but it also suggested that the family unit—headed by the father—was the political and cultural foundation of *chicanismo*. By implication, Chicanas were most important as caretakers of present-day activists and mothers of future revolutionaries. A 1971 Brown Beret advertisement made the implicit explicit by seeking to recruit only men. "The man we are looking for," the announcement read, "must have Huevos (nerve) a will to stand for what he believes."[109] Although translated as "nerve" by the newspaper, and literally meaning "eggs," *huevos*, like the English word "balls," is a slang term for testicles.

Many Chicanas, however, not only suggested that a new kind of man could emerge from the movement, they actively resisted their own exclusion and subordinate status. Indeed, one reason that the Brown Beret organization was seeking male recruits was that, by that time, most of the women members, frustrated by their lack of autonomy, had bolted to form an independent group called Las Adelitas de Aztlán.[110] "Adelitas" was the name given to the Mexican *soldaderas* who had fought alongside the male troops during that country's revolution. Chicanas thus continually revised the movement's cultural-nationalistic imagery to better fit them. In her regular columns for New Mexico's *El Grito del Norte*, for example, Enriqueta Vasquez reframed the notion of *la familia de la raza* to include an equal, if not starring, role for *la Chicana*. As a woman who had survived extreme poverty as a young girl (five of her twelve siblings had died in childhood), who had raised two children on her own as a divorced parent, and who had encountered blatant job discrimination, Vasquez was impatient with any implied subordination. Instead, she insisted that the Chicano family "must come up together." The role for a woman in the movement was not behind a man, she declared, but "alongside him, leading." Turning to the Mexican past as well as their own experiences as mothers, wives, and daughters, movement participants like Vasquez helped promote an understanding of Chicanas as defenders of their people, as equal partners in struggle.

Activism itself cemented that lesson. Through their participation in the Chicano movement, Chicanas came to appreciate their own talents. To be sure, Chicanas, like their male counterparts, often initially accepted what they saw as a natural division of labor along gender lines. Ironically, because the actual pasting and putting together of a newspaper was tedious work with little associated glory, that task—and much of the writing as well—often fell to women, like Valentina Valdez, the eloquent contributor to *El Grito del Norte*. Forming the backbone of the Chicano print media, Chicanas consequently authored some of the movement's most original and insightful political commentaries.

Along with viewing writing and secretarial skills as the domain of women, most movement participants saw food preparation as women's work. Thus, Lea Ybarra remembered how early in the movement Chicanas were often in the kitchen preparing food during a meeting while the male participants were discussing important business in the next room. (Often their ideas for fundraisers featured the women making even more food.) Ybarra distinctly remembered the day she overheard one male leader make a suggestion and thought to herself that not only had the same idea already occurred to her but she had a better one. After that, she was less content to stay in the kitchen. Nina Genera also decided to "stop making tortillas" as a result of her involvement in the movement.[111] Initially, she was so shy that when Chicano Draft Help began to perform skits, she only wanted to play the role of Richard Campos—the dead soldier who was silent and still. Before the war ended, however, in addition to approaching strangers in induction lines, Genera was playing major parts in skits and traveling across international borders to meet with Indo-Chinese women.

In fact, Genera and Ybarra, along with María Elena Ramirez, their actor colleague, were among a group of Third World women who traveled from the San Francisco Bay area in 1971 to meet with representatives from North Viet Nam in Vancouver, Canada. Just as anti-war activism contributed to a rethinking of what a man's role should be within the Chicano movement, such activism also helped Chicanas imagine what their roles might be if they were recognized as equals. At a time when some movement participants labeled feminism divisive to the Chicano movement, and even feminist Chicanas had difficulty "relating" to the politics and personalities of Anglo-American feminists, the women of Viet Nam seemed perfect role models. Ramirez, for example, in her interactions with Anglo-American feminists, had been disappointed, because too many, she felt, acted as if Chicanas needed their leadership and guidance. In contrast to such "abrasive" behavior, the Vietnamese were soft-spoken and respectful. She remembered the significance of the Vancouver meeting: "It was just like 'Wow.' We can find our own way to being liberated without following white women."[112]

Chicanas in Vancouver and elsewhere lauded the Vietnamese as tenacious, brave, and, above all, womanly warriors and leaders. To the married Genara, here was a feminist with whom she could identify. As described by another Chicana attendee, the Vietnamese were physically delicate, "small, about five feet tall," but extraordinarily gracious, "humble and kind." Yet their apparent gentleness and fragility did not in any way compromise their political resolve. "One sister from South Vietnam . . . had been an ordinary housewife when she was arrested," the same participant noted. "When she was finally released (six years later) she became a dedicated fighter for her people."[113] To Chicanas, Vietnamese women appeared to be both feminine and, as fearless contributors to their struggle, the equals of men. Perhaps that is why Vasquez, in a 1971 attempt to persuade Chicanas that their first loyalties remained with the Chicano movement and not with the "white women's liberation movement," once again made an example of Vietnamese women. Exaggerating to make her point, she wrote in a column entitled "*Soy Chicana Primero*" ("I Am First a Chicana"): "We have seen the Vietnamese woman fight for survival with a gun in one hand and a child sucking on her breast on the other arm."[114] Notable for their acceptance of many traditional values—movement women were going to be motherly and feminine—anti-war Chicanas nevertheless attempted to carve a space for women within a deeply culturally nationalistic and often patriarchal movement. Their struggle continued as the Chicano movement's anti-war crusade expanded.

Ultimately, what most impressed Ramirez about meeting the Vietnamese representatives in Vancouver, however, was that the struggle in Viet Nam seemed so similar to the Chicano one. Fundamentally, she recalled, it was about "people and land."[115] A strong identification with the Vietnamese struggle fueled Chicano anti-war activism. It amplified genuine concern about the suffering endured by the Vietnamese; it confirmed nascent or full-fledged anti-imperialists in their understanding of the war; it inspired Chicanas to model themselves after the Vietnamese women; it prompted movement participants to criticize the U.S. military and consequently forced them to develop a new vision of manhood independent of battlefield bravery.

Rejecting the traditional patriotism of the ethnic group, Chicano activists defiantly announced they would put their own struggle first. Both within and beyond the movement, the Chicano anti-war slogan with the broadest appeal was *¡La batalla está aquí!* Even in Texas, where activists had been reluctant to address the war issue for fear of alienating supporters, this idea, that the struggle for La Raza was in the American Southwest and not Southeast Asia, found a receptive audience. As casualties rose and anti-war sentiment spread across the country, moreover, a group of young people in Los Angeles, thinking about launching a specifically Chicano anti-war movement, had just such a message in mind.

CHAPTER 4

"I'd Rather Have My Sons Die for La Raza . . . than in Vietnam"

The Making of a Moratorium

In the early morning hours of September 16, 1969, a crowd of young people began to assemble in front of the downtown Los Angeles army induction center. Although Los Angeles's Mexican Americans tradition-ally had celebrated the date—Mexican Independence Day—with patri-otic parades and civic fiestas, these Chicano movement participants had gathered instead to declare their independence from the U.S. Selective Service System. Numbering nearly 100, the group of mostly college stu-dents formed a lengthy picket line in front of the center's doors to make clear their opposition to the ongoing war in Viet Nam. As urban youth, many of whom were African American or Mexican American, began arriving to be sworn into the service that morning, the demonstrators peacefully handed them anti-war leaflets. Then, just minutes before the main doors opened at 8 a.m., a twenty-three-year-old man stepped for-ward and explained why he, as a Chicano, was refusing to serve in Viet Nam. "I accuse the government of the United States of America of geno-cide against the Mexican people," he said. "Specifically, I accuse the draft, the entire social, political, and economic system . . . of creating a funnel which shoots Mexican youth into Viet Nam to be killed and to kill innocent men, women and children."[1]

According to the speaker, Rosalío U. Muñoz, a former student body president of the University of California at Los Angeles, the U.S. gov-ernment was guilty of inflicting psychological and cultural devastation upon Mexican American people at home while callously expending their lives overseas. Charging American society with exploiting the "machismo" of the Mexican American male overseas, Muñoz demanded that the government begin to address the deep-rooted social, economic, and racial problems that affected so many Mexican Americans at home. Until then, and until the Department of Defense stopped buying table grapes and deliberately undermining a boycott organized by the United Farm Workers, Muñoz announced, he intended to "boycott" the Selective Service System. Giving his girlfriend a kiss good-bye, Muñoz turned away from the crowd to enter the induction center and launch his battle as a draft resister.

Once inside, however, officials told Muñoz that his induction date had been postponed, a bureaucratic happenstance that rendered his show of draft resistance officially irrelevant. The demonstration was nonetheless significant. In the weeks and months following the September 16, 1969, demonstration, anti-war protest moved to the forefront of the Chicano movement in Los Angeles and across the Southwest. Genuinely opposed to American intervention, Chicano anti-war activists also adroitly used the war in Southeast Asia to focus attention on the plight of Mexican Americans in the American Southwest.

Beyond inaugurating this effort, the Mexican Independence Day gathering articulated the three major themes of organized Chicano anti-war protest. First, protesters linked the war in Viet Nam to the home front. As Muñoz made clear in his speech, Chicano anti-war activism was inseparable from such local community concerns as education, welfare rights, and police relations. Each of these social problems, he maintained, had "funneled" Mexican Americans to Viet Nam. A degrading educational system, for example, had failed to prepare Mexican Americans for college. The consequence was that few of them qualified for student draft deferments. Poverty only compounded the problem. Not only was full-time college attendance prohibitively expensive, Muñoz argued, but too many young men—caught between the lack of job opportunities and a degrading welfare system—joined the army out of economic desperation. Lastly, Muñoz denounced police brutality, arguing that a desire to escape that problem also prompted young men to enlist. "I accuse the law enforcement agencies of the United States of instilling greater fear and insecurity in Mexican youth than the Viet Cong ever could," he declared.

Second, the Mexican Independence Day protest was also grounded in Chicano cultural nationalism, in the advocacy of self-determination for people of Mexican origin within the United States. Instead of serving the

United States in the military, Muñoz proposed, young people should receive draft deferments to serve their people in the barrios. Convinced that the situation confronting Mexican Americans was both dire and unique, anti-war activists like Muñoz hoped that an independent Chicano anti-war effort would encourage community empowerment as much as help end the war. This overriding goal did not preclude borrowing tactics from the national anti-war movement—including protesting in front of induction centers. Later, the Brown Berets' participation at a national anti-war demonstration in San Francisco inspired them and other Chicano movement participants to plan a series of Chicano anti-war demonstrations in Los Angeles. Again borrowing from the mainstream peace movement, they called these demonstrations Chicano Moratoriums. Yet, despite instances of imitation and even cooperation, anti-war Chicanas and Chicanos, true to the nationalist origins of their movement, were always careful to champion their own concerns, to speak for themselves.

Third, Chicano anti-war activism encouraged the participation of people with diverse political outlooks. An emphasis on outreach and inclusiveness was evident from the start: Muñoz had drafted his speech with the help of several work colleagues and college friends (see Fig. 6). Near the close of 1969, Muñoz and other former college students joined forces with the Los Angeles Brown Berets to organize the first Chicano Moratorium march. The partnership brought together college-educated advocates of nonviolence and street-smart advocates of violence. As they built a broad-based movement, Chicano anti-war activists embraced such political diversity. Indeed, attendees at Chicano anti-war moratoriums soon ranged from a Mexican American candidate running for a congressional seat in the Democratic primary to Chicano Trotskyites who hoped the protest might help spark the longed-for revolution.

That wide embrace quickly proved useful, for once introduced to center stage, the previously untapped power of the war issue became an extraordinary organizational catalyst. For hundreds, and then thousands, of Mexican Americans, protest against a faraway war allowed them to focus their complaints about conditions at home. At the same time, by attempting to reconcile a sharp critique of U.S. actions at home and abroad with movement demands for government redress, anti-war activism exposed the central political dissonance between the Chicano movement's separatist assertions and its frequently integrationist goals. Inevitably, because Chicano anti-war activism addressed a topic that had generated much protest among Americans in general, it also

Figure 6. Rosalío Muñoz addresses a MEChA meeting on September 15, 1969. The night before he refused the draft, the former student body president of the University of California at Los Angeles asked Chicano members of the Movimiento Estudiantil Chicano de Aztlán to join his protest the following morning, a protest that marked the start of a sustained Chicano campaign against the draft and against the war. MEChA consistently supported both measures. Seated behind Muñoz are, in the far corner, Tony Salazar, president of UCLA's MEChA chapter, and Ramsés Noriega, a key behind-the-scenes organizer. Photo by George Rodriguez.

revealed the numerous tensions between white radicalism and Chicano nationalism. Most important, even as Chicano anti-war protest sought to foster unity within and beyond the Chicano movement, it exposed the fragility of coalition building through cultural-nationalistic appeals. In the end, Chicano anti-war activism showcased both the organizing strength and the inherent limitations of Chicano cultural nationalism.

A CHICANO ANTI-DRAFT CRUSADE

A month after the September 1969 protest, Muñoz found himself seated in front of his draft board being interviewed about his decision to refuse induction. With him was Ramsés Noriega, a UCLA graduate student in fine arts who had managed Muñoz's campaign for student body president the year before. To every question posed by his draft board, Muñoz responded in Spanish. Fully aware that Muñoz spoke perfect English, board members refused Noriega's attempt to serve as a translator. Apparently finding a young Mexican American woman who worked in the draft board office more trustworthy, they briefly utilized her services before cutting the entire interview short out of frustration. Despite the briefness of the encounter, Muñoz and Noriega left the building pleased. By refusing to speak in English, they had questioned the legitimacy of the draft board's power over Chicanos. They also had orchestrated yet another episode in Muñoz's public struggle with the Selective Service System. Partners in a Chicano anti-draft crusade, the pair was determined to raise awareness about the draft, and indirectly the war, among the entire Mexican American population.

As both later explained, their central aim was "mobilization." The word resonated within the context of the era's protest politics. Inspired by the size of recent civil rights demonstrations, most notably the 1963 March on Washington for Jobs and Freedom, several anti-war groups had adopted the word to underscore their commitment to massive anti-war demonstrations.[2] For their part, the shared aspiration of Muñoz and Noriega was to move unprecedented numbers of their fellow Mexican Americans to take action against the war and on behalf of the Chicano movement. Although by the fall of 1969 several Chicano activists from different states had either resisted the draft or obtained conscientious objector status, these were largely private decisions that had received little, if any, publicity.[3] In contrast, Muñoz sought out the spotlight from the start because both he and Noriega were interested in securing an audience for their anti-war stance that extended beyond Chicano movement circles.

Of the two, Muñoz was the latecomer to both Chicano and anti-war protest. Family tradition, however, blended higher education with activism. Both his parents were college graduates. During the 1930s, moreover, his Mexican immigrant father, Rosalío F. Muñoz, had been among the founders of a student group called Los Conquistadores on the campus of Arizona State Teachers College (now Arizona State University). Like members of the Mexican American Movement in Southern California, the Conquistadores had emphasized college attendance as a means of instilling ethnic pride and furthering ethnic uplift. In fact, the Conquistadores opened the first MAM chapter in Arizona and shared some members in common with the California group.[4] After graduation, Muñoz's father launched his career in Arizona before moving the family to California, where he went on to obtain a doctorate in educational psychology and eventually became a top-level administrator with the Los Angeles School District. Career promotions meant another move for the Muñoz family: from the eastside barrio of Lincoln Heights to the more upscale district of Highland Park. In fact, although Muñoz's anti-draft speech had indicted the welfare system, limited college prospects, and police harassment, Muñoz had depended upon other Mexican Americans working with him to provide these details. While not as well-off as most of his Anglo American classmates during his youth, Muñoz nonetheless had grown up in a middle-class milieu, in a family that stressed educational achievement, and, from the age of ten, in a neighborhood where Mexican Americans constituted a small, although growing, minority.[5]

Once enrolled at UCLA in 1964, Muñoz likewise became part of a small minority: he was one of no more than a few dozen Mexican American students on campus.[6] Not until the fall of 1967 did Mexican-origin students form the sufficient critical mass necessary to organize themselves into UMAS, or United Mexican American Students, a group that promoted college recruitment for minorities as well as the establishment of a Chicano Studies program.[7] Aware of UMAS, Muñoz was more interested in European intellectual history and student government. In fact, his speech refusing induction had been built along a series of "I accuse" statements that mimicked the letter written by the novelist Emile Zola in support of Alfred Dreyfus, the nineteenth-century French Jewish soldier who was unjustly accused of treason.[8] Echoing his high school experience, when he had successfully run for student body pres-

ident, as a sophomore at UCLA Muñoz also gained a seat as a representative on the student council. He remained active in student government throughout his college career, finally being elected student body
president in his senior year.

Initially, Muñoz was not, in his own words, very "Chicano-oriented."
The first Chicano student meeting he attended, he remembered, was conducted largely in Spanish, a language that, despite his use of it to defy his
draft board, he spoke only haltingly. Muñoz recalled feeling uncomfortable. A turning point occurred when a UMAS member emphasized to
him how Indian-looking his features were and told him that, whatever
Muñoz's politics, those features would remain unchanged. Soon Muñoz
began to play a more active role on behalf of Chicano students. As a
member of student government, he was able to acquire funding for various UMAS student-recruitment and student-retention projects. He also
joined Chicano students in a sit-in at the campus cafeteria to protest the
cafeteria's continued purchase of table grapes. In the spring of 1968,
Muñoz criticized a fraternity that had hosted a "Viva Zapata" party that
featured an altered Mexican flag in which a raised middle finger had
replaced the traditional eagle and serpent. Muñoz discovered he could be
a Chicano movement contributor despite his imperfect Spanish and relatively privileged background.

His election as student president for the 1968–69 school year all but
christened him as an up-and-coming Chicano leader. Reaching out to all
student voters, Muñoz's platform had stressed less minority-student concerns than issues of general student liberation, including an end to the
grading system and to the "in loco parentis" authority of university officials.[9] Nevertheless, during the campaign, Muñoz had identified himself
for the first time as "Rosalío Muñoz" instead of "Ross Muñoz," an indi-
cator of his own personal and political evolution. Then, in early 1969,
Muñoz appeared in a *Los Angeles Times* article written by the political
scientist Ralph Guzman. The accompanying photo depicted the student
leader seated in his office, wearing guarache sandals, with a big poster of
Emiliano Zapata in the background. Entitled "The Gentle Revolutionaries: Brown Power," Guzman's article explicitly suggested that Chicano
movement activists were less prone to violence—despite their admiration
of Zapata—than black power advocates. In that regard, Guzman had
approvingly quoted the student leader's sentiment that Mexican Americans "need a political regeneration . . . but not a violent one."[10]

Similarly, Muñoz's emergence as an anti-war activist had been gradual. His older brother Ricardo, who also had been responsible for taking

him to his first UMAS meeting, had brought him to his first anti-war rally in 1967. Yet Muñoz's recollection was that he had accepted his brother's invitation primarily because he wanted to hear the musical group that was performing that afternoon. Not until he became campus president did Muñoz take his first public stand against the war—by adding his name to a petition that a staff member within the Eugene McCarthy presidential campaign was circulating among college student presidents and campus newspaper editors. In signing a statement saying he intended to refuse to serve in the war, Muñoz joined hundreds of other student leaders in an act of solidarity. Muñoz later said that it was a comment made by Muhammad Ali that probably came closest to describing his own emerging attitude toward the conflict in Viet Nam. In February 1966, after the boxer had suddenly lost his draft exemption as a result of the lowered standards exemplified by Project 100,000, Ali had angrily told reporters, "I ain't got no quarrel with them Viet Cong."[11]

Approaching his own graduation—and consequent loss of a student deferment—in the spring of 1969, Muñoz became convinced that Mexican American draft-age youth could benefit from a Chicano version of Ali, someone who would pursue the draft issue, but from a Chicano movement standpoint. He had already decided that the approach of David Harris, founder of the well-known national anti-draft organization, the Resistance, would not do. Several months earlier, Harris had visited the UCLA campus and delivered a speech that, to Muñoz's mind, did not speak to Mexican Americans.[12] As Harris later acknowledged, the Resistance's message, geared toward middle-class whites, framed draft resistance as an individual moral decision. Muñoz, in contrast, saw the draft as a broad injustice that affected the entire Mexican American community. Nevertheless, like Harris, Muñoz had decided that trying to obtain another deferment after his graduation would be morally indefensible. Instead, despite risking incarceration and a heavy fine, Muñoz felt compelled "to make a statement" against the draft and the war.[13]

In this endeavor, Muñoz hoped that his rebuke of American society might prove especially powerful because it came from a young Mexican American man who had achieved success in an Anglo-dominated world but who was nonetheless able to see its flaws. He knew he could expect Chicano movement support for his draft refusal, but he also wanted his remarks to carry weight among the majority of Mexican Americans who did not consider themselves part of the Chicano movement. As expected, his draft refusal received extensive play in movement newspapers. But because he was a former student body president of UCLA, the *Los Angeles Times* also provided coverage. Despite his willingness to defy the draft—and to challenge a Mexican American tradition of military service—Muñoz still qualified as an old-fashioned role model in the Mexican American mold, especially given his college credentials. His decision was nevertheless a controversial one, even within his own family. Muñoz recalled that Thanksgiving 1969 was tense because an uncle, who had joined the extended family for the meal, had two sons enlisted in the U.S. Air Force. To Muñoz's relief, his grandmother, then in her nineties, avoided any potential conflict by assigning Muñoz a place of honor at the table, by her side.[14]

As he embarked upon his anti-draft campaign, Muñoz was also fortunate to have Ramsés Noriega by his side. The two had joined forces on the draft issue after Muñoz realized he was scheduled to report for induction on September 16th, a coincidence too good to squander. Good friends despite different personalities and talents, the two had worked together during the fraternity "Viva Zapata" controversy and Muñoz's student body campaign. Critical to their anti-draft effort, Noriega's political experience extended well beyond campus. As an organizer for the United Farm Workers in California's Coachella Valley in 1968, he had built support for the grape boycott there. A big man with a booming voice, Noriega was also a powerful speaker. Nevertheless, he preferred the role of master strategist to media spokesman: it was he who had envisioned building an entire campaign around the judicial prosecution of Muñoz for defying the draft. From the start, Noriega also realized that Muñoz—less physically intimidating and more mild-mannered—made a better public relations figure.

Born in Mexico and raised there until the age of twelve, Noreiga, like Muñoz, had also been a bit of an outsider among UCLA Chicano students, but for different reasons. A product of Mexican elementary schools that still dispensed the nationalist ideas of the Mexican revolution, Noriega enjoyed an extra measure of self-confidence about himself and his Mexican heritage. He was admiring but also somewhat dismissive of the incipient cultural nationalism among Mexican American students who were members of the campus organization UMAS. In a revealing contrast with Munoz, Noriega spoke of how UMAS members conducted their meetings in Spanish, but his recollection was that the Spanish used was "horrible . . . a real broken Spanish." Although he acknowledged that Chicano students seeking to reconnect with their ethnic roots "had a fire in them," he himself felt no compulsion to undertake the same identity quest.[15]

Beyond instilling ethnic pride, Noriega's Mexican upbringing had
taught him more painful lessons as well. During the greater part of his
childhood, his family had lived in the border town of Mexicali, where
Noriega saw—and experienced—harsh poverty. Years later, Noriega
recalled that Mexicali was such a hot and horrible place that the saying
in town was that if a local died and went to hell, his soul had better pack
a blanket: eternal flames might prove chilly in comparison to the heat of
Mexicali. To better their situation, in 1956 his family moved to the California interior valley town of Coachella, where Noriega attended high
school and also labored in the fields. Noriega remembered being deeply
touched after hearing Cesar Chavez speak for the first time in early 1966:
"My heart and my mind just started very strongly . . . thinking about the
idea of confronting this whole society." That was what appealed to Noriega about Chavez: "His spirit was one of confrontation."[16]

Noriega's earlier experience with the farmworkers' union served the
incipient draft crusade well. First, using his contacts from the union
movement, Noriega took Muñoz to meet with Chicano activists
throughout California to inform them of their cause and to seek their
advice even before the September demonstration. The consequence was
to ensure Chicano movement support across the state—and eventually
across the country—for their anti-draft effort. Likewise, Noriega's experience with the union influenced his decision to stay in the background.
The union's leaders were well aware that they were dependent upon
widespread support for their union boycotts and that many Mexican
Americans lacked political experience, so they had stressed the importance of training rank-and-file members to spread the word about the
union's cause. Noriega therefore liked to encourage other people to
speak in front of crowds or answer questions from the press. At one
meeting, Muñoz recalled, Noriega surprised one young man who had
volunteered to be the evening's projectionist by introducing him to the
audience as the evening's main speaker.[17] Within the anti-draft effort,
new members often became new spokespersons.

Between Noriega's organizing savvy and Muñoz's broad appeal, the
pair had some of the key ingredients for a successful crusade. Building
from Muñoz's draft refusal, their initial emphasis was not so much the
war as the draft.[18] Yet neither was interested in pursuing the nuts-and-
bolts of educating draft-age Chicanos concerning legal deferments.
They sought to focus the attention of the media and of Mexican Americans on the matter instead. It was Noriega's idea to record on camera
Muñoz's September speech boycotting induction. The film shot that day

became a fifteen-minute movie, with English and Spanish editions, called *Chale con el Draft*—the title in Chicano slang meant "Fuck the Draft."[19] Muñoz and Noriega began showing the film to various Mexican American political and civic clubs, War on Poverty agencies, and student groups.

The addition of music to the film no doubt enhanced its appeal on emotional and ethnic grounds. On screen, the solemn walk of Chicano protesters was initially accompanied by the mournful strains of "El Adios del Soldado," a popular song from the Mexican Revolution that tells of a soldier's promise to return to his love, which he does as a ghost after his death. Having emphasized the cost of war in young men's lives, the music then switched to the upbeat "Marcha de Zacatecas," a patriotic Mexican hymn written just before the turn of the century whose martial spirit underscored Muñoz's message about the fight being at home. Showing the film primarily to organizations that were already linked to the Chicano movement as part of an anti-draft/anti-war presentation, Muñoz and Noriega recalled that their point of view was readily accepted by sympathetic Mexican American and Chicano audiences.[20]

Throughout the fall of 1969, the pair continued to broadcast their central message, that the draft was particularly unfair to Mexican Americans, as widely as possible. Muñoz appeared on local television more than once. Working as a recruiter for the Claremont Colleges, about twenty-five miles east of Los Angeles, Muñoz attended an education conference in October and brought Noriega along. To Muñoz's surprise, he watched as Noriega, again manifesting his United Farm Workers' training, started cold-calling community organizations and Spanish-surnamed people from the city directory to drum up support for their cause. In that way, the pair came to know Fred Aviles, a Puerto Rican draft resister and advocate for island independence. Later that fall, Muñoz paid his way to Chicano conferences in Kansas City and Albuquerque to conduct workshops on the draft that were attended by several dozen people. In early November, he commenced a semi-fast, patterned after the fasts of Cesar Chavez. Protesting the draft, he ate little more than soup for a month and eventually dropped 30 pounds. Ordered that month by his draft board to reappear, Muñoz, again with Noriega's help, staged another demonstration in front of the induction center. Muñoz decided against entering the building, however, because he feared that his continued fast had left him in such a weakened condition that the Army would have reason to reject him as physically unfit. And Muñoz did not want the Army to refuse him; he wanted to refuse the Army. Only then could his plans to challenge the draft go forward.[21]

Geared more toward generating publicity than formulating policy, the anti-draft activities of Muñoz and Noriega nonetheless soon convinced many Chicano activists, already opposed to the war, of the need to take more concrete action. Toward that end, Bob Elias, a young journalist from Los Angeles and a new volunteer to the anti-draft effort, helped organize a conference in Denver in early December that attracted about seventy activists from several states. Labeled the National Chicano Anti-Draft Conference, the gathering forged a strong connection between Los Angeles Chicano anti-draft activists and members of Denver's Crusade for Justice, which played host to the event. Attendees, for example, vowed to place the draft and the war at the top of the agenda for the second Chicano Youth Liberation Conference, scheduled for Denver the following March.[22]

With less success, the young men in attendance also attempted to sketch out a Chicano plan of action toward the draft. In this regard, the conference exemplified the broader Chicano movement's competing visions of effecting social change: some activists advocated a complete rejection of U.S. society, while others demanded that Mexican Americans receive a fairer share of its bounty. And sometimes the same person embraced both positions. During his September speech refusing induction, for example, Muñoz had condemned the U.S. government on charges of genocide yet appealed to the same government to establish more programs along War on Poverty lines. A similar tension was evident at the December anti-draft conference. Pictures of the gathering showed participants raising their fists in a defiant Chicano power salute. A violent and unwarranted police beating suffered by two participants during the conference weekend no doubt only exacerbated feelings of alienation on the part of Chicano activists toward American society.[23] Nonetheless, the conference's main emphasis was on making the draft more egalitarian. Although three draft resisters, Muñoz, Chicago's Aviles, and Ernesto Vigil of Denver, who had mailed back his draft card nearly two years before, chaired the conference workshops, the conference itself did not advocate universal draft resistance. Workshop topics instead dealt with areas of potential reform. How might Mexican American representation on draft boards be improved? Did Chicanos who refused the draft know how to find experienced lawyers to help them? Was fighting for legislation to modify or abolish the draft a useful project?[24] Navigating between radical rhetoric and reform-minded politics, anti-draft activists struggled to define their relationship as Chicanos to the broader society.

The brainstorming resulted in a single, stillborn idea. For several weeks after the December gathering, Muñoz was designated in press accounts as head of a new organization called the "National Chicano Draft Board." The title was supposed to be a play on words: the organization was to draft young people into the movement—not the army—by establishing more Chicano-operated counseling centers. But that umbrella project, a labor-intensive approach that demanded tremendous dedication and offered little excitement, fizzled almost immediately. To be fair, questions of strategy and sustaining momentum troubled the draft resistance effort nationally, too.[25]

The Chicanos who gathered in Denver paralleled the national draft resistance movement in another important way: they evidently saw anti-draft activism as mainly the purview of men. Notably, Chicanas were not mentioned as a potential resource for the National Chicano Draft Board. Despite having worked as draft counselors throughout the Southwest, they had played no role in Muñoz and Noriega's initial anti-draft crusade. At the Denver conference, they were barely visible. A group picture of participants printed in the Crusade for Justice's newspaper, *El Gallo*, showed a single, unidentified woman among the crowd of men. The advent of draft resistance in the broader anti-war movement marginalized women as well. Automatically, in Alice Echols's phrase, "heroic action became the exclusive domain of men." Young women, whose lives were not at risk, were not allowed a voice in the decision-making."[26] In the Chicano anti-draft crusade, a similar trend was clear: men were to be leaders while women, if they were considered at all, were to be loyal supporters.

In fact, traditional gender roles had made an appearance from the start of the anti-draft crusade. During his September 16 demonstration, Muñoz had spoken about the "passion and suffering" of the archetypal Mexican woman in addition to the machismo of the Mexican man. By invoking such familiar images, Muñoz was attempting to reach out to an older generation beyond college campuses, but the stereotypes continued unabated at the anti-draft conference in Denver. Rodolfo "Corky" Gonzales, founder of the Crusade for Justice, for example, opened the conference with a familiar speech in which he said that Mexican American men had been entering the service to prove their "machismo and courage."[27] As the Chicano leader had both boasted and complained at a gathering the previous month, the United States was sending Chicanos to Viet Nam to take advantage of "the guts of the *mexicano* because we have proven that we have more guts than any other group that ever went to war."[28] Even as they opposed the war, conference participants continued to take pride in the military record of Mexican American men.

Despite the conference's articulated goals, the Chicano anti-draft crusade itself was soon subsumed into the broader Chicano anti-war effort. Already the attention of many conference participants had been diverted by national anti-war events that fall. On October 15, 1969, the date national anti-war activists had declared for a moratorium on business as usual, hundreds of thousands of Americans across the country had skipped work to participate in local anti-war rallies and memorial services. The following month, tandem anti-war demonstrations in San Francisco and Washington, D.C., sponsored by a national anti-war organization called the New Mobe, drew perhaps a quarter-million people on the West Coast and a half-million on the East. As Muñoz and Noriega considered the next stage of their crusade, therefore, they and other Chicano activists increasingly confronted the much larger and louder anti-war movement dominated by white radicals and liberals. And, increasingly, Chicano activists questioned how they could mold their opposition to the war to also further their goals of focusing Mexican Americans on the battle at home.

CULTURE CLASH

Just two days before the massive anti-war New Mobe rally in San Francisco that November, Muñoz was excited to receive an invitation to address the gathering. But as the rally that day dragged on, the crowd grew restless, and New Mobe organizers decided to drop the lesser-known Muñoz from the speaker's roster. Muñoz's recollection is that he was finally allowed to speak at the New Mobe rally that day only because Buffy Sainte Marie, a Native American singer, songwriter, and activist, had refused to perform until he was allowed his say. Muñoz's plight was not unique. Corky Gonzales, the dynamic leader of Denver's Crusade for Justice likewise received a last-minute invitation that was almost withdrawn. Both men had been eager to state their anti-war and pro-Chicano views in front of one of the most massive gatherings to take place during the Viet Nam War era. At the end of the day, however, conflicts between Chicano anti-war activists and the national anti-war movement overshadowed the potential for cooperation.[29]

For Chicanos dedicated to anti-war work, the rally that day turned out to be both an inspiration and a goad. On the one hand, the sheer enormity of the crowd provided an unparalleled form of encouragement to many Chicano movement attendees. "The Mobe was the most fantastic thing I ever saw," Bob Elias said years afterward in describing the vast sea of people in attendance. "It was so big, so giant. That's what really got us to saying we can do that."[30] Or, as David Sanchez, one of the founders of the Brown Berets, later explained, anti-war protest "was a trend, it was a national trend and we just made it into a Chicano trend."[31] On the other hand, Chicano activists were convinced that the national anti-war movement did not "relate directly to Chicanos."[32] In a later interview, Muñoz dated the origins of an independent Chicano anti-war effort to that November day in 1969. Mainstream peace activists had unwittingly exacerbated Mexican American vulnerability to the draft, Muñoz explained, by directing and limiting their anti-war message to people much like themselves. "We realized, around the time of the November 15 Moratorium [sic] that the main thing the white peace groups were doing was keeping whites out of the service," he told the Washington, D.C., alternative newspaper *Hard Times*. The consequences to him were obvious: "More Chicanos are in."[33]

At first glance, the New Mobe seemed an unlikely target for such an accusation. The New Mobe was the successor organization to the National Mobilization Against the War Committee, a vast coalition of politically left-leaning groups dedicated to stopping the war in Viet Nam but interested as well in promoting social justice. In 1967 the Mobilization had responded to a summer of violence in black communities across the nation by explicitly arguing that the war and civil rights amounted to *"only one struggle—for self-determination—and we support it in Vietnam and in black America."*[34] Although the original Mobe fell apart after the 1968 Democratic Convention, the following year, activist groups came together to form a New Mobe that endorsed the same linkage between domestic and international concerns. Thus, while the first demand of marchers in San Francisco and Washington was for an "immediate and total withdrawal from Vietnam," their second demand was for "self determination for Vietnam and black and minority people of America."[35] In San Francisco, moreover, organizers had made good on their commitment to that second goal—evincing their recognition of diversity within the United States—by incorporating representatives from the black, red, and brown power movements in the program.[36]

This fusing of minority concerns and opposition to the war had a long history within activist circles. One of the first organizations to speak out against the war was the Student Non-Violent Coordinating Committee (SNCC) in 1965. As a SNCC leader complained in the wake of a deadly voter registration drive in Mississippi, "There is no reason why black people should be fighting for free elections in Vietnam . . . when they don't have [free elections] in their own country."[37] Two years later, Martin Luther King Jr.'s decision to make public his private doubts about the war reflected a similar connection between home-front injustices and foreign affairs. Not only was the war inflicting destruction upon the peasants of Viet Nam, it was undercutting social programs and sending poor black men to fight and die, he argued.[38] By the turn of the decade, the conviction that domestic and international concerns were intertwined was popular among activists of all colors. Speaking to an Ivy League audience, for example, one historian of American foreign policy insisted that the domestic problems of "racism, poverty, inequality, and injustice" were every bit a part of the "crisis" confronting the nation as the continuing conflict in Indochina.[39]

Chicano speakers at the New Mobe that November embraced a similar point of view. Along with Denver's Gonzales and Rosalío Muñoz, Dolores Huerta, vice president of the United Farm Workers, also addressed the crowd that day. All three maintained that a desire for peace abroad was meaningless without an equal commitment to social justice at home. Thus, Huerta advocated continued support for the UFW boycott as well as freedom for Bobby Seale, chairman of the Black Panther Party, who was then under indictment on charges stemming from riots at the 1968 Democratic national convention. "If you cannot come out and demand that Bobby Seale be released; if you cannot come out and demand that corporate growers stop trying to destroy the farm-workers union," Huerta contended, "then you do not understand what the struggle for peace is all about." Gonzales similarly made clear that Chicano nationalism did not preclude cooperation with other like-minded groups. He spoke in favor of a "meaningful coalition" among all the anti-war constituencies gathered that day to further "a liberation movement for social change" across the country.[40] For his part, Muñoz continued to link the war in Viet Nam with domestic injustices.[41] All three Chicano speakers complimented the New Mobe's twin goals of stopping the war and ending racial injustice. Nevertheless, their inclusion on the stage that day provoked concern among some of the event's organizers.

Ultimately, the desire to be inclusive was less a priority for the embattled national anti-war movement than salvaging its reputation. Although polls suggested that years of fighting had turned many Americans against the war, an even greater number opposed the anti-war movement. Editors and reporters invariably had deemed "violent, bizarre, or countercultural behavior" more newsworthy than peaceful protests and so had helped fuel the widespread belief that Viet Nam demonstrators were spoiled, anti-American extremists.[42] So had President Nixon, who in his famous "Silent Majority" speech of November 1969 sharply distinguished between patriotism and protest. Nixon pledged to defend the nation's honor against an anti-war "minority" dedicated to "mounting demonstrations in the street." Strongly implying that his critics were being disloyal, Nixon also suggested that they were misguided as well, by reminding the American people that he had begun removing American troops from Viet Nam.[43]

Confronted with de-escalation on the war front and antagonism at home, anti-war organizers across the country faced a formidable task as they sought to sustain their efforts to end the war. Tactical disagreements between the New Mobe and another national anti-war group, the Vietnam Moratorium Committee, aggravated the problem. While the New Mobe countenanced civil disobedience and flashes of countercultural rebellion as part of its policy of inclusiveness, the Vietnam Moratorium Committee favored nonviolent, solemn, grassroots protests. One month earlier, the VMC had organized the cross-country October 15 Moratorium. Through hundreds of individual vigils held at churches, schools, and workplaces, the event had offered incontrovertible evidence that middle-class and respectable Americans opposed the war. Although the Vietnam Moratorium Committee had finally agreed to work with the more radical New Mobe to stage the November demonstrations, the VMC had also placed tremendous pressure upon the New Mobe to keep the November rallies decorous and peaceful.[44]

As a consequence, the two organizations argued bitterly over who to include on the roster of speakers.[45] Evidently, not only Chicanos felt the repercussions of these discussions. In his autobiography, *This Side of Glory*, David Hilliard recalled that, as a Black Panther, he had been censored. About the New Mobe on the West Coast, he wrote: "The anti-war movement is treating us like an anathema. Even the Bay Area Mobilization committee—of which we're a part—ignores and insults us, debating whether or not to let us speak, afraid of alienating protesters. And I'm constantly coached in what to say, how to appeal to these people."[46] Not part of the inner circle of New Mobe organizers, Chicano anti-war activists found themselves caught up in similar debates, without fully understanding why their presence had become a source of controversy.

The planned appearance of Corky Gonzales posed an even greater problem for the event's organizers than Muñoz. The Crusade for Justice had done battle with Denver's police and educational systems since 1966. Gonzales personally was a charismatic, fiery speaker. According to Bob Elias, rally organizers were fearful about what Gonzales might say, mostly because they were not that well acquainted with the various Chicano movement figures. "They thought he was going to talk about the [Brown] Berets," he said. "They stereotyped him."[47] Some New Mobe organizers on the West Coast apparently favored excluding the Denver activist altogether. Years later, Ernesto Vigil recalled that Gonzales had been included on the speakers' list only after a sectarian group, most likely the Socialist Workers Party, had lobbied the New Mobe for greater inclusiveness.[48]

The result of these behind-the-scenes debates was that Chicano activists were bolstered in their decision to build their own anti-war movement. Yet the November demonstration was the final nudge, not the root cause of Chicano anti-war independence. While the dictates of cultural nationalism contributed to the movement's quest for autonomy, resentment toward white activists predated the Fall of 1969. Just as participation in the New Mobe rally occasioned a sense among some Chicano activists of being patronized, previous interactions with the anti-war movement, the counterculture, and the sectarian left had prompted quite a few movement participants to be wary of white radicals. At the close of the 1960s, many Chicano activists felt alienated from Anglo-American activists on tactical, cultural, and political grounds.

To be certain, even the most culturally nationalistic Chicano movement participants often looked favorably upon the possibility of a collaboration between themselves and sympathetic white activists. Thus, Denver's Corky Gonzales once condemned white Americans as "blue-eyed devils," in the style of Malcolm X, but in the same speech he also praised white radical youth for their contributions to political change and coalition building.[49] Thus, in Texas, Chicano leaders distinguished between racist gringos and sympathetic Anglos. When it came to protesting the war, moreover, instances of actual convergence were commonplace. Chicano activists, for example, had participated extensively during the Vietnam Moratorium Committee's October protests. In Albuquerque that day, a three-thousand-person march was led by a group of Chicano students from the University of New Mexico, who carried a sign pairing the themes of racial and economic injustice: "Stop the Slaughter of Chicanos by the Racist Rich."[50] Movement representatives also spoke at anti-war rallies on the University of California campuses at Berkeley and Los Angeles.[51] As one UC Berkeley student activist recalled, Chicano contingents were routinely present at Bay area anti-war events.[52]

Such widespread participation, however, failed to address—much less allay—the particular concern of Chicano activists regarding the war, that Mexican Americans, especially those from poorer areas, were special targets of the war machine.[53] After graduation, for example, Muñoz could not fail to notice the gap in opportunity and savvy that existed between his Anglo friends from UCLA and the young Mexican American men from California's agricultural areas whom he met in his job as a college recruiter. In Los Angeles, the first group would laugh about the outrageous means they had devised to escape the draft; then, a few days later, the Mexican American boys would tell him that they were not even bothering to continue their education because they expected to be sent to Viet Nam.[54] In a similar vein, Chicano activists were resentful that college recruiters were so rarely seen in barrio high schools, where Army recruiters made routine stops.[55] Drawing upon such personal experience, Chicano movement participants questioned whether Anglo Americans who opposed the war appreciated the threat the draft posed to less fortunate Mexican Americans. Participation at the New Mobe only reinforced these doubts among Chicano activists regarding the "peace movement."

The "peace movement" label pointed to another difference in strategy between anti-war activism generally and Chicano opposition to the war. Although the mainstream anti-war movement represented a broad spectrum of people, pacifists had comprised an early and fundamental part of the national anti-war coalition. In contemporary discourse, moreover, all opponents of the war were "doves"—a bird that had symbolized peace since Biblical times. As an independent Chicano anti-war effort emerged in Los Angeles, Ramsés Noriega and Rosalío Muñoz, in still another instance of strategic borrowing from the UFW, likewise declared that they, too, embraced nonviolence. Their Brown Beret partners, however, did not. [56] They, like other Chicano activists, were convinced that their movement was a serious struggle, even a revolution, against racist oppression and economic injustice. As a result, many Chicano activists looked askance upon the very notion of a "peace movement."

Indeed, some Chicano groups stressed that they were opposed to the war, not dedicated to peace. Colorado's Crusade for Justice, for example, made such a distinction.[57] Although instances of actual physical confrontation were few during the course of the movement, many movement participants reserved the right to defend and protect themselves on principle. Such was the formal policy of the Brown Berets and a handful of other Chicano paramilitary groups, such as the Black Berets of Albuquerque.[58] Two years earlier, in New Mexico, still other Chicano activists associated with the Alianza's land-grant efforts had actually toted guns, an act for which they were not apologetic. "How can one guarantee complete non-violence when one lives in a completely VIOLENT country?" asked one supporter in 1969. Pointing a finger of blame at the "gringo," she explained: "With all the violence committed against Raza, I cannot stand by and relinquish my right to violence when I may see my neighbors and friends beaten."[59] Despite widespread admiration of Cesar Chavez among activists, few Chicano movement participants were willing to follow his example and unilaterally eschew the use of violence.

Like the peace movement, the counterculture inspired skepticism among Chicanos and Mexican Americans alike. When anti-war protestors gathered at San Francisco's Golden Gate Park during the New Mobe rally, they bumped up against the Haight-Ashbury district, in the 1960s a mecca for youth from around the country who wished to explore drug use and alternative lifestyles. Many participants in the counterculture had little interest in traditional politics per se, but instead sought to create a new personal reality through the pursuit of art, emotion, music, and acid. Yet, while the era produced plenty of Mexican American hippies, more conservative Mexican Americans had little patience with the counterculture's rejection of social and cultural conventions. This dim view of the counterculture certainly predated the New Mobe. For example, *El Grito,* a leading Chicano academic journal, recorded this conversation in early 1968 between several Mexican American men from San Jose (one of whom was a Viet Nam veteran) who were discussing a flyer that told of the disproportionate number of Mexican American war casualties:

> *Nacho:* Who was passing out those leaflets? Hippies?
> *Trini:* No. Chicanos were passing them out.
> *(Another Man):* They were decent people.
> *Nacho:* Oh? Decent?
> *(Other Man):* Yes. They were respectable people like you and me.

Apparently, to some Mexican American minds, hippies were by definition not respectable and, in some cases, even Chicanos might be of questionable character. After all, they sometimes experimented with the trappings of the counterculture by using marijuana and other drugs and growing their hair long.[61]

Accordingly, the major complaint of Chicano activists against the counterculture was not its embrace of social experimentation but its unwillingness to engage in politics. In 1968, for example, David Sanchez, of the Los Angeles Brown Berets, described his group as the antithesis of the counterculture. "Don't misunderstand the Chicano," he told a reporter. "We're not like the hippies with all this love and flower bullshit. We're fighters."[62] Likewise, a member of the Crusade for Justice, in an article published in *El Gallo,* compared the Mobe rally in San Francisco to a rock concert, proof to him that the mainstream anti-war movement lacked resolve. If they were interested in anything, he charged, the middle-class anti-war opponents who attended the rally were interested in taking care of their own: "With an electric guitar and a large ampliphiers [*sic*], you can control the student peace movement. . . . What it is doing is keeping [open] middle-class play grounds called 'College', while poor Chicanos keep providing the bodies for an unjust war. . . . The march on San Francisco was supposed to be a show of anti-war support, not a pop art festival."[63] Ironically, relations between Chicano movement participants and the most overtly political members of the national anti-war coalition—sectarian groups—were also plagued with mistrust.

Indeed, Chicano movement participants were often as wary of white sectarian radicals as they were dismissive toward white cultural radicals. Adamant that the Chicano movement was something unique and apart from white Europe as well as white America, a few Chicano activists automatically rejected Marxist theory as irrelevant to their cause. A far greater source of contention between Chicano activists and sectarian groups, however, was the tendency of these groups to take a patronizing attitude toward the Chicano movement. For example, the Maoist Progressive Labor Party, the same group that had contributed to the fatal internecine struggles within Students for a Democratic Society in 1969, repeatedly told Chicanos that their founding inspiration, cultural nationalism, was, like black power, a reactionary philosophy. Instead of emphasizing ethnic unity, the PLP insisted, Mexican Americans should support the workers' revolution. Although their dogmatic perspective made the PLP widely unpopular and ineffective, brash PLP members continued to voice this criticism at Chicano events.[64]

Instances of cooperation were more numerous with the Socialist Workers Party, a Trotskyite group that had broken away from the Socialist Party in 1937. At the start of the 1960s, the party had been reduced to a tiny organization which, like other Old Left groups, saw the political and social activism of the decade as a chance for recruitment and renewal.[65] Top SWP folk became leading anti-war activists. In contrast to the multifaceted concerns of the New Mobe organizers, however, SWP members insisted that anti-war demonstrations should remain focused on the single issue of stopping the war.[66] Yet the Socialist Workers Party also took a sustained interest in the Chicano movement, in small part because a few SWP members were Mexican Americans, in large part because the party viewed movement participants in general as potential SWP recruits. SWP stalwarts participated at many Chicano movement events, ranging from early student conferences to later symposiums on immigration reform.[67] The party's newspaper, the *Militant,* provided extensive coverage of the Chicano movement overall. And despite its reputation for narrowly focusing on the war, the party had apparently helped secure Corky Gonzales's appearance at the New Mobe, as Ernesto Vigil recalled. According to the *Militant,* only continued pressure from the SWP had ensured Gonzales's place on the speakers' platform that day, after New Mobe organizers attempted to withdraw his invitation.[68] Moreover, in the aftermath of that massive demonstration, Corky Gonzales, Rosalío Muñoz, and Bob Elias had all been invited to attend the founding conference, in Cleveland in June 1970, of the SWP-dominated National Peace Action Coalition.[69]

Notwithstanding these efforts, seemingly arcane political debates only estranged those Chicano activists who attended the NPAC conference. Invited to give one of the opening speeches, Muñoz recalled being surprised by his first encounter with sectarian politics, which were on grand display that weekend. During the anti-war march through the city that was one of the conference's events, for instance, Muñoz observed various participating groups displaying banners of Mao or Stalin. "I said, 'Jesus, what is this,'" he recalled. "It was so alien to what I was used to." The reception he received after giving another version of his initial anti-draft speech also indicated a divided gathering. For reasons that remained unclear to him, depending upon which slogan he issued different sections of the conference hall cheered.[70] Of course, the speech itself was yet another indication of the ideological distance between Chicanos involved in the anti-draft effort on the one hand and SWP members and other political radicals on the other. Concentrating upon domestic injustice, Muñoz's anti-draft declaration, while lamenting Vietnamese casualties, did not include an explicit critique of U.S. intervention nor a condemnation of U.S. imperialism, much less a refutation of the capitalist system.

People like Muñoz and Noriega were left-leaning but hardly committed to—or even that knowledgeable about—particular ideological lines. As they built their Chicano anti-war effort, Chicano activists tended to pick and choose from among the wide spectrum of alternative political views that flourished during the 1960s. By the close of that decade, Chicano movement participants in Los Angeles had decided that they were ready to mount their own demonstrations against the war, but their demonstrations would be crafted to fit their own political priorities and to inspire Mexican American activism at home.

THE FIRST MORATORIUM

On December 20, 1969, a contingent of about seventy Brown Berets in full-dress uniform—berets, army jackets, and dark pants for the men, brown skirts for the women—marched in formation down Michigan Avenue in an unincorporated section of East Los Angeles. They were leading the first large-scale Chicano protest march against the war to be held in the Los Angeles area, a protest that became the precedent for more than a dozen more rallies across the Southwest. Following the Berets, six Chicanos playing the role of pallbearers carried a replica of a coffin. Behind the mock funeral, a smaller group held aloft a large painting of a bloodied Chicano soldier with the rank of Private, who had been given the name J. J. Montez. Both the painting and the coffin were meant to symbolize all Mexican Americans who had died in Viet Nam. Following this dramatic vanguard, perhaps as many as a thousand more young people marched and chanted anti-war slogans.[71] Demonstrators at the front of the procession shouted *"¡Raza si!"* prompting those behind to thunder in return, *"¡Guerra no!"* Just before concluding at a local park, the demonstrators' route took a sharp, downhill turn. As their numbers filled the entire slope of the street, the protestors gave the distinct impression that, as far as the eye could see, Chicanas and Chicanos opposed the war in Viet Nam.[72]

This demonstration, advertised as a "March against Death," marked the largest Chicano protest against the war to date. In the wake of the November Mobe, Chicano student activists had joined with the barrio-based Brown Berets to form a Chicano anti-war effort that sought to address their specific concerns. Unlike the relatively unclear objectives of the Denver anti-draft conference that had been held a few weeks before, here was a specific—and more exciting—project to advance. While the name of their newfound organization, the Chicano Moratorium Committee, announced the group's demand for an immediate end to the war, their actions announced their commitment to the Chicano movement.

Despite this shared agenda, the young people who planned the December anti-war march nonetheless found themselves once again grappling with the possibilities and limitations of cultural nationalism as an organizing tool. Indeed, the Brown Berets, who cast themselves as fighters for the Chicano revolution, served to magnify the cultural-nationalist orientation of the anti-war effort. As they launched their own Chicano anti-war effort, Chicanos and Chicanas insisted that their anti-war stance derived specifically from their ethnic identity. Continuing to define their effort against the "white peace movement," they strove to construct an anti-war message they hoped would appeal to all Mexican Americans. Yet sharp differences regarding political style and strategy soon surfaced among various coalition members. As a result of the collaboration with the Berets, additional tensions revolved around the role of women. Although a number of anti-war activists persisted in their uncritical celebration of machismo, a few Beret women attracted to anti-war work began to demand inclusion and equality as organizers. Thus, even as they claimed to speak for an entire ethnic population, moratorium committee members faced the challenge of maintaining unity among their own small group.

Initially, the Brown Beret organization was a vital force within the coalition. Unlike the student group led by Muñoz and Noriega, which consisted of merely a handful of young men at the end of 1969, the Brown Berets' reputation as fearless defenders of the Chicano struggle had attracted scores of young men and women in chapters throughout the Southwest and beyond. The founding members of the original Los Angeles chapter had known each other since 1966, when they had all been part of Young Citizens for Community Action, a local service group whose primary interest was in educational reform. To indicate their emerging sense of ethnic pride, members had soon changed the group's name to Young Chicanos for Community Action. After opening La Piranya, a coffeehouse in East Los Angeles that became a central meeting place for young Mexican Americans to exchange ideas and hear visiting speakers talk about the Chicano movement, the YCCA members had found themselves the target of near constant law enforcement surveillance. The combined result was their further radicalization.[73]

The YCCA quickly adopted the trappings of a paramilitary organization. In 1968 its members took to wearing a military-style "uniform," beret included, which produced another name change. As the Brown Berets, members demonstrated on numerous occasions against police harassment and brutality, intervened to protect striking teens from baton-wielding law officials during the East L.A. high school "blowouts," and participated in several anti-war events.[74] Rejecting pacifism, the Brown Berets declared themselves to be soldiers, "the vanguard of the Chicano movement." Their fight, David Sanchez announced in the debut edition of the Beret publication, *La Causa,* was against "gabacho [white] oppression," which, the Beret leader explained, "must be stopped, because he [the white man] is a detriment to the Chicano spirit, culture, and existence."[75] By 1968, the duties of Beret membership included vowing to protect Mexican American rights and attending target practice and marching drills.[76]

The organization's increasingly aggressive stance attracted further police scrutiny. Just a month after the December moratorium march, Los Angeles police Sgt. Robert J. Thoms testified before a U.S. Senate subcommittee that the Brown Berets were "a militant brown power organization," which he defined as "an organization that is involved in the violent disruption of the establishment."[77] By then, official Washington had already taken note of the organization. In March 1968, the Federal Bureau of Investigation announced that the organization was controlled "by rabble rousing members of [the] Mexican American colony" and that it therefore posed "a definite threat to the security of the nation." A few months later, the group's attempts to recruit street youth spurred a further condemnation: another FBI memo suggested that most Brown Berets were "high school drop outs, dope addicts, militant racists and hoodlums."[78] In Los Angeles, local police decided that the organization merited both surveillance and infiltration.[79]

Law enforcement officials exaggerated the threat that the Berets posed. The Berets' militancy—and notoriety—derived primarily from their speech rather than their actions. Despite the frequent comparison to the Black Panthers, the Brown Berets never launched nor were they the target of a shoot-out with police. Although felony criminal charges were twice brought against individual members, all charges were eventually dropped.[80] According to Gloria Arellanes, one of the top-ranking Berets and an early supporter of the anti-war effort, talk of revolution was popular among members but very few seriously advocated engaging in violence. Those that did, she noted, failed to garner much support. Although she remembered with a certain fondness her days of chanting "Off the pig!" and engaging in target practice, Arellanes's recollection was that young people joined the Berets mostly because they sought a "place to belong," not a fight.[81]

That was also the experience of Hilda Quen Jensen (then Reyes), who joined the Brown Berets at the age of fifteen because she saw the organization as a positive alternative to joining a gang, which was what some of her friends were doing. She immediately paid a price. A participant in the blowouts at Roosevelt High School in 1968, Jensen posed for a photograph with bandoleers strapped across her chest. The picture soon became one of the iconic images of the Chicano movement, and she was permanently expelled from school for passing out book covers that featured the photograph. Still, years later, Jensen recalled that her time as a Beret was a "great experience . . . a learning experience" that allowed her to join in the struggle for justice in a concrete way. In addition to participating in a school boycott, along with other Berets she delivered food donations to striking farmworkers, helped launch a health clinic in East Los Angeles, and, eventually, protested the war. As Jensen remembered, after the San Francisco New Mobe, members of the Los Angeles chapter of the Brown Berets started holding frequent meetings to plan a Chicano anti-war demonstration. She suggested that the group visit East L.A. merchants to ask for donations, an idea that put Jensen in charge of the moratorium fundraising committee. While the initial reaction of merchants was, as she recalled, decidedly "mixed," the Brown Berets' rebel panache drew many young people, especially heretofore apolitical street youth, into the Chicano anti-war fold.[82]

Muñoz and Noriega and others involved in the anti-draft effort soon began attending the moratorium meetings. This coming-together benefited both sides. The anti-draft people brought their contacts from across the state and beyond. Despite their own predilection for nonviolence, Muñoz and Noriega recognized the Brown Berets' inherent appeal. From Noriega's perspective, the organization was responsible for swelling attendance at the December march and subsequent ones because "youth looked up to . . . the Brown Berets."[83] Similarly, Muñoz believed that "part of the success of the moratorium was that mixture of the . . . college youth movement and the grass roots kids in the Brown Berets."[84] The Brown Berets, in turn, believed that the student faction, especially Muñoz, the former student body president, could build bridges to the more moderate Mexican American organizations that were leery of the Berets' confrontational style. As one member recalled, "Muñoz, with his UCLA background and his conservative appearance, was able to draw the support from [community] groups that probably would not have supported us had it only been David [Sanchez]."[85]

Crucial as liaisons between the Berets and the student anti-war group were women like Jensen and, especially, given her greater employment experience, Arellanes. The daughter of a Mexican immigrant father and a California Native American mother, Arellanes had grown up in El Monte, a suburb roughly ten miles east of the city of Los Angeles. Race relations between Mexican Americans and Anglo Americans were often tense in El Monte: full-blown race riots had broken out at El Monte High School in 1963, during Arellanes's junior year there. A natural leader, Arellanes had been chosen by school officials to attend a special conference sponsored by the county of Los Angeles to discuss the problems of Mexican American youth. Later, she had served as a member of her school's Human Relations Club, whose aim was to reduce conflict between the two clashing groups. After graduation in 1964, Arellanes struggled through courses at East Los Angeles Community College before taking a job in a neighborhood anti-poverty program, a position that allowed her to hone her secretarial skills but that also stuck her behind a desk. For someone like herself, who wanted to make a difference, becoming a Brown Beret seemed an exciting possibility.[86]

Yet if the heady talk around La Piranya coffeehouse about social justice, Chicano pride, and the possibilities of cultural nationalism inspired young men and women alike, the ethos of the Brown Berets remained centered on male power and pride. The organization, for example, primarily promoted the recruitment of streetwise young toughs.[87] As expressed in the pages of their newspaper, the Brown Berets hoped to transform street fighters, particularly gang members and other *vatos locos* (crazy guys), into fighters for the movement. The evolution of the Berets into a self-proclaimed vanguard organization, moreover, inevitably prompted an increased emphasis on hierarchy and male-dominated authority.[88] Another manifestation of this tendency: most leaders of the organization were men. Appointed minister of finance and communications in early 1969, Arellanes was the sole exception to the rule of official male leadership. Still, the title of her position suggested its bookkeeping and secretarial origins.[89] In a reflection of the era as well as the organization, the main role of Beret women was to provide "clerical support, staff support," as Arellanes recalled. "In our minds,

we really thought this was a movement of Raza, [that] we were all
united," she continued. "Our philosophy was that we were all equal in
struggle, but we weren't."[90]

Several women Berets, however, eventually moved toward an independent social-action agenda. They first took center stage during the
summer of 1969 when the Berets cosponsored the opening of a free
health clinic in East Los Angeles, with Arellanes as the director. She
quickly banned male Berets from coming to the clinic during office
hours because clients found their presence so disruptive. That decision,
as well as her own reputation for being "aggressive," provoked a backlash: male Berets called Arellanes and her friends "women's libbers," a
label that implied ethnic-group betrayal because feminism was perceived as a white women's movement.[91] Tensions grew to be so grave
within the Los Angeles chapter that by December 1969 meetings were
sometimes held for men and women at different locations and times.[92]
Yet, if some men in the organization saw *chicanismo* and a push for
women's autonomy as irreconcilable, Arellanes recalled having trouble
reconciling the Brown Berets' continual talk of violence with her own
growing interest in health and healing. Looking back, Arellanes saw her
involvement in the Chicano Moratorium committee as a natural pro-
gression in her political development. The student faction at least
emphasized that the main purpose of the protest was to save Chicano
lives. Arellanes, who had lost a cousin in the war, soon became dedicated to Chicano anti-war work, along with other Beret women. Or, as
she explained, using a war metaphor, Chicanas were "breaking out of
traditional roles" and taking their place on the domestic "front lines."[93]
Thus, Arellanes appeared before the Los Angeles Police Commission
and successfully argued for a parade permit for the December march.
Aware that if she wore her Beret uniform she was likely to provoke a
negative response among the commissioners, she deliberately dressed in
civilian clothes, appearing, in her own words, as "Jane Doe Citizen."
Similarly, Arellanes strategically framed her appeal for the permit in the
most innocuous way. Mexican Americans, she convinced the commission, were entitled to memorialize their war dead.[94]

At the December march, the theme of honoring the war dead—a consistent motif at later events as well—predominated. As a publicity flier
for the march explained, the gathering would "honor of our Chicano
brothers, relatives, friends and loved ones who have been channeled into
the death pits of Vietnam."[95] While the term "death pits" conveyed
strong disapproval of the war, the announcement overall offered a great

deal of respect and sympathy for the sufferings borne by Mexican American soldiers and their families. Chicano demonstrators once again emphasized wartime sacrifice when they conducted a roll call of dead Mexican Americans soldiers before the march began. The exercise clearly echoed a national Vietnam Moratorium event two months earlier, during which protestors, passing in front of the White House, had announced the names of Americans who had died in Viet Nam. Aware that Mexican Americans had long taken pride in their group's military record, however, Chicano anti-war activists read the names of Mexican American war dead from previous conflicts as well as Viet Nam.[96] Finally, the route itself was a tribute to Mexican American military valor and sacrifice. Starting at a memorial built just after World War II to commemorate the thousands of Mexican Americans who had died during that conflict, the march ended at Eugene A. Obregón Park, which had been named after a Mexican American Marine—and Congressional Medal of Honor recipient—who had lost his life in Korea.[97] By honoring fallen soldiers, Chicano anti-war activists astutely tapped into long-standing ethnic pride in military service. Their goal, however, was to spur anti-war sentiment and to build the moratorium effort.

Demonstrators therefore offered a twist on tradition by pointing out that dying in Viet Nam and previous conflicts had *not* ensured Mexican Americans equal treatment. As during Muñoz's September 16 draft refusal ceremony, demonstrators used the anti-war demonstration as a springboard to address domestic injustices. A press announcement in advance of the march declared that the deaths of Mexican American servicemen in Viet Nam were "directly tied to oppression at home."[98] Eager to attract the greatest number of Mexican Americans to their cause, moratorium organizers broadened the scope of the event by featuring a variety of speakers at the rally after the march. Sharing the stage, for example, was a representative from the United Farm Workers, who updated the crowd on the union's struggle.[99] Also appearing was a local resident who had been beaten by members of law enforcement so severely during the East L.A. school blowouts the year before that he had required brain surgery. He spoke in favor of educational reform and against police abuse.[100] Although only one woman appeared on stage, she underscored the moratorium committee's central contention that the Chicano struggle for self-determination was more important than pursuing war in Southeast Asia. Alicia Escalante, the mother of two Brown Berets and head of the local chapter of the National Welfare Rights Organization, described the desperate poverty of some Mexican American families in the area. She then declared, to a round of cheers, "I'd rather have my sons die for La Raza and La Causa than in Vietnam."[101]

Reflecting the moratorium campaign's anti-draft origins, organizers also criticized the Selective Service System. Joining Rosalío Muñoz on stage that December was Manuel Gómez, the Bay Area poet and draft resister.[102] A page-long indictment against the war released by the moratorium committee two days before the march maintained that the draft remained unjust, despite its having been revamped by the Nixon administration the previous month. While maintaining student deferments until 1971, the new lottery system attempted to lessen the other class biases of the draft by choosing randomly among remaining nineteen-year-olds. Moratorium activists argued that because Mexican Americans comprised an overwhelmingly young population, with a median age of just twenty years, ethnic group members were still destined to bear an unfair burden of fighting in Viet Nam and future conflicts.[103] Nor were Chicano anti-war activists soothed by another Nixon administration reform specifically aimed at dampening anti-war protest: declining induction rates. They insisted that Mexican Americans remained particularly vulnerable to the draft. Again condemning the "racist nature of previous peace efforts," the indictment accused the "peace movement" of "educating white youth on why and how to avoid going to the war but not Chicanos."[104]

Indeed, the indictment seemingly condemned with as much fervor those white Americans who opposed the war as those who prosecuted it. According to the indictment, the construction of an independent Chicano anti-war effort had been necessary to address Mexican American concerns about the war that had been overlooked by Anglo-American anti-war activists. These included the familiar assertion that Mexican Americans were dying in disproportionate numbers. The press announcement further asserted that "a disproportionate number of men still in Vietnam are Mexican Americans." Lacking hard data, moratorium organizers apparently reasoned that if Mexican Americans were dying in disproportionate numbers, as Guzman's study suggested, they must be represented in the war zone in disproportionate numbers, too. The insinuation behind the grievance was that Anglo Americans had benefited disproportionately from troop withdrawals and the occasional release of prisoners of war. The indictment went on to make this point explicit by mentioning that among those Mexican Americans still in Viet Nam "was the first and longest held prisoner of war, Lt. Everett Alvarez, captured in 1964, whose release has not been negotiated while

those of many Anglos have."[105] With each accusation, anti-war organizers proposed a sharp Chicano-versus-Anglo divide.

Although left unspoken by the march's speakers, the political reality
was, of course, more complex. Cultural nationalism, while an integral
part of moratorium events, had its limits. Mexican Americans were no
more of a single opinion about the war than were Anglo Americans. A
Chicano activist in a brown beret and a Mexican American military man
in his green beret were likely to stand far apart politically, no matter their
shared ethnic backgrounds. Navy pilot Lt. Everett Alvarez personified
this lack of congruence. To moratorium organizers, Alvarez was a potent
example of how Chicanos bore an unfair amount of suffering as military
men. But Alvarez himself, imprisoned for more than five years by December 1969, always favored a more vigorous prosecution of the war. Determined to serve his country with honor, he was convinced that the P.O.W.s
who had accepted early release were traitors to those who remained.
Moreover, when his own sister, Delia, began to speak at anti-war rallies,
familial love did not sway his conclusion that her activism, and the anti-
war movement generally, was aiding and abetting the enemy.[106] Alvarez's
political attitudes regarding the war reflected both the year he was captured, 1964, and his successive years of physical and psychological pun-
ishment. Of course, moratorium organizers could not know his opinions
while he was in Viet Nam. His Mexican background alone dictated their
concern over his release. In a cultural-nationalist movement, ethnicity
was of necessity the prime building block. But ethnicity did not always
guarantee the affinity of viewpoints that Chicano movement participants
supposed.

When, at the moratorium rally, Muñoz demanded that more Mexican
Americans be appointed to draft boards, he demonstrated just such wish-
ful thinking. Muñoz wanted Chicano cases to be decided by other Mexican Americans and "not rednecks like on my draft board."[107] But a conservative Mexican American could spoil that scenario. For instance,
Salomón Baldenegro, a Chicano activist from Tucson, recalled that the
person who had blocked his attempt to receive conscientious objector
status in 1968 was a leading Mexican American businessman in town.
The businessman countered Baldenegro's plea by declaring that it was
impossible for any person of Mexican descent to be opposed to military
duty, first because Mexicans were Catholics and Catholics had been
fighting in wars since before the Crusades, and second because Mexican
boys were raised to be brave and macho and therefore they were culturally amenable to combat.[108] Granted that the businessman's historical

and sociological analyses were superficial, as a Mexican American he spoke with as much individual authority as Baldenegro did. To a Chicano resisting the draft, a fellow Mexican American with such views was no more likely to be helpful to his case than an Anglo draft board member, redneck or not. But Muñoz's criticism, and cultural nationalism, did not permit that possibility.

An array of powerful symbols and slogans of their Chicano heritage helped marchers ignore these contradictions. From the stylized Aztec eagle of the United Farm Workers' flag to the shouted chants of "Chicano Power!" to the brown of those wearing berets, demonstrators laid claim to a variety of inspirations. But here was another central limitation of cultural nationalism: it assumed that a shared cultural background would foster political harmony. Consequently, march organizers tended to dismiss any contrary opinions as not representative. Although a leader like Corky Gonzales liked to theorize that ethnic bonds would ultimately override class and political differences, the question remained: What if they did not?[109] Chicano movement participants most frequently resolved this conflict by labeling those Mexican Americans with whom they had conflicts as *vendidos,* or "sell-outs," to white America. Other popular terms activists used against their opponents included "Tío Taco," a Chicano version of "Uncle Tom," and "Malinche," the name of the indigenous woman who was given to the Spanish conqueror, Cortés, and became his translator.[110] Always, these terms implied traitor status, the same charge that several Brown Beret women had confronted because they had challenged the male hierarchy of the organization. Cultural nationalism thus always contained an either–or proposition. Either Mexican Americans sympathized with the aims and oratory of the Chicano movement or, some participants declared, they had abandoned their ethnic group.

The war in Viet Nam, ironically, temporarily provided a neutral ground for diverse factions within the Chicano movement. The war, Chicano activists could agree, was wrong. Unlike the debates over violence versus nonviolence, or machismo versus feminism, unlike the differences between the working-class activists who joined the Brown Berets and the college students who began the anti-draft campaign, opposing the war generated few tensions among the many people within the movement. Excited about the unity that an anti-war campaign could inspire, young Chicano activists in Los Angeles joined together in the moratorium committee to publicize their position in newspapers, speeches, and especially marches.

CHAPTER 5

"A Common Goal"

*The Chicano Moratorium March
of August 1970*

The sunny weather was the perfect complement to the exuberant mood pervading East Los Angeles's Whittier Boulevard on August 29, 1970 (see Fig. 7). That morning between 20,000 and 30,000 protesters had walked for more than three miles in a demonstration that the Los Angeles County Sheriff's Department, keeping a close eye on the proceedings, characterized as both "boisterous" and "cheerful."[1] One participant described the march as "intense, energetic, festive," and "defiant," while another called it simply "a very beautiful community expression."[2] For Rosalío Muñoz, the chairman of National Chicano Moratorium Committee, the day was a great triumph. He recalled receiving a bear hug along the way from Ruben Salazar, a well-known journalist and columnist for the *Los Angeles Times*. Salazar, who once had listened to committee members decry the *Times*'s lackluster coverage of the Chicano anti-war effort, congratulated Muñoz and the entire moratorium committee for the day's turnout. "You did it," he said. "You really did it."[3]

Organizers and other participants shared a feeling of accomplishment and optimism: the impressive gathering seemed to make palpable the Chicano movement goals of unity and pride. The procession was "such a high . . . a natural joy. . . . It was incredible the feeling," Irene Tovar, another member of the moratorium committee recalled. "Everybody was your brother, everyone had a common goal, a common purpose."[4] That day, "La Raza Unida" was no mere slogan, one movement newspaper contended, but "a spirit, alive and dynamic."[5] These analy-

Figure 7. Crowd of joyful marchers from Chicano Moratorium March, August 29, 1970. Although planners had hoped to attract 100,000 participants, the August march was still one of the largest assemblages of Mexican Americans ever. The diversity of the marchers was another triumph for moratorium organizers. Within this group shot, an Anglo American young man with frizzy blond hair raises his fist in a Chicano power salute, while the shirtless young man in the front of the crowd openly celebrates his Mexican roots by wearing an enormous sombrero. One sign identifies attendees from "El Paso"; another, insisting that "Che Lives and Is Walking Down Whittier Boulevard," pays tribute to a Chicano movement hero; and a third protests policy brutality, "They Shoot Chicanos, Don't They?" Photo by George Rodriguez.

ses spoke to the achievement of the organizers of the August moratorium march in assembling a broad protest coalition. Marchers that day included Chicano paramilitary outfits and Mexican American military veterans, rebellious teens and their worried parents, committed radicals and mainstream liberals. Carloads and busloads of Chicano activists from throughout California and other states attended. While most participants were young, entire families came to the demonstration, from grandparents to infants in strollers. Indeed, the phrase "Chicano Moratorium" soon came to mean more than an upcoming protest march or even a series of protests. To activists, the vast support for the moratorium campaign offered evidence of a swelling political consciousness, evidence that Mexican Americans were a "nation of people rising."[6]

Increasingly, this diverse group was making the sharp-edged connection between the war in Viet Nam and what they perceived to be a war at home. In Viet Nam, they questioned whether the Vietnamese forces were their enemy; at home, they were more convinced than ever that the police were. In the first half of 1970 several violent confrontations had taken place between law enforcement officials and ethnic Mexicans in Los Angeles. For those who had not been politicized by abstract revolutionary sentiments, or long-standing commitments to ethnic-group activism, or even by accumulated daily slights, police brutality against Mexican Americans and Mexican immigrants was proving to be an injustice impossible to ignore. To Chicano activists, local police aggression, like the war in Viet Nam, exemplified the power of the state working against the interests of Mexican-origin people. As Muñoz explained to one reporter a few days before the August anti-war march, "Just as everybody in the barrio has somebody in the war, just about everybody here has been harassed by the police or knows someone in prison."[7]

Unfortunately, the very pervasiveness of this problem caused the August 29th demonstration to end tragically. In the months before the August march the central refrain emanating from Los Angeles's National Chicano Moratorium Committee had been: "Our front line is not in Vietnam but in the struggle for social justice in the U.S."[8] Late on the afternoon of August 29, L.A. County Sheriff's deputies, joined by reinforcements from the city's police department, charged the park where the demonstration's concluding rally was being held, a decision that turned the demonstration into a battlefield. Within a matter of minutes, the day's tremendous feelings of hope, joy, and pride dissolved into fear, anger, and sorrow. The peaceful celebration turned into a tumultuous riot that eventually spilled out beyond the confines of the park. Ultimately, three people died as a result of the day's violence, including *Los Angeles Times* reporter Salazar. The violent outcome to the August march underscored like no other event that the struggle—indeed the war—was at home. From its rhetorical origins, the moratorium's organizing slogan had become an apt description for the day's brutal confrontation.

It was a confrontation from which the moratorium committee never fully recovered. Hoping to direct and shape community outrage in the wake of the national march, the committee instead underwent a process of internal fragmentation in the face of continued outbreaks of violence and an extensive law enforcement campaign that was designed to harass, intimidate, and discredit committee members. Although three more demonstrations occurred, none replicated the tantalizing brief success of the August march. For Chicano activists, challenging police power proved to be more complex, and more dangerous, than galvanizing anti-war sentiment. A day of unparalleled unity and tragedy, the National Chicano Moratorium March on August 29, 1970, marked both the pinnacle of organizational achievement for Chicano movement activists and their most serious setback.

THE MARCH

The people who began to gather at Belvedere Park at 10 a.m. that morning noticed that the lawns had been deeply watered the night before, leaving the ground soaked and muddy.[9] Yet little could dampen their spirits. The numbers pouring into the staging area and then traveling toward Whittier Boulevard constituted one of the largest assemblages of Mexican Americans ever. A jubilant, if somewhat straggly procession of thousands, they strolled en masse down Whittier Boulevard toward the site of the afternoon's rally in nearby Laguna Park. Although young people predominated, older Mexican Americans also participated.[10] Adding racial as well as regional diversity to the group were Native Americans from Alcatraz, Puerto Ricans from New York, and white and black activists from Los Angeles.[11] The diverse assembly of people evinced the massive coalition that Chicano anti-war activists had assembled.

An earlier Chicano moratorium demonstration in February had convinced leading activists that their anti-war campaign was capable of spurring such broad political mobilization. While the original moratorium in December had been mostly a local affair, the better-advertised February event drew some two thousand activists from throughout California and the Southwest. Proud of their ability to unite a still far-flung Chicano movement, members of the Chicano Moratorium Committee had added the word "National" to their title just before the February protest. Like geographic diversity, ethnic diversity was evident in February: marchers included a black delegation from the Che Lumumba branch of the Communist Party; a representative from the Young Lords, a Puerto Rican youth group similar to the Brown Berets; and Anglo-American members of the local Peace Action Council.[12] Most important to moratorium organizers was the support of members of their own ethnic group. Despite a downpour that day so heavy that inches of rain collected on the street, demonstrators encountered cheering Mexican American spectators whom they encouraged to join the march. Some did; others helped by proffering their umbrellas.[13] In addition, as requested by the moratorium committee, a number of merchants closed their shops that day in "honor of the war dead."[14]

The February demonstration convinced anti-war organizers that Mexican Americans were willing to back the moratorium committee's insistent demands for change, especially if respect for tradition was part of the package. No group captured this dual strategy better than Las Adelitas, a new "woman power" organization that made its debut at the February demonstration.[15] Dressed in black mourning clothes, Las Adelitas carried crosses inscribed with the names of dead Chicano soldiers. At the same time, the group, whose membership included many ex-Berets, had chosen a name that referred to the *soldaderas* of the Mexican Revolution. Hilda Quen Jensen wore a bandoleer, a leather belt filled with bullets, across her chest (see Fig. 8).[16] Familiar attitudes regarding the role of women and the role of the military thus served as a foundation for anti-war and even feminist protest. Framed in this way, moratorium protest offered something for women and men, radicals and liberals, young and old alike.

Nonetheless, an initial daunting task for the moratorium committee was addressing the legacy of the last major conflict that had affected Mexican Americans so greatly. As Rosalío Muñoz explained to a reporter shortly before the August march: "Chicanos came back from World War II" and "they put on their uniforms and medals, and they'd say, 'We served; you can't call me a wetback, you can't tell me where to go.'" But the consequence, Muñoz said, was that "we developed this cultural and psychological thing. You prove yourself . . . by going through the service." Therefore, the moratorium committee's "first priority was educating the community" to reconsider this practice, Muñoz declared.[17] Anti-war activists rejected military service as an avenue of social advancement and personal glory for Mexican American men.

Still, nothing in the moratorium message went directly against the conception—and acclamation—of Mexican American men as *muy machos*. In his *Militant* interview, for instance, Muñoz asserted that it was the "Chicano's machismo," as much as economic and social pressures, that had channeled Mexican Americans toward military life.[18] In addition, backers of the moratorium effort insisted that speaking out against the war was an act of courage. As a participant in the February moratorium patiently explained to a reporter, "We aren't shedding our machismo. We were proving our machismo by asking the establishment the tough question, 'Why are we dying overseas when the real struggle is at home?'"[19] Draft resistance was likewise a valiant endeavor. A young

Figure 8. Hilda Quen Jensen, Chicano Moratorium March, February 28, 1970. Jensen, whose last name was then Reyes, was among a group of women who had left the Brown Berets to launch their own organization, Las Adelitas. That day, they marched in black and carried crosses emblazoned with the names of Chicano war dead to convey a community-wide sense of mourning at mounting war casualties. Yet even as they invoked the familiar image of the silent, suffering, and pious Mexican woman, their group's name and the bullet-laced belt that Jensen donned paid tribute to the women fighters of the Mexican Revolution. That second image best represented their independence. Photo by Devra Weber.

Chicano scholar who thought highly of the moratorium effort reprised a familiar theme when he wrote: "To resist is in the strongest sense of the word a test of manhood, personal courage and honor, *machismo*."[20]

Expanding upon this idea, Chicana anti-war activists subtly recast the idea of machismo to define it as a positive male energy with unlimited potential for furthering social justice stateside. In an article supporting the Chicano Moratorium's 1970 anti-war campaign, for example, Enriqueta Vasquez, a writer for New Mexico's *El Grito del Norte*, recalled that during World War II Mexican Americans had listened to "El Soldado Razo," a song about a young private heading off to war. A generation later, however, the "real *soldado razo*," she wrote, was the Chicano who refused to kill his "brothers" in Viet Nam. Instead, he "knows his Machismo belongs to his people, to be used for his people, . . . to be used right here in the heartland of mi Raza, in Aztlán." Consequently, Mexican Americans were rethinking the traditional patriotism of the ethnic group. "We hear the first line of the Marine hymn . . . 'from the Halls of Moctezuma,'" she explained, "and we stop to wonder, 'What the hell were the Marines doing in the Halls of Moctezuma?'"[21] To Vasquez and other moratorium backers, opposing the war in Viet Nam was inseparable from the task of inspiring domestic politicization.

In this regard, widespread frustration and impatience among Americans in general regarding the war benefited the anti-war cause. Although the moratorium campaign incorporated many Chicano movement anti-war themes that had been prevalent for several years, it did so after five years of inconclusive fighting. Despite the president's repeated assurances that the war was winding down, moreover, in 1970 the war appeared to be expanding. On April 30, President Richard Nixon announced that U.S. troops had made an incursion into Cambodia. At universities across the country, new protests broke out. On May 4, National Guardsmen fired upon students at Kent State University in Ohio, killing four. MEChA students at California's San Fernando Valley State College demonstrated their frustration the next day: during a campus Cinco de Mayo rally, they burned an American flag.[22] Taking a more measured approach, the Congress of Mexican American Unity in Los Angeles drafted a letter to the president that urged Nixon to "alter your course and give more consideration to national issues that are tearing our country apart."[23]

At a time when support for the war was deteriorating across the country, one study concluded that Mexican Americans were even more opposed to the war's continuation than the general public. A few weeks before the August moratorium march, two Chicano researchers associated with the University of California at Santa Barbara polled three hundred Spanish-surnamed individuals in that town. They discovered that, compared with the general population, a higher percentage of respondents preferred the immediate withdrawal of American troops from Viet Nam, disapproved of President Nixon's Viet Nam policy, and supported student and anti-war protests. Suggesting that Mexican-origin people were casting a critical eye upon military service, a clear majority also said they would discourage their sons from entering the army.[24]

A Republican in the White House no doubt had an influence on the poll's anti-war findings.[25] The New Deal had cemented Mexican American loyalty to the Democratic Party.[26] Not until after the 1968 election did most Mexican American politicians serving in Washington became vocal opponents of the war, most notably, New Mexico Senator Joseph M. Montoya. Although in 1965 he had defended U.S. intervention "no matter what the cost," by 1969 he was urging Nixon to accelerate troop withdrawals because the war's price was too high in terms of lives and money.[27] Henry B. Gonzalez of San Antonio also noticeably upped his anti-war rhetoric once his long-time political ally and fellow Texan, Lyndon Baines Johnson, had left the presidency.[28] Closer to home for the rally's organizers, U.S. Representative Edward Roybal, a Democrat representing Los Angeles, had wholeheartedly endorsed the moratorium a few days before the August march.[29]

By mid-1970, the anti-war coalition included several older, more established organizations that were politically within the liberal tradition. A most surprising coup for the moratorium committee was the endorsement of the California G.I. Forum, the state branch of a civil rights organization that since World War II had promoted Mexican American inclusion by equating valor as soldiers with validation as citizens. At the group's June 1970 California convention, Viet Nam veterans had taken the lead in convincing their fellow members that the war was misguided.[30] Likewise, the Mexican American Political Association, under the leadership of state president Abe Tapia, who claimed to be a "new breed" of Mexican American, had joined the Chicano moratorium effort in time for the February demonstration.[31] In Los Angeles, one of the earliest supporters of the moratorium was the Congress of Mexican American Unity, an umbrella organization of more than three hundred ethnic advocacy groups ranging from barrio-based organizations to more traditional political action committees.[32] In 1970 the CMAU president was Esteban Torres, a local union leader and future

Democratic congressman. Shortly after the initial moratorium demonstration, in December 1969, one of the event's planners, Ramsés Noriega, had joined the organization in the hope of orchestrating a much broader campaign.[33]

CMAU participation provided practical benefits. The congress immediately contributed much-needed funds and secured a temporary office for the moratorium committee, which had been meeting at the Brown Beret headquarters in East Los Angeles. In addition, the CMAU's legitimacy and respectability soon rubbed off on the youth-dominated antiwar group. For its initial demonstration, the Chicano moratorium committee had obtained permission to march along a series of narrow residential streets. In contrast, supporters of future moratorium demonstrations requested permits for successive marches in the name of the CMAU and thus secured approval to proceed down Whittier Boulevard, the wide commercial strip that constituted the heart of Chicano East Los Angeles.[34] Long a contested space between law enforcement and Mexican American youth, being able to travel down this major thoroughfare was tantamount, at least for a few hours, to a Chicano takeover of part of the city. Or, as an article in the Brown Beret's Los Angeles newspaper *La Causa* enthusiastically declared, moratorium protest "liberated Whittier Blvd."[35] Indeed, in August, excited marchers soon took over the entire boulevard, even though the parade permit had allocated only half the street to the demonstration.[36]

An anti-war group dominated by white liberals likewise extended a helping hand to the moratorium committee. Throughout the Viet Nam War, the Peace Action Council of Southern California, an impressive coalition of religious, student, political, and labor interests, had coordinated most anti-war events in the Los Angeles area. Despite lingering accusations on the part of Chicano anti-war activists that the "white peace movement" was "institutionally racist," moratorium members readily accepted the PAC's financial and logistical support.[37] In June, as efforts to organize the August demonstration grew intense, the council secured for the moratorium committee more spacious and permanent office space. Like the Congress of Mexican American Unity, the PAC also contributed much-needed cash—in one case, holding a fundraiser that collected two thousand dollars. In addition, the group donated the sound equipment that was used during both the February and August rallies.[38]

Moratorium relations with groups from the sectarian left were more complicated. While welcoming help from all quarters, Chicano anti-war activists were careful to preserve their independence. Thus, the moratorium committee appreciated that the Socialist Workers Party had been one of the most consistent supporters of its efforts: SWP members marched in August as they had during both previous moratorium demonstrations in Los Angeles. Nonetheless, the Trotskyite group failed to endear itself to members of the anti-war committee after one party regular announced at a moratorium meeting that the committee should go to the Communists for money and to the SWP for guidance.[39] While the Socialist Workers Party deemed the moratorium effort representative of a "correct political outlook," some Chicano anti-war activists found the party's pervasive didacticism offputting.[40] Chicano anti-war activists had even less use for the Progressive Labor Party. As Muñoz later explained to a reporter, the "PLs" had dropped by a few moratorium meetings "months before" the August demonstration and had "put down our policies."[41] Specifically, the Maoist PLP charged that the moratorium slogan "Bring Our *Carnales* (Brothers) Home" was disruptive of working-class unity because it emphasized the return of Chicano soldiers instead of all G.I.s.[42] Despite this complaint, a handful of Progressive Labor Party members attended the August march. Suggesting how peripheral they were to the Chicano anti-war effort, they passed out leaflets emblazoned with the likeness of the Chinese leader Mao Zedong, while Chicano participants could be heard chanting "Viva Emiliano Zapata!" and "Viva Pancho Villa!"[43]

Although familiar with the radical left critique of American foreign policy, Chicano moratorium supporters preferred to emphasize the costs of the war at home. One exception was an anonymous polemic that appeared in the Brown Berets' *La Causa* on the day of the February moratorium protest. "The Vietnam War is the ultimate weapon of genocide of non-white peoples by a sick decadent *puto* [male prostitute] western culture," the polemic began. "The random genocide in the barrio, *campos* and ghettos is escalated to a calculated cold-blooded policy to enslave the Vietnamese people and rape their land of its resources." Glorifying the Vietnamese revolutionaries in their struggle against the "*gabacho* [white] invaders," the article concluded, "Let us learn from their example that to resist is to be a free man and to submit is to be a *puto* and thus a slave."[44] Although it contained a somewhat confusing use of metaphors (a *puto* culture raped), the insult overall was in keeping with the Brown Berets' hypermasculine, militant image. The tirade implicitly contrasted the mythical fighting spirit of Mexican men with the presumed effeminateness of Western culture. At the same time, the anti-war tirade, in its attempt to condemn the war as an imperialist venture, represented the views of only one faction within an ideologically divided Los Angeles chapter. Indeed, burdened by factional debates and other disputes, members of the Los Angeles-based chapter had become less involved in the day-to-day workings of the moratorium committee after the February demonstration. Uniformed, regimented, and marching in formation, Brown Berets nonetheless remained a notable presence during anti-war demonstrations.

Indeed, as the August demonstration drew near, by far the most important source of support for the moratorium committee remained other Chicano movement allies like the Berets. The moratorium committee, for example, benefited from the strong link it forged with MEChA, the Chicano student group that had been formed in Santa Barbara in 1969. MEChA contingents were readily evident during moratorium demonstrations across the state and in Los Angeles. For several college students within the moratorium committee, MEChA had been their introduction to the Chicano movement. In addition, like the Brown Berets before them, moratorium committee members enjoyed the backing of the Episcopal Church of the Epiphany in Lincoln Heights, whose pastor and congregation embraced a social justice policy.[45] Mexican American church members—including at least one World War II veteran—provided several key moratorium volunteers.[46] Finally, fresh from the February protest, Rosalío Muñoz and Ramsés Noriega traveled to Denver to attend the second annual Chicano Youth Liberation conference. Once again sponsored by the Crusade for Justice, the conference brought together several thousand young people from across the country, thus allowing moratorium organizers to strengthen contacts with activists in Denver and elsewhere.

Even more so than the previous year, the conflict in Viet Nam dominated the conference's empowerment agenda. The war's deleterious effect upon Mexican Americans was the subject of speeches, songs, poetry recitations, and theatrical *"actos."* In addition, a special anti-war workshop chaired by Muñoz and Noriega developed plans to stage a series of local protests across the Southwest as part of an extensive moratorium campaign that was to culminate in a massive march in Los Angeles that August.[47] When Muñoz shared the workshop's plans with the rest of the conference, the crowd broke out in approving claps and stomps. Soon, a thunderous chant filled the conference hall: *"¡Chale no!,* We won't go!"[48]

The Denver conference rewarded the moratorium committee with new members, including Katarina Davis del Valle, a native of Los Angeles. Born Katherine Maria Davis, the child of a Mexican immigrant mother and a light-skinned African American father, Davis del Valle was unaware of her father's ancestry until she was in her thirties. Identifying with neither Mexican American nor African American causes at first, she did sympathize as a youth with the Vietnamese who suffered bombing and disfigurement, in part because she herself suffered from a severe allergy that left her skin red and inflamed. When she was just sixteen, she had begun to research the war at the library and soon became involved in anti-war and then leftist political circles. The drama of the high school strikes in East Los Angeles the following year prompted Davis del Valle to volunteer her services at the offices of *La Raza* newspaper. Known then as "Kathy Davis" and, as she recalled, suffering from a misplaced sense of white guilt, she wanted to explore her Chicana identity. As a start, editor Eliezer Risco suggested that she change her name to "Katarina" and also encouraged her to use her mother's birth name.[49]

Still, until the Denver conference two years later, Davis del Valle remembered feeling torn between Marxism, which she considered a "white thing," and her loyalty to the Chicano movement. In Denver, a member of the Socialist Workers Party convinced her that she could be both "a Chicana and a Marxist [and] the whole world opened up to me." Catching a ride back to Los Angeles with Muñoz and Noriega, she put that discovery into action by becoming a dedicated member of the moratorium committee. Like most of the women involved in the anti-war group, Davis del Valle mainly did office work, although she was assigned the title of "co-chair of security" for the August demonstration. In another indication of the division of labor, at moratorium demonstrations prominent male members of the committee were likely to be up on stage, whereas women volunteers mostly offered logistical support.[50] Nevertheless, office work provided Davis del Valle with a special thrill one day shortly before the August march. She picked up the office phone to find that Western Union was calling to transmit a telegram of congratulations from the National Liberation Front of the People of Viet Nam. To Davis del Valle, Chicano anti-war activism perfectly reconciled her radical left and Chicano nationalist politics.[51]

In contrast to Davis del Valle, Irene Tovar was a committed liberal. Born in the Boyle Heights area of Los Angeles in 1938, one of Tovar's earliest memories was of U.S. servicemen banging on doors in her neighborhood looking for zoot-suiters. The violence convinced her parents to settle in Pacoima in the San Fernando Valley. Years later, Tovar still credited her parents, immigrants from Mexico, and in her father's case a veteran of the Mexican Revolution, with being her first political heroes. She was impressed by their compassion: Tovar remembered her father literally giving the coat off his back to a transient one cold day. Although her arrival at San Fernando Valley State College (later Cal State Northridge) at the age of eighteen pre-dated the Chicano movement, Tovar acted upon a professor's suggestion that she attend a black civil rights demonstration. Her pantheon of political heroes quickly expanded to include black leaders like James Farmer and Martin Luther King Jr., and Mohandas K. Gandhi, whose embrace of nonviolent resistance had inspired both. (To Tovar, the moratorium's policy of nonviolence was never merely strategic, but heartfelt.) Tovar spent the next dozen years working full-time, taking classes part-time, and volunteering on behalf of both the black civil rights movement and, as it emerged, the Chicano movement, too. By 1970, she was not only vice-president of the Greater Los Angeles Urban Coalition, a group dedicated to ending racial inequality and urban poverty, but she also had played a role as a community liaison in establishing one of the country's first Chicano Studies programs at her alma mater.[52]

Strongly opposed to the war in Viet Nam, Tovar joined the moratorium committee almost as soon as it was formed. Tovar had grown up hearing the story of Felix Longoria, the World War II soldier who had been denied burial in a small town in Texas because he was Mexican American. Long discussions in college, moreover, had convinced her that the conflict in Viet Nam was a civil war in which the United States had no business intervening. Bringing these two influences together, she did not understand why Mexican Americans should be dying overseas in a misguided war in Viet Nam when their own country still did not treat them as equals at home. Neither did her younger sister, Ramona. While Irene Tovar brought her stamina, political contacts, and organizational skills to the Los Angeles moratorium committee, Ramona Tovar coordinated support for the anti-war effort in the San Fernando Valley, where, in addition, she offered draft counseling. Although some older Mexican Americans disparaged anti-war activists as *"desgradecidos"* (ungrateful ones) and "Jane Fonda–types," Irene Tovar recalled, mostly the moratorium's policy of outreach worked. Supporters of the anti-war effort were a diverse group that ranged from young women like herself who had grown up very sheltered to profanity-loving gang members who suddenly stopped fighting to work for peace.[53]

Gilbert Cano, another member of the moratorium committee, understood how gang members might become converts to political activism.

Growing up in Los Angeles in a poor family headed by an alcoholic step-
father, Cano had been a gang member in his youth. When he joined the
service at the age of seventeen in 1956, he was certain that he was
headed toward an early death or prison, the fate of most of his friends.
Cano credited the U.S. Army with having saved his life. Not only was
he able to put the gang behind him, for the first time ever he could revel
in owning "three sets of underwear, two pair of boots . . . and [sleeping
on] sheets that didn't tear at the bottom when you got into bed." Once
discharged from the service, however, Cano felt adrift. In the late 1960s
he joined a War on Poverty agency, through which he met Rosalío
Muñoz. After the thoroughly Americanizing experience of the army,
Cano recalled the excitement of learning about the Chicano movement
and suddenly taking pride in his Mexican heritage. A "super-patriot"
until then, he also started to reconsider the merits of the war in Viet
Nam, especially given its toll upon working-class soldiers. Shifting his
loyalties, Cano stopped defending American foreign policy and started
promoting Chicano power.[54]

However their political biographies differed, members of the moratorium committee united around the central mission of mobilizing the
Mexican American population against the war and on behalf of the Chicano movement. With little money, but much enthusiasm, organizers
worked furiously to spread their anti-war message. One tactic was to
print thousands of anti-war flyers during the spring and summer of
1970. A representative example depicted a young soldier kneeling in
sorrow before a collection of white crosses. "We are of the opinion that
the millions upon millions spent . . . in a war that brings no benefits to
anyone," the text read, "should be spent in solving the unemployment
problem, [and the problems of] smog, drugs, housing . . . etc."[55] Members of the moratorium committee also continued to speak at countless
community halls, churches, private parties, and at peace group gatherings, often showing a film of the February protest as part of their presentation. That summer, the committee adopted an additional strategy:
holding impromptu rallies at local parks.

The strategy yielded results. As Cano recalled, most weekends a few
volunteers would set up a table laden with Mexican food and someone
would start strumming a guitar. Meanwhile, anti-war activists would
wander the park inviting people to drop by and learn about the war. To
Cano's delight, at work one day, an older Mexican American woman
told him that as a result of what she had learned at one of these park
events, she had decided to send her boy to Canada if he received a draft

notice. The contribution of Cano's own mother was another indication that the anti-war effort was reaching beyond Chicano movement participants. According to Cano, although his mother hated the word "Chicano" and complained that Cano's deep involvement in the moratorium campaign was making him a *"mitotero"* (busybody), unbeknownst to him at the time, she was one of the women cooking menudo and making tortillas for the park gatherings.[56]

The timing of the Chicano anti-war campaign, its careful recognition of the legacy of World War II, and, most important, its insistence that the struggle for Mexican Americans was at home and not in Viet Nam allowed the campaign to flourish in even a previously resistant quarter: Texas. Chicano moratoriums in Austin, San Antonio, and Houston, held during the summer of 1970, were well received. No doubt the way the moratoriums were advertised helped: "Raza backs rally to honor G.I.'s" read one headline.[57] Still, at the rally following the Houston demonstration, Bexar County Commissioner Albert Peña Jr., a well-known liberal politician who had served in the Navy during World War II, called the conflict in Viet Nam "a gringo war."[58] Mexican Americans confronted a different war. "The barrios are our Vietnam," he asserted.[59]

The decision to hold a series of local Chicano moratorium protests succeeded in building momentum for the moratorium campaign. In addition to those held in Texas, Chicano anti-war protests took place in Arizona, Colorado, Illinois, New York, and throughout the state of California, more than a dozen in all.[60] Participants at these events often then made plans to attend the big Los Angeles event on August 29, 1970. Indeed, members of the moratorium committee recalled the overwhelming task of locating housing for so many visitors as the August date approached.[61] Across the state especially, excitement ran high. As Joe Chacón, a Chicano movement participant from East Los Angeles College, recalled, in the weeks before August 29 the word "moratorium" was on everybody's lips in East Los Angeles. Yet upon traveling back home to California's Central Valley, he noticed the excitement about the anti-war event was just as high inland.[62]

The sheer magnitude of the forthcoming event, however, inspired a less positive outcome within the moratorium committee itself. Tensions developed among some members as they each jostled for the limelight.[63] On the day of the August demonstration, internal dissension spilled outward. The Brown Berets threatened to withdraw their support for the anti-war effort because, according to an article that appeared that day on the pages of *La Causa*, members of the moratorium committee were "ego-trippers and opportunist(s)" who had slighted the paramilitary organization.[64] Ultimately, however, the Berets decided that the moratorium was too important an event to ignore.

THE RALLY

After walking several hours in the hot sun, protestors entering Laguna Park "fell wearily—and gratefully—to the ground."[65] "Everyone [was] eager to find a spot on the grass, at last to sit and rest for a while," a marcher recalled.[66] Exhausted but triumphant, the crowd listened to musical performers before Rosalío Muñoz, in his role as chairman of the National Chicano Moratorium Committee, opened the post-march rally. "A year ago, when we started organizing against the war, there were very few us," Muñoz began. Now, as he stood before thousands of people, Muñoz asserted that "a powerful force for social change" had been created. While the conflict in Viet Nam remained of concern, he said, Mexican Americans needed to unite to tackle other problems. "We have to begin organizing on the issue of police brutality," he said. "We have to bring an end to this oppression."[67] In retrospect, his comments contained a tragic irony. Shortly afterward, the bulk of the demonstrators were running from the park in order to flee an assault by sheriff's deputies.

"Please everybody sit down. Nothing is happening back there," a voice announced from the stage, even as Muñoz continued to address the crowd. The speaker was wrong. A line of deputies had suddenly appeared on the edge of the park and had started pushing forward. Those on stage, at the opposite corner of the park, could see only some sort of movement of people that appeared to be heading their way. Desperate to quell any potential conflict, organizers once again asked for the crowd's cooperation. "Everybody sit down," the voice over the loudspeaker repeated three times, and then twice in Spanish, with increasing anxiety, "¡Siéntense!" "No queremos pedo" (Sit down! We don't want trouble).[68]

The confusion on stage was soon matched by confusion among the gathered demonstrators. "Swinging clubs they came, without a word, just swinging clubs and throwing gas," wrote one observer about the deputies' advance.[69] The sudden turn of events caught spectators "completely unaware."[70] According to Felix Martel, who headed a MAPA delegation from nearby San Bernardino, deputies "bore down" without warning. "People were seated and eating their lunches after the long march to the park and they were hot and tired," he said. "Suddenly, pandemonium broke lose."[71] A frightening stampede ensued as a crush of people were pushed toward the stage only to find the way blocked by a row of buses.[72] With the fear growing palpable and tear gas spreading through the air, thousands desperately scrambled to find an alternative escape. Or, as another Chicano witness at the park summarized the abrupt turn of events: "One minute mariachi, next minute mayhem."[73]

According to police officials, an earlier confrontation at a liquor store more than a block away from the rally site was the catalyst for their actions. Hot and thirsty, many marchers had crowded into the Green Mill Liquor Store, among only a handful of shops open that day (see Fig. 9). The owner, concerned that some people were leaving his store without paying, attempted to close his doors to make sure he collected money from everyone inside. According to the Sheriff's Department, after the store's silent alarm was tripped, patrol cars quickly responded with sirens blaring to what they thought was a "burglary in progress."[74] Suddenly confronted by a group of deputies who were hitting people indiscriminately in order to disperse the crowd, angry spectators pelted the deputies with bottles and rocks. Ernesto Vigil, an activist from Denver who had just bought a soda, watched the entire encounter from across the street. Under the impression that the skirmish had been quickly extinguished, he walked back to Laguna Park and toward a huge banner that read *"Abrazos No Balazos,"* the Chicano version of "Make Love, Not War."[75]

A few minutes later, Vigil and the other marchers were taken by surprise when they saw a line of deputies suddenly appear on the edge of the park and start to move forward toward the stage. According to an early Associated Press dispatch, "Deputies said that although only a handful of demonstrators had caused trouble, they had to clear everyone out of the park to disperse the troublemakers."[76] In fact, deputy sheriffs pushed the remnants of the small disturbance at the liquor store toward the huge, peaceful gathering. The disturbance spread as some curious and daring individuals rushed toward the corner of the park to see what was happening. Some threw rocks. Law enforcement quickly declared the entire assembly illegal and deputies forcefully began to remove the demonstrators. Later, the sheriff's department reported that a deputy sheriff who entered the crowd at this time was attacked: a Chicano apparently fired at him with the deputy's own weapon, missing the law enforcement officer's head by inches.[77]

The incident suggested the escalating level of the violence. Although the vast majority of those gathered in the park attempted to flee, some

Figure 9. Volunteers filling water bottles, Chicano Moratorium March, August 29, 1970. In another testament to the tremendous organizing effort in advance of the march, rows of plastic jugs of water await thirsty protestors who followed a route more than three miles long in the hot sun. Some merchants along Whittier Boulevard also passed out free sodas and other beverages to the demonstrators. The owner of the Green Mill Liquor store near the park where the march concluded, however, expected demonstrators inside his store to pay. The sheriff's department was called to settle the matter and chaos ensued. Photo by George Rodriguez.

young people stayed and fought. Chicano monitors quickly attempted to form a line between the deputies and protestors, but the human barrier was dispersed by a crossfire of tear-gas canisters, bottles, and physical blows. From the stage, Ramsés Noriega's booming voice could be heard repeating, "Hold your line! Hold your line!"[78] His words took on various meanings as events unfolded. At first a plea to law enforcement to maintain their distance, and then an encouragement to Chicano monitors under siege, Noriega's words also inspired the scores of young people who had decided to confront the sheriff's deputies directly.[79] Armed with "picket signs, magazines, flyers, purses, bottles, feet and fists," the youth temporarily repulsed the police advance.[80] As another observer recalled, "Young Chicanos were going up to police and landing one good body blow knowing that the police would immediately club them down."[81] Like many others that day, one young woman picked up a gas canister and threw it back toward the deputies in an effort to keep the stinging gas away from the panicked crowd.[82] Afterward, Chicano movement newspapers credited the fighting youth with providing demonstrators more time to escape harm.[83]

The police responded with even greater force. A Chicano filmmaker recorded what happened next to the young woman who had thrown the gas canister. As she was running *away,* a deputy swung his baton so hard against the base of her skull that her neck snapped forward and back before she collapsed on the ground.[84] A baton blow also blindsided a twenty-seven-year-old Coloradoan, an eight-year Army veteran, who has been occupied with helping a young boy get on his feet and out of the park. The Colorado veteran subsequently lost his eye.[85] One witness, forty-nine-year-old Enrique P. Nava, later testified that he twice saw a group of five or six deputies gang up on a single individual. In each case, he said, "all you could see was the batons going up and down, up and down, as fast as they could. . . . Then the prostrate form would be dragged away." Nava declared that violence perpetuated by law officers that day had left him "extremely shocked."[86]

The intensity of the response by both marchers and police officers was the result of long-simmering antagonisms between the two groups. In March 1970, a report issued by the U.S. Commission on Civil Rights had chronicled dozens of incidents of police abuse against Mexican Americans across the Southwest.[87] In Los Angeles, although Mexican Americans had confronted the problem of police brutality since before the zoot-suit hysteria of the 1940s, the problem seemed to intensify with the emergence of the Chicano movement.[88] Beginning with the formation of the Brown Berets and continuing through the first set of high school strikes in 1968, Chicano movement participants in Los Angeles had discovered that their willingness to engage in public protest made them frequent targets of official repression, harassment, and surveillance.[89] To law enforcement, the Chicano movement, especially to the extent that it appeared to echo the slogans and demands of black power advocates, was dangerously suspect.[90] The connection was transparent to one activist, who complained to a reporter that "the police have adopted a policy of pre-emptive strike" toward the Chicano movement. "They see the organization and militancy that's developing in this community and they are determined not to let it get as strong as the black movement has become," he asserted.[91]

Concurrent with the expansion of the moratorium campaign, a series of police assaults had aggravated already poor relations between activists and law enforcement officials in Los Angeles. Although the first moratorium demonstration, in December 1969, had taken place peacefully, four days later, a Christmas Eve protest organized by Católicos por la Raza, a group dedicated to making the Catholic hierarchy more responsive to the Chicano poor, had not. Determined to join a mass at St. Basil's Catholic Church—a celebration usually open to all—members of the group had been beaten back by L.A. County sheriff's deputies, some of whom were acting as ushers for the night's service.[92] Similarly, although the February moratorium demonstration had proceeded without incident, a week later, striking Chicano students at Roosevelt High School were pummeled by police using nightsticks. Police had also dragged teen-age girls by their hair.[93] As the moratorium committee went into organizational high gear that spring, the violence continued. In May, police who had been called to the campus of the University of California at Los Angeles after a student anti-war demonstration turned violent used the occasion to storm a building far away from the demonstration site. The building housed most of the school's minority student services. Without provocation, law enforcement officers had beaten Chicano faculty and students.[94]

Chicano activists involved in the anti-war campaign had spoken against police violence from the start. Refusing induction the previous September, for example, Rosalío Muñoz had blamed law enforcement for "funneling" young Mexican American men into the army by making the streets such a dangerous place for them. A victim of police brutality had appeared at the first moratorium demonstration in Los Angeles in December. At the February moratorium demonstration, the problem received even more attention. Among the speakers blasting law enforcement were Oscar Zeta Acosta and David Sanchez, the Brown Beret prime minister. Acosta, a flamboyant movement lawyer, was at the time a candidate for Los Angeles County Sheriff. His single campaign promise: to abolish the department and institute a "People's Protection Department" instead.[95] "They are killing us all over this damned place and we have to do something about it," he insisted. Similarly, Sanchez was angry about the recent death of a twenty-two-year-old Mexican American in police custody. To the dismay of some in the crowd, he asserted that achieving justice through politics was futile.[96] Indeed, public protest did not seem to alleviate the situation. That July, the police had shot and killed two Mexican nationals.

To Chicano activists, the double shooting underscored the extreme license that law enforcement officials displayed toward Mexican-origin people. Looking for a murder suspect on July 16, four police officers had entered a Los Angeles skid-row hotel and kicked open the door of a second-story apartment.[97] According to one of the officers, he caught a glimpse of a man trying to slip behind a second door and shouted a warning in English. When the young man approached him instead of halting, the police officer opened fire, immediately killing Guillermo Alcazar Sánchez. Hearing gunfire, several other residents in the apartment tried to escape. Three officers gathered on the street below fired and killed Sánchez's cousin, Gildardo Beltrán Sánchez, as he attempted to crawl through an apartment window. They later said they believed that their colleagues were in danger. In their early twenties, both cousins were Mexican nationals without documents who spoke only Spanish.[98] Compounding the senselessness of the tragedy, police soon discovered that their suspect never had been in the area nor had he anything to do with the murder in question.[99] In the wake of the killings, the Chicano moratorium committee joined other organizations to sponsor a march through downtown.[100]

Also among those dissatisfied with official police reports of the shooting was Ruben Salazar, a respected journalist for the *Los Angeles Times* and news director of KMEX, the local Spanish-language radio station. Born in Ciudad Juarez, Mexico, Salazar had immigrated to the United States with his family when he was as an infant. He had grown up in El Paso and become a naturalized citizen. By 1970, he was a seasoned journalist who had reported on the U.S. invasion of the Dominican Republic in 1965, spent time in Viet Nam covering the war, and headed the *Times*'s Mexico City bureau. Returning to Los Angeles in 1969 from

Mexico City, Salazar turned his attention to understanding the Chicano movement that had emerged in his absence. The following April, he narrowed his responsibilities for the paper to a weekly column so that he could focus his attention on his new job at KMEX. At both media institutions, he became an advocate for Mexican American grievances, including frequent complaints about law enforcement. In a March 1970 column, for instance, Salazar accused the Los Angeles Police Department of not doing enough to mend police–community relations.[101] As news director of KMEX, Salazar also provided extensive coverage of the Chicano student strike at Roosevelt High School, as well as the deaths of the Sánchez cousins.[102]

His reporting prompted official concern. In the wake of the Sanchez killings, two policemen paid Salazar a visit during which they complained that his reporting was hurting the department's image and quite possibly inciting the Mexican American community. Asked to tone down his coverage, Salazar instead wrote a column about the visit.[103] By then, he had begun researching a major exposé of the problem of police brutality. Three days before the August march, he met with several representatives of the U.S. Commission on Civil Rights to share "on the record" his concerns that law enforcement officials might try to discredit his reporting by, for example, planting drugs on him. Salazar also confided to friends that he believed he was being followed.[104] He definitely was being investigated; both the LAPD and the FBI had opened files on the reporter.[105]

The Federal Bureau of Investigation also closely monitored the Chicano anti-war effort. Paralleling the attitudes of local police agents, the FBI viewed youth and minority protest as threatening to the social order. The bureau therefore targeted "Mexican American militancy" for investigation along with the anti-war and black power movements.[106] FBI agents were present at most major Chicano events, and the bureau had opened files on every major Chicano leader and organization.[107] Sometimes FBI surveillance was more thorough than accurate. Agents in San Francisco, for example, reported upon an emerging Mexican American political effort called La Raza Oneida (instead of La Raza Unida).[108] Meanwhile, memos from the FBI director chided field agents for not taking a more aggressive stance against Chicano groups.[109] More ominously, at least one FBI document laid out a plan to "discredit violence-prone leaders" by manipulating feelings of "Chicano pride" and attacking activists who worked with black and white activists.[110] Although heavily censored, the FBI's file on the National Chicano Moratorium

Committee reveals that the bureau's interest in the organization echoed its determination to monitor and, if necessary, restrain the Chicano movement overall.[111]

Certainly, the August demonstration attracted the attention of the bureau. Of special concern to the FBI was that the national moratorium demonstration would coincide with a visit of President Richard Nixon to Southern California. Two days before the event, FBI agents were present when Chicano activists picketed an event Nixon was attending at the Los Angeles Music Center. (Implying that Nixon's Viet Nam policy was aimed at "saving face," mainly his own reputation, they carried signs that asked pointedly, if somewhat awkwardly, "Mr. Nixon, is your face worth our sons' lives?"[112]) A report from the Los Angeles office made clear that FBI agents were also at the August moratorium demonstration. The report began with a brief mention of the march's commencement at Belvedere Park; the remainder of the "urgent" dispatch was censored.[113] In a message to the Secret Service that day, however, the FBI revealed its concern that the Brown Berets were participating in the anti-war coalition.[114] More information about this connection was likely available via a San Diego police officer who, under police department orders to infiltrate the local chapter of the Brown Berets, had ended up leading that chapter's contingent to the August demonstration. His observations were passed to the FBI.[115] Beyond concerns about Nixon's proximity and the presence of the Brown Berets, the FBI apparently viewed any large demonstration with alarm. Agents already had closely followed an early Chicano moratorium march in San Francisco that May.[116]

Though they were not certain of FBI involvement, prior to the August march Chicano anti-war activists knew that they were under observation by police authorities. As early as February, marchers participating in the Chicano moratorium had noticed men whom they assumed to be plainclothes law enforcement officers photographing the entire demonstration.[117] More concretely, as the August demonstration drew near, police officers had taken to stopping cars with moratorium bumper stickers and questioning those inside.[118] Months after the march, Gil Cano bumped into a young man, now wearing an LAPD sergeant's uniform, who had been one of his most dedicated helpers *before* the August demonstration. The police officer unconvincingly offered that he had just joined the force and had been promoted quickly.[119] Accustomed to surveillance and low-level harassment, the Chicano moratorium committee also encountered infiltration.

Aware of how strained relations were between law enforcement and Mexican Americans, moratorium leaders redoubled their efforts to ensure a peaceful demonstration in August (see Fig. 10). In the wake of the Kent State shootings, and given the state of affairs locally, they understood that any large demonstration was potentially dangerous. To the credit of both Chicano anti-war activists and law enforcement agencies outside of Los Angeles, all of the Chicano anti-war demonstrations that had taken place elsewhere in the preceding months had occurred without incident. Hopeful of the same outcome, members of the Los Angeles moratorium committee met with representatives of the Sheriff's Department to plan the August march. (The demonstration's path fell entirely within the county.) They also arranged to have monitors participate in the march to keep the peace; the group of two hundred monitors included a contingent of lawyers and law students who would be able to provide legal advice in case of any conflicts.[120] In addition, just before the August march the moratorium committee distributed a flyer to marchers that was aimed at avoiding "a police attack." "Don't carry liquor or narcotics," the instructions read; "Be prepared at all times to retreat quickly and orderly." Imbued with a courtly sense of gender roles, the notice also urged men and official monitors to remember to protect the "women and weak" in the case of violence. If the worst should occur, the notice advised demonstrators to seek "a place of shelter until the 'troubles' subside, then leave directly for home."[121]

On the day of the march, a few demonstrators had explicitly challenged the moratorium committee's policy of nonviolence as well as police expectations of law and order. Issuing only a verbal threat as he marched down Whittier Boulevard, one young man chanted, "Come on, brother, pick up your gun!" to which his companions responded, "Down with the pigs!"[122] Although two witnesses later testified that a handful of protestors handed out pieces of pipe, none of the more substantive confrontations during the march featured pipes. Instead, around six or seven times during the three-hour procession, participants threw bottles, rocks, or smoke bombs at law enforcement officers who were stationed at nearly every cross street along the route.[123] Monitors quickly quelled these potential disturbances. Few among the marchers anticipated any further problems.

For this reason, the unexpected rush of the sheriff's deputies into the park instilled panic among most protestors but infuriated others. Indeed, several Chicano press accounts portrayed the conflict as a turning point in the making of a warrior-type Chicano who had vanquished

Figure 10. Chicana monitors, Chicano Moratorium March, August 29, 1970. Wearing brown armbands that identified them as monitors, these Chicanas are demonstrating their solidarity with the marchers passing in front of them. Behind them a row of photographers snaps away at the historic event. Later, in the face of claims by some police officials that the Chicano demonstrators had acted provocatively, participants pointed to the presence of two hundred monitors at the march and rally as evidence of their intent to keep the peace. Photo by George Rodriguez.

forever the stereotype of Mexicans as passive and docile.[124] For example, Lorenzo Vargas, a Chicano writer from San Diego, offered that participating in the August 29 march had precipitated an "evolution of consciousness" for him as a Chicano. Along the route, he had tried to stop one Chicano from throwing rocks at a sheriff's deputy, but his attitude grew more bellicose after witnessing the scene at the park: "I remember joining a line of people arm in arm to create a buffer zone between police and *raza*. But the police wouldn't wait; they kept massing, then all of a sudden they charged. It was horrible. I saw children crying, run over by police. Mothers were screaming, girls running in panic. There was gas and billyclubs. . . . I saw police kick and stomp Chicanos, run into people's houses and drag them out." After viewing these brutal incidents and others, Vargas decided to act. Using the present tense as if to make the moment come alive, he wrote: "I spot a fire station and a police car. I run, pick up a rock and soon the American flag is down and burning. The car couldn't be turned over, but it's burning."[125] For others as well, the conflict soon spread from the park.

Fleeing to Whittier Boulevard, angry youths shattered storefront windows and looted merchandise. Echoing assertions of pinpoint destruction proffered in the defense of African American rioters in earlier urban clashes, most Chicano movement accounts tried to excuse the theft and vandalism. "The looting of mostly furniture stores was done to build barricades to battle the police," explained one account.[126] Meanwhile, an article that appeared in the Crusade for Justice's newspaper, *El Gallo*, suggested that angry youths had deliberately attacked only stores "not owned by Chicanos or without signs in their windows expressing support for the moratorium." The same article also defended the looting as having resulted in an impromptu redistribution of wealth. The youths, it said, had robbed "jewelry stores and . . . [were] handing out money and jewelry to all Chicanos who passed by."[127] Similarly, an article from San Francisco praised the actions of "one young man who kicked open the door of a finance building, grabbled all the records and disperced [*sic*] them to the winds." "He knew that most of the bills" were owed by "his people."[128]

Deputies from the Sheriff's Department, along with reinforcement from the Los Angeles Police Department, attempted to turn back and punish the lawbreakers. Their announcements were fierce: "You must clear the streets! You must get back in your homes! If you throw an object, you are committing an assault on a police officer! If you throw an object, you will be shot!"[129] Despite such warnings, for at least five hours, the turmoil continued. Although police later estimated that no more than four hundred people had participated in the destruction, by the time the next morning dawned, one person was dead, two others were fatally wounded, thirty-one civilians and forty-three law enforcement officials were less seriously injured, and two patrol cars had been destroyed (see Fig. 11). The sheriff's department estimated that the damage from arson fires and looting topped $1 million. One hundred and fifty-two people had been arrested.[130]

Law enforcement used the power to arrest and detain broadly. In one notorious episode, police officers kicked, clubbed, and threatened members of the Colorado delegation before handcuffing more than twenty-five activists and hauling them to jail. Police had stopped the flatbed truck in which Corky Gonzales, leader of the Crusade for Justice, was riding because people allegedly were hanging off the sides of the vehicle.

Figure 11. Smoke billows from burning buildings along Whittier Boulevard, August 29, 1970. A few hours before, Whittier Boulevard, the heart of Mexican East Los Angeles, had been the scene of a triumphant and largely peaceful march. A minor skirmish at a liquor store, however, prompted deputies to forcefully clear the thousands of people who had gathered for a concluding rally at a park. To the surprise of law officers, young demonstrators met violence with violence, a response that soon spilled out beyond the park and onto the boulevard. Photo by George Rodriguez.

Discovering that Gonzales was carrying more than $300 in cash and claiming to have found a recently fired weapon, the police arrested everyone on the ludicrous charge of "suspicion of robbery."[131] For his part, Rodolfo Acuña, a Chicano Studies professor, was forcefully thrown against a deputy's squad car and arrested. Along with many others that day, Acuña, who had been trying to vouch for another demonstrator who was being arrested, was charged with "inciting a riot." For several hours, he waited with others on a bus parked in the heat outside a deputy's substation. When passengers dared to complain, deputies deliberately fired mace inside that bus and others, he recalled. Years later, Acuña maintained that the angry tone evident in the first edition of his textbook, *Occupied America,* was a product of his experiences that day.[132]

More violence soon occurred. Lynn Ward, a fifteen-year-old Brown Beret from the El Monte chapter, was hurled thirty-eight feet through a plate glass window after "unknown persons," according to the Sheriff's

Department, had tossed an explosive in a nearby trash can. Early reports were that the explosive was a tear gas canister. Ward died on September 9, 1970.[133] To his fellow Brown Berets, he had died defending his people. More murky were the circumstances surrounding the shooting of Angel Gilberto Díaz, thirty years old. The sheriff's department said that Diaz had driven his vehicle through two barricades at a high speed. Later explaining that the car constituted a "deadly weapon," deputies shot him in the head, whereupon Diaz had lost control of the vehicle and crashed into a utility pole. He died three days later without ever regaining consciousness.[134] What most stunned Los Angelinos that day, however, was the death of Ruben Salazar.

THE AFTERMATH

After covering the march, the rally, and the riot, Ruben Salazar and some colleagues had ducked into the Silver Dollar, a bar several blocks away from the park, to grab a beer before heading back to the station to write up the day's events for broadcast. As Salazar sat on a stool at the counter, a 10-inch tear-gas projectile slammed into his head. Sheriff Deputy Thomas Wilson later explained that he had fired into the bar because the Sheriff's department had received information that a person with a gun was inside. Witnesses offered a contrary recollection. The people in the doorway of the bar said that deputies were the only people with guns that they saw. They also said that the deputies had ordered them inside the building at gunpoint. A photograph taken by Raul Ruiz, of the Chicano newspaper *La Raza,* had captured people being forced into the building (see Fig. 12). Once inside, the bar's patrons were immediately surrounded by tear gas. Guillermo Restrepo, a witness and co-worker of Salazar's, said that Salazar had just finished telling him that he would follow him out the back door. A moment later the veteran newsman was slumped over with blood coming out of his head.[135]

Salazar's death horrified and outraged many Mexican Americans. Unlike so many who were injured that day, including the two fatally wounded youths, Salazar was a respected member of the establishment. At the very least, his death suggested the disregard with which police forces regarded Mexican American lives. Relations were so strained between law enforcement and Chicano activists, and the circumstances of Salazar's death so clouded, that many ethnic group members strongly suspected that Salazar's death had been deliberate. Yet they could not prove such allegations. The search for hard evidence spurred morato-

Figure 12. Cover of *La Raza* showing Los Angeles sheriff's deputy in front of
Silver Dollar bar, August 29, 1970. The deputy's stance appears to show that
he is aiming into a crowded bar; a few minutes later, another deputy fired a
tear-gas projectile into the bar, killing journalist Ruben Salazar. His death
made the August Chicano Moratorium March not just a symbol of Mexican
American opposition to the Viet Nam War, but also a symbol of how activists
were increasingly confronting a war at home. Source: *La Raza,* September
1970. Photo by Raul Ruiz.

rium demands for a full investigation into the day's violence. In the days
and weeks after the demonstration, several organizations issued similar
appeals in the hope that an impartial inquiry would reduce community
tensions and avert further violence.

Although the moratorium committee valiantly attempted to transform this widespread outrage into effective politics, continued violence,
internal disputes, and law enforcement opposition defeated the committee's hopes for redress. Seeking to move beyond the rhetoric of anti-war
protest to the reality of exposing police abuse, moratorium leaders soon
became mired in police counteraccusations that their protest had encouraged violent dissent. Unfortunately, a second moratorium event the following month lent credence to such accusations after it, too, ended violently. Under unprecedented pressure, the committee began to splinter
over questions of tactics and leadership. Police harassment and infiltration then compounded existing divisions among Chicanos by creating an

atmosphere of suspicion and tension. Consequently, the moratorium committee became less united and its efforts more diffuse just when the organization was confronted with not only its greatest political challenge but also a challenge from police officials to its very existence.

Profoundly shaken by the violence they had witnessed, moratorium leaders did not gather themselves for a press conference until two days after the August demonstration. On August 31, however, they announced their determination to fight against police brutality. Chairman Rosalío Muñoz spoke for many stunned Mexican Americans when he asserted that it was "more than ironic" that the "one man who could get our point across through the mass media is dead." To moratorium activists, however, the death of Salazar was part of a much larger problem. According to Muñoz, moratorium activists were therefore "committing ourselves to work full-time, for all of our lives if necessary, to bring [out] the police brutality of not only this incident, but the repression of our people beginning when we were invaded in Texas back in the 1830s. We are going to expose police agencies for what they are all across this country." In addition to calling for an investigation into the "police riot," Muñoz insisted that every person arrested during the August 29 disturbance be released. Describing East Los Angeles as enduring an "armed state of siege," Muñoz further demanded a reduction in the law enforcement presence in the area. In response, the mostly Chicano crowd roared its approval.[136]

Given the extent of public outrage, several Chicano activists concluded that the moratorium coalition had emerged from the events of August 29, 1970, stronger than ever before. Speaking on a local news program two days later, for example, Rodolfo Acuña lamented the actions of sheriff's deputies but still saw a positive side to the moratorium's tragic conclusion. "The police [sheriff's] department did more for us in terms of creating awareness and radicalizing our community than we could have done in several attempts," he contended.[137] Similarly, Dolores Small, a writer for San Bernardino's *El Chicano*, believed that the Chicano movement had gained recruits and maturity after being tested in the fires of August 29. "A bond of nationalism, that last week was symbolized by the hurled slogan and raised fist," she wrote, "has taken on the added strength of spirit and will of all Chicanos, even those not involved in the Chicano movement."[138]

Leading a team to get arrested demonstrators out of jail, Irene Tovar was likewise convinced that the moratorium committee was experiencing extraordinary support. On September 1, for example, a community planning meeting called by the moratorium committee drew an enormous crowd estimated at seven hundred people.[139] As Tovar recalled, not only were moratorium meetings attracting more people than ever before, but the crowds tended to include a wider range of ages, older people as well as younger activists. Raising bail money through an organization she helped establish, the Chicano Defense Fund, Tovar also measured support for the moratorium committee in terms of cold cash. Most donations, she recalled, came in the form of one- and five-dollar bills tossed into the hat during community meetings, although one anonymous Beverly Hills matron donated $14,000. Well-known in white and black liberal circles in Los Angeles, Tovar had circulated the message that the moratorium committee needed help.[140] Another manifestation of support was the legal team of white, black, and Mexican American defense lawyers that Tovar had quickly assembled through her political contacts. The lawyers were able to meet with the arrested demonstrators and secure their release.[141] As Tovar knew first-hand, distress at the demonstration's violent outcome clearly extended beyond the ethnic group.

Indeed, blacks and whites joined Mexican Americans in calling for a federal investigation into the events of August 29, particularly the death of Salazar. Thomas Bradley, then a member of the Los Angeles City Council and later mayor of the city, was one of the first people to issue this appeal two days after the march. He joined Manuel Ruiz, Jr. a recent nominee to the U.S. Civil Rights Commission, who had been a critic of police brutality in Los Angeles since the days of the zoot-suit violence.[142] California members of Congress, Democrats and Republicans, added their voices en masse to demands for an investigation on September 11.[143] By then, several community organizations and quasi-governmental agencies were also pressing the U.S. Justice Department to take action. The list of concerned groups ranged from the Los Angeles County Human Relations Committee to the Episcopal Diocese of Los Angeles to a new organization called Anglos for Chicanos.[144] An even greater number of Mexican American groups issued a similar appeal.[145]

Via telegrams and letters, other Mexican Americans presented their case for an investigation directly to President Nixon. "The Sheriffs acted with unwarranted force and without regard for the safety of innocent bystanders and citizens who were exercising their constitutional rights by peacefully demonstrating," read a petition signed by forty workers at a local health clinic. Meanwhile, a dozen Los Angeles professionals echoed the First Amendment argument in a telegram to the White

House. They cautioned that the events of August 29, 1970, had perilously endangered "freedom of expression and constitutional ideals." With even greater vehemence, seven California activists signed a letter warning that "the Mexican-American communities throughout the nation are shocked, disgusted, and fed up" with police abuse. "We have the right to know the truth," the letter insisted.[146]

Such appeals fell on deaf ears. Although President Richard Nixon, through his spokesman, quickly expressed sorrow at Salazar's death, the administration had less sympathy for Chicano demonstrators. Indeed, National Security Council adviser Henry Kissinger, coaching Nixon for his upcoming visit with the Mexican head of state Gustavo Díaz Ordaz on September 3 in San Diego, advised that the best policy was to ignore the recent violence. Regarding Salazar's death, Kissinger wrote, "There is no reason for you to take the initiative and bring it up."[147] The Justice Department, meanwhile, was more interested in investigating Chicano activists than law enforcement officials. On September 1, Attorney General John Mitchell placed a call to the FBI inquiring "as to whether there was any substance to the allegation some persons may have traveled interstate for the purpose of inciting a riot."[148] The U.S. Attorney in Los Angeles shared these concerns with the press the next day.[149]

By then, local officials had begun a campaign to isolate and discredit the moratorium committee. Speaking on August 30 from the city of Portland, Oregon, where he was a guest speaker at a convention of the American Legion, Los Angeles Police Chief Edward Davis was nonetheless certain that a "small group of hard-core subversives" had instigated the riot. "Ten months ago, the Communist Party in California said it was giving up on the blacks to concentrate on the Mexican Americans," he opined. "One percent can infiltrate and turn any group into a mob."[150] Sam Yorty, the mayor of Los Angeles, quickly chimed in with his own condemnation of "outside agitators." "The vast majority of people thought they were marching against the war," he stated. "They were used by other people who were not against the war but against the United States."[151] In his first press conference after the violence, Sheriff Peter J. Pitchess blamed the violence on "known dissidents who came to the location to incite and foment trouble." Rogue elements, he insisted, had committed "hundreds of provocative acts" during the demonstration.[152] In each case, local police officials portrayed the Mexican American population as at the mercy of dangerous radicals.

Mexican Americans on the street were inclined to disagree. Interviewed randomly by reporters in the days after the August demonstration, several residents of East Los Angeles gave Chicano demonstrators the benefit of the doubt. "There was no reason for the cops to charge our people like that," contended a thirty-six-year-old woman who assigned blame for the violence to law enforcement. "Whenever there's a hippie love-in, they have orgies going on, smoke pot and everything else and the cops don't charge them." Similarly, a college student who witnessed the day's events on television was certain that "Chicanos didn't plan this violence. We don't take our babies to a thing of terror and violence." Although a thirty-two-year-old man shared his dismay at the property damage that resulted from the riot, he also remarked: "I don't think the people who did the damage and who organized the demonstration were the same."[153] Even owners of damaged Whittier Boulevard businesses expressed more shock than anger. Regarding the rioters, one owner of a bakery commented, "They can't be Chicanos because they wouldn't do this too me."[154] Despite the smear campaign on the part of local authorities, the general Mexican American public initially appeared to view moratorium organizers and the bulk of the demonstrators as a separate and sympathetic group apart from the young people who had rioted.

The Chicano movement scored a public relations triumph, moreover, when the *Los Angeles Times* ran a series of photographs and articles about the circumstances of Salazar's death. Prominently displayed on the front page on September 4 was Raul Ruiz's photo of sheriff's deputies aiming their tear-gas cannons at unarmed people in the doorway of the Silver Dollar Café. Other photos ran inside the paper. *Times* staffers also interviewed Ruiz, along with his *La Raza* co-editor Joe Razo, whose eyewitness accounts and photographs had appeared the day before in *La Raza* under the headline "The Murder of Ruben Salazar." In an editorial that same day, the *Los Angeles Times* noted that the Sheriff's Department had refused to answer pressing questions. Most important, the *Los Angeles Times* asked, why were 10-inch tear-gas shells, designed to flush out suspects from behind barricaded walls, fired into the bar's doorway, which was blocked only by a curtain? "The sheriff owes the people he serves a full accounting," the editorial somberly concluded.[155] The editorial's conclusion foreshadowed a complaint voiced by moratorium supporters two days later: "Once again Chicano blood has been spilled and once again we are faced with official failure to respond."[156] Stung by the newspaper's coverage, Sheriff Pitchess lamely offered that Ruiz's photographs were "misleading." He also insisted that the upcoming Salazar inquest was the only proper forum for a "full accounting."[157]

The inquest's investigation, however, was inevitably a partial one. Almost lost amid the chorus of voices clamoring for answers was the moratorium committee's contention that the proper scope of any inquiry was not just the circumstances of Salazar's death but the actions of law enforcement throughout the day of the demonstration. Yet the inquest was a more focused proceeding. With seven local television stations carrying the entire proceedings live on a rotating basis and local newspapers printing daily stories, media coverage of Salazar's death soon dwarfed any attention that was paid to the broader Chicano concerns about police brutality.[158] Repeated questions by hearing officer Norman Pittluck about illegal behavior on the part of Mexican American demonstrators further undermined the Chicano agenda.[159] To moratorium sympathizers, such questions appeared to favor the Sheriff's Department, which continued to insist that deputies had demonstrated a "proper response" in the face of "combat conditions."[160] Offended by what they considered "irrelevant" testimony, a twenty-eight-member blue-ribbon committee headed by the Congress of Mexican American Unity's Esteban Torres twice interrupted the inquest on the first day of the proceedings by walking out in protest.[161]

Meanwhile, moratorium leaders directed their organizational energies to resuming their disrupted protest agenda. Shortly after the August demonstration, they announced their determination to stage another moratorium demonstration on September 16, Mexican Independence Day.[162] The date coincided with a parade that the Comité Mexicano Cívico Patriótico, a group of local businessmen and professionals, had sponsored for the preceding thirty-five years. Members of the conservative organization initially voted overwhelmingly to cancel their event, for fear that the occasion might become violent. The moratorium committee, however, with the CMAU's strong support, successfully lobbied the businessmen to reverse their decision and coordinate a joint celebration/demonstration. The new plan called for several contingents of National Chicano Moratorium demonstrators to march as part of the parade. To Rosalío Muñoz, the merger of moratorium protest with the traditional parade was welcome evidence of "unity among all segments of the local Mexican-American community."[163]

Counterbalancing such optimism was the widespread understanding that the potential for violence was greater than ever before. In the days immediately following the August demonstration, several violent clashes and even a small riot had occurred between Mexican American youth and police officials in the greater Los Angeles area and as far away as Barstow.[164] Although not directly related to a moratorium event, they indicated pervasive tensions. Resentment was also swelling closer to home. In the aftermath of the August demonstration, Chicano activists in East Los Angeles complained that deputies had taken to stopping them "right and left." Muñoz was frisked one afternoon as he left moratorium headquarters; others were arrested and then released.[165] At *La Raza* newspaper, Raul Ruiz declared, deputies constantly questioned people going in and out of the newspaper's office.[166] In San Fernando, Irene Tovar discovered that a police helicopter circled her home every night.[167] Angry at the constant harassment, moratorium supporters nevertheless once again met with representatives of the Sheriff's Department in advance of the Independence Day parade to ensure a peaceful gathering. Agreeing to the presence of sheriff's deputies along the parade route, they also recruited dozens of Chicano parade monitors to maintain order.[168]

Although the parade was a great success, the event's conclusion underscored the inability of the moratorium committee to hold each participant to a pacifist pledge. The moratorium contingent boasted several hundred members, many of whom wore badges that read "Nonviolence—16th of September Celebration." As the moratorium contingent passed by, moreover, the crowd began to cheer loudly.[169] Estimates are that the September 16th parade drew between 100,000 and 200,000 viewers, a massive turnout compared to previous years that some observers hailed as another sign of community support for the moratorium committee.[170] At the end of the march, however, another battle scene, albeit smaller, played out. A series of taunts between police and Chicanos quickly escalated into a riot after a few rock-throwing teens began smashing plate-glass windows and damaging patrol cars.[171] Before calm was restored that evening, one hundred people had been arrested, twenty buildings had been vandalized, and sixty-seven people, the vast majority of them law officers, had received mostly minor injuries.[172] Given police accusations that moratorium protest was synonymous with law-breaking and violent dissent, the conclusion of the September march was a grave blow to the moratorium committee.

Indeed, shortly after the march, conservative Mexican Americans began to denounce the moratorium. Chicano militants were "a bunch of punk kids," according to J. William Orozco, who served on the East Los Angeles Community College Board of Trustees and was a Republican Party activist. "The truth is they don't work, they just make trouble," Orozco offered.[173] Meanwhile, a local realtor named Alex Cota formed "Concerned Citizens of East Los Angeles," whose members passed out leaflets at East Los Angeles intersections praising the heroism of local law enforcement officers.[174] Attending the Salazar inquest as a private citizen, Cota's rejection of Chicano movement analysis and criticism was on full display. Taunted by Chicano youths, Cota heatedly replied, "¡Ustedes desgraciados!" (You ingrates!).[175]

Two weeks later, the inquest, like the parade, ended badly for Chicano movement supporters. While Chicano activists had awaited a clear condemnation of what they saw as a gross injustice, inquest jurors rendered a spilt and confusing verdict. As a group, the jurors evidently believed that the Sheriff's Department had exhibited "definite negligence" and that individual deputies had failed to use "discretion or prudence." A minority of the panelists, however, also felt bound by the hearing officer's arguably flawed instructions to render a ruling that all but exonerated Deputy Thomas Wilson and his colleagues.[176] Not just Chicano activists found the inquest a disappointment. As the Los Angeles Times noted, the proceeding left several important questions unanswered—most notably the Sheriff's Department policy regarding the use of 10-inch tear-gas shells. Despite earlier assurances, Sheriff Pitchess had refused to cooperate fully with the inquest proceedings.[177]

The split verdict permanently dashed Chicano hopes for a broader investigation into police actions that day. Citing the lack of unanimity among inquest panelists, Los Angeles District Attorney Evelle Younger a few days later announced his decision not to press criminal charges against Deputy Wilson.[178] The U.S. Commission on Civil Rights also declined to take any action, apparently convinced by a staff director that an investigation by the commission merely "would plow ground already well plowed" by the inquest.[179] Nor was any investigation forthcoming from the U.S. Justice Department. Having dedicated themselves to seeking justice in the emotion-filled days after the August march, the moratorium committee by October was searching for direction.

Meanwhile, the drama of August 29 and September 16 had drawn several newcomers to the moratorium committee, who insisted that turbulent times demanded a greater display of militancy. Not coincidentally, at least one of the new arrivals was a police plant. Under these circumstances, the long-standing tension between the moratorium's policy of nonviolence and the moratorium's policy of welcoming support from all quarters began to tear the committee apart.

Several founding members of the committee were dismayed by the changes they witnessed. According to Ramsés Noriega, the moratorium endured an influx of young people who "saw everything like a big party, they didn't understand the social and political thing of what was going on." Politically naive, these "individualist Chicano anarchist type(s)," Noriega said, comprised a "volatile group."[180] Rosalío Muñoz similarly recalled how a different crowd, "young, without jobs," began making an appearance at moratorium meetings. Using the committee's office as their personal hotel, they fought with the older members about using the phone to make long-distance calls and about using drugs on the premises. More ominously, they sometimes brought guns to meetings, Muñoz recalled.[181] Bob Elias likewise remembered that suddenly "your crazies [were] coming in, real wide-eyed crazies, gun-toting crazies."[182]

Almost alone, Ralph Ramirez, one of the original Brown Berets, sympathized with the new arrivals. Although the Los Angeles Berets had organized the first moratorium march the previous December, Ramirez himself had all but stopped attending meetings before August 29. Like so many of the new arrivals, the violence of that day had captured his attention. Years later, Ramirez summoned the phrase "lumpen proletariat" to describe the street youth, or *vatos locos*, who began to call the moratorium headquarters home. His hope was to shape the incipient political stirrings of these young men toward more productive ends. But whereas Ramirez saw an opportunity that fall for "more action, more community education [and] more marches," these newcomers, he admitted, were better prepared for "hand-to-hand combat."[183]

Most of the young rowdies remain nameless, with one exception—Eustacio "Frank" Martinez.[184] Originally from Texas, Martinez appeared at moratorium headquarters after August 29. A little more than a year later, he claimed to be an informant for the LAPD and the federal Bureau of Alcohol, Tobacco and Firearms. When he first appeared at moratorium headquarters, Martinez had immediately begun a campaign against Rosalío Muñoz, accusing him of being "not militant enough, and not going all the way." In October of that year, Martinez had proved his own willingness to do battle by leading a physical assault against Democratic Congressman John Tunney, who was in East Los Angeles campaigning for a Senate seat. That November, Martinez had sauntered outside of moratorium headquarters carrying a gun, flaunting the weapon to law enforcement agents who were maintaining a near-constant surveillance of the moratorium building. Immediately, a police raid had occurred that resulted in several Chicanos being arrested and injured. Shortly afterward, in a "stacked meeting," Martinez and his allies had ousted Muñoz from his position as chair.[185]

Although the ATF never confirmed Martinez's claim, Los Angeles police chief Edward Davis boasted years later on a television news show that the department had indeed employed an agent provocateur within the moratorium committee.[186] In a story that recalled the episode of Martinez displaying a gun in front of the police, Davis told a reporter, "We had a satellite that ah . . . went about. . . . We had this orbiting satellite. That's the way, I'll put it. And when they would walk out with brass knuckles, we made all these arrests, or an illegal gun or something. We were knocking them right and left."[187]

Despite these obstacles, the original members of the moratorium committee briefly overcame their differences at the end of 1970 when David Sánchez called Rosalío Muñoz and made a plea for unity. The factions held two more protests in January 1971. To hold these marches, the moratorium committee had to overcome another bout of red-baiting and intense criticism, which by this time was being voiced not just by Anglo American law enforcement officials but by an increasing number of Mexican American community leaders.[188] Both protests ended violently. At the second one, another person died, killed by sheriff's gunfire after a concluding rally erupted yet again in violence.[189] Afterward, even the most steadfast allies of the committee were calling for a "moratorium on moratoriums."[190]

Despite the hopes of activists that out of the tragedy of August 29 would come greater unity and politicization, Chicano movement participants failed to preserve their coalition in the face of continued violence and law enforcement repression. Although police infiltration and harassment corroded the workings of the moratorium committee during the fall of 1970, the fatal blow to the original anti-war coalition had been delivered on August 29, 1970. As Irene Tovar concluded years later, in the immediate aftermath of the national march, activists had experienced their moment of "greatest support," but the tragic violence that day had also "killed the spirit of activism" among many. Never again would so many Chicano movement participants unite in protest. In Tovar's words: "We paid for what we believed."[191]

Epilogue

In 1980 veterans of the Chicano movement held a march to mark the tenth anniversary of the Chicano Moratorium. One participant took the opportunity to write a poem that, referring to one of the last hot spots of the Cold War world, warned official Washington to temper its dismay that Russian troops had invaded Afghanistan the previous year. "*Yo soy Chicano* [I am a Chicano]," he wrote, "and I'm not willing / I'm not willing to leave Aztlán for Afghanistan."[1] Five years later, another anniversary march was held which once again mingled commemoration with protest: "Peace in Central America," read one flier advertising the event, "Justice at home!"[2] Ten years later, however, an "embarrassingly low turnout" for the twentieth-fifth anniversary march provoked some critics to deem protest out of fashion and Chicano movement priorities passé. The language of dissent of the previous generation, they said, spoke neither to new immigrants nor to younger Mexican Americans.[3] Ironically, that conclusion followed on the heels of the largest demonstration of ethnic Mexicans in the history of the United States. The moratorium anniversary crowd may have been smaller than expected, but in 1994 some 70,000 people, the vast majority of them Mexican Americans or other Latinos, had turned out to march in Los Angeles to protest Proposition 187, a California initiative that would have cut all educational and welfare benefits to illegal immigrants.[4] In nearby Santa Barbara, Chicano students opposed to the same measure infused an anti-war chant from an earlier era with new meaning when they shouted during a demonstration: "Hell No! We Won't Go!"[5] As these events made clear, in the decades since the moratorium campaign people of Mexican descent still had much to say regarding both domestic and international affairs. Contrary to any suggestion of irrelevance, at the start of a new century, as the United States embarked upon new military interventions in Afghanistan and Iraq, and as domestic problems continued, the concerns that Chicano movement participants had raised about the role of ethnic Mexicans in the United States and the role of the United States in the world appeared more pressing than ever.

At the height of the Chicano movement, these concerns had been deeply intertwined. A faraway war had profoundly influenced the ethnic group's struggle for equality. Movement participants, exploring their opposition to the conflict in Viet Nam, found themselves sharpening their protest against injustices at home. Critical of U.S. intervention, Chicano movement participants reconsidered an ethnic-group tradition of pride in military service. In examining the history of the conflict, activists forged a new understanding of themselves as similarly having endured a legacy of conquest and colonization. Eager to see the war end, members of the Chicano moratorium committee also sought to inspire ethnic Mexicans toward a politics of domestic protest in the hopes of furthering equality. That perhaps as many as 30,000 people had gathered together on August 29, 1970, was one measure of their success. United in their opposition to the war, the marchers that day were likewise united in their belief that, for Chicanos and Chicanas, the true front line was not in Southeast Asia but in the "struggle for social justice in the U.S."[6]

The tragic end to the moratorium campaign, however, placed the ultimate accomplishments of Chicano anti-war activism in doubt. Born in peaceful protest, the Chicano Moratorium had ended in death and destruction. For that reason, the memory of the moratorium remained powerful but bittersweet among many who marched that day. For these participants, the tragedy of August 29, 1970, symbolized above all the repressive and brutal nature of American society, the unwillingness of the "power structure" to countenance real change. Nevertheless, the moratorium was more than a lesson in defeat, a crystallization of injustice. Through the anti-war campaign, activists had organized one of the largest gatherings of Mexican-origin people in the history of the United States. The Chicano anti-war movement thus represented a dramatic test case of the power of Chicano cultural nationalism to unite diverse groups. Although cultural nationalism also contained inherent problems, activists succeeded in furthering political awareness among Mexican Americans and among Americans in general about the country's Mexican-origin population. Finally, in organizing the moratorium effort, Mexican Americans clearly put themselves on the right side of a wrong war. Despite the anti-war campaign's painful denouement, these achievements were significant.

After August 29, 1970, the committee members struggled mightily but in vain to direct all the energy and outrage that had been generated on that day toward positive ends. The moratorium organization quickly unraveled. While organizers unanimously agreed that stopping police brutality was their new priority, they could not agree upon tactics. At a time when "there was a lot of heat, there was a lot of confusion, there was a lot of anger," Chicano anti-war activists even disagreed about whether violence was part of the problem or part of the solution to the difficulties they faced. [7] From the start, moratorium organizers had maintained a policy of peaceful nonviolence. To the credit of many, more than a dozen peaceful moratorium protests had been organized across the Southwest and beyond during the spring and summer of 1970. Even after the brutal onslaught of the deputy sheriffs at Laguna Park on August 29, 1970, the vast majority of Chicano demonstrators had simply tried to flee. The small minority who had counterattacked, however, revealed that some young people were more than ready to eschew nonviolence under certain circumstances. In the wake of the national march, especially given the heightened emotions on both sides, subsequent demonstrations became occasions for yet more violence and destruction. No matter that police officials routinely engaged in fierce repression and provocation, clashes with law enforcement always damaged the moratorium committee's reputation more. Even before another demonstrator died violently, on January 31, 1971, the Los Angeles committee had started to hemorrhage membership and support. By then a shadow of its former self, the National Chicano Moratorium Committee collapsed shortly thereafter.

For organizers of the moratorium effort, the war in Viet Nam proved tremendously useful yet ultimately limiting as a rallying cry. "The battle is here," a successful slogan, striking in its simplicity and emotional suasion before August 29, 1970, failed as an action blueprint after that fateful day. On the one hand, the brutal repression at the park that day convinced many within the movement and beyond that the "battle" was truly at home. On the other, addressing that repression plunged young movement participants into a losing contest against entrenched authorities who had at their disposal the power and legitimacy of the state.

Among protestors, rage and desperation accelerated. After the final moratorium march in the city, on January 31, 1971, one Chicano participant wrote: "The fact that the police have started a war in East Los Angeles is the reason Chicanos have united to form moratoriums and fight oppression." Calling the confrontation between law enforcement and movement demonstrators a "war," the writer continued: "When I saw two Chicanos go down from gunshot blasts I wished for some means of destroying the pigs. But I knew that I could do nothing but throw rocks and sticks to satisfy my frustration."[8] Here was a war that Chicano youth would lose.

In fact, the violence that began on August 29, 1970, stretched the analogy between the war in Southeast Asia and the Chicano struggle for social justice to its breaking point. Solidarity with Vietnamese villagers was useful for the Chicano movement because the injustices the villagers suffered were so stark, and because the mounting number of Mexican American deaths, coupled with horrific Vietnamese suffering, increasingly called into question the war's purpose and continuation for ethnic Mexicans. For the Chicano movement, the faraway nature of the conflict in Viet Nam further safeguarded the war's utility as metaphor. Chicano movement activists could identify with the Vietnamese and, by doing so, could feel reinforced in their vision of themselves as members of Aztlán. They could claim with pride that they too were a brown-skinned people, with a similar history of conquest and colonization, who were daring to confront the same powerful enemy. But neither the inspirational idea of Aztlán nor the parallels between the Mexican American struggle and events in Viet Nam could offer much guidance or protection once a confrontation was actually underway at home. Organizers of the National Chicano Moratorium Committee seemed to have learned as much when they came together for a final protest in May 1971. Several former members of the committee were among those participating in La Marcha de la Reconquista, a trek that carried them across the length of California, from Calexico to Sacramento. Notably, when the marchers entered the Los Angeles area, they walked nearly forty miles straight through the city, rather than stopping and risking an encounter with police officers or sheriff's deputies.[9] Although the march was dedicated to reconquest, and implicitly to advancing the Chicano homeland of Aztlán, most Chicano movement participants by then recognized that Aztlán was a fantasy compared to the real power of the U.S. government and local law enforcement agencies. In the City and County of Los Angeles, they had encountered matters of life and death.

Those harsh experiences help explain the trajectory of the Chicano movement after 1970. Most prominently, cultural nationalism began to lose ground to socialism. This leftward shift paralleled developments within other 1960s social movements that became more radical with the passage of time as members experienced firsthand the reach of American judicial and police power. To be certain, the Chicano movement had always shared a few members with sectarian groups, and many more movement participants had studied Marxism with interest. Thus, in 1969, the San Francisco Bay Area attendees at the Denver Youth Conference had critiqued nationalism as a "reactionary" ideology.[10] During the 1970s, however, a handful of Chicano Marxist organizations emerged. In Los Angeles, for example, the Maoist August Twenty-ninth Movement, founded in 1974, took its name, though not its membership, from the moratorium effort.[11] The following year, El Centro de Acción Social Autonóma, Hermandad General de Trabajadores (Center for Autonomous Social Action, General Brotherhood of Workers, better known by its acronym, CASA) declared itself to be a Marxist–Leninist organization. Founded as a social service agency for immigrant workers in 1969, CASA made the switch after its members became engaged in a lengthy legal battle to defend "Los Tres," three activists who were involved in the shooting of a federal agent; the young men claimed entrapment.[12] Grappling with such injustices, many movement participants broadened their analysis to consider class as well as race as a source of Chicano oppression.[13]

The conviction that class conflict offered a "correct theory" of analysis, however, did not prevent Chicano Marxists from repeating some of the same missteps as their cultural-nationalist brethren.[14] As socialists tended to place the Chicano movement even more firmly within an international context, for example, facile comparisons proliferated. "We salute the victorious struggle," read one headline that appeared in a leftist student publication after North Vietnamese troops finally triumphed. Just as the Vietnamese had won their battle for "self-determination," the paper suggested, so too would the Chicano people one day.[15] In a similar vein, as part of a battle for control of the Chicano political party, El Partido de la Raza Unida, the Crusade for Justice hosted in 1973 a rival Raza Unida National and International Conference that declared Chicano support for leftist revolutions across the globe. In the complete absence of any ties to individual revolutionaries, some conference organizers nonetheless naively hoped that a guerilla or two might attend the gathering.[16] In this case, an international emphasis did distract from local issues. The quick splintering of the Raza Unida Party at the national level, moreover, highlighted a continuing dilemma for the Chicano movement that radical left politics aggravated: the difficulty of achieving political unity.[17] Despite the shared belief that the solution was revolution not reform, Chicano Leninists and Chicano Maoists not only engaged in fierce debates for much of the 1970s but both also sparred with non-Marxist movement participants.[18]

At the heart of these ongoing evolutions and divisions within the Chicano movement were deep differences of opinion among activists wrestling with the dilemma of what to do next. Indeed, the bitter coda of the moratorium campaign only intensified that challenge. In the early, heady days of self-discovery and incipient organizing, activists had joyfully addressed the question "What is a Chicano?" After 1970, the question became much tougher: "What is the Chicano movement?" In search of direction, shortly after the final moratorium demonstration, *La Raza* newspaper in Los Angeles ran an editorial that pleaded with Chicano activists "to begin defining what we mean" by such terms as "self-determination," "local community control," and "liberation." Reflecting the crisis atmosphere in Los Angeles and the massive frustration of many movement participants, the newspaper asked: "Is the Chicano community basically interested in obtaining a piece of the pie by its protests? Is revolution really possible, and if so, what forms must it take? What do we mean by revolution? Does power really come out of the gun? Is our struggle against oppression only a Chicano struggle or is it a class struggle?"[19] Even at moments of great unity, such as the August 29, 1970, moratorium march, Chicano activists had advocated different answers. By concentrating on the more immediate task of mobilizing the Mexican-origin population, the moratorium campaign had succeeded in papering over such fissures, but only for a while.

Political differences remained, not only within the movement, but also beyond it. During the spring of 1970, for example, Chicano movement activists struggled to explain why Army Capt. Ernest L. Medina, a native of New Mexico, was facing murder charges. Medina had been the commanding officer on the ground during the My Lai massacre two years before, when American soldiers killed perhaps as many as three hundred Vietnamese civilians. For anti-war activists, accepting Medina as one of their own meant offering tortured explanations as to how the army officer's actions that day no doubt reflected a desperate attempt to win approval from a racist, oppressive society. At best, Medina was "a dupe of the establishment."[20] While this interpretation of American patriotism as pathology was in keeping with the Chicano movement's harshest condemnations of both American imperialism and racism, the Medina case also bluntly demonstrated the limits of the anti-war movement's attempt to politicize Mexican Americans against the war.[21] After August 29, 1970, at the same time that moratorium activists were raising money to bail out arrested demonstrators, Medina was visiting Los Angeles on a fundraising trip, asking fellow Mexican Americans to contribute to his defense coffers. Apparently, to those who did, he remained an embattled hero.[22]

Clarifying that cultural nationalism always promised more than it delivered in terms of ethnic unity, the Medina case furthermore exposed the resiliency of an earlier tradition that esteemed military service. Notably, when the National Chicano Moratorium Committee joined in the traditional Mexican Independence Day Parade just two weeks after the August demonstration, anti-war activists marched in a parade that included a U.S. Navy recruitment float.[23] Five years later, Mexican American mothers in Sacramento rededicated the statue they had erected in 1951 to honor their sons who had died in the Korean Conflict. While the original statue's inscription had been written in Spanish, the rededicated statue included a plaque that paid tribute in English to "American servicemen of Hispanic descent and all others who sacrificed their lives to protect the freedoms we now enjoy."[24] More than ever, the statue advertised ethnic legitimacy and belonging. The overlapping notions of military service, pride, and belonging also continued to strike a chord with the citizens of Edinburg, Texas, near the Mexican border. They repeatedly commemorated Alfredo "Freddy" C. Gonzalez, a U.S. Marine and the posthumous recipient of the Congressional Medal of Honor, who had been killed in Hue City in 1968 at the age of twenty-one. In an echo of the World War II era, Gonzalez's life became the focus of a permanent exhibition at the county museum; his name also soon adorned both a local elementary school and an American Legion post.[25]

In the early 1990s Mexican American veterans of World War II, Korea, and Viet Nam launched a broader effort to honor all Latino Congressional Medal of Honor recipients. While the style of the proposed monument, a twenty-foot-high, Aztec-like pyramid, recalled Chicano aesthetics, the sculpture to be placed at the top of the monument would display a political motif that Chicano activists had contested. Monument advocates in Los Angeles wished to see a depiction of Eugene Obregón, a Los Angeles native and Congressional Medal of Honor recipient, protecting the life of his good friend and fellow Marine, Bert M. Johnson, an Anglo Texan. As the League of United Latin American Citizens noted in its 2002 resolution supporting the continuing memorial effort, Obregón, who died at the age of twenty in Korea so that Johnson might live, "exemplifies the loyalty and brotherhood which should exist among all Americans, regardless of race or nationality."[26] According to the league's resolution, battlefield sacrifice served as a compelling example of social unity and, implicitly, equality. Despite the massive display of Chicano anti-war protest on August 29, 1970, these ideas remained popular among many Mexican Americans.

Yet if Chicano activists failed to topple tradition, they did present a dramatic alternative. Rejecting American patriotism, activists pledged their allegiance to the Chicano movement instead. Indeed, for many movement participants, cultural nationalism became a new form of patriotism, a compelling and even cathartic replacement. It clearly inspired similar sentiments of belonging and pride. Guided by this organizing philosophy, Chicanos and Chicanas openly celebrated their Mexican, and, specifically, their indigenous cultural inheritance. They demanded to know more about Mexican accomplishments throughout history. Declaring Aztlán to be their true homeland, some even boasted about their willingness to defend it. Within the movement, the imagery of Aztec warriors merged with well-known stories of Mexican American battlefield bravery to instill movement activists with a clear notion that Chicano youth were fighters ready to take on the system.

Often inspirational, Chicano cultural nationalism nevertheless could be just as problematic as American nationalism. Whenever an anti-war event became simply an opportunity to brag about the historic toughness and "machismo" of Mexican men, for example, anti-war activists were not rethinking a tradition of military service as much as uncritically appropriating it. That appropriation, moreover, often contained the disturbing assumption that ethnic Mexicans were inherently superior to Anglo Americans. While no doubt a momentarily gratifying idea to a people who had long been told they were inferior, fixed identities also undercut the possibility of progress and change. From this vantage point, the "gringo" was always going to be the enemy. The logical consequence of that assumption was evident in a series of bombings that occurred in Los Angeles starting in September 1970.[27] The following January, on the eve of the final moratorium march, a bomb exploded in the men's restroom of a federal building in Los Angeles, killing a janitor. Although the death was an accident, a group called the Chicano Liberation Front soon claimed credit and justified the violence as a blast against oppression.[28] At its worst, Chicano cultural nationalism harbored racist and destructive tendencies.

It also harbored the potential for sexual exploitation. If one of the dangers of a movement that embraced warrior imagery was the risk of fostering violent confrontation, another was the way it looked at women as commodities in the service of the revolution. Given that the violence movement participants perpetrated was a small fraction of the violence visited upon them, far more central to the experience of many movement participants was the temptation for some male activists to interpret cultural nationalism as a license for them to embrace their internal "macho" character. Bemoaning his failure to uphold the cultural-nationalist goal of ethnic group loyalty, for example, Oscar Zeta Acosta, the Chicano movement lawyer and featured speaker at the February 1970 moratorium demonstration, published a "Love letter to the Girls of Aztlán" that confused his sexual pleasure with a revolutionary agenda.[29] "I never saw a girl of Aztlán that I did not love," Acosta wrote in the summer of 1970 with apparent regret, "yet the women I fucked and those I wanted to fuck for the most part were white, lightly colored, or at least Spanish which is one hell of a note for a son of the revolution." An advocate of *la familia de la raza*, Acosta's vision was intensely biological. It depended upon Chicanas accepting his sexual overtures to keep him from procreating with "colorless broads." Yet Chicanas, by pursuing feminist ideals, were also in danger of becoming "colorless," he warned. Acosta dismissed such ideals as culturally inauthentic, precepts "copied from some white woman's notes." Casting his letter as an effort to preserve authentic Chicano "language, tradition, [and] culture," Acosta actually had little patience for the cultural value that many traditional Mexican families placed upon womanly purity and virginity before marriage. Instead, he encouraged Chicanas, for his good and the good of the revolution, to abandon the "sad idea" that "brown girls must keep their lovely legs locked."[30] Acosta was being deliberately provocative, but the logic of cultural nationalism guided his ideas.

To assume that cultural nationalism was only a collection of counterproductive tendencies, however, would be a mistake. It was much more. Despite the limitations and problems inherent in cultural nationalism, the Chicano movement was truly liberating for thousands of people of Mexican descent, half of whom were women. First, the movement's recognition that American society was rent through with profound structural inequities liberated many Mexican Americans from a shameful sense that they alone were to blame for their "backward conditions."[31] Second, the Chicano movement demanded an end to racism, both external and internal. Quick to object to contemporary manifestations of discrimination and prejudice, movement activists also addressed centuries of internalized racism. Third, the Chicano movement, and Chicano anti-war activism in particular, boldly disputed what had become a narrow and unproductive Mexican American civil rights strategy.

One accomplishment of the Chicano movement was to demand a fresh perspective from those who sought to understand the obstacles to ethnic-group progress. Before the advent of the Chicano movement, few social scientists knew anything at all about people of Mexican descent and among those who did the general agreement was that Mexican culture was the real problem. Most academicians assumed that people of Mexican descent shared a set of values and traditions that together constituted a "culture of poverty," and some specifically lamented that, despite the experience of World War II, the Mexican American population remained "an extreme example of a minimally assimilated people."[32] In contrast, Chicano movement participants viewed assimilation as the problem, not the solution. Impatient with repeated attempts to examine the supposed cultural inadequacies of the Mexican-origin population, they pointed the finger of blame at the shortcomings of American institutions. For that reason, along with a celebration of Chicano culture, the Plan de Aztlán contained a rudimentary analysis of economic exploitation as part of its understanding of the contours of Chicano liberation. Always basic to Chicano protest against the war, moreover, was a critique of fundamental structural inequities in U.S. society. Inferior schools, low-wage jobs, a lack of political representation, and even police brutality all contributed to Mexican American vulnerability to the draft, Rosalío Muñoz had insisted. Emphasizing these points, the moratorium committee had succeeded in raising political awareness, not just about the war in Viet Nam but also about the chronic social problems ethnic Mexicans faced within the United States.

This greater awareness among movement participants in general contributed to Chicano demands for relevant education. During the movement, student activists eagerly sought the development of college courses that spoke directly to their experience and the problems that ethnic Mexicans confronted. As outlined in 1969's *El Plan de Santa Bárbara*, which gave birth to MEChA, a key source of support for the moratorium effort, the movement's aspirations for higher education featured the establishment of Chicano Studies programs.[33] Often noted as one of the most-enduring legacies of the Chicano movement, Chicano Studies programs quickly appeared on most campuses of the University of California as well as those within the California State University system.[34] Elsewhere in the Southwest, campus protest spurred the founding of similar academic and outreach programs. As a result, during the decade of the 1970s, new fields, such as Chicano history, blossomed. With success came continued struggle: at the mercy of the university in terms of hiring, funding, and tenure, Chicano Studies programs often proved to have a complex relationship to their founding goals of advancing Chicano liberation through education, research, and protest.[35] Nevertheless, in 2003 the Chicana and Chicano Studies Department at the University of California at Santa Barbara announced plans to offer a doctorate in Chicano Studies, the first of its kind in the country. Enrollment in the program was to begin in 2005.[36]

Another prominent accomplishment of Chicano cultural nationalism concerned race. Quick to object to instances of Anglo-American discrimination, Chicano movement participants also addressed the problem of internalized racism. Proudly identifying with their indigenous past, and, more often than not, with the Vietnamese, they, more than any generation of Mexican Americans before them, became comfortable in public in their own skins. Although some Mexican Americans had forged political alliances with African Americans as early as the 1950s, Chicanas and Chicanos a decade later forthrightly removed themselves from the white race. In essence, they accepted majority society's frequent classification and even rejection of ethnic Mexicans as non-white but viewed this non-white categorization as a point of pride versus an obstacle to overcome. Along the way, they sometimes idealized pre-Columbian civilizations, at least as much as earlier generations had glamorized the Spanish conquistadors. Nonetheless, Chicano movement participants also broke through a central legacy of conquest: the notion of white racial superiority. While the Chicano movement focused upon the wars of 1836 and 1848, that racial hierarchy had been an integral part of Mexican culture long before then: its origins dated back to the original conquest of the Aztecs by the Spanish, begun in 1519.

Addressing internalized racism, moreover, contributed to a fundamental turn in Mexican American attitudes toward immigrants. Into the 1960s, leading Mexican American scholars and activists alike had spoken nonchalantly about the problem of the "wetback."[37] For most of the twentieth century, moreover, the recognition of common bonds of culture had competed with a real fear among Mexican Americans that new arrivals were likely to "inflame and reinforce the negative stereotypes Americans already held about Mexicans."[38] Yet, just as Chicano movement participants sympathized more with the Vietnamese fighters than with the American military, Chicano activists promoted identification with immigrants from Mexico, both documented and undocumented, over their own status as American citizens. The willingness of activists to see themselves as inhabitants of Aztlán furthered the perception that they were politically, culturally, and racially united with their cousins to the south. The slogans of CASA, the immigrants' rights group in Los Angeles, were telling of how Chicano activists sought to erase the border: "*Somos Un Pueblo Sin Fronteras*" (We Are a People Without Borders) and "*Somos Uno Porque America Es Una*" (We Are One Because America Is One). Influenced by the call for justice embedded in the Chicano movement, moreover, in the 1970s organizations like the League of Latin American Citizens and the American G.I. Forum, which had once vigorously distinguished between U.S. citizens and non-citizens, adopted a much more sympathetic outlook toward these immigrant "brothers."[39] The switch came just in time for the hundreds of thousands of new immigrants who entered the United States from south of the border during the decades of the 1960s and 1970s. The majority of these immigrants were from Mexico, although starting in the 1980s (and as a direct result of U.S foreign policy in the region), thousands of immigrants from Central America also began to enter the United States.[40] Spurred in part by the 1965 Immigration Act that permitted unlimited entry for the purpose of family reunification, the phenomenon also reflected a surge in illegal immigration in subsequent decades.[41]

As the popularity of new ideas regarding race and immigration during the 1970s suggested, the Chicano movement, particularly as exemplified by Chicano anti-war activism, challenged a long-standing tripod of citizenship that had rested upon whiteness, masculinity, and military service. While countervailing tendencies had appeared at times, the dominant trend for Mexican American civil rights activists since before World War II was to show how successfully members of their ethnic group had emulated the idealized American citizen, who was white, assimilated, and ready to serve *his* country. This strategy won some concrete victories against segregation, even as it contributed to a general self-silencing among many Mexican American political leaders about matters of U.S. foreign policy. Not willing to be silent about the war in Viet Nam, Chicano movement activists forthrightly interrogated the value of entering the armed forces, the course of U.S. foreign policy, and the cost of citizenship. Why, movement participants asked, more than a hundred years after the first Mexicans had become American citizens, did ethnic group members continue to feel the need to prove their loyalty? In what ways did the conquest of 1848 parallel the colonial experience of the Vietnamese? Why were Mexican Americans once again benefiting from equal-opportunity front lines when elsewhere discrimination remained? The result was an accelerating critical view of U.S. military operations and service among movement participants.

An emerging feminist consciousness among Chicanas played an instrumental role in the reexamination of masculinity that inevitably followed. Despite (or because of) the blatant sexism on the part of some Chicanos, women activists increasingly demanded respect as equals. Two poems captured the political and cultural shift. Amid the procession of male warriors in Corky Gonzales's well-known 1967 epic poem, *I Am Joaquin*, the only woman mentioned by name is the Catholic Virgin of Guadalupe/Aztec goddess Tonantzin. Otherwise, women appear in the poem as nameless iconic figures, twice huddled beneath black shawls. But in 1971 a poem by the Chicana feminist Ana Montes celebrated "La Nueva Chicana" who had cast off that silent and humble position. She was "a bare-headed girl fighting for equality," an "unshawled girl living for a better world."[42] Often inspired by the example set by Vietnamese women who fought against American occupation, Chicanas sought to break out of their supporting roles within the movement. Just as important, they disputed the conventional wisdom regarding men's roles. As a placard carried by one older woman marching in the February 1970 moratorium demonstration read: "*Yo Quiero Hijos, No Heroes*" (I want sons, not heroes).[43] While the safe and familiar role of mother framed the demonstrator's politics, that framing did not take away from the larger significance of her protest: Chicanas rejected the glorification of Mexican American wartime exploits, especially against the Vietnamese people. As mothers, sisters, and feminists, they recognized that meeting the cultural expectations of manly behavior on the battlefield and off had the ability to oppress Chicanos and Chicanas alike. This message, moreover, affected the broader movement. As early as 1968, a recruitment appeal for a New Mexico self-defense group called Los Comancheros challenged potential members: "Listen, you think you are so macho because you fight with your blood brother, because you get drunk, because you treat women like things." The appeal continued: "We don't need machos. We need guys with fresh blood and fresh ideas."[44]

By providing an opening that permitted new ideas about culture, about race, and even about gender roles to emerge and flourish, Chicano cultural nationalism promoted a sense of liberation among movement participants and served to heighten political awareness about ethnic Mexicans beyond the movement. Thus, even as the Chicano movement waned, mainstream politicians flirted with Chicano rhetoric, and both mainstream parties made renewed attempts to court the Mexican American vote.[45] In 1976 Democratic presidential candidate Jimmy Carter surprised many when he directly reached out to Hispanic voters in Southern-inflected but grammatically correct Spanish.[46] With less success, his opponent, President Gerald Ford, attempted to make a similar appeal by eating a tamale, still wrapped in its corn husk, at the Alamo in San Antonio.[47] While at times achingly superficial, these efforts recognized the newfound electoral clout of Mexican Americans. Indeed, aided by new provisions of the Voting Rights Act in 1970 and 1975, the registration of many new Chicano voters, for the Democratic Party mainly, was another enduring, if unintended, legacy of the Chicano movement.[48] In 1967 California did not have a single Mexican American state representative, and Texas claimed only ten.[49] In 2004 these two states, which still boasted the largest ethnic Mexican populations in the country, had twenty-five and thirty-seven Latino representatives, respectively, the vast majority of whom were Democrats.[50] Nationwide, congressional representation for Mexican Americans jumped from three to fifteen, all but one Democrats.[51] Movement protest was the start of this trend. A generation later, the size and continuing growth of the Latino population suggested it would continue.

Although the moratorium campaign ultimately failed in its larger goal of using anti-war organizing as a springboard toward building a broader-based movement for social justice, Chicano anti-war activism contributed to these accomplishments. Events at the start of the twenty-first century, moreover, confirmed the continuing relevance of the Chicano movement's critical outlook on U.S. politics and society. Domestically, stubborn problems remained, including the backlash against immigration. Internationally, after the deadly attacks on the World Trade Center in New York City on September 11, 2001, the United States embarked on a "global war on terrorism," in the words of President George W. Bush, a massive militarization that soon committed American troop in large numbers to wars in Afghanistan and then Iraq.[52] Mindful of both these trends, Rosalío Muñoz, who had chaired the 1970 Chicano anti-war committee, and Jorge Mariscal, a literature professor at the University of California at San Diego, whose own military service in Viet Nam had turned him against that conflict, drafted a Chicano anti-war cyber-petition. Its demands: "No first strike against Iraq or anywhere else! Fund peace, not war! *La Raza Humana, sí. Guerra no!*"[53] Meanwhile, the U.S. Army, facing increased manpower demands, upped its recruit-ment of Latino soldiers, particularly immigrants. Together these events revealed that, at the crossroads of domestic inequality and U.S. foreign policy, a fundamental debate continued over who was to be an American citizen, under what circumstances, and at what price.

Within the United States, equality of opportunity proved elusive. In 2002, according to the most recent census data, Mexican-origin people in particular and Latinos in general continued to lag far behind the majority U.S. population in terms of educational obtainment and in-come. A generation after Chicano movement activists decried the "push-out" rate of Mexican American youth, one 2002 estimate placed the Latino dropout rate in the state at 55.3 percent.[54] Dividing the umbrella term "Latino" into its constituent parts of Puerto Ricans, Cubans, Cen-tral and South Americans, and Mexicans further revealed that, nation-ally, the Mexican-origin population's high school graduation rate was the lowest of any Latino group, at 50.6 percent. In comparison, 88.7 per-cent of "non-Hispanic whites" over the age of twenty-five were high school graduates.[55] Low levels of educational achievement, in turn, translated into low-paying jobs. In 2002 Latinos were twice as likely as non-Hispanic whites to work in service-sector jobs or as common labor-ers. Within the Latino group, the ethnic Mexican population again con-fronted a particularly bleak situation: it had the lowest percentage of workers earning more than $35,000, just 23.6 percent, and one of the highest percentages of families living below the poverty level, 22.8 per-cent.[56] While these statistics obscured the impact of the arrival during the 1980s and 1990s of millions of immigrants from Mexico and elsewhere, a look at the native-born population alone in comparison to the general U.S. population still revealed sizeable education and income gaps.[57]

More important, the cascade of negative consequences limited oppor-tunities for immigrants and citizens alike. In 1996, an anthropologist sur-veying similar census data had summarized his findings as revealing "the distribution of sadness."[58] One unfortunate consequence of pervasive poverty and a lack of education among Latinos was a rise in deadly gang warfare beginning in the 1970s.[59] The ongoing war at home directly con-tributed to another unfortunate fact: while Latinos were invariably underrepresented on college campuses, they were too often over-represented in prisons.[60] Starting in the 1980s, moreover, advocates of immigration restriction proved eager to exploit evidence of Latino poverty and criminality. The resulting flurry of anti-Mexican and anti-immigrant sentiments they generated was another persistent sadness confronting the Latino population. Although judicial decision soon overturned Proposition 187, individual Anglo Americans were angry enough in 2003 to begin to form their own private militias in Arizona and elsewhere to patrol the U.S.–Mexican border. Linking their crusade to the Bush administration's post–September 11 efforts to improve "homeland security," militia members were open about their willingness "to defend the border in a patriotic way" against a perceived immigrant invasion.[61]

As the new century dawned, the U.S. military offered that the answer to all these problems—the lack of opportunities and, implicitly, the immigrant backlash—was armed service. In 2001, as he left his position as Secretary of the Army, Louis Caldera, the son of immigrant Mexican parents, viewed his efforts to recruit a new generation of Hispanic Americans to the military as one of the major accomplishments of his two-and-a-half-year tenure.[62] In a bilingual propaganda blitz aimed at Latinos and Latinas alike, Caldera had promoted the Army as offering unparalleled opportunity and education for Mexican-origin people. Given that doors to college campuses were open to fewer and fewer after the dismantling of most affirmative-action policies, Caldera's campaign contained a bitter irony. From the viewpoint of military recruiters, however, much work remained to be done. Unlike Africans Americans, whose percentage representation in the military was more than twice their percentage in the general population, Latinos were actually underrepresented.[63] According to Department of Defense figures, "Hispanics" (the military's term) made up 8.27 percent of all total active duty troops in 2000, whereas Hispanics were 13 percent of the total military-age population of 18–44-year-olds in the country. The same report revealed, however, that Latinos were also drastically underrepresented in the officer ranks. In 2000 only 3 percent of Latinos were commissioned officers; the rest served in the enlisted ranks, "the military's working class," according to one critic. In comparison, 14.9 percent of the total armed forces were officers.[64] No doubt the low level of education among Latinos helped explain this discrepancy. At the same time, that so many Latinos were not college-bound heightened their appeal from the military's perspective. Young people in college rarely pursued military careers.[65] In 2002 the Army renewed its outreach efforts toward Latinos. As James P. McLaurin III, deputy assistant secretary of the Army, explained while in

San Antonio to celebrate Hispanic Heritage Month, "Hispanics repre-
sent approximately 22 percent of our recruiting market."[66] The statistic
was disproportional: at the time, enlistment-age Latinos, those between
the ages of eighteen and twenty-four, made up only 15 percent of the
nation's enlistment-age population.[67]

In contrast to the anti-immigrant sentiments that flourished elsewhere, the armed forces warmly welcomed immigrants. In a deliberate
attempt to make military service an attractive option to them, immigrant recruits received a fast track to citizenship. In 1994, the same year
that Proposition 187 was on the ballot in California, a change in federal
law provided that immigrant soldiers could be eligible for citizenship
after three years of legal residency versus five years for civilians.[68] After
September 11, 2001, moreover, President Bush signed an executive
order stating that any legal immigrant on active duty could immediately
apply for citizenship.[69] Technically, military service was an option for
legal residents only. Yet, against a backdrop of anti-immigrant propos-
als, including a plan to deny citizenship to the U.S.-born children of illegal arrivals, the military's promise of inclusion and protection found a
receptive audience among immigrants in general.[70] In 2003 immigrants,
about a third of whom were from Mexico and other Latin American
countries, comprised an estimated 5 percent of the armed forces.[71]

After the United States went to war against Iraq in March 2003, the
connection between U.S. citizenship and military service grew stronger—
and more poignant. Tellingly, dozens of people a day were soon descend-
ing upon the U.S. embassy in Mexico City, under the mistaken impression that if they volunteered to fight in Iraq on behalf of the United States,
they too would be automatically eligible for citizenship.[72] These offers
revealed that many Latin Americans, eager to escape their own desperate
poverty, still viewed the United States as a land of opportunity. Yet even
as polls indicated considerable initial Latino support for the conflict, warfare also clarified the price of belonging.[73] The first casualty in the Iraqi
war was a twenty-seven-year-old Guatemalan who had entered the
United States illegally several years before, gained asylum, and joined the
Marines less than a year before he died. In recognition of his military service and death in combat, José Gutiérrez was offered citizenship posthumously. So were other immigrant soldiers in the weeks to follow.[74]

During the Chicano movement, activists had angrily questioned why
military service was one of the few opportunities for advancement for
people like Gutiérrez. That the question remained pertinent at the start
of a new century spurred an appreciation of the Chicano movement's

energetic and creative attempt to rethink the role and history of ethnic Mexicans in the United States and to restructure the conditions that limited ethnic-group progress. Rejecting those old parameters of American citizenship, the Chicano movement had invigorated the struggle for social justice among ethnic Mexicans. Determined to shake up the status quo, movement participants had crafted a new identity that interwove a profound reinterpretation of U.S. history with an incisive critique of U.S. foreign policy. At its best, in the words of Jorge Mariscal, "the term Chicano/a meant the exact opposite of blind patriotism."[75] At its best, the Chicano movement inspired many young people of Mexican descent to recognize their oppression and work toward positive change in their communities. The best impulses within Chicano cultural nationalism also propelled movement participants into a broader and more profound engagement with the world. "Because we know who we are, our nationalism becomes internationalism," Manuel Gómez had written shortly before resisting the draft.[76] For many participants within the Chicano movement, cultural nationalism was a forceful catalyst that instilled within them a hunger for social justice that indeed included all of *la raza humana.*

In 2004, many activists remained politically committed. Supporters of the moratorium effort had carved out careers as writers, professors, union leaders, social-welfare advocates, and elected officials. Some, post-*movimiento,* became political radicals, while others decided that they could exert the most influence by agitating within the system. Still others continued to explore their indigenous heritage with greater study and care. Not surprisingly, news of U.S. military interventions abroad also preoccupied anti-war activists of a generation ago. Relocated from northern New Mexico to Northern California, Elizabeth "Betita" Martínez, for example, became active in a San Francisco-based organization called Latinos Contra la Guerra. Meanwhile, Carlos Montes, a former Brown Beret who had attended the original Chicano Moratorium march in December 1969, headed a similar Los Angeles-based group called Latinos Against the War. Colorado's Ernesto Vigil likewise remained as fiercely critical of U.S. foreign policy as he had been more than three decades before when he had resisted the draft. In August 2002, he had traveled from Denver to Los Angeles to attend another combined protest/commemoration event that activists had dubbed Chicano Moratorium 2002. There, Vigil had spoken with familiarity about the likely loss of domestic liberties during wartime.[77] "These are grave times," he warned.[78] His passion for activism likewise remained; he urged those attending the conference to continue to organize—to protest U.S. military intervention abroad and to work at home to improve the lives of everyday people. For him, and others inspired by the earlier activism, "*¡Raza sí! ¡Guerra no!*" continued to resonate with purpose and meaning.

Notes

ACKNOWLEDGMENTS

1. Valerie Richardson, "Chicano Group Denied Funding," *Washington Times*, 9 May 2004, www.washingtontimes.com/national/20040509–123652–1592r.htm.

INTRODUCTION

1. Alvarez, interview.
2. Alvarez and Pitch, *Chained Eagle*, 2.
3. "Interview with Delia Alvarez, POW Sister," *La Raza* 1, no. 8 (April 1972): 37.
4. Alvarez, interview.
5. Young, *The Vietnam Wars*, 117–20; Alvarez and Pitch, *Chained Eagle*, 4–5, 23–24.
6. Alvarez, interview.
7. Ibid.
8. Ibid.; Raul Ruiz, "The POW," *La Raza* 1, no. 8 (April 1972): 30–31.
9. "Sister of Longest-Held POW Starts Protest," *Regeneración* 1, no. 10 (1971): 19.
10. Ibid.
11. Alvarez, interview.
12. Federal Bureau of Investigation, Freedom of Information Act document, Subject: "La Raza Unida," file no. 100–62747–96, "Rally against war, racism and repression, 5/20/72."
13. Alvarez, interview.

14. Rose Del Castillo Guilbault, "Brother and Sister, at War," *San Francisco Chronicle*, 24 February 1991, 4.

15. Alvarez and Pitch, *Chained Eagle*, 49.

16. For an analysis that evaluates the significance of opposing the Viet Nam War for the gay liberation movement, see Suran, "Coming Out Against the War."

17. Martin Luther King Jr.'s 1967 speech, "Beyond Vietnam," most famously captured African American concerns about the war (see "Beyond Vietnam," box 1, folder 24, Social Protest Collection). For Asian American protest, see Wei, *The Asian American Movement*, 38–41.

18. Nevertheless, the literature about the Viet Nam anti-war movement has little to say about Mexican Americans. Neither "Mexican American" nor "Chicano" appeared in the index of DeBenedetti's *An American Ordeal*. Nor did a collection of essays on the Viet Nam anti-war movement make mention of the moratorium effort, despite the authors' intentions to include oft-ignored voices, including women and G.I.s (see Small and Hoover, *Give Peace a Chance*). In contrast, Fred Halstead's 1978 book, *Out Now!*, contained a few pages on the moratorium. A top Socialist Workers' Party spokesman, Halstead was most intent on crediting the SWP for inspiring the Chicano Moratorium (*Out Now!*, 506–7). Most recently, in *The War Within*, Tom Wells devoted one sentence to the Chicano protest.

19. On black power, see Tyson, *Radio Free Dixie*; Cleaver and Katsiaficas, *Liberation, Imagination, and the Black Panther Party*; Van Deburg, *A New Day in Babylon*; and for a journalistic account, Pearson, *The Shadow of the Panther*. See also Taylor, *Vietnam and Black America*.

20. Until that time, only a Los Angeles march of Catholics on the feast day of the Virgin of Guadalupe, on December 8, 1934, had drawn a larger crowd of ethnic Mexicans. An estimated forty thousand marchers participated in a manifestation of religious sentiment encouraged by local clergy to oppose the anticlerical leanings of the post-revolutionary Mexican government (see Sánchez, *Becoming Mexican American*, 167–70).

21. Among the scholars who argue that the Chicano movement prompted a new racial identity, see Haney López, *Racism on Trial*; and San Miguel, *Brown, Not White*.

22. The pertinent literature on each topic is extensive, so the following is necessarily a partial list. On American citizenship, see Kerber, *No Constitutional Right to be Ladies*; Schudson, *The Good Citizen*; and Smith, *Civic Ideals*. On how Latinos had forged a sense of belonging, a "cultural citizenship," that extended beyond traditional political boundaries, see Flores and Benmayor, *Latino Cultural Citizenship*. On manhood, see Rotundo, *American Manhood*. Investigations of Latino and Mexican masculinity include Zinn, "Chicano Men and Masculinity,"; Mirandé, *Hombres y Machos*; and Gutmann, "A (Short) Cultural History of Mexican Machos." For an African American perspective on manhood, see Hine and Jenkins, *A Question of Manhood*. Regarding race and, specifically, whiteness, important studies include Roediger, *The Wages of Whiteness*; and Jacobson, *Whiteness of a Different Color*. Finally, for works that examine race in direct relation to ethnic Mexicans, see two works by Neil Foley,

"Becoming Hispanic" and *The White Scourge*; and Haney Lopez, *White By Law*.

23. Studies that foreground the linkages between masculinity, military service, and citizenship include O'Leary, *To Die For*; and Snyder, *Citizen-Soldiers and Manly Warriors*, the last three chapters of which address the American experience in particular. Also see Powell, *Gender and Power*, especially 135–36, 152–54; and Powell, *Masculinities*.

24. Ford, *Americans All!*; Mershon and Schlossman, *Foxholes and Color Lines*. The trend continued in 2001; see Dansby, Stewart, and Webb, *Managing Diversity in the Military*, 231–64.

25. *LULAC News*, vol. 13, no. 4 (October 1946), 17, in the LULAC Archives.

26. For the African American experience during World War II, see Buchanan, *Black Americans in World War II*; Capeci, *The Harlem Riot of 1943*; Sitkoff, "Racial Militancy and Interracial Violence in the Second World War"; Dalifume, "The 'Forgotten Years' of the Negro Revolution"; and Wynn, *The Afro-American and the Second World War*. For Native Americans, see Bernstein, *American Indians and World War II*. For World War II's contribution toward gay liberation, see D'Emilio, *Sexual Politics, Sexual Communities*; and Berube, *Coming Out Under Fire*. For the experience of women, see Hartmann, *The Home Front and Beyond*; and Gluck, *Rosie the Riveter Revisited*. Finally, for works that examine Mexican immigration at mid-century, see Scruggs, *Braceros, "Wetbacks," and the Farm Labor Problem*; and Galarza, *Merchants of Labor*.

27. Alvarez, interview; Rose Del Castillo Guilbault, "Brother and Sister, at War," *San Francisco Chronicle*, 24 February 1991, 4.

28. Genera, interview.

CHAPTER 1: "TO BE BETTER AND MORE LOYAL CITIZENS"

1. *A Medal for Benny*. Thanks to Paul Buhle for pointing me toward this film.

2. Shull and Wilt, *Hollywood War Films*, 139.

3. *Hispanics in America's Defense*, 11.

4. Ibid., 52–57. Eleven was the number of Mexican American recipients, although *Hispanics in America's Defense* tallied a total of 12 "Hispanic" recipients by including Harold Gonsalves, a Californian whose father was born in Massachusetts, evidently of Portuguese descent. Other lists include Rudolph B. Dávila, who was born in Texas of mixed Spanish–Philippine descent. Many of these lists appear on line, including, for example, one found as part of "Hispanic Online—Hispanic Heritage Plaza 2002," at http://www.hispaniconline.com/hh02/history_heritage_hisp_medal_of_honor.html, accessed 21 July 2003. Short biographies of Mexican Americans who received the Congressional Medal of Honor during World War II and the Korean Conflict comprise much of Morin, *Among the Valiant*.

5. For a case study, see García, "Americans All."

6. Perales, *Are We Good Neighbors?* 79, 217.

7. Ibid., 80.

8. Hernández Alvarez, *A Demographic Profile of the Mexican Immigration to the United States,* 477.

9. Martinez, "Mexican Immigration to the U.S.," 1.

10. Meier and Ribera, *Mexican Americans, Americans Mexicans,* 69–102; Camarillo, *Chicanos in a Changing Society*; Montejano, *Anglos and Mexicans in the Making of Texas*; Griswold del Castillo, *The Los Angeles Barrio*; De León, *The Tejano Community*; De León, *They Called Them Greasers*; Haas, *Conquests and Historical Identities in California*; and Monroy, *Thrown Among Strangers.*

11. Martinez, "Mexican Immigration to the U.S.," iv.

12. Meier and Ribera, *Mexican Americans, Americans Mexicans,* 154.

13. Balderrama and Rodríguez, *Decade of Betrayal*; Hoffman, *Unwanted Mexican Americans in the Great Depression,* 83–142; and Sánchez, *Becoming Mexican American,* 213–15.

14. Hoffman, *Unwanted Mexican Americans in the Great Depression,* 41–44.

15. Hernández Alvarez, *A Demographic Profile of the Mexican Immigration to the United States,* 477. The 2.5 million estimate is found in Gómez-Quiñones, *Chicano Politics,* 31. Other estimates are lower. In 1943 the federal Office for the Coordinator for Inter-American Affairs estimated that people of Mexican descent in the five southwestern states numbered just over two million (2.15 million), while Carlos Castañeda, a regional director for the Fair Employment Practices Commission during the war, estimated that the Southwest's population of Mexican-origin people, based on the 1940 census, was just under two million (1.89 million) (see Nash, *The American West Transformed,* 10; and Perales, *Are We Good Neighbors?* 92–93). The U.S. census historically has severely undercounted people of Mexican descent.

16. Gutiérrez, *Walls and Mirrors,* 53.

17. Orozco, "The Origins of the League of United Latin American Citizens (LULAC)," 134.

18. *Mexicans in California,* 166–67, 140.

19. Blum, *V Was for Victory,* 26–28, 205; Garcia, *Rise of the Mexican American Middle Class,* 74; García, *Mexican Americans,* 26–27; McWilliams, *North From Mexico,* 213; Meier and Ribera, *Mexican Americans, Americans Mexicans,* 158; Fuller, *The Mexican Housing Problem in Los Angeles,* 4.

20. Navarro, *The Cristal Experiment,* 20; Pycior, *LBJ and Mexican Americans,* 10–15.

21. Daniel, *Chicano Workers and the Politics of Fairness,* 72.

22. Garcia, *Rise of the Mexican American Middle Class,* 72–74.

23. As quoted in Escobar, *Race, Police, and the Making of a Political Identity,* 30.

24. Vargas, "Tejana Radical," 560.

25. Ibid., 553–80; Vargas, *Proletarians of the North*; McWilliams, *North From Mexico,* 195; Weber, *Dark Sweat, White Gold.*

26. Historians of the Mexican American experience have written extensively on LULAC, in no small part because of the organization's rich documentary record that spans from its founding to present-day activities. Secondary sources

on LULAC include Sandoval, *Our Legacy,* whose unpublished manuscript on the history of LULAC was made available from the organization. Also see Orozco, "The Origins of the League of United Latin American Citizens (LULAC)"; Márquez, *LULAC;* García, *Mexican Americans,* 25–61; and García, *Rise of the Mexican American Middle Class,* especially 250–300. For a brief but sharp critique of LULAC, see Montejano, *Anglos and Mexicans in the Making of Texas,* 232–33.

27. Weeks, "The League of United Latin-American Citizens," 264.

28. Márquez, *LULAC,* 36.

29. W. E. Leonard, "Where Both Bullets and Ballots Are Dangerous," *Survey,* 28 October 1916, 88–87, quoted in Shelton, "Political Conditions Among Texas Mexicans Along the Rio Grande," 10.

30. Skerry, *Mexican Americans,* 45; Weeks, "The League of United Latin-American Citizens," 265, 275.

31. See De León, *They Called Them Greasers,* especially chap. 5, "Disloyalty and Subversion."

32. Vargas, "Tejana Radical," 568.

33. Weeks, "The League of United Latin-American Citizens," 265.

34. Almaguer, *Racial Fault Lines,* 258. The 1930 U.S. Census was an exception in that it considered people of Mexican descent a group distinct from the "white" population. Almaguer suggested that the temporary reclassification of Mexican Americans as a separate group labeled "Mexican" in the 1930 census may have been an indication of widespread anti-Mexican sentiment. Mexican Americans returned to the white category in the 1940 census, and not until the 1980 census did the U.S. government provide a box to check for those who wished to identify themselves as being of "Spanish/Hispanic origin descent."

35. Márquez, *LULAC,* 31–32. See also García, "Mexican Americans and the Politics of Citizenship."

36. Foley, *The White Scourge,* 62.

37. Edward A. Gutierrez, "Darkness Lifts to the Dawn," *LULAC* News (April 1939), 12, quoted in Fincher, *Spanish Americans as a Political Factor in New Mexico,* 94.

38. Orozco, "Alice Dickerson Montemayor," 436.

39. Garcia, *Rise of the Mexican American Middle Class,* 255.

40. Christian, "Joining the American Mainstream," 594.

41. Sáenz, *Los méxico-americanos en la gran guerra.*

42. Orozco, "The Origins of the League of United Latin American Citizens (LULAC)," 127.

43. O'Leary, *To Die For,* 8.

44. Weeks, "The League of United Latin-American Citizens," 259.

45. As quoted in Muñoz, *Youth, Identity, and Power,* 32.

46. Mexican American Movement Handbook, n. d., by The Supreme Council of the Mexican American Movement, in box 1, folder 16, Mexican American Movement Collection.

47. Muñoz, *Youth, Identity, and Power,* 33. For more on MAM, see Sánchez, *Becoming Mexican American,* 254–58.

48. Sánchez, *Becoming Mexican American,* 248–49.

49. García, *Mexican Americans,* 161.

50. Both letters are in box 93, folder 1, of the Dennis Chavez Collection.

51. For more on Chavez, see Lujan, "Dennis Chavez and the Roosevelt Era"; and Gómez and Coy, *Chavez, El Senador.*

52. Takaki, *Double Victory.*

53. McWilliams, *North From Mexico,* 27–276.

54. Gluck, *Rosie the Riveter Revisited,* especially chaps. 4 and 9; Garcia, *Rise of the Mexican American Middle Class,* 302.

55. Muñoz, *Youth, Identity, Power,* 57.

56. White, "What the Negro Thinks of the Army," 71.

57. *Spanish Speaking Americans in the War.*

58. Ralph C. Guzman's experience serving in the U.S. Navy, for example, was negative (see Levy, *Cesar Chavez,* 84).

59. Tuck, *Not with the Fist,* 221.

60. Ibid., 226.

61. Kibbe, *Latin Americans in Texas,* 227.

62. *Spanish Speaking Americans in the War.*

63. Griffith, *American Me,* 265.

64. *Spanish Speaking Americans in the War.*

65. Quotation from a veteran is in *The Men of Company E.*

66. *Hispanics in America's Defense,* 52–57.

67. Griffith, *American Me,* 264. See also Kibbe, *Latin Americans in Texas,* 223; García, *Mexican Americans,* 209; Perales, *Are We Good Neighbors?* 90; and McWilliams, *North From Mexico,* 260.

68. Kibbe, *Latin Americans in Texas,* xix; Burma, *Spanish-Speaking Groups in the United States,* 30; Morin, *Among the Valiant,* 34–35.

69. Burma, *Spanish-Speaking Groups in the United States,* 30.

70. The U.S. Department of Defense estimates that between 250,000 and 500,000 Hispanics participated in the conflict, and so comprised from 2 to 5 percent of all troops. As used by the Defense Department, "Hispanics" is a term that includes Puerto Ricans and other Latinos, but during World War II it predominantly meant Mexican Americans. (The Department of Defense knows that 53,000 Puerto Ricans served.) In 1940 Mexican Americans probably accounted for no more than 2 percent of the total U.S. population. According to the 1940 U.S. census, the total U.S. population was just over 132 million, while an estimate by Gómez-Quiñones puts the total U.S. Mexican-origin population at 2.5 million. Determining the number of Mexican Americans in the United States during World War II with more precision is difficult, given the unreliable nature of census data (see note 7). Although contemporaries (and scholars, subsequently) have suggested disproportionate rates of service for the ethnic group, such was the case only if Mexican Americans served in numbers beyond the lower-end quarter-million estimate or if the total population of Mexican-origin people in the United States was well under 2.5 million (see *Hispanics in America's Defense,* 27; Gómez-Quiñones, *Chicano Politics,* 31).

71. Broyles-González, *El Teatro Campesino,* 36–40.

72. Humberto González, "I remember . . .", *The Mexican American,* July 1972, 2.

73. Morin, *Among the Valiant*, 51.

74. George Mariscal mentioned Hero Street briefly in *Aztlán and Viet Nam*, 28. The best source for information on the street is The Street of Heroes website, http://www.herostreetusa.org, where a series of newspaper articles has been collected (accessed on 12 July 2001).

75. Mariscal, *Aztlán and Viet Nam*, 27.

76. This quotation is from an interview with Herrera that appeared in the *Pueblo (Colorado) Chieftan* in June 1995. It is available at http://www.homeofheroes.com/profiles/profiles_herrera.html (accessed 18 December 2002).

77. Burma, *Spanish-Speaking Groups in the United States*, 259.

78. Humberto González, "I remember . . .", *The Mexican American*, July 1972, 2.

79. Blum, *V was for Victory*, 198.

80. Garcia, *Rise of the Mexican American Middle Class*, 302.

81. The FEPC's lackluster record regarding ethnic Mexicans, in particular, is the subject of Cletus E. Daniel's *Chicano Workers and the Politics of Fairness*.

82. Meier and Ribera, *Mexican Americans, Americans Mexicans*, 167.

83. Santillan, "Rosita the Riveter," 138.

84. Ibid., 137.

85. "Latin American Juvenile Delinquency in Los Angeles, Bomb or Bust?" box 15, folder 10, Manuel Ruiz Papers.

86. The 1943 riots are well covered in Escobar, *Race, Police, and the Making of a Political Identity*, 233–43. See also Mazón, *The Zoot-Suit Riots*; McWilliams, *North From Mexico*, 244–53; Nash, *The American West Transformed*, 110–20; and Adler, "The 1943 Zoot-Suit Riots," 142–58.

87. Morin, *Among the Valiant*, 56.

88. Adler, "The 1943 Zoot-Suit Riots," 155.

89. Minutes of CCLAY meeting, 3 August 1942, box 3, folder 7, Ruiz Papers.

90. Escobar, *Race, Police, and the Making of a Political Identity*, 265.

91. Telegram, Hector E. Valdez to J. T. Canales, 21 May 1943, box 67, folder marked "Correspondence, J. T. Canales, 1942–1943," Sanchez Papers.

92. Letter, Leocardio Duran to Governor Coke Stevenson, 16 October 1943, box 67, folder marked "Correspondence, ACLU, 1942–1943," Sanchez Papers.

93. Mariscal, *Aztlán and Viet Nam*, 29. As Mariscal noted, to his father's great dismay, Douglas Herrera refused to serve in Viet Nam.

94. Letter, John J. Herrera to Manuel C. Gonzales, 16 September 1943, box 67, folder marked "Correspondence, ACLU, 1942–1943," Sanchez Papers.

95. Telegram, Hector E. Valdez to J. T. Canales, 21 May 1943; and letter, Leocardio Duran to Governor Coke Stevenson, 16 October 1943; both in box 67, folder marked "Correspondence, J. T. Canales, 1942–1943," Sanchez Papers.

96. Letter, J. T. Canales to George I. Sanchez, 22 May 1943, box 67, folder marked "Correspondence, J. T. Canales, 1942–1943," Sanchez Papers.

97. "Bomb or Bust?" Ruiz Papers.

98. Kibbe, *Latin Americans in Texas*, 121, 208.

99. Foley, *The White Scourge*, 206–7. Mexico did not allow braceros to enter Texas under the original contract-worker program, which expired in 1947 (see Craig, *The Bracero Program*, 51).

100. Marin, "Mexican Americans on the Home Front," 79.

101. Letter, M. C. Gonzales to George I. Sanchez, 20 October 1943, box 67, folder marked "Correspondence, ACLU, 1942–1943," Sanchez Papers.

102. Letter, M. R. González to M. C. Gonzales, 15 October 1943, box 67, folder marked "Correspondence, ACLU, 1942–1943," Sanchez Papers.

103. Blum, *V Was for Victory*, 198.

104. "Fair Employment Practice: A Cornerstone to Foreign Policy," address delivered by Senator Dennis Chavez, 19 June 1945, box 78, folder 28, Chavez Collection.

105. Perales, *Are We Good Neighbors?* 137–38.

106. Kibbe, *Latin Americans in Texas*, 1–6.

107. *LULAC* News, July 1945, 6.

108. Perales, *Are We Good Neighbors?* 130–31.

109. Griffith, *American Me*, 265; *Hispanics in America's Defense*, 54.

110. Perales, *Are We Good Neighbors?* 156–57.

111. Griffith, *American Me*, 266.

112. Perales, *Are We Good Neighbors?* 250–51, 253, 257.

113. Allsup, *The American G.I. Forum*, 41. See also, Carroll, *Felix Longoria's Wake*. The most recent biography on the American G.I. Forum's founder is García, *Hector P. García*.

114. Allsup, *The American G.I. Forum*, 41.

115. Gutiérrez-Jones, *Rethinking the Borderlands*, 157. The limits of Johnson's willingness to back the Longoria family is the subject of Robert Caro's "The Compassion of Lyndon Johnson," *The New Yorker*, 12 April 2002, 56–77.

116. Allsup, *The American G.I. Forum*, 98.

117. San Miguel, *"Let Them All Take Heed,"* 116.

118. Letter, Hector P. Garcia to Major Hugh B. Taylor, 3 November 1948, box 143, folder 48, Garcia Collection.

119. Ramos, *A People Forgotten, A Dream Pursued*, 7.

120. The popularity of queen contests is documented in the Forum publications *The Forum News Bulletin* and *The Forumeer*.

121. See, e.g., *LULAC* News, October 1945, 5; and June 1947, 15; García, *Mexican Americans*, 49.

122. For Ochoa, see Foley, "Becoming Hispanic," 63; for cooperation between LULAC and the NAACP, see Allsup, *The American G.I. Forum*, 67.

123. García, *Mexican Americans*, 56–58.

124. Ibid., 49–51. Convicted in a second trial, Hernández's sentence was reduced to twenty years in prison.

125. Tuck, *Not with the Fist*, 221.

126. Gómez-Quiñones, *Chicano Politics*, 44–48.

127. For an analysis that traces how Mexican American women used their traditional roles as a springboard to broader activism within the Community Service Organization, see Rose, "Gender and Civic Activism in Mexican American Barrios," 177–200. Although Rose argued for a greater appreciation of women's participation, she also noted that "while wives were often out of the public eye, many men in the organization enjoyed positions of visibility and recognition in the community" (181).

128. Garcia, *A World of Its Own*, 237–40.

129. Gilbert, *Another Chance*, 87; Rosenberg and Rosenberg, *In Our Times*, 33.

130. Dallek, *Lone Star Rising*, 316.

131. Burma, *Spanish-Speaking Groups in the United States*, 107; Gómez-Quiñones, *Chicano Politics*, 42.

132. Briegel, "Alianza Hispano-Americana and Some Mexican-American Civil Rights Cases in the 1950s," 180. In 1963 the Texas town of Kennedy closed its municipal pool rather than allow Mexican Americans to use it (see García, *Viva Kennedy!*, 50).

133. Cashman, *African Americans and the Quest for Civil Rights*, 124–30.

134. Ulibarrí, *Mayhem Was Our Business*, 31.

135. Garcia, *Rise of the Mexican American Middle Class*, 313.

136. Thomas S. Sutherland, "Texas Tackles the Race Problem," *Saturday Evening Post*, 12 January 1952.

137. Martínez, *Mexican-Origin People in the United States*, 37.

138. For more about this deportation campaign, see García, *Operation Wetback*.

139. García was born in Villa Costaño, Coahuila, Mexico (Morin, *Among the Valiant*, 144). Morin mistakenly wrote that Herrera was born in El Paso, Texas, but Herrera emigrated from the town of Carmago in the state of Chihuahua with his uncle when he was an infant (see Silvestre Herrera, Medal of Honor, http://www.homeofheroes.com/profiles/profiles_herrera.html [accessed 18 December 2002]).

140. Gutiérrez, *Walls and Mirrors*, 162.

141. Ibid., 164.

142. Allsup, *The American G.I. Forum*, 51.

143. Ibid., 55.

144. *LULAC News*, October 1953, 9.

145. The statue, with its original dedication, can be seen in Sacramento on Tenth Street across from the State Capitol. I would like to thank Lucy G. Barber for pointing out the statue to me.

146. For more about Hero Street, see the Hero Street website, http://www.herostreetusa.org (accessed 12 July 2001). For a tally of Korean-era Mexican American Medal of Honor recipients, see Morin, *Among the Valiant*, 260–76.

147. Gutiérrez, "Chicanos and Mexicanos Under Surveillance," 33–38, 43–44.

148. García, *Mexican Americans*, 201, 210, 213–14, 218–19.

149. *Forum News Bulletin*, August 1953, 8, among the unprocessed papers in the Garcia Collection.

150. Márquez, *LULAC*, 62.

151. *Giant*.

152. Gutiérrez-Jones, *Rethinking the Borderlands*, 75.

153. Allsup, *The American G.I. Forum*, 99.

154. The American G.I. Forum's response to the Daughters of the American Revolution captured members' readiness to defend Mexican Americans from

discrimination (see Allsup, *The American G.I. Forum*, 99); regarding optimism among members of the League of United Latin American Citizens, see Márquez, *LULAC*, 57.

CHAPTER 2: "NEW WIND FROM THE SOUTHWEST"

1. Moore and Guzman, "New Wind from the Southwest," 645–46.
2. Ibid., 647.
3. This analysis inevitably builds upon the historical interpretations of several historians who have examined the Mexican American experience from a generational perspective, most prominently Mario T. García, who described the politics of what he termed the Mexican American generation in his book, *Mexican Americans: Leadership, Ideology and Identity, 1930–1960*. García also distinguished the "Mexican American generation" from a preceding "Immigrant generation" and succeeding "Chicano generation," in "La Frontera: The Border as Symbol and Reality in Mexican American Thought." Yet, whereas García, for example, portrayed 1960 as a clear dividing line between two political generations, this chapter, by looking at how the ethnic group responded to the Viet Nam War, reveals that tensions occurred not only between Chicano movement organizers and leaders of more established Mexican American organizations but also within individual Mexican American and Chicano groups during the decade of the 1960s.
4. Caro, *The Years of Lyndon Johnson*, 168–69; Dallek, *Lone Star Rising*, 80.
5. "Remarks of LBJ at the Swearing-In Ceremony of Vicente T. Ximenes," 9 June 1967, Fred Panzer Aide File, box 382, White House Central Files [hereafter WHCF], LBJ Library; Speech of the President at El Paso, 28 October 1967, Executive HU2, box 7, WHCF, LBJ Library; "LULAC week proclaimed by LBJ," box 11, Scrapbook 11.1, Garcia Collection.
6. Dallek, *Lone Star Rising*, 369.
7. Johnson, Introduction, 7.
8. Grebler, Moore, and Guzman, *The Mexican-American People*, 18–19, 143–44, 181, 197–98, 249–52.
9. Pycior, *LBJ and Mexican Americans*, 155–56.
10. *Carta Editorial*, 3 July 1963, 7. Issues of *Carta Editorial* can be found on microfilm in the Chicano Studies Library, University of California, Berkeley.
11. *Carta Editorial*, 5 April 1965, 5. In another expression of support, in 1960 the national convention of the American G.I. Forum passed a resolution in support of the sit-ins conducted by civil rights workers opposing segregation in the South (García, *Viva Kennedy!*, 45–46.
12. Matusow, *The Unraveling of America*, 361; Farber, *The Age of Great Dreams*, 111.
13. Pycior, *LBJ and Mexican Americans*, 163.
14. Van Deburg, *A New Day in Babylon*, 4.
15. Grebler, Moore, Guzman, *The Mexican-American People*, 7. Edward. J Escobar made a similar point in Edward J. Escobar, "The Dialectics of Repres-

sion: The Los Angeles Police Department and the Chicano Movement, 1968–1971" *Journal of American History* 79 (March 1993): 1490.

16. As quoted in Pycior, *LBJ and Mexican Americans*, 163.

17. Grebler, Moore, and Guzman, *The Mexican-American People*, 15. For a general discussion of minority voting rights, see Thernstrom, *Whose Votes Count?*

18. Quezada, *Border Boss*, 13–14; Navarro, *The Cristal Experiment*, 29; Skerry, *Mexican Americans*, 45; Foley, *From Peones to Politicos*, 17–24, 91–95, 99–102.

19. Grebler, Moore, and Guzman, *The Mexican-American People*, 115.

20. Santillan, "Third Party Politics," 150; Regalado, "Latino Empowerment in Los Angeles," 94.

21. Steven J. Roberts, "Mexican-American Hostility Deepens in Tense East Los Angeles," *New York Times*, 4 September 1970, 20.

22. Grebler, Moore, Guzman, *The Mexican-American People*, 561.

23. Moore, *Mexican Americans,* 52. The 12 percent figure is from the 1960 census; the 15 percent is from the 1970 census.

24. Grebler, Moore, Guzman, *The Mexican-American People*, 566; Gómez-Quiñones, *Chicano Politics*, 15.

25. *Carta Editorial*, 12 October 1965, 4–5.

26. Ibid. In fact, the only California outpost of the Russians, Fort Ross, was established well north of the Republic of Mexico in 1812 and abandoned as unprofitable in 1839.

27. *Carta Editorial*, 8 April 1966, 1.

28. *Carta Editorial*, 26 May 1967, 2.

29. Pycior, *LBJ and Mexican Americans*, 170.

30. Telegram, David S. North to Hector P. Garcia, 11 October 1967, box 100, folder 58, Garcia Collection. About raising expectations, also see Pycior, *LBJ and Mexican Americans*, 166, 169, 170.

31. Remarks of the President at the Swearing-In Ceremony for Vicente T. Ximenes; and Memo, President to Cabinet Members and Vicente T. Ximenes, 9 June 1967, Executive FG 687, box 386, WHCF, LBJ Library.

32. Memo, Vicente T. Ximenes to the President, 7 March 1968, Executive HU2, box 7, WHCF, LBJ Library.

33. Most notably, in 1967 LULAC and the American G.I. Forum were named the organizational heads of a $5 million poverty program called Project SER (Service, Employment, and Redevelopment; in Spanish, *ser* means "to be"). In early 1968 Johnson declared a "LULAC Week" to honor "a group of patriotic, devoted Americans who, for 39 years, have taken an active concern in the well-being and the future of . . . Spanish-speaking Americans." That same year, Johnson appointed the Forum's founder to be a member of the U.S. delegation to the United Nations and to be the first Spanish-surnamed member of the United States Civil Rights Commission (see "LULAC week proclaimed by LBJ," box 11, Scrapbook 11.1; and "Dr. Garcia appointed to Civil Rights Commission," box 10, Scrapbook 12.1, both in Garcia Collection; and Allsup, *The American G.I. Forum*, 140–41.

34. Memo, Chris Aldrete, Special Assistant to the Chairman of the Democratic National Committee, Hispanic Political Affairs, to John Criswell, 8 August 1967, Executive HU2, WHCF, LBJ Library. Aldrete was also a member of the League of United Latin American Citizens and the American G.I. Forum.

35. Memo, Joe Califano Jr. to the President, 28 December 1969, Executive HU2/MC, box 23, WHCF, LBJ Library. The president's reply, dated 31 December 1966, is on a yellow slip of paper stapled to the memo.

36. Memo, John W. Gardner to the President, 11 February 1967, Executive HU2/MC, box 23, WHCF, LBJ Library.

37. Memo, Harry McPherson to the President, 17 February 1967, Harry McPherson Aide File, WHCF, LBJ Library. See also a letter dated 4 October 1967 and written by Dr. George I. Sanchez to White House aide David S. North refusing his invitation to come to El Paso. Sanchez called the gathering in El Paso a "consolation prize" that had been offered instead of a White House conference "planned and staffed by Mexican Americans" (box 21, folder marked "Joint Conference on Mexican Americans, 1967–1968," Sanchez Papers.

38. Yellow slip of paper stapled to Memo, McPherson to President, 17 February 1967, WHCF, LBJ Library.

39. Memo, Joe Califano to the President, 13 February 1967, Executive HU2/MC, box 23, WHCF, LBJ Library.

40. *The Forumeer*, November 1967, 2. Issues of *The Forumeer* can be found on microfilm in the Chicano Studies Library, University of California, Berkeley.

41. Texas Inter-Agency Committee on Mexican American Affairs, *The Mexican Americans*, 240.

42. Muñoz, *Youth, Identity, Power*, 176.43. *The Forumeer*, November 1967, 3.

44. Unger, *Best of Intentions*, 50, 66, 311–12.

45. Matusow, *The Unraveling of America*, 251; Fairclough, "Martin Luther King, Jr. and the War in Vietnam," 27.

46. García, *Memories of Chicano History*, 226.

47. *El Paso Times*, 27 October 1967, 1-A.

48. "Beyond Vietnam," speech given by Martin Luther King Jr. at Riverside Church, New York City, 4 April 1967, box 1, folder 24, Social Protest Collection.

49. *El Paso Times*, 28 October 1967, 3-A.

50. *El Paso Times*, 29 October 1967, 5-E.

51. Memo, Vicente T. Ximenes to Marvin Watson, 5 February 1968, Executive FG 687, box 386, WHCF, LBJ Library.

52. Vigil, interview. Vigil's letter was printed in full in *El Gallo*, 10 May 1968, 2. The Chicano Studies Library at the University of California, Berkeley has *El Gallo* on microfilm.

53. Genaro Garcia, interview.

54. Herring, *America's Longest War*, 10.

55. LaFeber, *The American Age*, 520.

56. Young, *The Vietnam Wars*, 82.

57. Berman, *Planning a Tragedy*, 8–9.

58. Young, *The Vietnam Wars*, 160. The decision of the Johnson administration to increase American troop involvement is the focus of Logevall, *Choosing War*.

59. For LBJ's doubts, see Beschloss, *Reaching for Glory*, 194, 213, 216, 353, 365, 378–80, 382.

60. Young, *The Vietnam Wars*, 230.

61. The anti-war movement is addressed in DeBenedetti, *An American Ordeal*; Wells, *The War Within*; and Heineman, *Campus Wars*.

62. Gómez-Quiñones, *Chicano Politics*, 45. To reduce suspicion, organizations as different as the American G.I. Forum and the Alianza Federal de Mercedes, which fought for land in New Mexico under the leadership of Reies López Tijerina, included a clause in their founding documents denying membership to communists (see Allsup, *The American G.I. Forum*, 51; and Gardner, *¡Grito!* 96).

63. "Remarks by the Honorable Joseph M. Montoya before the Western Regional Conference of the Young Democrats," 4 September 1965, box 37, folder 39; "Strong in Conflict—Steadfast through Ordeal," speech presented to the Veterans of Foreign Wars, 24 June 1967, box 38, folder 37; both in Montoya Papers.

64. *La Luz*, September 1976, 20.

65. *La Opinión*, 1 January 1965, 6; 29 June 1965, 6. For additional editorials in support of Johnson's early Viet Nam policy, see the editorials for 9 February, 25 April, 3 June, 12 August, and 29 July 1965. All editorials are on page 6.

66. Márquez, *LULAC*, 68.

67. Letter, Hector P. Garcia to the President, 6 April 1967, Vicente T. Ximenes Name File, box X-1, WHCF, LBJ Library.

68. *Carta Editorial*, 23 November 1965, 3.

69. Newspaper clippings from the *San Antonio Express News*, 2 July 1966 and the *Corpus Christi Caller*, 3 July 1966, box 8, Scrapbook 8.3, Garcia Collection.

70. See, e.g., a list dated 11 October 1969 tallying the Laredo war dead, in box 64, folder 48, Garcia Collection. Dr. Garcia himself also collected newspaper articles with the names of war dead. In 1969, Octavio I. Romano V., the University of California at Berkeley anthropologist, compiled a list of Spanish-surnamed war dead, which appeared on the pages of the journal *El Grito* that fall.

71. Pycior, *LBJ and Mexican Americans*, 192.

72. Letter, Vicente T. Ximenes to Robert S. McNamara, 12 July 1967, Vicente T. Ximenes Name File, box X-1, WHCF, LBJ Library.

73. Letter, Hector P. Garcia to the Armed Forces Professional Division, 9 August 1967, box 51, folder 64; telegram, Hector P. Garcia to Lyndon B. Johnson, 2 January 1968, box 100, folder 58; clipping from *Corpus Christi Caller*, 20 January 1968, box 51, folder 64; all in Garcia Collection.

74. Letter, S. B. Sanchez to Robert R. Sanchez, 27 December 1967, box 86, folder 47, Garcia Collection. The letter does not indicate S. B. Sanchez's rank.

75. Letter, Pat Vasquez Jr. to his father, 30 April 1967, box 53, folder 49, Garcia Collection.

76. Letter, Mario R. Vasquez to Lyndon B. Johnson, 26 July 1967, box 53, folder 49, Garcia Collection.

77. *La Opinión,* 22 April 1967, 6; and 5 November 1967, sec. 2, p. 2.

78. *La Opinión,* 24 June 1967, 1.

79. Marcia Miranda-Arrizón's 1998 Master's thesis, "Building Herman (a)dad," is the best source on Francisca Flores's life.

80. *Carta Editorial,* 23 November 1965, 3.

81. *Carta Editorial,* 10 August 1965, 1.

82. García, *Memories of Chicano History,* 274.

83. *Congressional Quarterly Almanac* 23 (90th Cong., 1st sess., 1967): 944.

84. *El Malcriado,* 12 April 1967, 24.

85. Guzman's findings were published in *La Raza Yearbook 1968,* 33, but were circulated among Mexican American and Chicano activists before then. Additional casualty information, from December 1967 to March 1969, echoed Guzman's original findings. The supplemental report was printed in *La Raza 1969,* 12–16. A copy of Guzman's finding, with accompanying data, can be found in box 2, folder 38, Social Protest Collection. In 1989 two geographers, Brady Foust of the University of Wisconsin–Eau Claire and Howard Botts of the University of Wisconsin–Whitewater, looked at Spanish-surnamed casualties during the Viet Nam War across the country. They also discovered that casualties were disproportionate, but to a much lesser degree. Whereas Guzman looked specifically at Spanish-surnamed casualties from the five southwestern states, where the Spanish-surnamed population constituted 11.8 percent of the population in 1960, Foust and Botts looked at Hispanic casualties nationwide at a time when the 1970 census estimated the Hispanic population to be 4.6 percent of the total U.S. population. Relying upon the U.S. Census Bureau's Spanish Surname List, in no year did they estimate that Hispanic casualties nationwide ever comprised more than 6 percent of the total war casualties. Yet Foust and Botts also stated, "Given the undercount produced by the Spanish surname data file, the percentage contribution of Hispanics to total casualties is certainly much higher" (Foust and Botts, "Age, Ethnicity, and Class in the Vietnam War").

86. Guzman, *La Raza Yearbook 1968,* 33.

87. Appy, *Working-Class War,* 35.

88. Letter, Hector P. Garcia to Colonel Morris Schwartz, 12 November 1966, box 129, folder 61, Garcia Collection.

89. Draft of a letter from Hector P. Garcia to Lyndon Johnson, no date but written sometime after 9 January 1968, box 129, folder 61, Garcia Collection. See also letter, Lewis B. Hershey, Director of the Selective Service, to Vicente T. Ximenes, Chairman of the Inter-Agency Committee on Mexican American Affairs, 20 February 1968; and letter, Hector P. Garcia to Colonel Morris Schwartz, 9 July 1967, in the same folder.

90. *People's World,* 30 March 1968, 3.

91. Draft of a letter from Garcia to Lyndon Johnson, no date but written sometime after 9 January 1968, box 129, folder 61, Garcia Collection.

92. Message, Larry Levinson to the President, 9 September 1967, Confidential FG 282, box 33, WHCF, LBJ Library.

93. Appy, *Working-Class War,* 25, 37.

94. Grebler, Moore, and Guzman, *The Mexican-American People*, 117; U.S. Commission on Civil Rights, California Advisory Committee, *Education and the Mexican American Community in Los Angeles County*, 4; Galarza, Gallegos, and Samora, *Mexican-Americans in the Southwest*, 46.

95. Appy, *Working-Class War*, 32–33.

96. *El Malcriado*, 12 April 1967, 24.

97. Members of the Alianza claimed that the district attorney had broken the law by improperly arresting them when he charged them with trespassing on federal forest land and, while there, causing a nuisance. On October 22, 1966, Tijerina and other members had camped out at the Echo Amphitheater in the Kit Carson National Forest and held a mock trial for two forest rangers who tried to remove them. (Acuña, *Occupied America*, 3rd ed., 340; Nabokov, *Tijerina and the Courthouse Raid*, 33; Gardner, *¡Grito!* 30–84).

98. Clark Knowlton, "The New Mexican Land War," *The Nation*, 17 June 1968, 793. Knowlton, a sociologist, wrote several articles on the Alianza, including "Violence in New Mexico: A Sociological Perspective" and "Reies L. Tijerina and the Alianza Federal de Mercedes: Seekers after Justice."

99. Gardner, *¡Grito!* 17.

100. Nabokov, *Tijerina and the Courthouse Raid*, 18.

101. Gardner, *¡Grito!*, 141.

102. Recent works on the Chicano movement include García, *Chicanismo*; and Chávez, *"¡Mi Raza Primero!"* For Southern California, see also the focus of Marin, *Social Protest in an Urban Barrio*; Gómez-Quiñones, *Mexican Students por la Raza*; Rosen, *Political Ideology and the Chicano Movement*; and Santillan, *La Raza Unida*. Overviews of the Chicano movement include Muñoz, *Youth, Identity and Power*; and Gómez-Quiñones, *Chicano Politics*, especially chap. 2, entitled "Liberalism: The Chicano Movement." Chicanas are the focus of Bernal, "Chicana School Resistance and Grassroots Leadership"; and Espinoza, "Pedagogies of Nationalism and Gender." For more about Chicano third-party politics, see García, *United We Win*; and Navarro, *The Cristal Experiment*. The predecessor organization to La Raza Unida Party in Texas is the focus of Navarro, *Mexican American Youth Organization*. Finally, recent memoirs by Chicano movement participants include Gutiérrez, *The Making of a Chicano Militant*; and Treviño, *Eyewitness*.

103. See a similar point in "The Little Strike that Grew into La Causa," *Time*, 4 July 1969, 16–21.

104. *La Causa*, 15 December 1969, 5.

105. Grebler, Moore, and Guzman, *The Mexican-American People*, 16.

106. Muñoz, *Youth, Identity, Power*, 3.

107. Navarro, *Mexican American Youth Organization*, 115.

108. The title of José Angel Gutiérrez's 1968 Master's thesis is "La Raza and Revolution: The Empirical Conditions of Revolution in Four South Texas Counties." A founding member of MAYO, he received his Master's degree from St. Mary's University, San Antonio.

109. García, *United We Win*, 17; Muñoz, *Youth, Identity, Power*, 119.

110. Marin, *Social Protest in an Urban Barrio*, 140; Fields and Fox, "The Brown Berets," 211–12.

111. Chávez, *"¡Mi Raza Primero!"* 45.

112. Gardner, *¡Grito!* 217–25.

113. Pycior, *LBJ and Mexican Americans*, 226–27; Rodriguez, "Cristaleño Consciousness," 158.

114. Federal Bureau of Investigation, Freedom of Information Act document, Subject: "Crusade for Justice," file no. 105-176910-17, "News service clipping, United Press International article, no date."

115. The history of black–brown relations during the 1960s and 1970s remains largely unexplored. Brief mentions can be found in Acuña, *Occupied America*, 3rd ed., 309–10; Galarza, Gallegos, and Samora, *Mexican Americans in the Southwest*, 61–64; and Gómez-Quiñones, *Chicano Politics*, 95.

116. For Chavez, see Levy, *Cesar Chavez*, 197. Tijerina's Alianza passed an anti-war resolution at its 1966 convention (see Nabokov, *Tijerina and the Courthouse Raid*, 218–19). Corky Gonzales spoke at an anti-war rally in Denver in August 1966, a decision, according to one researcher, that marked "his entry into the files of the FBI" (see Vigil, *The Crusade for Justice*, 27).

117. *El Informador*, 2 December 1967, 1.

118. García's *Viva Kennedy!* is the most extensive treatment of the campaign.

119. Information about Gonzales's early career can be found in Vigil, *The Crusade for Justice*, especially 15–28. Also see Marin, *A Spokesman for the Mexican American Movement*.

120. Gonzales, notes from conversation. In 1987, a car accident left Gonzales with short-term memory loss; under the circumstances, I decided against taping the interview. The connection between war and profit, however, was one that Gonzales repeatedly stressed during an afternoon's visit.

121. Vigil, *The Crusade for Justice*, 28.

122. Vigil did not ask for the label and is not sure he was the first, although he was certainly one of the first Chicanos to refuse the draft (*El Gallo*, 10 May 1968, 1–2).

123. "Draft Conference," *El Gallo*, January 1970, 3.

124. *El Gallo*, 31 August 1967, 1.

125. Levy, *Cesar Chavez*, 197.

126. *El Malcriado*, 12 April 1967, 5.

127. Letter, Jesus Hernandez to the President, 22 November 1967, Executive TR 125 File, WHCF, LBJ Library.

128. Baldenegro, interview.

129. Montes, notes from conversation; García, *Memories of Chicano History*, 224.

130. Homer D. C. Garcia, notes from conversation.

131. Ibid. See also Navarro, *Mexican American Youth Organization*, 88; and García, *United We Win*, 16.

132. García, *United We Win*, 24; Navarro, *Mexican American Youth Organization*, 100.

133. "Race Hate," *Congressional Record* (3 April 1969): 8590–91; "Foundation Responsibility," *Congressional Record* (16 April 1969): 9308–09.

134. Homer D. C. Garcia, interview.

135. Andrade, interview.

136. Military installations in or near San Antonio included Fort Sam Houston, Kelly Air Force Base, Lackland Air Force Base, and Randolf Air Force Base. Laughlin Air Force Base is 150 miles east; Fort Bliss in El Paso and Fort Hood north of Austin are other large army installations.

137. Homer D. C. Garcia, interview.

138. Navarro, *Mexican American Youth Organization*, 183.

139. García, *United We Win*, 16.

140. Compean, interview.

141. Gutiérrez recounts his encounters with his local draft board in *The Making of a Chicano Militant*, 113–14.

142. Andrade, interview; Genaro García, interview.

143. Typewritten transcript of an article from the *San Antonio Inferno*, misdated as 8 January 1967 (versus 1968), in box 13, folder 13, Galarza Papers.

144. "Mexican American United Conference: LA RAZA UNIDA," box 13, folder 13, Galarza Papers.

CHAPTER 3: "BRANCHES OF THE SAME TREE"

1. Baldenegro, interview.

2. *El Plan Espiritual de Aztlán,* reprinted in Garcia, *Chicano Politics,* 170–73.

3. *La Causa,* December 1970.

4. According to the 1960 census, 54.8 percent of the Spanish-surnamed population in the Southwest was native-born of native parents, while 29.8 percent was native-born with at least one immigrant parent (Grebler, Moore, and Guzman, *The Mexican-American People,* 30).

5. Grebler, Moore, and Guzman, *The Mexican-American People,* 150. According to the 1970 census, only 5.4 percent of the Mexican American population had obtained a college education (Moore, *Mexican Americans,* 70).

6. Gómez, interview.

7. Gonzales, *I Am Joaquín,* 3–20.

8. Ibid., 13.

9. For more on the history and meaning of "Chicano," see Gómez-Quiñones, "Toward a Perspective on Chicano History," 3; and Fox, *Hispanic Nation,* 120–21.

10. *La Raza,* 1 January 1969, 12.

11. Vasconcelos's essay, *La Raza Cósmica,* first appeared in 1925. It has been republished several times since, most recently in 1999 by the Centro de Estudios Generales, Universidad Nacional, in Heredia, Costa Rica.

12. "Who is a Chicano? And what is it the Chicanos Want?" originally appeared in the *Los Angeles Times* on February 6, 1970. The column was reprinted in Salazar, *Border Correspondent,* 235–37.

13. From the Preamble to *El Plan Espiritual de Aztlán,* reprinted in Garcia, *Chicano Politics,* 170.

14. *Chicano Student News,* 25 August 1968, 3.

15. *Bronce* was published in 1969 in Oakland. *Raza de Bronce* was published in 1973 at the University of California, San Diego campus. The Mexican

American Political Association also briefly published a newsletter, entitled *Prensa de Bronce,* in 1969 in Los Angeles. All of these titles and publishing information are available through the California Digital Library. Copies of *Bronce* are also available on microfilm in the Chicano Studies Collection of the Ethnic Studies Library at the University of California, Berkeley.

16. García, *United We Win,* 35, 41.

17. Campean, *La Raza Unida Party in Texas,* 5.

18. Leroy F. Aarons, "The Chicanos Want In," *Outlook,* 11 January 1970.

19. Baldenegro, interview.

20. *Inside Eastside,* 15–29 September 1968, 7.

21. "Tale of La Raza," *Bronze,* 25 November 1968, 2.

22. *The Militant,* 24 July 1970, 7.

23. Muñoz, *Youth, Identity, Power,* 33.

24. García, *Mexican Americans,* 43. According to García, the date of the speech was uncertain, but it was apparently delivered in the late 1930s or early 1940s.

25. Klor de Alva, "Aztlán, Borinquen, and Hispanic Nationalism," 148.

26. Chávez, *The Lost Land,* 8.

27. From the Preamble of *El Plan Espiritual de Aztlán,* reprinted in Garcia, *Chicano Politics,* 170.

28. Ibid.

29. Ibid.

30. Grebler, Moore, and Guzmán, *The Mexican-American People,* 113.

31. From the Preamble to *El Plan Espiritual de Aztlán,* reprinted in Garcia, *Chicano Politics,* 170. As such a viewpoint suggested, Chicano movement activists also were rethinking the ethnic group's stance on immigration.

32. Ibid., 172. Klor de Alva made a similar point in "The Invention of Ethnic Origins and the Negotiation of Latino Identity," 58. According to Klor de Alva, the set of cultural contrasts put forth by movement participants included humanism versus materialism, communal property versus private property, community versus alienation, and, finally, "a life of sacrifice focused on others" versus "seductive capitalism focused on the self."

33. Steiner, *La Raza,* 389.

34. Gonzales, *I Am Joaquín,* 3.

35. Armas, "La Familia de la Raza," 44.

36. *El Grito del Norte,* 7 December 1970, 2.

37. Fields and Fox, "The Brown Berets," 212.

38. *El Gallo,* December 1967, 8.

39. From a December 1969 letter written by Manuel Gómez refusing induction. Gómez's letter was printed in several Chicano movement newspapers, including *La Verdad,* May 1970, 14. It can also be found in Martínez and Longeaux y Vásquez, *¡Viva La Raza!* 287–89.

40. Gómez, interview.

41. Ibid.

42. Gómez letter, in Martínez and Longeaux y Vásquez, *¡Viva La Raza!* 287–89.

43. Ibid.

44. Gómez, interview.

45. Gómez letter, in Martínez and Longeaux y Vásquez, ¡Viva La Raza! 287–89.

46. Gómez, interview; The Militant, 2 May 1969, 9.

47. Valdez Martinez, interview.

48. El Grito del Norte, 10 August 1970, 6, 8.

49. El Grito del Norte, 10 August 1969, 6–8; 14 September 1969, 8–9.

50. El Grito del Norte, 10 August 1969, 6.

51. El Grito del Norte, 10 August 1969, 8.

52. El Grito del Norte, 14 September 1969, 9.

53. Chicano Student Movement, September 1968, 7.

54. Echo, 14 July 1970, 14.

55. Católicos por la Raza, January 1970, 8.

56. A similar point was made by at least one African American anti-war activist; see Wells, The War Within, 273.

57. Mariscal, Aztlán and Viet Nam, 231. Translations are by George Mariscal.

58. Ibid., 248.

59. Muñoz, Youth, Identity, Power, 5, 131.

60. Barrera, Ornelas, and Muñoz, "The Barrio as an Internal Colony," 490.

61. Gómez-Quiñones, "Toward a Perspective on Chicano History," 6.

62. Acuña, Occupied America, 1st ed., 7, 3.

63. La Causa, December 1970, 7.

64. Manual Gómez used the word "model" (Gómez, interview). As early as 1964, theater director Luis Valdez, after visiting the island, upheld Fidel Castro as a leader for all Mexican Americans (Muñoz, Youth, Identity, Power, 52).

65. El Grito del Norte, 19 May 1969, 8–9; 14 June 1969, 12–13.

66. El Gallo, May 1972, 3.

67. For debates among campus groups, see Muñoz, Youth, Identity, Power, 90–94.

68. Gómez, interview. See also the 29 August 1970 edition of La Causa. As pressures mounted in the days before a massive anti-war march in East Los Angeles, the Beret newspaper warned: "The left wing, the right wing, the socialists, the democrats, and every other damn foreign ideology has attempted to prostitute the Chicano movement for there [sic] own purposes of perpetuating caucasoid madness. We are not right wing or left wing, we are Chicanos."

69. La Causa, March 1971, 7.

70. Elizabeth Martínez, interview.

71. Ibid.

72. Sutherland, Letters from Mississippi.

73. Elizabeth Martínez, interview; Martínez, The Youngest Revolution.

74. Elizabeth Martínez, interview.

75. Other people on the trip were Frank Joyce, a civil rights activist, and feminist Charlotte Bunch.

76. El Grito del Norte, 29 August 1970, 4, 14.

77. Ibid., 1.

78. Muñoz, Youth, Identity, Power, 52.

79. Mooney and Majka, *Farmers' and Farm Workers' Movements*, 81 (quotation), 163.

80. According to a later state report, Bud Antle, without consulting the field workers and probably against their wishes, had signed a "sweetheart" contract with the Teamsters instead of bargaining with the farmworkers' union (Mooney and Majka, *Farmers' and Farm Workers' Movements*, 166–67; see also *El Malcriado*, 1 January 1971, 2–3; 15 January 1971, 4–5; and Crockcoft, *Outlaws in the Promised Land*, 183).

81. *Vietnam Campesino* in Luis Valdez and the Teatro Campesino, *Actos* (Fresno, Calif.: Cucaracha Productions, 1971), 105–110.

82. Ibid., 110, 123–124, 126–128, 130, author's translation.

83. *Soldado Razo*, in Valdez and the Teatro Campesino, *Actos*, 131–45. In 1999 an independent film based upon the play was produced by Kinan Valdez, Luis Valdez's son; the film was called *Ballad of a Soldier*.

84. *The Militant*, 25 December 1970, 13.

85. Newspaper clipping from *San Antonio Evening News*, 16 October 1969, 2, in box 2, folder marked "Vietnam Moratorium, San Antonio," Bernal Papers.

86. Navarro, *Mexican American Youth Organization*, 176, 193.

87. Shockley, *Chicano Revolt in a Texas Town*, 164.

88. Andrade, interview.

89. Ibid.

90. Ybarra, interview.

91. Genera, interview.

92. Ibid.

93. Ybarra, interview.

94. Ibid.

95. Genera, interview.

96. Ybarra, interview.

97. The words of the ballad appeared in *Bronze*, January 1969, 9. Ybarra was an editor for the Oakland-based newspaper.

98. Ybarra, interview.

99. Ybarra and Genera, *La Batalla Está Aquí*, 6–7.

100. Ybarra, interview.

101. Ybarra and Genera, *La Batalla Está Aquí*, 2, 6–8.

102. Ibid., 6–7. The booklet listed such examples. Ybarra, in her interview, said all were drawn from encounters she and Genera had with Mexican Americans during their anti-war work.

103. Ybarra, "Too Many Heroes: The Oral Histories of Chicano Vietnam Veterans."

104. Ybarra and Genera, *La Batalla Está Aquí*, 7.

105. Ibid., 6.

106. *El Alacrán*, 15 June 1970, 4.

107. "From El Barrio to Viet Nam," *El Barrio*, 1970.

108. As quoted in Mariscal, *Aztlán and Viet Nam*, 142, 242–43, 246.

109. *La Causa*, 28 February 1970, 5.

110. The split is detailed in Espinoza, "Pedagogies of Nationalism and Gender," 133–43. As Espinoza pointed out, the emphasis on male militancy was clear from the start. In one 1968 recruitment ad that featured a revolutionary male figure, the phrase "Girls too . . ." appeared as an apparent afterthought (ibid., 24).

111. Genera, interview.

112. Mary Ellen Ramirez, interview.

113. *El Grito del Norte,* 5 June 1971, page K.

114. *El Grito del Norte,* 26 April 1971, 11, 14.

115. Mary Ellen Ramirez, interview.

CHAPTER 4: "I'D RATHER HAVE MY SONS DIE FOR LA RAZA . . . THAN IN VIETNAM"

1. Muñoz, interview. Muñoz's speech refusing the draft was published in several Chicano newspapers, including Los Angeles's *La Raza* (10 December 1969, 6).

2. Among the anti-war groups that included "mobilization" in their title was the Spring Mobilization Committee to End the War, the Student Mobilization Committee, the National Mobilization Committee to End the War In Vietnam, and its successor organization, the New Mobe. For the influence of the civil rights movement, see the comments of Sydney Peck in Wells, *The War Within,* 92–93. For more on the inspirational 1963 march, see Barber, *Marching on Washington,* especially ch. 5.

3. By September 1969 a partial list of draft resistors included José Sanchez from Los Angeles; Denver's Ernesto Vigil, and Tucson's Salomón Baldenegro. Richard Santillan, now a professor at California State Polytechnic University at Pomona, had obtained conscientious objector status.

4. Documents pertaining to Los Conquistadores can be found in the Chicano Research Collection, Hayden Library, Arizona State University. In yet another connection, Muñoz's aunt, Rebecca, who was active in both groups, later married Felix Gutiérrez, the editor of MAM's *Mexican American Voice.*

5. Muñoz, interview; "Rosalío F. Muñoz, 91, Leading Latino Education, L.A. District Official," *Los Angeles Times,* 28 May 2004, B-12 [home edition].

6. Muñoz estimated that probably no more than fifty or sixty Mexican Americans attended UCLA his first year (Muñoz, interview). The estimate might be generous. In 1967 the total Mexican American student population at the University of California was only seventy students, according to a state report (see U.S. Commission on Civil Rights, California Advisory Committee, *Education and the Mexican American Community in Los Angeles County,* 4).

7. Like many other Mexican American campus groups, UMAS changed its name, to MEChA (El Movimiento Estudiantil Chicano de Aztlán) in 1969.

8. Hemmings, *The Life and Times of Emile Zola,* 164.

9. Reflective of the countercultural tenor of the era, candidate Muñoz also suggested: "Let's decorate the campus with student art and graffiti: there are plenty of blank walls that need murals, plenty of potential sculpture gardens on

campus. Take over the lawns with picnics, ball games, folk-dancing, guerrilla theatre and just plain grooving on the grass" (*Daily Bruin,* 7 October 1968, 6).

10. "The Gentle Revolutionaries, Brown Power," *West,* 26 January 1969, 9.

11. Hauser, *Muhammad Ali,* 143–45; Marqusee, *Redemption Song,* 162; Muñoz, interview.

12. Excerpts of Harris's speech were printed in the *Daily Bruin,* 28 October 1968, 1.

13. Wells, *The War Within,* 127–28; Muñoz, interview.

14. Muñoz, interview.

15. Noriega, interview.

16. Ibid.

17. Muñoz, interview.

18. Noriega, interview.

19. Thanks to Jorge Mariscal for the translation. As Mariscal also once pointed out, the title should have been "Chale con *la* draft."

20. Muñoz, interview; Noriega, interview.

21. Muñoz, interview; Noriega, interview; "Youth Again Refuses Draft," *Los Angeles Times,* 29 November 1969, sec. 2, p. 29.

22. Muñoz, interview; Noriega, interview; Elias, interview.

23. The two participants who suffered the beating were Bob Elias and Ernesto Vigil. For more about the run-in with police, see Vigil, *The Crusade for Justice,* 116.

24. Details of the gathering can be found in "Draft Conference," *El Gallo,* [January 1970?], 3.

25. Wells, *The War Within,* 266.

26. Echols, "'Women Power' and Women's Liberation," 173; see also Adams, "The Women Who Left Them Behind."

27. "Draft Conference," *El Gallo,* [January 1970?], 3.

28. Audio tape of Corky Gonzales speaking at a Chicano conference held at California State College, Hayward, November 13 or 14, 1969. Ernesto Vigil loaned the author a series of tape recordings of Gonzales speaking.

29. Muñoz, interview; and e-mail correspondence from Rosalío U. Muñoz, 16 August 2002, in the author's possession; Ernesto Vigil, telephone conversation, 20 September 1993; Halstead, *Out Now!* 506–7; *The Militant,* 7 November 1969, 7; and *The Militant,* 9 November 1969, 7.

30. Elias, interview.

31. Sanchez, interview.

32. "Symposium closes tonight," *The Daily Pioneer,* 14 November 1969.

33. Ginny Berson, "Tierra o Muerte: Chicanos Fight for Nationhood," *Hard Times,* August 24–31, 1970.

34. Quoted in DeBenedetti, *An American Ordeal,* 188; italics in original.

35. *People's World,* 27 September 1969, 3. Other goals were to protest antiballistic missile construction and to allow free speech for G.I.s.

36. The roster of speakers included Ralph Albernathy of the Southern Christian Leadership Conference, David Hilliard, chief of staff of the Black Panther Party, and Mad Bear Anderson, a Native American advocate (*People's World,* 22 November 1969, 1).

37. "Stokeley Carmichael Responds to Vital Questions America Asks," box 4, folder 31, Social Protest Collection.

38. "Beyond Vietnam," speech given by Martin Luther King Jr. at Riverside Church, New York City, 4 April 1967, box 1, folder 24, Social Protest Collection.

39. "The Indo-China War," Walter LaFeber speech given at Cornell University, May 1970. A copy is in the author's possession. Thanks to Bob Buesell for providing it to me.

40. *People's World*, 22 November 1969, 1.

41. Muñoz, interview.

42. DeBenedetti, *An American Ordeal*, 229, 253–54, 264; Small, *Covering Dissent*, 161.

43. Nixon, "Nixon's Address to the Nation on the War in Vietnam".

44. Wells, *The War Within*, 389–90.

45. DeBenedetti, *An American Ordeal*, 261.

46. Hilliard, *This Side of Glory*, 260. Not that the coaching did any good. Hilliard advocated killing Nixon, a suggestion that brought shouts of disapproval from the crowd.

47. Elias, interview.

48. Ernesto Vigil, telephone conversation, 20 September 1993. Fred Halstead, a leading SWP member, offered a similar account in his history of the antiwar movement (Halstead, *Out Now!* 506–7).

49. Audio tape of Corky Gonzales speaking in Los Angeles, no date. Ernesto Vigil loaned the author a series of tape recordings of Gonzales speaking.

50. *El Grito del Norte*, October 1969, 3.

51. *People's World*, 18 October 1969, 1.

52. Ybarra, interview.

53. Appy argued that even if deaths of blacks (and Hispanics, by implication) were not disproportional in Viet Nam, the war was still largely fought by working-class men (see *Working-Class War*, 28–38).

54. Muñoz, interview.

55. In 1970 Crystal City High School in Crystal City, Texas, banned Army recruiters from visiting the school after Chicanos took over the school board (Shockley, *Chicano Revolt in a Texas Town*, 164).

56. Chavez, "Birth of a New Symbol," 209.

57. Vigil, *The Crusade for Justice*, 114.

58. "Las Gorras Negras," *Venceremos Papel*, 1 July 1971, 14.

59. Enriqueta Vasquez, "¡Despierten Hermanos!," *El Grito del Norte*, 14 August 1969.

60. *El Grito* 1 (Spring 1968): 19.

61. Social use of marijuana among some Mexican Americans also predated the popularity of the drug in the 1960s (see Bullington, "Drug Use Patterns in a Chicano Community," 118–20; and Carey, "Marijuana Use Among the New Bohemians," 91–92).

62. Bryan, "The Story of the Brown Berets," reprinted in *El Gallo*, April 1968, 5 (originally printed in an alternative Los Angeles newspaper called *Open City*, date unknown).

63. *El Gallo,* [January 1970?], 5.

64. The PLP's contribution to the demise of Students for a Democratic Society is retold in Wells, *The War Within,* 303–5. For strained relations with Chicanos, see William J. Drummond, "How East L.A. Protest Turned Into Major Riot," *Los Angeles Times,* 16 September 1970, 24.

65. Isserman, *If I Had a Hammer,* 185. Isserman estimated that in 1960 the larger Socialist Party probably had no more than one thousand active members.

66. Wells, *The War Within,* 18, 399; Unger, *The Movement,* 193.

67. Gómez-Quiñones, *Chicano Politics,* 146–50. For information about the SWP in Texas, see García, *United We Win,* 213–15.

68. *The Militant,* 7 November 1969, 7; and 9 November 1969, 7.

69. "National Peace Action Coalition" conference summary, in Social Protest File, box 1, file 48, Social Protest Collection. Also among the list of sponsors were two Puerto Ricans and an Asian American.

70. Muñoz, interview.

71. The number participating is a rough estimate. *The Militant* said 1,500. The Brown Beret paper, *La Causa,* two months later, said 2,000. Muñoz recalled a crowd numbering between 500 and 1,000. Carlos Montes, who was the Brown Beret minister of communication and spoke at the rally, estimated 500.

72. *People's World,* 27 December 1969, 1; Muñoz, interview.

73. A detailed account of the origins of the Brown Berets can be found in Chávez, "Birth of a New Symbol," 205–22.

74. Chavez, "Birth of a New Symbol," 282; Escobar, "The Dialectics of Repression," 1495–96; Dial Torgerson, "Brown Power Unity Seen Behind School Disorders," *Los Angeles Times,* 17 March 1968, reprinted in García, *Chicano Politics,* 220.

75. *La Causa,* 23 May 1969, 8.

76. The information about target practices and marching drills can be found, along with the recollections of several prominent women Berets, in Espinoza, "Revolutionary Sisters."

77. U.S. Senate, Committee on the Judiciary, *"Extent of Subversion in the New Left: Testimony of Robert J. Thoms,"* 23, 33.

78. Federal Bureau of Investigation, Freedom of Information Act document, Subject: "Brown Berets," file no. 105-178715, "Memorandum to Mr. W. C. Sullivan from Mr. W. R. Wannall, 3/26/68," and "Memorandum to Mr. W. C. Sullivan from Mr. W. R. Wannall, 6/5/68."

79. Escobar, "The Dialectics of Repression," 1497–98.

80. Four Brown Berets were among thirteen Chicanos indicted on felony conspiracy charges stemming from their participation in the Los Angeles high school strikes of 1968. They initially confronted sixty-six years in prison, but the charges were dropped two years later (Muñoz, *Youth, Identity, Power,* 68, 71). In the second case, in April 1969, several Berets were accused of setting fires in a downtown hotel while Governor Ronald Reagan was in the building speaking on education and "Latin youth." A police officer testified during the trial that he had infiltrated the Brown Beret organization, encouraged the arson, and participated in setting the fires. After an involved legal process, all charges were dropped against the Chicano accused (*Los Angeles Times,* 10 August 1971, part

II, 2; and 11 August 1971, part II, 1; Escobar, "The Dialectics of Repression," 1498).

81. Arellanes, interview.

82. Jensen, written responses to written questions exchanged over e-mail.

83. Noriega, interview.

84. Muñoz, interview.

85. Marin, *Social Protest in an Urban Barrio,* 205.

86. Arellanes, interview.

87. Chavez, "Birth of a New Symbol," 215–16; Espinoza, "Revolutionary Sisters," 23–24.

88. Espinoza makes this point in her seminal account of the relationship between men and women and between feminism and nationalism within the Brown Berets (see Espinoza, "Revolutionary Sisters"). My account owes much to her analysis and to my interview with Gloria Arellanes.

89. Espinoza, "Revolutionary Sisters," 29.

90. Arellanes, interview.

91. Ibid. Also see Chávez, "Birth of a New Symbol," 217. According to author F. Arturo Rosales, years later, one former Brown Beret remained convinced that feminism was a "CIA plot," that Gloria Steinem was an FBI agent, and that both had worked to undermine Chicano cultural nationalism (see Rosales, *Chicano!* 182; the book is a companion volume to a four-part television documentary series of the same name).

92. Arellanes, interview; Chávez, "Birth of a New Symbol," 215; and Espinoza, "Revolutionary Sisters," 33.

93. As quoted in Espinoza, "Pedagogies of Nationalism and Gender," 132.

94. Arellanes, interview.

95. "Chicano Moratorium," reprinted in *La Raza,* 10 December 1969, 6.

96. Arellanes, interview.

97. On the WWII monument's construction, see Sánchez, *Becoming Mexican American,* 274. For more information about Eugene Obregón, see Morin, *Among the Valiant,* 260–61.

98. "Release on: Chicano Moratorium, December 18, 1969," box 30, Hernandez Collection.

99. "Chicano Moratorium," *El Machete,* 8 January 1970.

100. Escobar, "The Dialectics of Repression," 1484.

101. *People's World,* 27 December 1969, back page.

102. Ibid.

103. The median age of the Spanish-surnamed population in the Southwest was mentioned in Grebler, Moore, and Guzman, *The Mexican-American People,* 13.

104. "Release on: Chicano Moratorium, December 18, 1969," box 30, Hernandez Collection.

105. Actually, Alvarez spent eight-and-a-half years as a P.O.W., while U.S. Army Captain Jim Thompson was held prisoner for nine years. During the war, however, few people were aware of Thompson's fate (Alvarez and Pitch, *Chained Eagle*; Philpott, *Glory Denied*).

106. Alvarez and Pitch, *Chained Eagle,* 233–34, 245.

107. *People's World*, 27 December 1969, back page.

108. Baldenegro, interview.

109. Steiner, *La Raza*, 385.

110. For examples of the use of the word *vendido* by Chicano movement participants, see, for example, *People's World,* 7 March 1970, 4; and *El Grito del Norte,* 10 August 1970, 8. In April 1972 the Crusade for Justice's newspaper, *El Gallo,* printed a speech by Corky Gonzales that captured this extensive vocabulary: "We cannot be blinded to the *vendidos,* the right-wingers, the Tio Tacos, the exploiters, and the Malinches of the nation." Chicana feminists later reclaimed La Malinche, whom the Spanish called Doña Marina, as a heroine. A classic essay in this regard is Del Castillo, "Malintzin Tenepal."

CHAPTER 5: "A COMMON GOAL"

1. The *Los Angeles Times* reported the lower figure based upon police reports (see Charles T. Powers and Jeff Perlman, "One Dead, 40 Hurt in East L.A. Riot," *Los Angeles Times,* 30 August 1970, 19). Higher estimates appeared in Chicano movement publications, including *Regeneración* (vol. 1, no. 6, [1970], inside page editorial entitled "The Time is Now") and the front page of the September 1970 edition of *El Gallo* (date incorrectly listed as June 1970).

2. Agustin Garza, "La Raza—Su Espíritu y Su Lucha," *La Voz del Pueblo–El Enterado,* Joint Special Edition, September 1970, 5; *La Raza Nueva,* radio show hosted by Moctezuma Esparza and broadcast on KPFK radio station, Chicano Studies Library, University of California at Los Angeles (the *La Raza Nueva* tape mentions no date, but apparently the recording took place just a day or two after the August march). The tape is part of the collection of the Chicano Studies Library, University of California at Los Angeles.

3. Muñoz, interview.

4. Tovar, notes from conversation.

5. Agustin Garza, "La Raza—Su Espíritu y Su Lucha," *La Voz del Pueblo–El Enterado,* Joint Special Edition, September 1970, 5.

6. "National Chicano Moratorium," *La Voz del Pueblo* (San Diego), August 1970, 1.

7. Curtis J. Sitomer, "Chicanos to Push Rights Theme," *Christian Science Monitor,* 25 August 1970.

8. "National Chicano Moratorium," *La Voz del Pueblo* (San Diego), August 1970, 1.

9. KMEX, *Viente Años Despues.* This Spanish-language television station in Los Angeles produced the documentary to mark the twentieth anniversary of the Chicano Moratorium.

10. The parents of Richard Santillan, a Chicano movement participant in Los Angeles and a conscientious objector to the draft, were among the marchers. They also attended Chicano Moratorium 2002, a multi-event, multimedia commemoration of the original Chicano Moratorium (Santillan, notes from conversation).

11. Scenes of the march captured in the KMEX documentary *Viente Años Despues* show marchers carrying signs that refer to Alcatraz and Puerto Rico.

Also see William J. Drummond, "How East L.A. Protest Turned Into Major Riot," *Los Angeles Times*, 16 September 1970, 24. A photograph by George Rodriguez showed that an unidentified black man carried one end of the large banner that read National Chicano Moratorium at the very front of the march.

12. For African American moratorium participation, see *People's World*, 7 March 1970, 4; for the Young Lords, see *The Militant*, 16 January 1970, 3; and Muñoz, interview. Also see the first issue of *La Raza* (vol. 1, no. 1 [March 1970]: 3).

13. The amount of rain is clear in the motion picture *March in the Rain*; the mention of umbrellas appears in *People's World*, 7 March 1970, 4.

14. *La Causa*, 28 February 1970, 1.

15. *People's World*, 7 March 1970, 4.

16. *La Raza* 1, no. 1 (March 1970): 10.

17. Froben Lozada, "The Chicano Moratorium—how it developed," *The Militant*, 4 September 1970, 6; the interview took place before August 29 but was not printed until September because the paper was closed for three weeks during a vacation period for staff.

18. Ibid.

19. Salazar, *Border Correspondent*, 244.

20. Vera, "Observations on the Chicano Relationship to Military Service in Los Angeles County, " 35.

21. *El Grito del Norte*, 29 August 1970, 2. *"Soldado razo"* or *"raso,"* from the verb *arrasar,* meaning "to level," roughly translates as a "buck private."

22. Acuña, "Remembering August 29, 1970."

23. Marin, *Social Protest in an Urban Barrio*, 203; *La Opinión*, 13 May 1970, 3.

24. Ornelas and Gonzalez, "The Chicano and the War," 25–31. The researchers divided their respondents by sex and age. "Youths" were those between the age of 15 and 21, while those over 21 were categorized as adults.

25. In 1968 Hubert Humphrey received 87 percent of the Mexican American vote for president, compared to Nixon's 10 percent (Levy and Kramer, *The Ethnic Factor*, 79).

26. Meier and Ribera. *Mexican Americans, Americans Mexicans*, 207.

27. "Remarks by the Honorable Joseph M. Montoya before the Western Regional Conference of the Young Democrats," 4 September 1965, box 37, folder 39; "Montoya Assails Pres. Nixon, Gov. Cargo; Cites Need for Greater Leadership," press release from the offices of Senator Joseph M. Montoya, 28 March 1969, box 39, folder 32; and "Vietnam," no date, box 39, folder 61, all in Montoya Papers.

28. Although Gonzalez endorsed a United Nations peace effort in 1967, that same year he also voted against an explicit anti-war resolution that called for a ban on the use of federal funds to carry out military operations in North Viet Nam. After Nixon's election, however, Gonzalez introduced a bill that would have prevented the executive from sending draftees into combat except in declared wars (see *Congressional Quarterly Almanac*, vol. 23, 90th Cong., 1st sess. (Washington, D.C.: Congressional Quarterly, 1967), 10-H; Rodriguez, *Henry B. Gonzalez*, 165; and *Congressional Weekly Report*, vol. 24, no. 15 (9 April 1971): 798).

29. "Roybal Backs Chicano Viet Moratorium," *Los Angeles Times,* 25 August 1970, sec. 2, p. 4; "Respalda Ed Roybal la marcha Pro-Moratoria," *La Opinión,* 28 August 1970, 3.

30. California 1970 Convention of the American G.I. Forum, box 13, folder 1, Galarza Collection. The anti-war resolution had originated in Colton, California, about an hour inland from Los Angeles, where Viet Nam veterans dominated the local chapter. The role of the Colton chapter was revealed in a 1974 *Forumeer* article, which stated that at the organization's 1971 national convention "a militantly-worded anti-war resolution . . . sponsored originally by the Viet Nam-veteran-led Colton, Calif. GI Forum passed unanimously with no discussion whatsoever" (*The Forumeer,* October 1974, 4).

31. *People's World,* 14 September 1968, 2.

32. *People's World,* 28 February 1970, 1; *La Opinión,* 13 May 1970, 3. An important source of information on the Congress of Mexican American Unity is the Antonio Hernandez Collection, Chicano Studies Library, University of California, Berkeley.

33. "Congress of Mexican American Unity, Steering Committee Meeting, January 8, 1970," box 37, Hernandez Collection.

34. Ibid. Also see "Minutes, June 24, 1970," box 37, Hernandez Collection.

35. *La Causa,* 22 May 1970, 6.

36. Dick Main, "There Was Nothing Peaceful In East L.A. March, Pitchess says," *Los Angeles Times,* 1 September 1970, 1.

37. *La Causa,* 22 May 1970, 6.

38. Muñoz, interview.

39. Ibid.

40. *The Militant,* 4 September 1970, 7; Antonio Camejo, "Lessons from the L.A. Chicano Protest," *The Militant,* 16 October 1970, 9; Muñoz, interview.

41. Drummond, "How East L.A. Protest Turned Into Major Riot," *Los Angeles Times,* 16 September 1970, 24.

42. Antonio Camejo, "Lessons of the L.A. Protest," *The Militant,* 16 October 1970, 9–12; *Los Angeles Times,* 16 September 1970, 1.

43. "Man Pushed Into Bar at Gunpoint, Salazar Inquest Told," *Los Angeles Times,* 24 September 1970, 23; "Nuestra Batalla No Está en Vietnam, Está Aquí," Special Moratorium edition, *La Raza* 1, no. 3 (September–October 1970).

44. *La Causa,* 28 February 1970, 1. A similar article published by a Brown Beret chapter in San Diego advocated armed struggle (see "Chicano Moratorium," *El Grito de Aztlán,* 30 June 1970).

45. Chávez, "Birth of a New Symbol," 208.

46. Nancy Tovar, notes from conversation. Tovar's husband, Rudy Tovar, a Church member and World War II veteran, was recognized for his work on behalf of the Moratorium along with other volunteers during Chicano Moratorium 2002.

47. *People's World,* 5 April 1970, 15.

48. *People's World,* 11 April 1970, 9.

49. Davis del Valle, interview.

50. Arellanes, interview. Irene Tovar, who was also a member of the moratorium committee, made the same point (Irene Tovar, interview).

51. Davis del Valle, interview.

52. Irene Tovar, interview; Irene Tovar, notes from conversation.

53. Irene Tovar, interview.

54. Cano, notes from conversation.

55. A copy of the flier in is the author's possession, a gift from Rosalío U. Muñoz.

56. Cano, notes from conversation.

57. "Raza backs rally to honor G.I.'s," *Papel Chicano*, 8 August 1970, 1.

58. *Echo*, 28 July 1970, 1.

59. *Papel Chicano*, 8 August 1970, 4.

60. A partial list derived from Chicano press reports includes the California cities of San Diego, Santa Barbara, San Francisco, Oakland, San Bernardino, Fresno, and Riverside, as well as the Texas cities of San Antonio, Austin, and Houston, in addition to New York, Chicago, Denver, and, in Arizona, the tiny border town of Douglas.

61. Irene Tovar, inteview; Davis del Valle, interview.

62. Chacón, interview.

63. Irene Tovar, interview.

64. "National Chicano Moratorium Goes Sour in Last Moratorium Effort," *La Causa*, 29 August 1970, 5.

65. Frank del Olmo, "Anatomy of a Riot," *Los Angeles Times,* 30 August 1970, sec. 1, p. B.

66. Drummond, "How East L.A. Protest Turned Into Major Riot," *Los Angeles Times,* 16 September 1970, 1.

67. KPFK recording of Chicano Moratorium rally, 29 August 1970, East Los Angeles Public Library. Rosalío Muñoz and other speakers can be heard on the tape. The tape was played on August 23, 2002, during the Chicano Moratorium 2002 film night.

68. Ibid.

69. *Regeneración* 1, no. 6 (1970): 1.

70. "Chicano Moratorium," Special Moratorium edition, *La Raza* 1, no. 3 (September–October 1970)–.

71. Dolores Small, "Peaceful March Turns to Violence," *El Chicano*, 4 September 1970, 1.

72. National Chicano Moratorium Committee press release, 31 August 1970, box 62, folder 7, Galarza Collection; Drummond, "How East L.A. Protest Turned Into Major Riot," *Los Angeles Times,* 16 September 1970, 25.

73. Joe Bautista, "A 'Police Riot' in East Los Angeles," *El Chicano*, 4 September 1970, 1.

74. Charles T. Powers and Jeff Perlman, "One Dead, 40 Hurt in East L.A. Riot," *Los Angeles Times,* 30 August, 1970, 1.

75. Vigil, interview. Also, many thanks to Hermino Gonzales, a moratorium volunteer, who shared some pictures he had taken of the August demonstration with me; the banner with the slogan appeared in several of them.

76. "Hispano Rally Erupts," *Denver Post,* 30 August 1970.

77. Drummond, "How East L.A. Protest Turned Into Major Riot," *Los Angeles Times,* 16 September 1970, 25.

78. KPFK recording of Chicano Moratorium rally, 29 August 1970, East Los Angeles Public Library.

79. Electronic mail message to author from Rosalío Muñoz, 5 September 2002.

80. López, "Amigos de Aztlannet.com."

81. Baca, "The Day the Police Rioted!"

82. The young woman can be seen throwing a tear gas canister in the film *Viente Años Despues.*

83. See, e.g., "Puercos Attack La Raza," *El Machete,* 29 October 1970, 4.

84. The baton assault appears in "Quest for a Homeland," the first episode of the four-part series *Chicano!: History of a Mexican American Civil Rights Movement.*

85. "LA Police Attack Chicano Moratorium—Two Die," *El Gallo,* September 1970, 2; the masthead carries the erroneous date of June 1970. Also, Federal Bureau of Investigation, Freedom of Information Act document, Subject: "National Chicano Moratorium Against the War," file no. 100–459861, "LHM [letterhead memorandum] regarding Mexican Independence Day Celebration, from SAC [Special Agent in Charge] Denver to FBI Director, 16 September 1970."

86. Paul Houston and Dave Smith, "Inquest Hears Witness Tell How Salazar Died," *Los Angeles Times,* 19 September 1970, sec. 2, p. 10. Nava was the brother of Julian Nava, the incoming president of the Los Angeles Board of Education.

87. U.S. Commission on Civil Rights, *Mexican Americans and the Administration of Justice in the Southwest.*

88. Escobar, *Race, Police, and the Making of a Political Identity.*

89. For more examples of beatings, as well as instances of harassment and surveillance, see Escobar, "The Dialectics of Repression," 1496–1500.

90. Escobar, "The Dialectics of Repression," 1494.

91. Steven J. Roberts, "Mexican-American Hostility Deepens in Tense East Los Angeles," *New York Times,* 4 September 1970, 20.

92. Richard A. Martinez, interview, 42–47. Also see the organization's newspaper, *Católicos por la Raza,* January 1970.

93. Escobar, "The Dialectics of Repression," 1499; Ruben Salazar, "Latin Newsmen, Police Chief, Eat . . . Fail to Meet," *Los Angeles Times,* 13 March 1970, sec. 2, p. 7.

94. Escobar, "The Dialectics of Repression," 1499.

95. Vigil, *The Crusade for Justice,* 137.

96. *People's World,* 7 March 1970, 4. According to a Chicano watchdog group, this young man was the sixth Mexican American to die at the jail under suspicious circumstances during the previous year. A list of names of the people who died under suspicious circumstances is found in box 14, folder 24, of the Bert Corona Collection.

97. Escobar, "The Dialectics of Repression," 1500.

98. "Una Tragedia De Errores," *La Opinión,* 19 July 1970, 1.

99. "La muerte de los dos mexicanos," *La Opinión,* 19 July 1970, 1.

100. "Demostración Ayer De MexicoAmericanos," *La Opinión,* 19 July 1970, 1.

101. Salazar, *Border Correspondent,* 6–25, 244–46.

102. Ibid., 245; Escobar, "The Dialectics of Repression," 1501.

103. Ruben Salazar, "A Beautiful Sight: The System Working the Way It Should," *Los Angeles Times,* 24 July 1970, sec. 2, p. 7.

104. Robert Lopez, "Journalist's Death Still Clouded by Questions from Friends," *Los Angeles Times,* 26 August 1995, 1.

105. Salazar, *Border Correspondent,* 31; Escobar, "The Dialectics of Repression," 1499–1501.

106. "Mexican American Militancy" was one of several categories used to track dissent among Mexican-origin people in the United States. Another was "Internal Security—Spanish American." Chicano activists were also filed under the "Rabble Rouser " and "Agitator" indices. The most detailed study of government surveillance of a single Chicano movement organization is Vigil's *Crusade for Justice.* For more about FBI surveillance of social and minority protest during the 1960s and 1970s, see Churchill and Vander Wall, *Agents of Repression*; O'Reilly, *"Racial Matters"*; and Donner, *The Age of Surveillance.*

107. Thousands of pages of documents released under the Freedom of Information Act to the author make clear that the FBI maintained files on the Crusade for Justice, the Brown Berets, the Raza Unida Party, the Congress of Mexican American Unity, and the Chicano Moratorium, among other organizations. These files contain reports about Chicano protest demonstrations, conferences, and individual leaders.

108. Federal Bureau of Investigation, Freedom of Information Act document, Subject: "Raza Unida," file no. 100–627471, Memos from SAC [Special Agent in Charge] San Francisco, 3 March 1970, 23 March 1970, and 31 March 1970.

109. Federal Bureau of Investigation, Freedom of Information Act document, Subject: "Brown Berets," file no. 52–88699, two memos from the Director, FBI to SAC Los Angeles, regarding reported theft of machine gun, 5 March 1968, and 18 March 1968; and Subject: "Brown Berets," file no. 105–196274, "Memo from the Director, FBI to SAC Milwaukee, 7 August 1969.

110. Federal Bureau of Investigation, Freedom of Information Act document, Subject: "La Raza Unida," file no. 100–62747, "Survey of Mexican American organizations, 9/29/70."

111. Out of 577 pages reviewed, 477 were released. Many of the released pages had passages, sometimes amounting to almost the entire page, blanked out. The most frequent reason cited for withholding Chicano Moratorium files was that the material was exempt in "the interest of national defense or foreign policy." Evidently, the Chicano Moratorium was additionally suspect because it was an anti-war group; its files were cross-listed under "VIDEM," Vietnam Demonstrations. Thanks to Ernesto Vigil for noting the frequent use of the national security exemption.

112. Federal Bureau of Investigation, Freedom of Information Act document, Subject: "National Chicano Moratorium Against the War," file no. 100–459861,

report from the FBI's Los Angeles bureau entitled "National Chicano Moratorium, August 29, 1970, Internal Security–Spanish American."

113. Federal Bureau of Investigation, Freedom of Information Act document, Subject: "National Chicano Moratorium Against the War," file no. 100–459861, "FBI teletype from Los Angeles to Director, 29 August 1970."

114. Federal Bureau of Investigation, Freedom of Information Act document, Subject: "National Chicano Moratorium Against the War," file no. 100–459861, "Teletype from Director, FBI to U.S. Secret Service, 29 August 1970," four pages, three withheld.

115. Ferriss and Sandoval, *The Fight in the Fields*, 154.

116. Federal Bureau of Investigation, Freedom of Information Act document, Subject: "National Chicano Moratorium Against the War," file no. 100–459861, Teletype from San Francisco to the Director (FBI), relaying observations of agents present at San Francisco Chicano Moratorium, 30 May 1970.

117. García, *Memories of Chicano History*, 276.

118. Elias, interview.

119. Gil Cano, electronic message to the author, 18 September 1970, in the author's possession. Bob Elias and Gloria Arellanes mentioned the same infiltrator in their interviews.

120. Gómez-Quiñones, *Chicano Politics*, 126.

121. Press release by the National Chicano Moratorium for the August 29, 1970 March, box 37, Hernandez Collection.

122. "Nuestra Batalla No Está En Vietnam, Está Aquí," *La Raza*, Special Moratorium Edition, September 1970.

123. Dave Smith, "Woman Scores Both Deputies and Militants," *Los Angeles Times*, 25 September 1970, 3; Drummond, "How East L.A. Protest Turned Into Major Riot," *Los Angeles Times*, 16 September 1970, 24.

124. See, e.g., "Rebellion in Los Angeles," *La Verdad*, September 1970, 2; "L.A. Moretorium [*sic*]—Riot or Revolt?", *¡Basta Ya!* October 1970, 2.; *La Voz del Pueblo–El Enterado*, September 1970, 5; Dolores Small, "Peaceful March Turns to Violence," *El Chicano*, 4 September 1970, 1.

125. Lorenzo Vargas, "Chicano: Evolution of Consciousness," *Raza de Bronce*, 26 February 1973, 2.

126. *La Verdad*, September 1970, 3.

127. "LA Police Attack Chicano Moratorium—Two Die," *El Gallo*, September 1970, 2 (the masthead carries the erroneous date of June 1970).

128. "L.A. Moretorium [*sic*]—Riot or Revolt?", *¡Basta Ya!* October 1970, 2.

129. Doug Robertson, "How Can It Happen on My Street, to My Family?" *Los Angeles Herald-Examiner*, 30 August 1970.

130. *La Opinión*, 1 September 1970, 1; Memo from Theodore H. Von Minden, Chief, Patrol Division East to Sheriff Peter J. Pitchess, 31 August, 1970, box 302, folder 10, Debs Collection.

131. Robert Kistler, "Police Reports Over Militant's Arrest Conflict," *Los Angeles Times*, 31 August, 1970, 3.

132. *La Raza Nueva*, radio show hosted by Moctezuma Esparza and broadcast on KPFK radio station, Chicano Studies Library, University of California at Los Angeles; Acuña, "Remembering August 29, 1970."

133. Charles T. Powers and Jeff Perlman, "One Dead, 40 Hurt in East L.A. Riot," *Los Angeles Times*, 30 August 1970, 19; Paul Houston, "Boy, 15, Dies of Riot Injuries," *Los Angeles Times*, 10 September 1970, 1.

134. "Eyewitness to a Murder," *La Voz del Pueblo–El Enterado*, Joint Special Edition, September 1970, 2; Richard Vasquez, "Second Victim of Riot Dies," *Los Angeles Times*, 2 September 1970, 3.

135. Transcripts of tape-recorded interviews with Hector Franco and Guillermo Restrepo, box 62, file 7, Ruiz Papers.

136. KPFK recording of National Chicano Moratorium Committee press conference, 31 August 1970, Chicano Studies Library, University of California at Los Angeles. The audience response can be heard on the tape. For a printed version of the prepared portion of Muñoz's speech, see "A Statement by the National Chicano Moratorium Committee," 31 August 1970, box 62, folder 7, Galarza Collection.

137. *La Raza Nueva*, radio show hosted by Moctezuma Esparza and broadcast on KPFK radio station, Chicano Studies Library, University of California at Los Angeles.

138. Dolores Small, "Peaceful March Turns to Violence," *El Chicano*, 4 September 1970, 1.

139. "Piden a la communidad que se mantenga en calma," *La Opinión*, 1 September 1970, 1.

140. Irene Tovar, interview.

141. Acuña, "Remembering August 29, 1970."

142. Paul Houston, "U.S. Inquiry Urged," *Los Angeles Times*, 1 September 1970, 1.

143. "Salazar Probe," *Los Angeles Times*, 17 September 1970, 27. Drafted by Democratic Senator Alan Cranston and Democratic Representative Edward Roybal, a letter to the U.S. Department of Justice was signed by nineteen additional California congressmen—including two Republicans.

144. Paul Houston, "East L.A. Fete Canceled 1st Time in 35 Years," *Los Angeles Times*, 5 September 1970, sec. 2, p. 1; Paul Houston, "Chicanos Will Resume Violence Halted Rally," *Los Angeles Times*, 3 September 1970, 1. Still other groups demanding an outside investigation were the local branch of the Urban Coalition, the California State Advisory Commission to the U.S. Commission on Civil Rights, and four local Roman Catholic priests (see U.S. Commission on Civil Rights, California Advisory Committee, *Police–Community Relations in East Los Angeles, California*, 31).

145. Several Chicano groups also united in a coalition to press for an inquiry. The coalition was called the National Chicano Coordinating Committee and included representatives from the Southwest and Midwest Councils of La Raza, the National Chicano Media Council, the National Urban Coalition, the Mexican American Legal Defense Fund, and labor unions. Still other groups demanding an investigation were PORQUE? (Project to Organize, Research, [and] Question Unknown Evidence), a local effort, and, from Texas, the national office of the League of United Latin American Citizens (Press Releases of the National Chicano Coordinating Committee, box 62, file 7, Galarza Collection; the PORQUE project proposal, box 38, folder 6, Corona Collection;

also see *Regeneración* 1, no. 6, [1970]: 17–18; Paul Houston, "U.S. Says it is Probing Reports that Outsiders Fomented Riot," *Los Angeles Times,* 2 September 1970, 1; and *La Opinión,* 1 September 1970, 1).

146. The petition, the telegram, and the letter are all in the folder marked "[Gen] HU 3–1/LG, L-R," Subject Files "HU," box 37, White House Central Files, Nixon Presidential Materials.

147. "Memorandum for the President" from Henry A. Kissinger in first folder of four marked "Mexico Nixon/Ordaz 20–21 August 1970," box 948, VIP visits, National Security Council Files, Nixon Presidential Materials.

148. Federal Bureau of Investigation, Freedom of Information Act document, Subject: "National Chicano Moratorium Against the War," file no. 100–45861, "Teletype to Director, San Diego from Los Angeles, 9/2/70."

149. Paul Houston, "U.S. Says it is Probing Reports that Outsiders Fomented Riot," *Los Angeles Times,* 2 September 1970, 3.

150. "Davis Blames Subversives," *Los Angeles Times,* 31 August 1970, 14.

151. "Yorty Gives Nixon His Views on Riot," *Los Angeles Times,* 5 September 1970, sec. 2, p. 10.

152. Dick Main, "There Was Nothing Peaceful In East L.A. March, Pitchess says," *Los Angeles Times,* 1 September 1970, 19.

153. Richard Vasquez, "Barrio Residents Describe Riot Reactions," *Los Angeles Times,* 6 September 1970, 1.

154. Doug Robertson, "How Can It Happen on My Street, to My Family?" *Los Angeles Herald-Examiner,* 30 August 1970.

155. Series of articles and photos in the *Los Angeles Times,* 4 September 1970, 1, 3. The editorial appeared in sec. 2, p. 8.

156. National Chicano Coordinating Committee Press Release "Sunday AM Sept. 6," box 62, File 7, Galarza Collection. The press release was also published in *Regeneración* (vol. 1, no. 6 [1970]: 17–18).

157. "Pitchess Discounts Value as Evidence of Riot Pictures," *Los Angeles Times,* 4 September 1970, 2.

158. Paul Houston, "TV Channels Will Provide Full Coverage of Salazar Inquest," *Los Angeles Times,* 9 September 1970, 1. The *Los Angeles Times* carried daily coverage. A young Tom Brokaw reported for the local NBC affiliate.

159. See, e.g., Paul Houston and Dave Smith, "Witness at Salazar Hearing Charges Bias," *Los Angeles Times,* 18 September 1970, 1.

160. Paul Houston, "Younger Plans No Charge," *Los Angeles Times,* 15 October 1970, 1.

161. Paul Houston and Dave Smith, "Mexican American Observers Walk Out of Salazar Inquest," *Los Angeles Times,* 11 September 1970, 1.

162. Paul Houston, "East L.A. Fete Canceled 1st Time in 35 Years," *Los Angeles Times,* 5 September 1970, sec. 2, p. 1.

163. Frank Del Olmo, "Chicano Group Reverses Stance on Parade," *Los Angeles Times,* 11 September 1970, 3.

164. "Rioting Spreads," *Los Angeles Times,* 31 August 1970, 1; "Relative Calm of Riot Areas Marked by Sporadic Incidents," *Los Angeles Times,* 2 September 1970, 3.

165. "Chicanos Hit Sheriff Searches in East L.A.," *Los Angeles Times*, 5 September 1970, 10; Steven J. Roberts, "Mexican-American Hostility Deepens in Tense East Los Angeles," *New York Times*, 4 September 1970, 20.

166. "Photos of Café Shooting Taken by Community Paper's Editors," *Los Angeles Times*, 4 September 1970, 3.

167. Irene Tovar, interview.

168. Dial Torgerson, "U.S., Sheriff Officials, Civilians Will Monitor East L.A. Parade," *Los Angeles Times*, 16b September 1970, 3.

169. "Violencia al terminar el desfile," *La Opinión*, 17 September 1970, 3; *Regeneración* 1, no. 9 (1970): 2.

170. Antonio Camejo, "L.A. Chicanos assail war," *The Militant*, 25 September 1970, 16; "Lessons of the L.A. Protest," *The Militant*, 16 October 1970, 9–12. The *Los Angeles Times* reported 150,000 and then 200,000.

171. "Sheriff's Deputy, Civilian Shot in Melee After East L.A. Parade," *Los Angeles Times*, 17 September 1970, 1; David Lamb, "'Chicano Power' Chants Shouted by Demonstrators," *Los Angeles Times*, 17 September 1970, 1.

172. Minden to Peter J. Pitchess, Sheriff, 17 September 1970, box 298, folder 2, Debs Collection; and news reports.

173. *Glendale (Calif.) News-Press*, 18 September 1970, 1. The importance that the newspaper gave Orozco's criticism was revealed by the article's placement above the banner on the front page.

174. *Regeneración* 1, no. 6 (1970): 7.

175. Dave Smith and Paul Houston, "Men Pushed into Bar at Gunpoint," *Los Angeles Times*, 24 September 1970, 3.

176. Four members of the seven-member panel ruled that Salazar's death "was at the hands of another person"; three ruled the death was an "accident" (see "Jury Splits 4–3," *Los Angeles Times*, 6 October 1970, 1; "Salazar Verdict: It Confuses Many," *Los Angeles Times*, 6 October 1970, 1; and "Salazar Jurors See Verdict as a Slap at Deputies," *Los Angeles Times*, 8 October 1970, 1).

177. "Salazar Facts Still Unknown," *Los Angeles Times*, 7 October 1970, sec. 2, p. 6; see also Chávez, *"¡Mi Raza Primero!"* 71–72.

178. Paul Houston, "Younger Plans No Charge," 15 October 1970, *Los Angeles Times*, 1.

179. Official Memorandum from Howard A. Glickstein, staff director to the United States Commission on Civil Rights, 29 October 1970, box 18, folder 2, Ruiz Papers.

180. Noriega, interview.

181. Muñoz, interview.

182. Elias, interview.

183. Ramirez, interview.

184. Donner, *The Age of Surveillance*, 347–48.

185. Ibid.; *Los Angeles Free Press*, 2–10 February 1972, 1; "Chicano Moratorium leader says he was a federal agent," newspaper article, n.d., in file marked "Police," Santillan Collection; Escobar, "The Dialectics of Repression," 1505. See also Chávez, *"¡Mi Raza Primero!"* 72–73.

186. A request through the Freedom of Information Act about this matter

Notes to Pages 182–188

generated a two-sentence statement saying that some under-aged Brown Berets once drank wine.

187. Citizens Research and Investigation Committee and Tackwood, *Glass House Tapes*, 136–37. While the people interviewed mentioned seeing guns, no one mentioned seeing brass knuckles.

188. "Se Opone a la Violencia un fuerte grupo de ELA," *La Opinión*, 13 January 1971, 3; "Que Explotan a los rojos a los demostrantes 'chicanos,'" *La Opinión*, 15 January 1971, 3; *Los Angeles Times*, 12 January 1971, sec. 2, p. 6.

189. "Rosalío Muñoz, culpa a la policía del Sheriff," *La Opinión*, 1 February 1970, 1; "January 31st Massacre," *La Raza* 1, no. 5 (February 1971); Chávez, *¡Mi Raza Primero!* 74–75.

190. *Regeneración* 1, no. 9 (1970): 2.

191. Irene Tovar, interview.

EPILOGUE

1. Tomás Gaspar, "It Will be Here," *La Gente de Aztlán*, October 1980, 6.

2. Rosalío U. Muñoz provided the author with a copy of this flier.

3. David E. Hayes-Bautista and Gregory Rodriguez, "The Chicano Movement: More Nostalgia than Reality," *Los Angeles Times*, 17 September 1995, 6.

4. Patrick J. McDonnell and Robert J. Lopez, "L.A. March Against Prop 187 draws 70,000," *Los Angeles Times*, 17 October 1994, 1.

5. I was on campus taking part in the demonstration when I heard the chant.

6. "National Chicano Moratorium," *La Voz del Pueblo*, August 1970, 1.

7. Muñoz, interview.

8. J. T. Ruiz, "La Marcha de la Justica," *El Alacrán*, March 1971, 4.

9. Sanchez, *Expedition Through Aztlán*, 41–43. See also Chávez, *¡Mi Raza Primero!* 77–79.

10. *People's World*, 12 July 1969, 2.

11. Muñoz, *Youth, Identity, and Power*, 94–95.

12. Chávez, *¡Mi Raza Primero!* 99–107.

13. For an early analysis of these ideological developments within the Chicano movement, see Garcia, "The Chicano Movement and the Mexican American Community."

14. For "correct theory," see Muñoz, *Youth, Identity, and Power*, 154.

15. "We Salute the Victorious Struggle," *El Comité Estudiantil del Pueblo*, May 1975, 1. Similarly, María Elena Ramirez, who had once lent her theatrical talents to an anti-draft effort in the San Francisco Bay Area, only abandoned her conviction that Maoism was the solution to Chicano oppression after a trip to China in 1972, when government officials there pointed out to her that the success of the Chinese revolution had depended upon the support of millions of peasants in a largely agrarian society whereas Mexican Americans constituted a minority within an industrialized nation. Ramirez good-naturedly conceded that maybe some reassessment was in order (María Eléna Ramirez, interview).

16. *El Gallo*, November–December 1973 and January 1974, 4–5.

17. For an account of the national party's disintegration, see García, *United We Win*, 135–48.

18. Muñoz, *Youth, Identity, and Power*, 94–95.

19. *La Raza* 1, no. 5 (February 1971): 86.

20. See Delfino Varela, "The Making of Captain Medina," *Regeneración*, vol. 1, no. 1 (1970), 8–13; and the less sympathetic "Pobrecito Captain Medina, a Dupe of the Establishment," *La Causa*, 22 May 1970, 15.

21. Thanks to Dionne Espinoza for this important insight.

22. Mariscal, *Aztlán and Viet Nam*, 257. In addition, the American G.I. Forum passed a resolution in support of Medina at their 1971 national convention (see "G.I. Forum Votes to Aid Capt. Medina," *La Voz del Pueblo*, July–August 1971, 6.

23. Antonio Camejo, "L.A. Chicanos assail war," *The Militant*, 25 September 1970, 16.

24. The plaque commemorating the rededication is visible at the foot of the statue, which resides across from the State Capitol on Tenth Street in Sacramento.

25. Leatherwood and Garza, "Alfredo Cantu Gonzalez" entry. In 1996, the Navy followed suit, commissioning the USS *Alfredo Gonzalez*, a guided-missile destroyer and the first U.S. warship named after a Mexican American.

26. Eugene A. Obregón / Medal of Honor Campaign, Aztecanet, http://www.azteca.net/cmhlatino/. A resolution in support of building this monument can be found at the League of United Latin American Citizens website, http://www.lulac.org/Issues/Resolve/2002/40%20Eugene%20Obregon.html.

27. "Bomba en el Palacio de Justicia de Los Angeles," *La Opinión*, 6 September 1970, 1.

28. Escobar, *Race, Police, and the Making of a Political Identity*, 1508.

29. Oscar Zeta Acosta also defended Corky Gonzales after his arrest on August 29, 1970.

30. Oscar Zeta Acosta, "A Love Letter to the Girls of Aztlán," *Con Safos*, Summer 1970, 29. Carl Gutiérrez-Jones made a similar point about Acosta's "tendency to transform women into a commodity exchanged among men." In his insightful analysis of Acosta's written work, Gutiérrez-Jones concluded, that, from Acosta's perspective, "to be a Chicano (male) means to sleep with Chicanas" (Gutiérrez-Jones, *Rethinking the Borderlands*, 130–31).

31. Muñoz, *Youth, Identity, and Power*, 33.

32. Coined by the anthropologist Oscar Lewis, the term "culture of poverty" enjoyed wide popular use after it appeared in his books, beginning with *Five Families: Mexican Case Studies in the Culture of Poverty*. For the use of this term by Mexican American researchers, see Galarza, Gallegos, and Samora, *Mexican-Americans in the Southwest*, 57. The comment about minimal assimilation can be found in Kluckhorn, *Variations in Value Orientation*, 26. For a devastating critique of the extant social science literature on Mexican Americans, see Romano-V., "The Anthropology and Sociology of Mexican-Americans." Ignacio M. García called the "reinterpretation of the Chicano experience," including the rejection of the culture of poverty thesis, as one of four critical steps toward a Chicano political consciousness (see his *Chicanismo*, especially 43–47).

33. Chicano Coordinating Council on Higher Education, *El Plan de Santa Bárbara*.

34. Muñoz, *Youth, Identity, Power*, 84.

35. Ibid., 155–63.

36. "UCSB to Establish Nation's First Chicano Studies Ph.D. Program," University of Santa Barbara press release, 4 August 2003, http://www.instadv.ucsb.edu/release/Display.aspx?PKey = 1013. Originally, enrollment was planned to start in 2004, but according to the UCSB Chicano Studies Department, enrollment is now set to start in Fall 2005 (see http://www.chist.ucsb.edu/phd/index/shmtl).

37. Galarza, Gallegos, and Samora, *Mexican-Americans in the Southwest*, 20, 33.

38. Gutiérrez, *Walls and Mirrors*, 60.

39. Ibid., 191, 194.

40. *Profile of the Foreign-Born Population in the United States: 1997*, 10–12.

41. Gonzales, *Mexicanos*, 226–28; Martínez, *Mexican-Origin People in the United States*, 39.

42. Montes, "La Nueva Chicana," 19. For an appraisal of the role of Chicana feminism within the Chicano movement, see Gutiérrez, "Community, Patriarchy, and Individualism." Male resistance to change was the focus of Martínez, "Chingón Politics Die Hard."

43. *La Raza* 1, no. 1 (March 1970): 10.

44. "For Machos Only," *El Grito del Norte*, 24 August 1968, 1.

45. Gómez-Quiñones, *Chicano Politics*, 176.

46. Bourne, *Jimmy Carter*, 319–20, 333–34.

47. That incident and more recent outreach efforts can be found in Radelat, "Road to Power."

48. García, "The Chicano Movement: Its Legacy for Politics and Policy," 94.

49. For Mexican American political representation in 1967 at the state level, see Grebler, Moore, and Guzman, *The Mexican-American People*, 561.

50. For data about California, see Joe Rodriguez, "Latina Lawmakers Make their Mark," *San Jose Mercury News*, 29 May 2003, http://www.bayarea.com/mld/mercurynews/news/columnists/joe_rodriguez/5971823.htm; and "Latino Legislative Caucus Homepage," http://democrats.assembly.ca.gov/Latino Caucus/. Information about Latino representation in Texas can be found at the "Legislative Reference Library of Texas," http://www.lrl.state.tx.us/legis/profile78.html; and http://www.lrl.state.tx.us/legis/members/roster.cfm.

51. Grebler, Moore, and Guzman, *The Mexican-American People*, 561. According to the Congressional Research Service, the 108th Congress had a record twenty-five Hispanic members (http://www.senate.gov/reference/resources/pdf/RS21379.pdf). Biographical information from each representative's Web page indicated how many of these were of Mexican origin and their party affiliation.

52. On March 12, 2003, the president signed an executive order establishing two Global War on Terrorism medals for members of the armed forces. The White House published the executive order as a press release at http://www.whitehouse.gov/news/releases/2003/03/20030312-6.html.

53. A copy of the petition is in the author's possession. The petition and its signatories can also be found at http://lists.quantumimagery.com/pipermail/ sdcpj/2002-October/000216.html.

54. According to the California Department of Education, while the population of Latino ninth-graders during the 1997–98 academic year was 180,969, only 103,795 Latinos graduated from public high schools in the state four years later (California Department of Education, Educational Demographics Office, "Graduation Rates in California Public Schools by Ethnic Group"). Many thanks to Lisa Chavez for helping me locate this information and make sense of it.

55. Different from the California statistics above, the U.S. Census calculated the dropout rate as the percentage of people over the age of 25 who had not completed high school (see *The Hispanic Population in the United States* (March 2002), 5. The entire report can be accessed on the Internet at http://www.census.gov/prod/2003pubs/p20–545.pdf.

56. Ibid., 6. Only Puerto Ricans had a higher percentage of people living below the poverty level, at 26.1 percent.

57. Vélez-Ibañez, *Border Visions*, 187–88.

58. Ibid., 182.

59. Ibid., 189–92. See also William Overend, "Fresno Triples Its Anti-Gang Forces, *Los Angeles Times,* 25 February 2002, B-6.

60. On June 18, 1990, *Time* magazine ran a cover story on "Child Warriors." The profile of child soldiers across the globe included an article on gang warfare in Los Angeles. According to the California Department of Corrections, in 2002, Hispanics made up 35.4 percent of the state's prison population. According to U.S. census data, Hispanics made up 32.4 percent of the state's general population (see California Department of Corrections, www.corr.ca .gov/CDC/facts_figures.asp; and U.S. Census Bureau, http://quickfacts .census.gov/qfd/states/06000.html). See also "Crime Statistics Paint a Gloomy Picture for Latino Communities," *Arizona Report* 1 (Winter 1997), a publication of the Mexican American Studies and Research Center at the University of Arizona; and a Bureau of Justice Statistics press release, 17 August 2003, "More than 5.6 Million U.S. Residents Have Served or Are Serving Time in State or Federal Prisons," http://www.ojp.usdoj.gov/bjs/pub/press/piusp.01pr.htm.

61. Max Blumenthal, "Vigilante Injustice," *salon.com,* 22 May 2003, http://www.salon.com/news/feature/2003/05/22/vigilante/index.html.

62. Caldera, "Secretary of the Army Louis Caldera '78 Says Farewell." For more about the Army's recruiting efforts among Hispanic youth, see Jorge Mariscal, "Chicano POWs Returned Home," *La Prensa San Diego,* 7 May 1999, http://www.laprensa-sandiego.org/archieve/may07/pow.htm.

63. In the early 1990s, African Americans made up 23 percent of the armed forces, but only 11 percent of the general population (McAlister, *Epic Encounters*, 254).

64. These statistics and more appeared in U.S. Department of Defense, "Population Representation in the Military Service, Fiscal Year 2000," especially tables B-25; B-34, B-47, and B-49. (http://dod.mil/prhome/poprep2000/).

Many thanks to Mr. Rick Janhkow for pointing me toward the Department of Defense report and guiding me through it.

65. Steven A. Holmes, "Is This Really An All-Volunteer Army?" *New York Times*, 6 April 2003, sec. 4, p. 1.

66. Macarena Hernandez, "Pentagon courts Hispanics" *San Antonio Express-News*, 10 October 2002, 3B.

67. U.S. Department of Defense, "Population Representation in the Military Service, Fiscal Year 2000," table B-3, http://dod.mil/prhome/poprep2000/.

68. David W. Chen and Somini Sengupta, "Not Yet Citizens But Eager to Fight for the U.S.," *New York Times*, 26 October 2001, 1.

69. Steven A. Holmes, "Is This Really An All-Volunteer Army?" *New York Times*, 6 April 2003, sec. 4, p. 1.

70. Leading the effort in this regard was Representative Brian Bilbray, Republican from San Diego, who served in the U.S. Congress between 1995 and 2001. He repeatedly sponsored legislation to change birthright citizenship.

71. Chaleampon Ritthichai, "Immigrant Soldiers," *Gotham Gazette*, May 2003, http://www.gothamgazette.com/article/immigrants/20030501/11/368. See also Tim Weiner, "Latinos Gave Their Lives to New Land," *New York Times*, 4 April 2003, B-10.

72. Weiner, "Latinos Gave Their Lives to New Land," *New York Times*, 4 April 2003, B-10.

73. One early estimate by Republican pollsters was 70 percent (see Earl Ofari Hutchinson, "Latinos Say 'Yes' to Iraq War, But Why?" 7 April 2003, Alternet.org, http://www.alternet.org/story.html?StoryID = 155571).

74. Simon Crittle, "In Death, A Marine Gets His Life Wish," *Time*, online edition, 28 March 2003, http://www.time.com/time/world/article/0,8599,438626,00.html. Gutiérrez had also hoped that once he was a U.S. citizen, he could sponsor his sister's citizenship application. She remained in Guatemala after his death, cut off from the income he had once sent her.

75. Jorge Mariscal, "Cannon Fodder, Latinos likely to be on the front lines of the next war," *LatinoLA.com*, 14 October 2002, http://www.latinola.com/story.php?story = 528. In this article, Mariscal came to a similar conclusion about the Chicano movement's significance. As he wrote: "[The Chicano movement] meant a radical analysis of U.S. history and foreign policy coupled with a commitment to progressive activism."

76. Gómez, interview.

77. Author's notes of Ernesto Vigil speaking before attendees of the Chicano Moratorium 2002. He spoke at the film night and during a scholars' panel, 23 and 25 August 2002.

78. Ernesto Vigil, "Commentary."

Bibliography

ORAL HISTORY INTERVIEWS

Conducted by Author:

Alvarez, Delia. Tape-recorded. San Francisco, Calif., 14 February 2002.
Andrade, Erasmo. Tape-recorded. Austin, Texas, 1 June 1994.
Arellanes, Gloria. Tape-recorded. El Monte, Calif., 15 December 2002.
Baldenegro, Salomón. Tape-recorded. Tucson, Ariz., 24 January 1993.
Cano, Gilbert. Notes from conversation. Los Angeles, Calif., 25 August 2002.
Chacón, Joe. Tape-recorded. Los Angeles, Calif., 16 April 1993.
Compean, Mario. Tape-recorded. Yakima, Wash., 29 August 1999.
Davis del Valle, Katarina. Tape-recorded. Sacramento, Calif., 18 January 2002.
Elias, Bob. Tape-recorded. Los Angeles, Calif., 19 April 1993.
Garcia, Homer D. C. Notes from conversation. San Jose, Calif., 23 March 1993.
Garcia, Genaro. Tape-recorded. Austin, Texas, 11 June 1994.
Genera, Nina. Tape-recorded. Hayward, Calif., 12 March 1997.
Gómez, Manuel. Tape-recorded. Irvine, Calif., 15 March 1997
Gonzales, Rodolfo. Notes from conversation. Denver, Colo., 27 November 2001.
Gutiérrez, José Angel. Tape-recorded. Dallas, Texas, 6 June 1994.
Jensen, Hilda Quen. Written responses to written questions. July and August 2003.
Martínez, Elizabeth. Tape-recorded. San Francisco, Calif., 15 January 1993.
Montes, Carlos. Notes from telephone conversation, 20 September 1993.
Muñoz, Rosalío U. Tape-recorded. Los Angeles, Calif., 15 and 28 May 1993.
Noriega, Ramsés. Tape-recorded. San Diego, Calif., 1 November 1993.
Ramirez, María Elena. Tape-recorded. Union City, Calif., 19 March 1997.

Ramirez, Ralph. Tape-recorded. Los Angeles, Calif., 30 October 1993.

Sanchez, David. Tape-recorded. Los Angeles, Calif., 20 April 1993.

Santillan, Richard. Notes from conversation. Los Angeles, Calif., 25 August 2002.

Tovar, Irene. Tape-recorded. San Fernando, Calif., 14 December 2000.

Tovar, Irene. Notes from conversation. San Fernando, Calif., 2 December 2002.

Tovar, Nancy. Notes from conversation. Los Angeles, Calif., 24 August 2002.

Valdez Martinez, Valentina. Tape-recorded. Tierra Amarilla, N.M., 22 August 1997.

Vazquez, Enriqueta Longeaux. Tape-recorded. San Cristobal, N.M., 23 August 1997.

Vigil, Ernesto. Tape-recorded. Denver, Colo., 22 March 1993.

Ybarra, Lea. Tape-recorded. Fresno, Calif., 19 January 1993.

All materials related to the above interviews are in the author's possession. A few words about methodology: during the tape-recorded interviews, I almost always asked about the person's family background, their involvement in the Chicano movement, and their opposition to the Viet Nam War. I asked other questions, too, a long and varied list, depending upon what preliminary information I had gathered from Chicano movement newspapers, other media sources, various archival documents, and secondary works. A few interviews were not recorded; most of these transpired from chance meetings at conferences, with me deciding to take notes after a conversation had turned toward matters pertinent to my research. One exception to this general process was Hilda Quen Jensen. Just before the manuscript was completed, I found out that she was living in Alabama. Not able to make a last-minute trip to visit her, I asked her questions and received her responses via e-mail so that I might have a written record. Finally, I attempted to engage in a "feminist practice of oral history" by frequently sharing my work in progress—a methodology that often required follow-up phone calls and/or e-mail correspondence.

Conducted by Carlos Vásquez:

Martinez, Richard A. 1990.

Navarro, Armando. 1989.

Santillan, Richard. 1989.

These interviews were conducted as part of the UCLA Oral History Program for the California State Archives State Government Oral History Program. Transcripts available at the California State Archives, Sacramento, Calif., and other repositories.

ARCHIVAL SOURCES

Joe Bernal Papers. Benson Latin American Collection, University of Texas, Austin.

Dennis Chavez Collection. Center for Southwest Research, University of New Mexico, Albuquerque.

Chicano Movement Collection. Houston Metropolitan Research Center, Houston Public Library.

Bert Corona Papers. Department of Special Collections, Stanford University Libraries, Stanford, Calif.

Ernest E. Debs Collection. Special Collections Library, California State University, Los Angeles.

Ernesto Galarza Papers. Department of Special Collections, Stanford University Libraries, Stanford, Calif.

Dr. Hector P. Garcia Collection. Special Collections Library, Texas A & M University, Corpus Christi.

Speeches of Rodolfo "Corky" Gonzales. Audiotape Recordings. Private collection of Ernesto Vigil, Denver, Colo.

José Angel Gutiérrez Papers. Benson Latin American Collection, University of Texas, Austin.

Antonio Hernandez Collection. Chicano Studies Library, University of California, Berkeley.

Lyndon B. Johnson, Papers of the President, Lyndon Baines Johnson Library, Austin, Texas.

League of United Latin American Citizens (LULAC) Archives. Benson Latin American Collection, University of Texas, Austin.

Mexican American Movement Collection. Special Collections Library, California State University, Northridge.

Joseph M. Montoya Papers. Center for Southwest Research, Zimmerman Library, University of New Mexico.

Nixon Presidential Materials. National Archives, College Park, Maryland.

Edward R. Roybal Collection. Special Collections Library, California State University, Los Angeles.

Manuel Ruiz Papers. Department of Special Collections, Stanford University Libraries, Stanford, Calif.

George I. Sanchez Papers. Benson Latin American Collection, University of Texas, Austin.

Richard Santillan Collection. Chicano Studies Library, University of California, Berkeley.

Social Protest Collection. Bancroft Library, University of California, Berkeley.

NEWSPAPERS AND NEWSLETTERS

Most of the Chicano movement newspapers cited below can be found on microfilm in the Chicano Studies Library, University of California, Berkeley.

Agenda (Washington, D.C.)
Amigos (Tucson)
Arizona Report (Tucson)
¡Basta Ya! (San Francisco)
Bronze (Fresno/San Jose/Oakland)
Caracol (Houston)
Carta Editorial (Los Angeles)
Católicos por la Raza (Los Angeles)

Chicano Student Movement (Los Angeles)
Chicano Student News (Los Angeles)
Christian Science Monitor
Chicano Times (San Antonio)
Congressional Quarterly Almanac
Congressional Record
Congressional Weekly Report
Con Safos (Los Angeles)
Daily Bruin (University of California, Los Angeles)
Daily Pioneer (California State University, Hayward)
Denver Post
East Los Angeles Tribune/Commerce Tribune
Echo (Austin)
El Alacrán (publication of the MEChA chapter at California State University, Long Beach)
El Barrio (San Diego/Oakland)
El Chicano (Compton, Calif.)
El Chicano (San Bernardino, Calif.)
El Comité Estudiantil Chicano de Aztlán (Los Angeles)
El Enterado (Berkeley)
El Gallo (Denver)
El Paso Times
El Grito (Berkeley)
El Grito de Aztlán (San Diego)
El Grito del Norte (Española, N.M.)
El Informador (Berkeley)
El Machete (Los Angeles)
El Malcriado (Delano, Calif.)
The Forumeer (San Jose)
Glendale (Calif.) News-Press
Hard Times (Washington, D.C.)
Hispanic Magazine (online)
Inside Eastside (Los Angeles)
La Causa (Los Angeles)
La Gente de Aztlán (Los Angeles)
La Luz (Denver)
La Opinión (Los Angeles)
La Raza (Los Angeles)
La Raza Yearbook (Los Angeles)
La Verdad (San Diego)
La Voz del Pueblo (Berkeley)
La Voz del Pueblo (San Diego)
La Voz del Pueblo–El Enterado (Hayward and Richmond, Calif.)
Los Angeles Free Press
Los Angeles Times
LULAC News (Texas)
LatinoLA.com (online)

Mexican American (Odessa, Texas)
The Militant
The Nation
The New Yorker
Outlook (magazine supplement of the *Washington Post*)
Papel Chicano (Houston)
People's World
Raza de Bronce (San Diego)
Regeneración (Los Angeles)
Rolling Stone
Salon.com (online)
San Antonio Evening News
San Antonio Express-News
San Jose Mercury News
San Francisco Chronicle
Saturday Evening Post
Time.com (online)
Venceremos Papel (Albuquerque)
Washington Post
Washington Times.com (online)
West (magazine supplement of the *Los Angeles Times*)

OTHER SOURCES

Acuña, Rodolfo F. *Occupied America: The Chicano's Struggle for Liberation.* 1st ed. San Francisco: Canfield Press, 1972.
———. *Occupied America: A History of Chicanos.* 3rd ed. New York: Harper Collins, 1988.
———. "Remembering August 29, 1970." *La Prensa San Diego,* 6 September 2002, http://www.laprensa-sandiego.org/archieve/september06–02/person.htm.
Adams, Nina A. "The Women Who Left Them Behind." In *Give Peace a Chance,* edited by Melvin Small and William D. Hoover. Syracuse: Syracuse University Press, 1992.
Adler, Patricia Rae. "The 1943 Zoot-Suit Riots: Brief Episode in a Long Conflict." In *The Mexican Americans, An Awakened Minority,* edited by Manuel P. Servín. New York: Macmillan, 1974.
Ahari, Mohammed E., ed. *Ethnic Groups and Foreign Policy.* New York: Greenwood Press, 1987.
Allsup, Carl. *The American G.I. Forum.* Austin: Mexican American Studies Center, University of Texas, 1982.
Almaguer, Tomás. *Racial Fault Lines: The Historical Origins of White Supremacy in California.* Berkeley: University of California Press, 1994.
Alvarez, Everett, Jr., and Anthony S. Pitch. *Chained Eagle.* New York: Donald I. Fine, 1989.
Ambrecht, Biliana C. S. *Politicizing the Poor: The Legacy of the War on Poverty in a Mexican-American Community.* New York: Praeger, 1976.

Anaya, Rudolfo A., and Francisco Lomelí. *Aztlán: Essays on the Chicano Homeland*. Albuquerque: N.M.: Academia/El Norte Publications, 1989.

Appy, Christian G. *Working-Class War*. Durham: University of North Carolina Press, 1993.

Armas, Jose. "La Familia de la Raza." *De Colores: A Journal of Emerging Raza Philosophies* (Albuquerque, N.M.) 3, no. 2 (1976): 11–44.

Austin, Joe, and Michael Nevin Willard, eds. *Generations of Youth: Youth Cultures and History in Twentieth Century America*. New York: New York University Press, 1998.

Baca, Herman. "The Day the Police Rioted! Remembering 32 Years Ago." http://www.azteca.net/aztec/cmora.html.

Baca-Zinn, Maxine. "Political Familism: Toward Sex Role Equality." *Aztlán* 6 (Spring 1975): 13–26.

Bailey, Thomas A. *The Man in the Street: The Impact of American Public Opinion on Foreign Policy*. New York: Macmillan, 1948.

Balderrama, Francisco E., and Raymond Rodríguez. *Decade of Betrayal: Mexican Repatriation in the 1930s*. Albuquerque: University of New Mexico Press, 1995.

Barber, Lucy G. *Marching on Washington: The Forging of an American Political Tradition*. Berkeley: University of California Press, 2002.

Baritz, Loren. *Backfire: A History of How American Culture Led Us into Vietnam and Made Us Fight the Way We Did*. New York: Ballantine Books, 1985.

Barrera, Mario, Charles Ornelas, and Carlos Muñoz. "The Barrio as an Internal Colony." In *People and Politics in Urban Society*, edited by Harlan Hahn. Beverly Hills, CA: Sage Publications, 1972.

Berman, Larry. *Lyndon Johnson's War: The Road to Stalemate in Vietnam*. New York: W. W. Norton, 1989.

———. *Planning a Tragedy: The Americanization of the War in Vietnam*. New York: Norton, 1982.

Bernal, Dolores Delgado. "Chicana School Resistance and Grassroots Leadership: Providing an Alternative Framework for the 1968 East Los Angeles Blowouts." Ph.D. diss., University of California, Los Angeles, 1997.

Bernstein, Alison R. *American Indians and World War II: Toward a New Era in Indian Affairs*. Norman: University of Oklahoma Press, 1991.

Berube, Allan. *Coming Out Under Fire: The History of Gay Men and Women in World War Two*. New York: Free Press, 1990.

Beschloss, Michael R., ed. *Reaching for Glory: The Johnson White House Tapes, 1964–1965*. New York: Simon and Schuster, 2001.

Blight, David W. *Frederick Douglass' Civil War: Keeping Faith in Jubilee*. Baton Rouge: Louisiana State University Press, 1989.

Blum, John Morton. *V Was for Victory: Politics and American Culture during World War II*. New York: Harcourt Brace Jovanovich, 1976.

Bourne, Peter G. *Jimmy Carter: A Comprehensive Biography from Plains to Postpresidency*. New York: Scribner, 1997.

Breitman, George, ed. *By Any Means Necessary: Speeches, Interviews, and a Letter by Malcolm X*. New York: Pathfinder, 1970.

Briegel, Kaye. "Alianza Hispano-Americana and Some Mexican-American Civil Rights Cases in the 1950s." In *The Mexican Americans, An Awakened Minority*, edited by Manuel P. Servín. New York: Macmillan, 1974.

Broyles-González, Yolanda. *El Teatro Campesino*. Austin: University of Texas Press, 1994.

Buchanan, A. Russell. *Black Americans in World War II*. Santa Barbara, Calif.: Clio Press, 1977.

Bullington, Bruce. "Drug Use Patterns in a Chicano Community." Ph.D. diss., University of California, Los Angeles, 1974.

Burma, John H. *Spanish-Speaking Groups in the United States*. 1954. Reprint, Detroit: Blaine Ethridge Books, 1974.

Caldera, Louis. "Secretary of the Army Louis Caldera '78 Says Farewell." *Assembly Online* (newsletter of the Association of Graduates of the U.S. Military Academy)March/April 2001, http://www.aog.usma.edu/PUBS/ASSEMBLY/010304/caldera.htm.

California Department of Education, Educational Demographics Office. "Graduation Rates in California Public Schools by Ethnic Group, 1984–85 through 2001–02," http://www.cde.ca.gov/demographics/reports/statewide/ethgrate.htm.

Camarillo, Albert. *Chicanos in a Changing Society: From Mexican Pueblos to American Barrios in Santa Barbara and Southern California, 1848–1900*. Cambridge, Mass.: Harvard University Press, 1979.

———. "Research Note on Chicano Community Leaders: The G.I. Generation." *Aztlán* 2 (Fall 1971): 145–50.

Capeci, Jr., Dominic J. *The Harlem Riot of 1943*. Philadelphia: Temple University Press, 1977.

Carey, J. T. "Marijuana Use Among the New Bohemians." In *The New Social Drug*, edited by D. E. Smith. Englewood Cliffs, N.J.: Prentice-Hall, 1970.

Caro, Robert A. *The Years of Lyndon Johnson: The Path to Power*. New York: Knopf, 1982.

Carroll, Patrick. *Felix Longoria's Wake: Bereavement, Racism, and the Rise of Mexican American Activism*. Austin: University of Texas Press, 2003.

Cashman, Sean Dennis, *African Americans and the Quest for Civil Rights, 1900–1990*. New York: New York University Press, 1997.

Chávez, Ernesto. "Birth of a New Symbol: The Brown Berets' Gendered Chicano National Imaginary." In *Generations of Youth: Youth Cultures and History in Twentieth Century America*, edited by Joe Austin and Michael Nevin Willard. New York: New York University Press, 1998.

———. *"¡Mi Raza Primero!" (My People First!): Nationalism, Identity, and Insurgency in the Chicano Movement in Los Angeles, 1966–1978*. Berkeley: University of California Press, 2002.

Chávez, John R. *The Lost Land: The Chicano Image of the Southwest*. Albuquerque: University of New Mexico Press, 1984.

Chicano Coordinating Council on Higher Education. *El Plan de Santa Bárbara: A Chicano Plan for Higher Education*. Oakland, Calif.: La Causa Publications, 1969.

Chicano!: History of a Mexican American Civil Rights Movement. Television documentary. Executive producer José Luis Ruiz. National Latino Communication Center, 1996.

Christian, Carole E. "Joining the American Mainstream: Texas's Mexican Americans during WWI." *Southwestern Historical Quarterly* 92 (April 1989): 559–95.

Churchill, Ward, and Jim Vander Wall. *Agents of Repression: The FBI's Secret Wars Against the Black Panther Party and the American Indian Movement.* Boston: South End Press, 1988.

Citizens Research and Investigation Committee, and Louis Tackwood. *Glass House Tapes: The Story of an Agent Provocateur and the New Police Intelligence Complex.* New York: Avon, 1973.

Cleaver, Kathleen, and George Katsiaficas, eds. *Liberation, Imagination, and the Black Panther Party.* New York: Routledge, 2001.

Cohen, Bernard C. *The Public's Impact on Foreign Policy.* Boston: Little, Brown, 1973.

Compean, Mario. *La Raza Unida Party in Texas: Speeches, by Mario Compean and José Angel Gutiérrez.* Introduction by Antonio Camejo. New York: Pathfinder Press, 1970.

Craig, Richard B. *The Bracero Program: Interest Groups and Foreign Policy.* Austin: University of Texas Press, 1971.

Crockcoft, James D. *Outlaws in the Promise Land.* New York: Grove Press, 1986.

Dalifume, Richard M. "The 'Forgotten Years' of the Negro Revolution." *Journal of American History* 55 (June 1968): 90–106.

Dallek, Robert. *Lone Star Rising: Lyndon Johnson and His Times, 1908–1960.* New York: Oxford University Press, 1991.

Daniel, Cletus E. *Chicano Workers and the Politics of Fairness: The FEPC in the Southwest, 1941–1945.* Austin: University of Texas Press, 1991.

Dansby, Mickey R., James B. Stewart, and Schuyler C. Webb, eds. *Managing Diversity in the Military: Research Perspectives from the Defense Equal Opportunity Management Institute.* New Brunswick, N.J.: Transaction Publishers, 2001.

Davis, Mike. *City of Quartz.* New York: Random House, 1992.

De León, Arnoldo. *The Tejano Community, 1836–1900.* Albuquerque: University of New Mexico Press, 1989.

———. *They Called Them Greasers: Anglo Attitudes Towards Mexicans in Texas, 1821–1900.* Austin: University of Texas Press, 1993.

DeBenedetti, Charles, and Charles Chatfield, assisting author. *An American Ordeal: The Antiwar Movement of the Vietnam Era.* Syracuse, N.Y.: Syracuse University Press, 1990.

Del Castillo, Adelaida R. "Malintzin Tenepal: A Preliminary Look into a New Perspective." In *Essays on la mujer,* edited by Rosaura Sanchez. Los Angeles: University of California Chicano Studies Center, 1977.

D'Emilio, John. *Sexual Politics, Sexual Communities: The Making of a Homosexual Minority in the United States, 1940–1970.* Chicago: University of Chicago Press, 1983.

Donner, Frank J. *The Age of Surveillance: The Aims and Methods of America's Political Intelligence System.* New York: Random House, 1981.

Echols, Alice. "'Women Power' and Women's Liberation: Exploring the Relationship between the Antiwar Movement and the Women's Liberation Movement." In *Give Peace a Chance,* edited by Melvin Small and William D. Hoover. Syracuse: Syracuse University Press, 1992.

Escobar, Edward J. "The Dialectics of Repression: The Los Angeles Police Department and the Chicano Movement, 1968–1971." *Journal of American History* 79 (March 1993): 1483–1514.

———. *Race, Police, and the Making of a Political Identity: Mexican Americans and the Los Angeles Police Department, 1900–1945.* Berkeley: University of California Press, 1999.

Espinoza, Dionne. "Pedagogies of Nationalism and Gender: Cultural Resistance in Selected Representational Practices of Chicana/o Movement Activists, 1967–1972." Ph.D. diss., Cornell University, 1996.

———. "'Revolutionary Sisters': Women's Solidarity and Collective Identification among Chicana Brown Berets in East Los Angles, 1967–1970." *Aztlán* 26 (Spring 2001): 17–58.

Fairclough, Adam. "Martin Luther King, Jr. and the War in Vietnam." *Phylon* 45 (1984): 19–39.

Farber, David. *The Age of Great Dreams: America in the 1960s.* New York: Hill and Wang, 1994.

Federal Bureau of Investigation. Documents released in response to Freedom of Information Act request for information on the Crusade for Justice, the Brown Berets, the Raza Unida Party, the Congress of Mexican American Unity, and the National Chicano Moratorium Committee.

Fields, Rona M., and Charles J. Fox. "The Brown Berets." In *Chicano Politics: Readings,* edited by F. Chris García. New York: MSS Information Corp., 1973.

Fincher, E. B. *Spanish Americans as a Political Factor in New Mexico, 1912–1950.* 1950. Reprint, New York: Arno Press, 1974.

Flores, William V., and Rina Benmayor. *Latino Cultural Citizenship: Claiming Identity, Space, and Rights.* Boston: Beacon Press, 1997.

Foley, Douglas E. *From Peones to Politicos: Ethnic Relations in a South Texas Town, 1900–1977.* Austin: Center for Mexican American Studies, University of Texas, 1977.

Foley, Neil. "Becoming Hispanic: Mexican Americans and the Faustian Pact with Whiteness." In *Reflexiones 1997: New Directions in Mexican American Studies,* edited by Neil Foley. Austin: Center for Mexican American Studies, University of Texas at Austin, 1998.

———. *The White Scourge: Mexicans, Blacks, and Poor Whites in Texas Cotton Culture.* Berkeley: University of California Press, 1997.

Ford, Nancy Gentile. *Americans All!: Foreign-Born Soldiers in World War I.* College Station: Texas A & M University Press, 2001.

Foust, Brady, and Howard Botts. "Age, Ethnicity, and Class in the Vietnam War: Evidence from the Casualties File." Unpublished conference paper, 1989 (in the author's possession).

Fox, Geoffrey. *Hispanic Nation: Culture, Politics, and the Constructing of Identity*. Tucson: University of Arizona Press, 1996.

Fuller, Elizabeth. *The Mexican Housing Problem in Los Angeles*. 1920. Reprint, New York: Arno Press, 1974.

Galarza, Ernesto. *Merchants of Labor: The Mexican Bracero Story*. Charlotte, N.C.: McNally and Loftin, 1964.

Galarza, Ernesto, Herman Gallegos, and Julian Samora. *Mexican-Americans in the Southwest*. Santa Barbara, Calif.: McNally and Loftin, 1969.

García, Alma M. *Chicana Feminist Thought: The Basic Historical Writings*. New York: Routledge, 1997.

Garcia, David. *Requiem 29*. Motion Picture. 1970. (Chicano Studies Research Library, University of California, Los Angeles)

Garcia, F. Chris, ed. *La Causa Política: A Chicano Politics Reader*. Notre Dame, Ind.: University of Notre Dame Press, 1974.

———. *Chicano Politics: Readings*. New York: MSS Information Corp., 1973.

García, Ignacio M. *Chicanismo: The Forging of a Militant Ethos among Mexican Americans*. Tucson: University of Arizona, Press, 1997.

———. *Hector P. García: In Relentless Pursuit of Justice*. Houston, Texas: Arte Público Press, 2002.

———. *United We Win: The Rise and Fall of the Raza Unida Party*. Tucson: Mexican American Studies and Research Center, University of Arizona Press, 1989.

———. *Viva Kennedy!: Mexican Americans in Search of Camelot*. College Station: Texas A & M Press, 2000.

García, John A. "The Chicano Movement: Its Legacy for Politics and Policy." In *Chicanas/Chicanos at the Crossroads: Social, Economic, and Political Change*, edited by David R. Maciel and Isidro D. Ortiz. Tucson: University of Arizona Press, 1996.

García, Juan Ramon. *Operation Wetback: The Mass Deportation of Mexican Undocumented Workers in 1954*. Westport, Conn.: Greenwood Press, 1980.

Garcia, Matt. *A World of Its Own: Race, Labor, and Citrus in the Making of the Greater Los Angeles Area, 1900–1970*. Chapel Hill: University of North Carolina Press, 2001.

García, Mario T. "Americans All: The Mexican American Generation and the Politics of Wartime Los Angeles, 1941–1945." In *The Mexican American Experience: An Interdisciplinary Anthology*, edited by Rodolfo O. De La Garza et al. Austin: University of Texas Press, 1985.

———. "La Frontera: The Border as Symbol and Reality in Mexican American Thought." *Mexican Studies/Estudios Mexicanos* (Summer 1985): 214–20.

———. *Memories of Chicano History: The Life and Narrative of Bert Corona*. Berkeley: University of California Press, 1994.

———. *Mexican Americans: Leadership, Ideology, and Identity, 1930–1960*. New Haven, Conn.: Yale University Press, 1989.

———. "Mexican Americans and the Politics of Citizenship: The Case of El Paso, 1936." *New Mexico Historical Review* 59 (April 1984): 187–204.

Garcia, Richard A. "The Chicano Movement and the Mexican American Community, 1972–1978: An Interpretative Essay." *Socialist Review* 8 (July–October 1978): 117–36.

———. *Rise of the Mexican American Middle Class: San Antonio, 1929–1941.* College Station: Texas A & M University Press, 1991.

Gardner, Richard. *¡Grito!: Reies Tijerina and the New Mexico Land Grant War of 1967.* Indianapolis: Bobbs-Merrill Company, 1970.

Giant. Motion Picture. George Stevens, producer. Warner Brothers. 1956.

Gilbert, James. *Another Chance: Postwar America, 1945–1968.* New York: Knopf, 1981.

Gitlin, Todd. *The Sixties: Years of Hope, Days of Rage.* Toronto: Bantam Books, 1987.

Gluck, Sherna Berger. *Rosie the Riveter Revisited.* Boston: Twayne Publishers, 1987.

Gluck, Sherna Berger, and Daphne Patai, eds. *Women's Words: The Feminist Practice of Oral History.* New York: Routledge, 1991.

Gómez, Arthur R., and Cissie Coy. *Chavez, El Senador.* Albuquerque, N.M.: Dennis Chavez Foundation, 1988.

Gómez-Quiñones, Juan. *Chicano Politics: Reality and Promise.* Albuquerque: University of New Mexico Press, 1990.

———. *Mexican Students por la Raza: The Chicano Student Movement in Southern California, 1967–1977.* Santa Barbara, Calif.: La Causa Publications, 1978.

Gonzales, Manuel G. *Mexicanos: A History of Mexicans in the United States.* Bloomington: Indiana University Press, 1999.

Gonzales, Rodolfo. *I Am Joaquín / Yo Soy Joaquín.* Illustrations by Yermo Vasquez. N.p., 1967.

Grebler, Leo, Joan W. Moore, and Ralph Guzman. *The Mexican-American People: The Nation's Second Largest Minority.* New York: Macmillan, 1970.

Griffith, Beatrice. *American Me.* Boston: Houghton Mifflin, 1948.

Griswold del Castillo, Richard. *The Los Angeles Barrio, 1850–1890: A Social History.* Berkeley: University of California Press, 1979.

Gutiérrez, David G. *Walls and Mirrors: Mexican Americans, Mexican Immigrants, and the Politics of Ethnicity.* Berkeley: University of California Press, 1995.

Gutiérrez, José Angel. "Chicanos and Mexicanos Under Surveillance: 1940 to 1980." *Renato Rosaldo Lecture Series 2: 1984–1985.* Tucson: Mexican American Studies and Research Center, 1985.

———. *The Making of a Chicano Militant: Lessons from Cristal.* Madison: University of Wisconsin Press, 1998.

Gutiérrez, Ramón A. "Community, Patriarchy and Individualism: The Politics of Chicano History and the Dream of Equality." *American Quarterly* 45 (March 1993): 44–72.

Gutiérrez-Jones, Carl. *Rethinking the Borderlands: Between Chicano Culture and Legal Discourse.* Berkeley: University of California Press, 1995.

Gutmann, Matthew C. "A (Short) Cultural History of Mexican Machos." In *Gender Matters: Rereading Michelle Z. Rosaldo,* edited by Alejandro Lugo and Bill Maurer. Ann Arbor: University of Michigan Press, 2000.

Haas, Lisbeth. *Conquests and Historical Identities in California, 1769–1936.* Berkeley: University of California Press, 1999.

Halstead, Fred. *Out Now!* New York: Monad Press, 1978.

Hammerback, John C., Richard J. Jensen, and José Angel Gutiérrez. *A War of Words: Chicano Protest in the 1960s and 1970s.* Westport, Conn.: Greenwood Press, 1985.

Hammond, William M. "United States Army in Vietnam." In *Public Affairs: The Military and the Media, 1962–1968.* Washington D.C.: Center for Military History, United States Army, 1988.

Haney López, Ian F. *Racism on Trial: The Chicano Fight for Justice.* Cambridge, Mass.: Harvard University Press, 2003.

———. *White By Law: The Legal Construction of Race.* New York: New York University Press, 1996.

Hartmann, Susan M. *The Home Front and Beyond: American Women in the 1940s.* Boston: Twayne Publishers, 1982.

Hauser, Thomas. *Muhammad Ali: His Life and Times.* New York: Simon and Schuster, 1991.

Heineman, Kenneth J. *Campus Wars.* New York: New York University Press, 1993.

Hemmings, F. W. J. *The Life and Times of Emile Zola.* New York: Charles Scribner, 1977.

Hernández Alvarez, José. *A Demographic Profile of the Mexican Immigration to the United States, 1910–1950.* Berkeley: International Population and Urban Research, 1966.

Herring, George C. *America's Longest War: The United States and Vietnam, 1950–1975.* 2nd ed. New York: McGraw-Hill, 1986.

Hilliard, David, with Lewis Cole. *This Side of Glory.* Boston: Morris and Brown, 1993.

Hine, Darlene Clark, and Earnestine Jenkins, eds. *A Question of Manhood: A Reader in U.S. Black Men's History and Masculinity.* Bloomington: Indiana University Press, 1999.

The Hispanic Population in the United States: March 2002. Current Population Reports. Series P-20, Population characteristics; no. 545. Washington, D.C.: U.S. Department of Commerce, Bureau of the Census, 2003.

Hispanics in America's Defense. [Washington, D.C.?]: Office of the Deputy Assistant Secretary of Defense for Military Manpower and Personnel Policy, [1990].

Hoffman, Abraham. *Unwanted Mexican Americans in the Great Depression: Repatriation Pressures, 1929–1939.* Tucson: University of Arizona Press, 1974.

Hosokawa, William. *Nisei: The Quiet Americans.* Rahway, N.J.: Quinn and Boden, 1969.

Howes, Craig. *Voices of the Vietnam POWs: Witnesses to Their Fight.* New York: Oxford Press, 1993.

Isserman, Maurice. *If I Had a Hammer.* New York: Basic Books, 1987.

Jacobson, Matthew Frye. *Whiteness of a Different Color: European Immigrants and the Alchemy of Race.* Cambridge, Mass: Harvard University Press, 1998.

Jameson, Elizabeth, and Susan Armitage, eds. *Writing the Range: Race, Class, and Culture in the American Women's West.* Norman: University of Oklahoma Press, 1997.

Johnson, Lyndon. Introduction to *Among the Valiant,* by Raul Morin. Alhambra, Calif.: Borden Publishing, 1963.

Kahin, George McTurnan. *Intervention: How America Got Involved in Vietnam.* New York: Knopf, 1986.

Kearns, Doris. *Lyndon Johnson and the American Dream.* New York: Harper and Row, 1976.

Kerber, Linda K. *No Constitutional Right to Be Ladies: Women and the Obligations of Citizenship.* New York: Hill and Wang, 1998.

Kibbe, Pauline R. *Latin Americans in Texas.* 1946. Reprint, New York: Arno Press, 1974.

Klor de Alva, J. Jorge. "Aztlán, Borinquen, and Hispanic Nationalism." In *Aztlán: Essays on the Chicano Homeland,* edited by Rudolfo A. Anaya and Francisco Lomelí. Albuquerque: N.M.: Academia/El Norte Publications, 1989.

———. "The Invention of Ethnic Origins and the Negotiation of Latino Identity, 1969–1981." In *Challenging Fronteras: Structuring Latina and Latino Lives in the U.S.,* edited by Mary Romero, Pierrette Hondagneu-Sotelo, and Vilma Ortiz. New York: Routledge 1997.

Kluckhorn, Florence R. *Variations in Value Orientation.* New York: Row, Peterson, 1961.

KMEX, *Veinte Años Despues: Extraños en Nuestra Propia Tierra [After Twenty Years: Strangers in Our Own Land].* Television Documentary. Los Angeles, 1990.

Knowlton, Clark. "The New Mexican Land War." *The Nation,* 17 June 1968, 793.

———. "Reies L. Tijerina and the Alianza Federal de Mercedes: Seekers after Justice." *Wisconsin Sociologist* 22 (Fall 1985): 133–44.

———. "Violence in New Mexico: A Sociological Perspective." *California Law Review* 58: 1054–84

KPFK Radio Station, Los Angeles. Coverage of Chicano Moratorium press conferences. 31 August 1970. Chicano Studies Library, University of California at Los Angeles.

———. Coverage of Chicano Moratorium rally. 29 August 1970. East Los Angeles Public Library.

Kurtz, Donald V. "Politics, Ethnicity, Integration: Mexican Americans in the War on Poverty." Ph.D. diss, University of California, Los Angeles, 1970.

LaFeber, Walter. *The American Age: United States Foreign Policy at Home and Abroad since 1750.* New York: W. W. Norton, 1989.

———. "The Indo-China War." Speech given at Cornell University, May 1970 (copy in author's possession).

Leatherwood, Art, and Alicia A. Garza. "Alfredo Cantu Gonzalez" entry. *The Handbook of Texas Online*. http://www.tsha.utexas.edu/handbook/online/articles/view/GG/fgoqp.html.

Levering, Ralph B. *The Public and American Foreign Policy, 1918–1978*. New York: Morrow, 1978.

Levy, Jacques E. *Cesar Chavez: Autobiography of La Causa*. New York: W. W. Norton, 1975.

Levy, Mark R., and Michael S. Kramer. *The Ethnic Factor: How America's Minorities Decide Elections*. New York: Simon and Schuster, 1972.

Lewis, Oscar. *Five Families: Mexican Case Studies in the Culture of Poverty*. New York: Basic Books, 1959.

Logevall, Fredrik. *Choosing War: The Lost Chance for Peace and the Escalation of War in Vietnam*. Berkeley: University of California Press, 1999.

López, Ralph Urbina. "Amigos de Aztlannet.com." Copy in author's possession. (The article originally appeared as part of the Aztlannet.com Web site, now defunct, which provided extensive coverage of Chicano Moratorium 2002.)

Lowi, Theodore J. *The End of Liberalism: Ideology, Policy, and the Crisis of Public Authority*. New York: W. W. Norton, 1969.

Lujan, Roy. "Dennis Chavez and the Roosevelt Era, 1933–1945." Ph.D. diss., University of New Mexico, 1987.

Lunch, William L., and Peter W. Sperlich. "American Public Opinion and the War In Vietnam." *Western Political Quarterly* 32, no. 1 (1979): 21–44.

Maciel, David R., and Isidro D. Ortiz, eds. *Chicanas{hrs}/{hrs}Chicanos at the Crossroads: Social, Economic, and Political Change*. Tucson: University of Arizona Press, 1996.

March in the Rain. Motion picture. Claudio Fenner-López, producer. 1970

Marín, Christine. "Mexican Americans on the Home Front: Community Organizations in Arizona During World War II." *Perspectives in Mexican American Studies* 4 (1993): 79–91.

Marin, Marguerite V. "Protest in an Urban Barrio: A Study of the Chicano Movement." Ph.D. diss., University of California, Santa Barbara, 1980.

———. *Social Protest in an Urban Barrio: A Study of the Chicano Movement*. Lanham, Md.: University of America Press, 1993.

Mariscal, George. *Aztlán and Viet Nam: Chicano and Chicana Experiences of the War*. Berkeley: University of California Press, 1999.

Mariscal, Jorge. "Chicanos and Chicanas say, 'No a la Guerra.'" *Counter-Punch*, 10 October 2002, http://www.counterpunch.org/mariscal1010.html.

———. "When Chicano POWs Returned Home." *La Prensa San Diego*, 7 May 1999. http://www.laprensa-sandiego.org/archieve/mayo7/pow.htm.

Márquez, Benjamin. *LULAC: The Evolution of a Mexican American Political Organization*. Austin: University of Texas Press, 1993.

Marqusee, Mike. *Redemption Song: Muhammad Ali and the Spirit of the Sixties*. London: Verso, 1999.

Martínez, Elizabeth. *500 Años del Pueblo Chicano/500 Years of Chicano History in Pictures*. Albuquerque, N.M.: SouthWest Organizing Project, 1991.

———. "Chingón Politics Die Hard: Reflections on the First Chicano Activists Reunion." *Z Magazine*, April 1990, 46–50.

Martínez, Elizabeth, and Enriqueta Longeaux y Vásquez. *¡Viva La Raza!: The Struggle of the Mexican American People*. New York: Doubleday, 1974.

Martínez, Elizabeth Sutherland. *The Youngest Revolution: A Personal Report on Cuba*. New York: Dial Press, 1969.

Martinez, John Ramon. *Mexican Immigration to the U.S.* San Francisco: R and E Research Associates, 1974.

Martínez, Oscar J. *Mexican-Origin People in the United States: A Topical History*. Tucson: University of Arizona Press, 2001.

Matusow, Allen J. *The Unraveling of America: A History of Liberalism in the 1960s*. New York: Harper and Row, 1984.

Mazón, Mauricio. *The Zoot-Suit Riots: The Psychology of Symbolic Annihilation*. Austin: University of Texas Press, 1984.

McAlister, Melani. *Epic Encounters: Culture, Media, and U.S. Interests in the Middle East, 1945–2000*. Berkeley: University of California Press, 2000.

McWilliams, Carey. *North From Mexico*. 1949. Reprint, New York: Greenwood Press, 1968.

A Medal for Benny. Motion picture. Paul Jones, producer. Paramount, 1945.

Meier, Matt S., and Feliciano Ribera. *Mexican Americans, American Mexicans: From Conquistadores to Chicanos*. New York: Hill and Wang, 1993.

The Men of Company E. Motion picture. Alfredo Lugo and Jose Luis Sedano, producers. Whittier, Calif.: Mestizo Production Associates, 1983.

Mershon, Sherie, and Steven L. Schlossman. *Foxholes and Color Lines: Desegregating the U.S. Armed Forces*. Baltimore, Md.: Johns Hopkins University Press, 1998.

The Mexican Americans: A New Focus on Opportunity. Testimony Presented at the Cabinet Committee Hearings on Mexican American Affairs. El Paso, Texas: Inter-Agency Committee on Mexican American Affairs, 1967.

Mexicans in California: Report of Governor C. C. Young's Mexican Fact-Finding Committee. 1930. Reprint, San Francisco: R and E Research Associates, 1970.

Miranda-Arrizón, Marcia. "Building Herman(a)dad: Chicana Feminism and the Comisión Feminil Mexicana Nacional." Master's thesis, University of California, Santa Barbara, 1998.

Mirandé, Alfredo. *Gringo Justice*. Notre Dame, Ind.: University of Notre Dame Press, 1987.

———. *Hombres y Machos: Masculinity and Latino Culture*. Boulder, Colo.: Westview Press, 1997.

Mirandé, Alfredo, and Evangelina Enríquez. *La Chicana: The Mexican American Woman*. Chicago: University of Chicago Press, 1979.

Monroy, Douglas. *Thrown Among Strangers: From Indians to Mexicans on the Landscape of Southern California, 1769–1900*. Berkeley: University of California Press, 1999.

Montejano, David. *Anglos and Mexicans in the Making of Texas, 1836–1986*. Austin: University of Texas Press, 1987.

Montes, Ana. "La Nueva Chicana." In *Chicana Feminist Thought: The Basic Historical Writings,* edited by Alma M. García. New York: Routledge, 1997.

Mooney, Patrick H., and Theo J. Majka. *Farmers' and Farm Workers' Movements: Social Protest in American Agriculture.* New York: Twayne Publishers, 1995.

Moore, Joan W. *Mexican Americans.* 2nd ed. Englewood Cliffs, N.J.: Prentice-Hall, 1976.

Moore, Joan W., and Ralph Guzmán. "New Wind from the Southwest." *Nation,* 30 May 1966, 645–48.

Morales, Armando. *Ando sangrando.* La Puente, Calif.: Perspectivas Press, 1972.

Morin, Raul. *Among the Valiant.* Alhambra, Calif.: Borden Publishing, 1963.

Morse, George Donnelson. *Vietnam: An American Ordeal.* Englewood Cliffs, N.J.: Prentice-Hall, 1990.

Muñoz, Carlos, Jr. *Youth, Identity, and Power: The Chicano Movement.* London: Verso Press, 1989.

Nabokov, Peter. *Tijerina and the Courthouse Raid.* Albuquerque: University of New Mexico Press, 1969.

Nash, Gerald. *The American West Transformed: The Impact of the Second World War.* Bloomington: Indiana University Press, 1985.

Navarro, Armando. *The Cristal Experiment: A Chicano Struggle for Community Control.* Madison: University of Wisconsin Press, 1998.

———. "The Evolution of Chicano Politics." *Aztlán* 5 (Spring/Fall 1974): 72–82.

———. *Mexican American Youth Organization: Avant-garde of the Chicano Movement in Texas.* Austin: University of Texas Press, 1995.

———. "El Partido de la Raza Unida in Crystal City: A Peaceful Revolution." Ph.D. diss., University of California, Riverside, 1974.

Nixon, Richard. "Nixon's Address to the Nation on the War in Vietnam: 'The Silent Majority' Speech, November 3, 1969." Watergate.Info, http://www.watergate.info/nixon/silent-majority-speech-1969.shtml.

O'Leary, Cecilia Elizabeth. *To Die For: The Paradox of American Patriotism.* Princeton, N.J.: Princeton University Press, 1999.

O'Reilly, Kenneth. *"Racial Matters": The FBI's Secret File on Black America, 1960–1972.* New York: Free Press, 1989.

Ornelas, Charles, and Michael Gonzalez. "The Chicano and the War: An Opinion Survey in Santa Barbara." *Aztlán* 2 (1971): 23–35.

Orozco, Cynthia E. "Alice Dickerson Montemayor: Feminism and Mexican American Politics in the 1930s." In *Writing the Range: Race, Class, and Culture in the American Women's West,* edited by Elizabeth Jameson and Susan Armitage. Norman: University of Oklahoma Press, 1997.

———. "The Origins of the League of United Latin American Citizens (LULAC) and the Mexican American Civil Rights Movement in Texas, with an Analysis of Women's Political Participation in a Gendered Context, 1910–1929." Ph.D. diss., University of California, Los Angeles, 1992.

Pearson, Hugh. *The Shadow of the Panther: Huey Newton and the Price of Black Power in America.* Reading, Mass.: Addison-Wesley, 1994.

Pelayo, Jaime. "The Chicano Movement and the Vietnam War." Senior thesis, Yale University, 1997.

Perales, Alonso S. *Are We Good Neighbors?* 1948. Reprint, New York: Arno Press, 1974.

Philpott, Tom. *Glory Denied: The Saga of Jim Thompson, America's Longest Held Prisoner of War.* New York: Norton, 2001.

El Plan Espíritual de Aztlán. In *Chicano Politics: Reading,* edited by F. Chris García, 170–73. New York: MSS Information, 1993.

Polenberg, Richard. *War and Society: The United States, 1941–1945.* Philadelphia: J. B. Lippincott, 1972.

Powell, R.W. *Gender and Power: Society, the Person, and Sexual Politics.* Stanford, Calif.: Stanford University Press, 1987.

———. *Masculinities.* Berkeley: University of California Press, 1995.

President's Committee on Civil Rights. *To Secure These Rights.* Washington, D.C: Government Printing Office, 1947.

Profile of the Foreign-Born Population in the United States: 1997. Current Population Reports. Series P-23, Special studies; no. 195. Washington D.C.: U.S. Department of Commerce, Economics and Statistics Administration, Bureau of the Census, [1999].

Pycior, Julie Leininger. *LBJ and Mexican Americans: The Paradox of Power.* Austin: University of Texas Press, 1997.

Radelat, Ana. "Road to Power." *Hispanic Magazine,* May 2003, http://www .hispanicmagazine.com/2000/may/Features/.

Ramos, Henry A. J. *A People Forgotten, A Dream Pursued: The History of the American G.I. Forum, 1948–1972.* N.p.: G.I. Forum, 1983.

Raúlsalinas. *Un Trip through the Mind Jail y Otras Excursions.* San Francisco: Editorial Pocho-Che, 1980.

La Raza Nueva. Radio show. Moctezuma Esparza, host. Broadcast on KPFK radio station, [August 30/31?], 1970. Chicano Studies Library, University of California at Los Angeles.

Quezada, J. Gilberto. *Border Boss: Manuel B. Bravo and Zapata County.* College Station: Texas A & M Press, 1999.

Regalado, James A. "Latino Empowerment in Los Angeles." In *Latino Empowerment: Progress, Problems, and Prospects,* edited by Roberto E. Villareal, Norma G. Hernandez, and Howard D. Neighbor. New York: Greenwood Press, 1988.

Rendón, Armando. *Chicano Manifesto: The History and Aspirations of the Second Largest Minority.* New York: Macmillan, 1971.

Rodriguez, Eugene, Jr. *Henry B. Gonzalez: A Political Profile.* New York: Arno Press, 1976.

Rodriguez, Marc Simon. "Cristaleño Consciousness: Mexican-American Activism Between Crystal City, Texas, and Wisconsin, 1963–1980." In *Oppositional Consciousness: The Subjective Roots of Social Protest,* edited by Jane J. Mansbridge and Aldon Morris. Chicago: University of Chicago Press, 2001.

Roediger, David R. *The Wages of Whiteness: Race and the Making of the American Working Class.* London: Verso Press, 1991.

Romano-V., Octavio I. "Spanish Surnamed War Dead, Vietnam." *El Grito* 3, no. 1 (Fall 1969): 6–31.

Romero, Mary, Pierrette Hondagneu-Sotelo, and Vilma Ortiz, eds. *Challenging Fronteras: Structuring Latina and Latino Lives in the U.S.* New York: Routledge, 1997.

Rose, Margaret. "Gender and Civic Activism in Mexican American Barrios." In *Not June Cleaver: Women and Gender in Postwar America, 1945–1960,* edited by Joanne Meyerowitz. Philadelphia: Temple University Press, 1994.

Rosen, Gerald Paul. "The Development of the Chicano Movement in Los Angeles." *Aztlán* 4 (Spring 1973): 155–83.

———. *Political Ideology and the Chicano Movement: A Study of the Political Ideology of Activists in the Chicano Movement.* San Francisco: R and E Associates, 1975.

Rosenberg, Norman L., and Emily S. Rosenberg. *In Our Times: America Since World War II.* 5th ed. Englewood Cliffs, N.J.: Prentice Hall, 1995.

Rotundo, E. Anthony. *American Manhood.* New York: Basic Books, 1993.

Sáenz, J. Luz. *Los méxico-americanos en la gran guerra y su contingente en pró de la democracia, la humanidad, y la justicia.* San Antonio, Texas: Artes Gráficas, 1933.

Salazar, Ruben. *Border Correspondent: Selected Writings, 1955–1970.* Berkeley: University of California Press, 1995.

San Miguel, Guadalupe, Jr. *Brown, Not White: School Integration and the Chicano Movement in Houston.* College Station: Texas A & M Press, 2001.

———. *"Let Them All Take Heed": Mexican Americans and the Campaign for Educational Equality in Texas, 1910–1981.* Austin: University of Texas Press, 1987.

Sanchez, David. *Expedition Through Aztlán.* La Puente, Calif.: Perspectivas Publications, 1970.

Sánchez, George J. *Becoming Mexican American.* New York: Oxford University Press, 1993.

Sandoval, Moíses. *Our Legacy: The First Fifty Years.* N.p.: League of United Latin American Citizens, n.d.

Santillan, Richard. *La Raza Unida.* Los Angeles: Tlaquilo Publications, 1973.

———. "Rosita the Riveter: Midwest Mexican American Women during World War II, 1941–1945." *Perspectives in Mexican American Studies: Mexican Americans in the Midwest* 2 (1989): 115–45.

———. "Third Party Politics: Old Story, New Faces." In *Chicano Politics: Readings,* edited by F. Chris García. New York: MSS Information Corp., 1973.

Schudson, Michael. *The Good Citizen: A History of American Civic Life.* New York: Martin Kessler Books, 1998.

Scruggs, Otey. *Braceros, "Wetbacks," and the Farm Labor Problem: Mexican Agricultural Labor in the United States, 1942–1954.* New York: Garland Publishers, 1988.

Servín, Manuel P. *An Awakened Minority: The Mexican-Americans.* 2nd ed. New York: Macmillan, 1974.

———, comp. *The Mexican Americans: An Awakening Minority, [by] Manuel P. Servín.* Beverly Hills: Glencoe Press, 1970.

Shelton, Edgar Greer, Jr. "Political Conditions Among Texas Mexicans Along the Rio Grande." Thesis, University of Texas, 1946.

Shockley, John Staples. *Chicano Revolt in a Texas Town.* Notre Dame, Ind.: University of Notre Dame Press, 1974.

Shull, Michael S., and David Edward Wilt. *Hollywood War Films, 1937 to 1945.* Jefferson, N.C.: McFarland and Co., 1996.

Sitkoff, Harvard. "Racial Militancy and Interracial Violence in the Second World War." *Journal of American History* 58 (1971): 661–81.

Skerry, Peter. *Mexican Americans: The Ambivalent Minority.* New York: The Free Press, 1993.

Small, Melvin. *Covering Dissent: The Media and the Anti-War Movement.* New Brunswick, N.J.: Rutgers University Press, 1994.

———. *Johnson, Nixon, and the Doves.* New Brunswick, N.J.: Rutgers University Press, 1988.

Small, Melvin, and William D. Hoover, eds. *Give Peace a Chance.* Syracuse, N.Y.: Syracuse University Press, 1992.

Smith, Rogers M. *Civic Ideals: Conflicting Visions of Citizenship in U.S. History.* New Haven, Conn.: Yale University Press, 1997.

Snyder, R. Claire. *Citizen-Soldiers and Manly Warriors: Military Service and Gender in the Civic Republican Tradition.* Lanham, Mass.: Rowman and Littlefield, 1999.

Spanish Speaking Americans in the War: The Southwest. Washington, D.C.: Office of the Coordinator of Inter-American Affairs, [1942?].

Steiner, Stan. *La Raza: The Mexican Americans.* New York: Harper, 1970.

Suran, Justin David. "Coming Out Against the War: Antimilitarism and the Politicization of Homosexuality in the Era of Vietnam." *American Quarterly* 53 (September 2001): 452–88.

Sutherland, Elizabeth. *Letters from Mississippi.* New York: McGraw Hill, 1965.

Takaki, Ronald T. *Double Victory: A Multicultural History of America in World War II.* Boston: Little, Brown, 2000.

Taylor, Clyde. *Vietnam and Black America: An Anthology of Protest and Resistance.* Garden City, N.Y.: Anchor Press, 1973.

Texas Inter-Agency Committee on Mexican American Affairs. *The Mexican Americans: A New Focus on Opportunity:* Testimony presented at the Cabinet Committee Hearings on Mexican American Affairs, El Paso, Texas, 1967.

Thernstrom, Abigail M. *Whose Votes Count? Affirmative Action and Minority Voting Rights.* Cambridge, Mass.: Harvard University Press, 1987.

Thompson, Hunter S. "Strange Rumblings in Aztlán." *Rolling Stone* 81 (29 April 1971): 30–37. Reprinted in *The Great Shark Hunt* (New York: Summit Books, 1979).

Tirado, Miguel David. "Mexican American Community Political Organization: The Key to Chicano Political Power." *Aztlán* 1 (Spring 1970): 53–78.

Treviño, Jesús Salvador. *Eyewitness: A Filmmaker's Memoir of the Chicano Movement*. Houston, Texas: Arte Público Press, 2001.

Tuck, Ruth. *Not with the Fist*. New York: Harcourt, Brace, 1946.

Tyson, Timothy B. *Radio Free Dixie: Robert F. Williams & the Roots of Black Power*. Chapel Hill: University of North Carolina Press, 1999.

U.S. Commission on Civil Rights. *Mexican Americans and the Administration of Justice in the Southwest* [a report]. Washington, D.C.: Government Printing Office, 1970.

U.S. Commission on Civil Rights. California Advisory Committee. *Education and the Mexican American Community in Los Angeles County: A Report of an Open Meeting*. Sacramento: The Committee, 1968.

————. *Police–Community Relations in East Los Angeles, California: A Report of the California State Advisory Committee to the United States Commission on Civil Rights*. [Los Angeles]: The Committee, 1970.

U.S. Congress. Senate. Committee on the Judiciary. *"Extent of Subversion in the New Left: Testimony of Robert J. Thoms"*: *Hearings before the Subcommittee to Investigate the Administration of the Internal Security Act and Other Internal Security Laws of the Committee on the Judiciary*. 91st Cong., 2nd sess., 20 January 1970.

Ulibarrí, Sabine R. *Mayhem Was Our Business—Memorias de un Veterano*. Tempe, Ariz.: Bilingual Press, 1997.

Unger, Irwin. *Best of Intentions: The Triumph and Failure of the Great Society under Kennedy, Johnson, and Nixon*. New York: Doubleday, 1996.

————. *The Movement: A History of the New Left, 1959–1972*. New York: Dodd, Mead, 1974.

Valdez, Luis, and the Teatro Campesino. *Actos*. Fresno, Calif.: Cucaracha Productions, 1971.

Van Deburg, William L. *A New Day in Babylon: The Black Power Movement and American Culture, 1965–1975*. Chicago: University of Chicago Press, 1992.

Vargas, Zaragosa. *Proletarians of the North: A History of Mexican Industrial Workers in Detroit and the Midwest, 1917–1933*. Berkeley: University of California Press, 1993.

————. "Tejana Radical: Emma Tenayuca and the San Antonio Labor Movement during the Great Depression." *Pacific Historical Review* 66 (November 1997): 553–80.

Vasconcelos, José. *La Raza Cósmica*. 1925. Reprint, Heredia, Costa Rica: Centro de Estudios Generales, Universidad Nacional, 1999.

Vélez-Ibáñez, Carlos G. *Border Visions: Mexican Cultures of the Southwest United States*. Tucson: University of Arizona Press, 1996.

Vera, Ron. "Observations on the Chicano Relationship to Military Service in Los Angeles County." *Aztlán* 1 (Fall 1970): 27–37.

Vigil, Ernesto. "Commentary." Copy in author's possession. (This article originally appeared as part of a now defunct Web site.)

————*The Crusade for Justice: Chicano Militancy and the Government's War on Dissent*. Madison: University of Wisconsin Press, 1999.

Villareal, Roberto E., Norma G. Hernandez, and Howard D. Neighbor, eds. *Latino Empowerment: Progress, Problems, and Prospects.* New York: Greenwood Press, 1988.

Weber, Devra. *Dark Sweat, White Gold: California Farm Workers, Cotton, and the New Deal.* Berkeley: University of California Press, 1994.

Weeks, O. Douglas. "The League of United Latin-American Citizens: A Texas-Mexican Civic Organization." *Southwestern Political and Social Science Quarterly* 10 (December 1929): 257–78.

Wei, William. *The Asian American Movement.* Philadelphia: Temple University Press, 1993.

Wells, Tom. *The War Within.* Berkeley: University of California Press, 1994.

White, Walter. "What the Negro Thinks of the Army." *Annals of the American Academy of Political and Social Science* 33 (September 1942): 67–80.

Wynn, Neil A. *The Afro-American and the Second World War.* New York: Holmes and Meier, 1976.

Ybarra, Lea. "Conjugal Role Relationships in the Chicano Family." Ph.D. diss., University of California at Berkeley, 1977.

———. "Too Many Heroes: The Oral Histories of Chicano Vietnam Veterans." Paper presented at the National Association of Chicana and Chicano Studies Conference, Tucson, Ariz., April 2001.

Ybarra, Lea, and Nina Genera. *La Batalla Está Aquí: Chicanos and the War.* Rev. ed. El Cerrito, Calif.: Chicano Draft Help, 1972. First published 1970.

Young, Marilyn B. *The Vietnam Wars, 1945–1990.* New York: HarperPerennial, 1991.

Zinn, Maxine Baca. "Chicano Men and Masculinity." *Journal of Ethnic Studies* 10 (1982): 29–44.

Index

Compositor: Sheridan Books, Inc.
Indexer: Roberta Engleman
Text: 10/13 Sabon
Display: Sabon
Printer and binder: Sheridan Books, Inc.